MW00760823

Runaway State-Building

Runaway State-Building

Patronage Politics and Democratic Development

CONOR O'DWYER

The Johns Hopkins University Press

Baltimore

© 2006 The Johns Hopkins University Press
All rights reserved. Published 2006
Printed in the United States of America on acid-free paper

2   4   6   8   9   7   5   3   1

The Johns Hopkins University Press
2715 North Charles Street
Baltimore, Maryland 21218-4363
www.press.jhu.edu

Library of Congress Cataloging-in-Publication Data
O'Dwyer, Conor, 1972–
Runaway state-building : patronage politics and democratic development /
Conor O'Dwyer.
p.   cm.
Includes bibliographical references and index.
ISBN 0-8018-8365-2 (hardcover : alk. paper)
1. New democracies. 2. Democratization. 3. Bureaucracy. 4. Patronage,
Political. 5. Nation-building. 6. Poland—Politics and government—
1989– 7. Czech Republic—Politics and government—1993– 8. Slovakia—
Politics and government—1993– I. Title.
JC423.O26 2006
320.9—dc22   2005029018

A catalog record for this book is available from the British Library.

Contents

Figures and Tables

FIGURES

TABLES

Preface

Patronage politics is a phenomenon as important as it is difficult to research. In new democracies, such as those in Eastern Europe, Latin America, East Asia, and Africa, it is a particularly pressing problem because these countries often already face problems of "stateness" and performance legitimacy. Yet, at a time when even political conservatives have come to recognize the importance of the state (see, for example, Fukuyama 2004) and when observers of new democracies from Brazil to Indonesia have noted both the prevalence and harmful consequences of patronage politics, it has proven difficult to study the relationship between democratization and state-building cross-nationally and systematically. Differences in starting points, international context, economic development, political culture, institutional structure—to name just a few—have made it difficult to establish the relevant baselines for comparison. Attempts to establish such baselines using large-N statistical techniques have run aground because of the challenge of collecting data about and constructing measures of so sensitive a variable as political corruption. This book uses a carefully chosen political setting, postcommunist Eastern Europe, to overcome the problems that have plagued comparative research on the topic of patronage in state administrations. The cases of these new democracies offer leverage on an old question, how the patronage pressures unleashed by democratization shape the construction of postauthoritarian states.

Postcommunist Eastern Europe presents a rare opportunity to overcome these difficulties because the shared experience of communism imposed political similarities across countries, and the collapse of that system in 1989 marked a common starting point for postcommunist state-building. Given these similarities, the baselines for comparison are unusually clear, and intensive case-study analysis—with all the advantages it affords in terms of data collection and nuanced measurement—is possible. It hardly needs saying that the region also offers plenty of opportunities to encounter the phenomenon of patronage-infused state-building.

In its analysis of three formerly communist countries, this book finds some confirmation for the prevailing wisdom about patronage politics and democratic development. But it also indicates the need to refine that wisdom. Pressures for political patronage are strongest in countries where democratization precedes the consolidation of the apparatus of state. This is the situation in which most, though not all, of the new democracies in Eastern Europe, Latin America, East Asia, and Africa find themselves. The surprising success of a small number of postcommunist democracies in constraining political patronage suggests, however, that the sequencing of democratization vis-à-vis state consolidation is not destiny. Uncontrolled patronage poses the biggest threat to state-building in democracies whose party systems are underinstitutionalized, volatile, and unpredictable. Such systems do not generate quality party competition and, hence, do not provide voters with the information and leverage to hold governing parties accountable. In new democracies whose party systems institutionalize rapidly, however, robust party competition can mitigate, though not eliminate, the pressure for political patronage even where democratization preceded state consolidation.

Ultimately, for democracy's advocates the lessons of the postcommunist experience are heartening. Parties' never-ending quest for political advantage in newly opened electoral arenas need not lead to unaccountable government and bloated, politicized states; if electoral competition offers voters intelligible choices among familiar actors, it will enable them to hold governments accountable and lead to a more effective state.

I am deeply indebted to many individuals and organizations who contributed generously to the writing of this book. It began at the University of California, Berkeley, under the able and inspiring direction of Chris Ansell, John Connelly, Steve Fish, Ken Jowitt, and Jonah Levy. A great many friends and colleagues also helped me form my ideas. Thanks, in particular, to Mieczysław Boduszyński, Erin Carr, Linda Cook, Lara Deeb, Ken Foster, Vanna Gonzales, Tomek Grabowski, Mary Alice Haddad, Laura Henry, Abby Innes, Wade Jacoby, Andrew Janos, Juliet Johnson, Janelle Kerlin, Andrej Krickovic, Dan Kronenfeld, Enita Kushi, Soumita Lahiri, Michael Martinez, Grigore Pop-Eleches, Alberta Sbragia, Ben Smith, Sherrill Stroschein, Ned Walker, Lucan Way, Larry Winner, Deborah Yalen, and Daniel Ziblatt. I am also grateful to the many people who helped me in my field research in Poland, the Czech Republic, and Slovakia over extended stays from 1999 to 2001. They provided not only invaluable guidance but also, in many cases, a place to stay. Special thanks to Andrzej Tarłowski, Kazimiera Tarłowska, Norbert Malszewski, Jana Grittersová, Jan Gritters, Gustav and Peter Matijek, Pavel Černoch, Marek Jiruše, Pavla Nováková, and Pavel and Šárka Hoffman. The manuscript benefited enormously from the suggestions of Henry Tom and the editorial board at the Johns Hopkins University Press, as well as Claire McCabe Tamberino and Glenn Perkins.

I would like to extend my deep gratitude to the following institutions for supporting this research: the Jacob Javits Fellowship, the Foreign Language and Area Studies Fellowship, the Berkeley Center for German and European Studies, and the Berkeley Program in Soviet and Post-Soviet Studies. The Academy Scholars program at Harvard University provided a year of intellectual (and financial) support as I transformed the research into a book. A significant part of this support came in the form of feedback from Jorge Dominguez, Margarita Estevez-Abe, Susan Pharr, and Robert Putnam's comparative politics field seminar: my thanks to them.

Finally, I would like to thank my family for their constant encouragement and support. I owe a special debt to my wife Ingrid, my emotional support and last line of editorial advice; without her there would be no book. I dedicate it to her.

Acronyms

For political parties, the letters from the original language were used to form the acronym.

ANC	African National Congress (South Africa)
AWS	Electoral Action Solidarity (Poland)
BBWR	Non-Party Bloc to Support Reform (Poland)
BSP	Bulgarian Socialist Party
CBOS	Center for Public Opinion Research (Poland)
CCM	Chama cha Mapinduzi (Tanzania)
ČSSD	Czech Social Democratic Party
DS	Democratic Party (Slovakia)
DU	Democratic Union (Slovakia)
ECU	European Currency Units
EU	European Union
GHIC	General Health Insurance Company (Czech Republic)
GHIF	General Health Insurance Fund (Slovakia)
GNP	gross national product
HDZ	Croatian Democratic Union
HSD-SMS	Movement for Self-Governing Democracy-Association for Moravia and Silesia
HZDS	Movement for a Democratic Slovakia
INEKO	Institute for Economic and Social Reforms (Slovakia)
Kč	Czech crowns
KDH	Christian Democratic Movement (Slovakia)
KDS	Christian Democratic Party (Czech Republic)
KDU-ČSL	Christian Democratic People's Party (Czech Republic)
KIE	Committee for European Integration (Poland)
KMT	Kuomintang (Taiwan)

KPN	Confederation for an Independent Poland
KSAP	National School of Public Administration (Poland)
KSČM	Communist Party of Bohemia and Moravia
LPR	League of Polish Families
MFA	Ministry of Foreign Affairs
MITI	Ministry of International Trade and Industry (Japan)
NATO	North Atlantic Treaty Organization
NDB	New Democracies Barometer
NGO	nongovernmental organization
NIK	Supreme Audit Office (Poland)
NUTS	Nomenclature des Unités Territoriales Statistiques (EU)
ODA	Civic Democratic Alliance (Czech Republic)
ODS	Civic Democratic Party (Czech Republic)
OECD	Organization for Economic Cooperation and Development
OF	Civic Forum (Czech Republic)
OPZZ	All-Poland Trade Union
PC	Center Understanding (Poland)
PHARE	Poland and Hungary Action for the Reconstruction of the Economy (EU)
PiS	Law and Justice Party (Poland)
PO	Citizens' Platform (Poland)
PR	proportional representation
PRI	Institutional Revolutionary Party (Mexico)
PRL	Polish People's Republic
PSL	Polish Peasant Party
SDK	Party of the Democratic Coalition (Slovakia)
SDKÚ	Slovak Democratic and Christian Union
SDL'	Party of the Democratic Left (Slovakia)
SdRP	Social Democracy of Poland
SDSS	Social Democratic Party of Slovakia
SK	Slovak crowns
SLD	Democratic Left Alliance (Poland)
SMK	Party of the Hungarian Coalition (Slovakia)
SNS	Slovak Nationalist Party
SO	Self-Defense (Poland)
SOP	Association for Civic Understanding (Slovakia)
SPR-RSČ	Association for the Republic-Republican Party of Czechoslovakia
UD	Democratic Union (Poland)

UDF	Union of Democratic Forces (Bulgaria)
UP	Union of Labor (Poland)
US	Freedom Union (Czech Republic)
UW	Freedom Union (Poland)
VPN	Public Against Violence (Slovakia)
WHO	World Health Organization
ZChN	Christian National Union (Poland)
ZRS	Association of Workers of Slovakia
ZS	Slovak Green Party

Runaway State-Building

Introduction

We still have not fully realized that, since 1989, we have not simply been reforming the state, we have been building it.

Aleksander Smolar (April 2004), political scientist and advisor to several post-1989 Polish governments (quoted in Kurski 2004)

As democratization sweeps across new parts of the globe—from Latin America to Africa, Eastern Europe to East Asia—it is hard not to be struck by the variety and diversity of the world's new democracies. Their political culture, path of democratic transition, previous democratic experience, and level of economic development are just a few of the differences that contribute to their conspicuous diversity. Yet a great number of these new democracies have a common feature: because of their politicization, the very state institutions meant to facilitate effective government seem just as likely to frustrate it.

Nowhere is the tension between democratic politics and the development of the state more apparent than in formerly communist nations. If the fall of communism in Eastern Europe confounded the expectations of both scholars and political actors in 1989, much of the region's political development since the fall has proven equally surprising. Particularly unexpected is the evolution of state bureaucracies after communism. The first surprise is that severing the close links between the Communist Party and the state has not reduced bureaucratic bloat.[1] On the contrary, many bureaucracies have grown dramatically ten years after revolutions that were against an overweening and monolithic state apparatus.[2] For all their expansion, these states continue to underperform, and in some cases have even declined, in their capacity for governance (Ganev 2001). This pattern of runaway state-building—rapid expansion in the size of the state administration without appreciable gains in its effectiveness—is visible in much, though not all, of the region.[3] The second big surprise is the variation in state-building outcomes. Despite similarities

in terms of their recent history, political institutions, level of economic development, political culture, and geopolitical context, a small minority of these states
have not expanded significantly but have achieved superior governance to that of
their neighbors.

The appearance of runaway state-building in much of Eastern Europe is one of
the great ironies of political development after communism, but perhaps more important, it provides a close to controlled setting for exploring a phenomenon evident in a great many of the world's new democracies. The goal of this book is to
make use of the research opportunity offered by the confluence of the fall of communism, introduction of democratic politics, and re-building of the state in Eastern Europe and to analyze the relationship between government, opposition, and
the state in democratic and democratizing systems.

To explain the variation in state-building trajectories among postcommunist
states, this book advances a more general argument about the relationship between
political parties and the state in new democracies. Runaway state-building is a consequence of patronage politics in party systems whose underinstitutionalization
precludes robust party competition.[4] The number of personnel expands most, and
the ability to build administrative capacity lags behind farthest, in those new democracies where party system development has stalled and where party competition
does not provide voters the means to discipline the government. Runaway state-
building is patronage-driven state-building, a potential problem wherever democratization occurs in the context of an unconsolidated state.[5]

In analyzing why runaway state-building has occurred in much of Eastern Europe, this book provides a framework for untangling the causal relationships between party competition, political patronage, and the state which have long formed
a focal point of comparative politics research and theorizing (Geddes 1994; Shefter
1994; Skowronek 1982). As Barbara Geddes (1994) recounts, the Brazilian state in its
various democratic interludes seesawed between periods of effective policymaking
and debilitating patrimonialism, depending on the robustness of party competition.
The inability to control patronage politics provided some of the most serious challenges to Asia's new democracies in the 1980s and 1990s, as the Philippines and Indonesia vividly illustrate (Thompson 1996; Montinola 1999; Tan 2004). Africa has
faced endemic political corruption (Rothchild and Chazan 1988), and the problems
stemming from such corruption are still evident after the continent's wave of democratization in the 1990s (Gyima-Boadi 2004). Anarchic party competition led to
rampant patronage politics in the French Third Republic, and dominant-party politics in postfascist Italy led to chronic state bloat (Shefter 1994). Even U.S. history,
which contributed the terms *spoils system* and *urban machine* to the literature on pa-

tronage politics, offers many examples of political parties that used state resources for their own internal party-building (Shefter 1994). Finally, recent scholarship on southeastern Europe in the 1970s and 1980s suggests a strong link between the quality of party competition and the politicization of the state (Ziblatt and Biziouras 2005).

Some may wonder: why call this state-building at all? Certainly, I am departing here from the conventional usage of the term, which refers to the process by which a state gains greater power over or autonomy from society—by war-making or by bureaucratizing (Tilly 1985; Silberman 1993, 1–4). In either case, expansion implies increasing state capacity. In contrast, runaway state-building is not driven by inter-state competition or bureaucrats seeking legal-rational legitimation, but by elected politicians seeking patronage resources for the task of party-building. Thus, in runaway state-building, a bigger state is a sign of both patronage and state *under*development (Kitschelt 2000; Piattoni 2001, 200–206; Scott 1969).[6]

When does state-building become runaway state-building? The answer hinges on the concurrent phenomena of rapid expansion of the state administration and the failure to achieve commensurate gains in effectiveness. But what are the criteria for assessing rapid growth and effectiveness? It is not my intention to fix absolute threshold limits for runaway state-building which could apply across history and across the globe. It makes more sense to understand the concept of runaway state-building in relative terms, to use it as means for constructing specific cross-national comparisons framed within a certain geographical and historical context.[7] For example, in the context of the decolonization of Africa after World War II, African states A and B grew much more rapidly than African states C and D. In Eastern Europe, looking at countries that are very similar in most relevant respects, the Polish and Slovak states grew much more rapidly than the Czech and Hungarian ones. Within the context of postcommunist Eastern Europe, one can establish a baseline for what would be considered very rapid growth: a rapid rate of expansion is one in which the size of the state administration doubles within ten years or less.[8] By this measure, Poland, Slovakia, Bulgaria, and many of Russia's regions would meet the first criterion for classification as runaway states, but Hungary and the Czech Republic, which presumably faced the same basic structural constraints, would not. This rule of thumb may not be useful in other contexts—for example in comparing the growth of city administrations in the United States in its age of machine politics—but one might still use the concept of runaway state-building to compare American cities and to test the hypothesis that their expansion is the result of how local-level party systems developed. It is a matter of establishing the right baseline for a particular context.

But how much of runaway state-building is "runaway" and how much is state-building? Even in the most patronage-dominated political systems, some portion of administrative expansion will serve functional needs—to provide more state services, for example—rather than political ones. As Chapter 1 discusses, a considerable part of these states' postcommunist expansion is certain to have been the result of the transition to a market economy. It is probably impossible to determine, a priori, how much state-building was functional and how much was political in any given case. It is, however, quite possible to make an accurate post facto assessment by establishing a comparative baseline using countries facing the same geopolitical and economic structural constraints. If, for example, Eastern European states of similar levels of economic development facing the same task of transforming a command economy at the same time experienced wildly different rates of state expansion, then it is plausible that functional imperatives were not the only ones at work. If, furthermore, there are both strong theoretical reasons and a raft of empirical evidence suggesting that patronage politics is more widespread in those countries whose administrations expanded most rapidly, then the case for patronage-led state-building becomes stronger still. As in all comparative politics research, it is necessary to set wide confidence intervals and to subject apparent relationships to tight scrutiny. It is also necessary, of course, to have area-specific knowledge in order to frame the right comparisons.

What exactly is expanding: personnel, institutions, spending? This is a topic addressed in detail in Chapters 1 and 2, but for now the important thing to note is that prior theory and area-specific knowledge must determine which units to compare. This book focuses on the state administration, the policy-implementing heart of the state, but even within this category I concentrate on several units to compare its overall development across countries. For example, Chapter 2 examines the number of national-level personnel, while Chapter 5 looks separately at local-level personnel. This decision is driven by theoretical considerations (it only makes sense to talk about patronage-led state expansion if government decisions can affect hiring patterns within a given part of the state) and area-specific knowledge (national-level governments do not make hiring decisions at the local level in these countries). Chapters 4 and 6 investigate institutions and spending on specific policies. The more that trends in these areas of comparison point in the same direction, the more robust the assessment of the character of state expansion will be.

Because the effectiveness of the state administration is difficult to measure empirically, this book does not rest its characterization of state effectiveness on any one indicator. Instead, it uses a battery of indicators. If these point in the same direction, and if they are properly contextualized historically and geographically, then I take them as valid measures of effectiveness. An effective state is one whose administration displays the following four characteristics: predictable career paths, an ethic of professionalism, a clear recognition and enforcement of the distinction between public means and private gain, and political autonomy.[9] Chapter 3 describes how I used interviews to evaluate postcommunist state administrations on these criteria. I corroborate this set of indicators with those constructed by other scholars, particularly, a recent cross-national indicator of the quality of governance created by the World Bank called "government effectiveness" (Kaufmann, Kraay, and Mastruzzi 2003). This is described in detail in Chapter 1, but in brief, it is a composite measure of the capacity of the state administration to implement government policies. I then use policy case studies of health care and social security to assess a state's ability to provide benefits according to its own predefined criteria and legal commitments. As with the rate of state expansion, it makes more sense to assign individual states relative values on the effectiveness variable than to attempt to come up with an absolute measure that can apply across different regions and time periods. If a state is expanding rapidly, while at the same time receiving low scores on all of these indicators, I consider it a case of runaway state-building.[10]

Why does patronage politics matter? What are the costs of runaway state-building? There are, of course, the costs of unnecessary and underutilized administrative personnel. In countries engaged in economic catch-up, these are wasted resources, representing public investment that never occurred. But more important than the wage costs are the less visible, though much greater, costs to state capacity. Patronage is an external shock to the process of bureaucratic rationalization that social scientists since Max Weber have identified as the core attribute of state-building (Weber 1978; Silberman 1993; Skocpol 1985). As Peter Evans and James Rauch (1999; 2000) have shown in their comparison of state organization in 35 less developed countries, bureaucratic rationalization (or as they put it, "Weberianness") is the linchpin of effective state governance and, in the long term, brings higher economic growth rates. Of course, state capacity is only one of a number of factors affecting long-term economic growth, and transition economies may initially post impressive growth rates as they complete macroeconomic reforms that require little active state regulation (Evans and Rauch 1999, 761).[11] Without effective states, however, these growth rates are hard to sustain in the medium to long term, especially as governments turn to the more regulation-intensive elements of economic productivity—for example, education, health care, and industrial policy. Even in the short run, an ineffective state means that a less developed country is not living up to its economic potential. Rampant patronage politics weakens the foundations of democracy itself, particularly in new democracies. By undermining state effectiveness, patronage deprives government parties of a necessary tool to deliver on the policies of their campaign programmes, which in turn breeds general disillusionment with democracy. At the extreme, this "Weimar scenario" means democracy in form but not in content. Such "electoral democracies" may find it difficult to weather internal challenges from nondemocrats and, should they arise, waves of reverse democratization (Huntington 1997).

Postcommunist Eastern Europe constitutes perhaps the ideal research platform for examining patronage-led state-building because it includes a wealth of cases that offer both wide variation and the opportunity for controlled comparisons. I focus on three new democracies in which regime change necessitated a radical reorientation and rebuilding of the state bureaucracy: Poland, the Czech Republic, and Slovakia. Each typifies one of the major possible trajectories of party-building and state development, while at the same time controlling for a host of other causal factors.[12] Focusing on a small number of countries, using multiple measures, and comparing across several policy areas allows me to mitigate the difficulties of measurement and data collection that plague research—especially statistically driven research using big cross-national samples—on political corruption. In order to document the difficult, and in many cases stalled, transformation of the state from communist-style *nomenklatura* apparatus to professional and meritocratic bureaucracy, I conducted over 100 interviews in Polish, Czech, and Slovak with officials at all levels of their respective state administrations. To create comparable measures of state size, I consulted closely with the Polish, Czech, and Slovak national statistical offices to gather new data on state employment, salaries, and spending.[13]

In Poland, which has battled party fragmentation and government instability since the spectacular demise of the Solidarity movement in the early 1990s, the number of personnel in the national-level state administration doubled between 1990 and 1997. In Slovakia, where party system development was derailed by the rapid rise of an autocratic, machine-style party, the national-level administration also nearly doubled in the short space of seven years. In neither country was the explosive expansion in state size matched by an (at least roughly) commensurate increase in state capacity. By contrast, the national bureaucracy of the Czech Republic, whose party system consolidated early in the postcommunist period, expanded little in the same period. This difference is all the more striking in light of measures of state capacity that rank the Czech administration more highly than the Polish and Slovak ones—both in absolute terms and relative to the beginning of the transition (Kaufmann, Kraay, and Mastruzzi 2003).

Runaway state-building occurs when party-building and state-building become intertwined, creating ideal conditions for patronage politics. New democracies often are characterized by weak civil societies and states delegitimized by their un-democratic past; such problems are particularly acute in Eastern Europe and the former Soviet Union. The public's disengagement from politics constitutes a severe obstacle to party-building strategies based on popular mobilization, while the dele-gitimization of the state presents a tempting opportunity for party-building based on influence over recruitment to and promotion in the state bureaucracy. These two social facts generate strong pressures for parties to substitute patronage for mass support in building their own organizations. This patronage swells the state ad-ministration, politicizes its personnel, and hobbles its effectiveness.

This argument would seem to fly in the face of pluralist theories of politics, whose basic premise is that elections enable voters to "vote the rascals out" (Pow-ell 1989; 2000). If the public disapproves of official corruption, why should the in-troduction of electoral competition not increase government accountability to voters and lead to more rationalized state-building?[14] I argue that electoral com-petition can constrain patronage-led state-building when it is robust and insti-tutionalized—restrictive conditions for this region. *Robust competition* implies that no party is dominant. *Institutionalization* means that elections present voters the choice among a manageable number of stable parties with familiar coalition-build-ing preferences (Mainwaring 1999, 3–4; Mair 1997; Toole 2000, 458; Shabad and Slomczynski 2004; Kreuzer and Pettai 2003). Party systems that meet these criteria provide the conditions for building coherent governments and credible opposi-tions. Only rarely have postcommunist party systems provided these conditions, however. Some have been dominated by political machines. Others have been highly fragmented and volatile. In either case, competition has done little to rein in wide-scale patronage.

In many ways, the 1989 revolutions in Eastern Europe represented a telescoped version of Martin Shefter's (1994) celebrated thesis about the sequencing of state- and party-building:[15] if party-building precedes the consolidation of state bureau-cracies, then party-builders incline toward patronage-based strategies.[16] Because electoral competition was introduced *before* the consolidation of the postcommu-nist state administrations, the door was open to patronage politics, enabling un-derdeveloped and resource-hungry parties to raid the administration for their own party-building. Like the nineteenth- and early-twentieth-century Italian and Amer-ican cases Shefter (1994) and Epstein (1967, 104–11) describe, postcommunist coun-tries faced the challenge of reconciling the processes of building democratic party structures and modern state bureaucracies. The revolutions of 1989 brought a sud-den and complete expansion of suffrage. New party structures had to be established and built up. The discredited, but not disbanded, Communist Parties had to rebuild sprawling party apparatuses for a changed political landscape.[17] The dual transformations from a centrally planned to a market economy and from a Leninist to a democratic regime necessitated major restructuring of the state administration at the same time that governing elites were seeking to build a party political base for themselves.

The sequencing thesis is the best answer that comparative politics has as to why patronage politics occurs in some countries and not in others, and it correctly predicts the strong predisposition to patronage-led state-building that has occurred in Eastern Europe. Yet the sequencing thesis is not sufficient to explain the *variation* in state-building in Eastern Europe. It is not enough simply to know the sequencing of democratization and state consolidation; electoral competition also constrains party behavior. This book reappraises the sequencing hypothesis from a party-competitive, pluralist perspective. Such a perspective rests on Schumpeter's understanding of democracy as a mechanism for translating representation into governance through competitive elections and government accountability (Schumpeter 1950).[18] Of course, the Schumpeterian perspective also highlights the difficulties in accomplishing this translation. One of its key insights is to show how some forms of pluralist party competition frustrate effective government: the logic of party competition in Poland and Slovakia furnish two good examples. By showing the sequencing framework's limitations, this book points to ways in which it may be refined, strengthened, and made more applicable to new cases.

The second task of this book is to explain how patronage affects not just the size but also the organization of state administrations, especially their effectiveness. If, in Weberian terms, bureaucracy is an organizational form that derives its legitimacy from legal-rationalism, then patronage represents a patrimonial form of legitimization. Instead of establishing their authority on professional credentials and policy-making expertise, state officials depend on personal connections to politicians for their positions, budgets, and material resources. In contrast to bureaucratic rationalization, patronage-led state-building is neither propelled by routinization and knowledge accumulation nor characterized by predictability and impersonalism. Rather it is unpredictable, personalized, and unconstrained by past commitments. As a result, patronage-based bureaucracies are less effective than Weberian ones (Evans and Rauch 1999; 2000). Of the three countries at the focus of this book, only the Czech Republic—whose more robust party competition has offered greater restraint on patronage by the parties of government—has begun to develop the features of bureaucratic organization. In contrast, the more prevalent and more sweeping patronage made possible by Poland and Slovakia's dysfunctional party competition has arrested the process of bureaucratization in those countries' state administrations.

Patronage-led state-building is a problem that in different geographic and historical contexts has long fascinated political scientists, sociologists, and historians. Understanding why states fail to build capacity is also a pressing practical problem. As the record of the developmental states in Asia attests, states can become the agents of modernization and progress in the less developed world (Johnson 1982; Wade 1990; Amsden 1989); therefore, the opportunity costs of runaway state-building are potentially enormous. Though scholars have drawn attention both to the incomplete institutionalization of party systems and to the problem of bloated, ineffective state administration in new democracies, the tendency has been to treat these separately. This book, by contrast, sees them as interrelated phenomena.

This book also corrects a curious shortcoming of the preponderance of literature on the global wave of democratization in the 1980s and 1990s—its unswerving focus on the causes and prerequisites for successful democratic transition to the exclusion of analyzing the state (Ganev 2001). The argument here takes democratization as its starting point and then looks to its effects on other aspects of political development. Successful democratization is not the endpoint of transitions from authoritarianism: the very fact of democratization may create new problems of political development, problems the countries of postcommunist Eastern Europe are just now beginning to address.

PLAN OF THE BOOK

Chapter 1 lays out the theoretical framework, and the following chapters develop the threads of the argument empirically through close comparisons of Poland, the Czech Republic, and Slovakia.

Chapter 2 focuses on political parties. It describes how robust party competition served to discipline governing parties in the Czech Republic but failed to do so in Poland and Slovakia. Telling this story provides a novel means to both conceptualize and empirically measure the robustness of party competition in democratizing systems.

Chapter 3 turns to the other side of the argument, the development of the national-level state administration in terms of size and effectiveness. It documents the hypertrophic growth of the Polish and Slovak state administrations in the 1990s, in contrast to the restrained expansion of the Czech state. The second part of the chapter presents extensive field interviews with state officials, politicians, and policy experts from 1999 to 2001.

Chapter 4 examines state decentralization: how national governments handle decentralization gets to the heart of the relationship between party competition and state-building. Do governments treat such "reform" as a way to create new offices without devolving real power? Because of its interest to the European Union (EU), decentralization also provides an excellent means to assess the influence of the EU on postcommunist state-building. Contrary to the institutional convergence predicted by much of the conventional wisdom, the demands of EU enlargement can produce very different institutional outcomes in the postcommunist states which reflect how domestic party politics can twist the intentions of EU incentives and pressures. In the absence of robust party competition, government parties often use the EU as cover for patronage-enhancing "reforms." This case study highlights the influence of the EU in placing certain reforms on the state-building agenda and the limits of EU conditionality in controlling the course of those reforms.

Chapter 5 analyzes the development of local state administrations, which because of their insulation from national politics, are excluded from the analysis of the previous chapters. This very insulation, however, makes the local-level state a perfect comparison for testing the explanatory power of rival political-cultural hypotheses about state-building. For example, a bureaucratic culture hypothesis would predict the same pattern of state-building at the local and national levels in each country, regardless of the robustness of local party competition. The data reveal, however, that the rate of *local* state expansion in the Czech Republic *is no less* than that in Poland. Because local-level party competition in the Czech Republic is underinstitutionalized, it is unable to constrain patronage politics by local governments. The expansion of *local-level* Czech state administration is the exception that proves the rule.

Chapter 6 asks how far the argument can be extended to other areas of the state. How useful is the party competition framework, which works so well for the development of the state administration, in explaining the development of the postcommunist welfare state? This chapter presents case studies of two important areas of welfare policy: pension systems and health care. Though the analysis shows one key difference—that state expansion came in the form of expenditure rather than personnel growth—the general outlines of state-building are the same. The greatest expansion and the least effective welfare policy administration occurred in those countries where party competition was least robust.

Chapter 7 tackles the question: how well does this book's theoretical framework travel to other new democracies? Using the categories developed in the previous chapters' analysis of the emblematic Polish, Czech, and Slovak cases, it presents a large-N analysis of state effectiveness and party system development in contemporary Latin America, Africa, Asia, and the rest of Eastern Europe.

The conclusion addresses three questions that spring from the previous chapters' analysis of state-building and democratization in Poland, the Czech Republic, and Slovakia. First, are there institutional mechanisms for strengthening party competition and constraining party patronage in new democracies? Second, how sustainable is runaway state-building over the long term? Finally, what are its implications for the study of comparative politics?

CHAPTER ONE

The Concept and Causes of Runaway State-Building

The stakes in the new democracies in Eastern Europe are large, with the state, in effect, being up for grabs. Whoever comes to power is not only in a position to determine that most crucial of resources, the rules of the game, but also in a position to control the new bureaucracies and new government agencies. Given that much will now start from scratch, there are few if any legacies which will need to be accommodated. Party, inevitably, will make a difference.

Peter Mair (1997, 172)

This chapter lays out the theoretical framework driving the comparisons at the core of this book. It first presents the broad outlines of runaway state-building in the core case studies: Poland, the Czech Republic, and Slovakia. More detailed measures are set forth in Chapter 3. Before presenting a model linking party competition to patronage politics, the focus of Chapter 2, the current chapter briefly sets forth the major rival hypotheses for the phenomenon of runaway state-building in the countries compared here. The last section of the chapter presents a framework for analyzing the impact of patronage on the effectiveness of the state administration.

THE PHENOMENON

As a unit of analysis, the state is one of the more contentious and sprawling within social science. Any study of state-building runs into the problem of how widely or narrowly to define the state itself. Define it too broadly and one's theory need incorporate a multitude of variables in order to explain something like the magnitude of expansion, for different elements of the state, such as the educational system and the military, may expand for different reasons. This problem is accentuated when there are only a few cases and including many variables wipes out analytical leverage. Define the state too narrowly and one's causal inferences will not be generalizable.

To test the hypothesis that the magnitude and character of administrative expansion is determined by the capacity of party competition to constrain patronage, I have settled on the following balance between these internal and external validity considerations: I define the state bureaucracy as the set of nonelected, publicly funded positions of administration of the central government and its branch offices. At the level of the national administration, this includes the central ministries and offices, their branch offices, the territorial administration of the central government, state inspectorates, and tax offices. This is the heart of the state, the apparatus of administration that translates government policies into practice, that oversees the collection of tax revenues, and that represents the authority of the central government in the far-flung provinces (Weber 1978; Skocpol 1985; Tilly 1985; Silberman 1993).

This definition of the state also lends itself particularly well to studying the dynamics of patronage politics in countries undergoing simultaneous democratization and state-building.[1] The state administration constitutes the set of positions most directly linked to the policies of the national government for their organizational character, composition, and functioning. It is here that the Communist Party's *nomenklatura* system left its strongest mark on organizational culture. Since the fall of communism ended the *nomenklatura* system, it is now seen by both administrative officials and the public as an abuse of power to place political appointees in mid- and lower-level bureaucratic posts.[2] In practice, however, there have been few formal or informal constraints on such appointments by the governing parties. The only effective constraint is a credible opposition party or parties, which voters can use to punish government parties that push patronage too far. Thus, the state administration became the spoils of national-level party competition in the postcommunist era. If one cannot establish a relationship between patronage politics and expansion in this part of the state, it is unlikely that one can establish one in other parts.

It is important to be clear about what is not included in this definition of the state, and why it is not included. First, I am not (initially) looking at the local state

administration.[3] Local governments were established in Poland, the Czech Republic, and Slovakia in 1990. From their inception, they were granted autonomy from
the central government in the hiring of personnel and guaranteed their own resource base through fixed formulas for sharing tax revenues with the center. Therefore, examining national-level party politics cannot be expected to explain local administrative expansion. Second, my definition does not include the military, though
it does include administrative positions in the Ministry of Defense and the Ministry
of the Interior. To include the military apparatus of the state would introduce a
whole range of international factors, clouding the intended focus on domestic politics. State-owned enterprises are also excluded since their development is driven in
large part by market forces.

Last, my definition excludes personnel employed in state welfare services. The
reason, again, is not that patronage is absent from this sphere but simply that its link
to personnel expansion is less direct than in the state administration. In comparison
to the state administration, welfare agencies have proved less open to patronage
since 1989. As I discuss later in this chapter, whereas state administrative positions
have been relatively well-paid since 1989, those in the welfare state have been noto-
riously underpaid, which makes them unattractive for patronage.[4] Moreover, welfare agencies were less directly linked to the *nomenklatura* system during the communist era.[5] Even lower-level positions in the welfare system—such as nurses and
teachers—require a greater degree of specialized knowledge and professional expertise than those in the administration, which serves as a barrier to patronage.

Figure 1.1 shows the cumulative growth in the number of personnel in the
national-level state bureaucracies in Poland, the Czech Republic, and Slovakia from
1993 to 2000.[6] The number of personnel in Slovakia and Poland grew by 71 and 55
percent, respectively. If one takes 1990 as the baseline, the Polish state administration doubled between 1990 and 1996. In other words, it took only seven years for the
number of personnel in both the Polish and the Slovak state bureaucracies to dou-
ble in size. Not only is expansion of this magnitude and speed extraordinary in comparison with Western Europe and the United States, it far outstrips the growth of
the neighboring Czech state. The Czech administration barely budged, increasing
by only 16 percent.[7]

In addition to its magnitude, the timing of expansion differed greatly. Slovakia's
was concentrated in a two-year period, while Poland's was constant over time. The
differing periodization of state expansion in Poland and Slovakia reflected how their
logics of party competition each structured patronage. As I describe below, in Slovakia patronage was tied to a single political machine and very much depended on
the political fortunes of that one party. When that party needed patronage, it

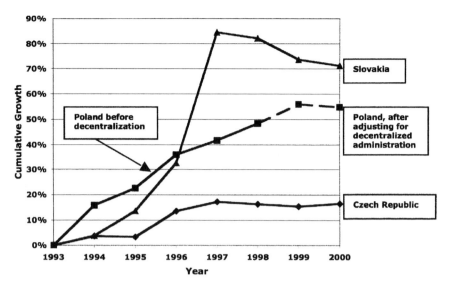

Fig. 1.1. Cumulative Growth of National-Level State Administrative Personnel. See Appendix 1 for sources

splurged. In Poland, by contrast, patronage was shared out among many parties and was a general feature of the system regardless of who sat in the government. This created a dynamic of steady, inexorable state growth.

One might surmise that the Slovak and Polish state administrations expanded so much not because of patronage but because they were adding capacity while the Czechs were not. However, if new personnel were added because they met real needs and were meritocratically selected, then the effectiveness of the state administration should have risen in at least rough proportion to its growth in size. In my interviews with state officials from 1999 to 2001 (presented in Chapter 3), this was certainly not the picture of Slovak and Polish state-building that emerged. Nor do other independently collected data, such as Kaufmann, Kraay, and Mastruzzi's "Governance Matters III" survey (2003), suggest that Poland or Slovakia have built state capacity commensurate with the magnitude of expansion.[8] Table 1.1 presents each country's score on their index of "government effectiveness," a measure that "combine[s] into a single grouping responses [in surveys of area specialists and policy experts] on the quality of public service provision, the quality of the bureaucracy, the competence of civil servants, the independence of the civil service from political pressures, and the credibility of the government's commitment to policies" (2003, 3).[9] As these data show, the fastest growing states of Poland and Slovakia were not those with the most capacity at the end of the 1990s. Nor were they the states

TABLE 1.1.
Government Effectiveness Scores by Country and Year

Country	1996	2000
Czech Republic	0.60	0.71
Poland	0.47	0.39
Slovakia	0.18	0.28

SOURCE: Kaufmann, Kraay, and Mastruzzi (2003)

that made the greatest gains in capacity relative to their starting points. This is the definition of runaway state-building: hypertrophic expansion with no discernable gain in capacity.

WHAT CAUSES RUNAWAY STATE-BUILDING? RIVAL HYPOTHESES

What are other possible explanations for runaway state-building in postcommunist countries, and among these three countries in particular? The comparative politics literature suggests a number of alternatives. The aim here is not to rule them out definitively, only to show their shortcomings before setting forth a patronage explanation that offers the best fit for the variation observed.

Some have pointed to economic factors. One variant of this argument is that postcommunist states have grown as a result of acquiring new tasks in the transformation from a command to a market economy (Bartkowski 1996). While this explanation accounts for some of the expansion, the magnitude and rapidity of Polish and Slovak expansion seem above and beyond the demands of economic restructuring; after all, the transition obviated tasks such as central planning at the same time that it introduced new ones. More importantly, why has the magnitude of state expansion varied so much between these three countries, which are at similar points in the economic transition?[10] It is questionable to assume, as this explanation implicitly does, that the restructuring of the state to handle its new tasks occurs in an instrumentally rational, efficient manner. One cannot assume that there is a constituency for administrative reform in these countries that is sufficiently organized to thwart the ambitions of political parties seeking to benefit from state restructuring.

A second variant of the economic explanation invokes Wagner's Law, which holds that economic development generates demand for greater levels of government services (Gimpelson and Triesman 2002; Wagner 1883). Over the long term, it seems hard to argue with this proposition, but how much can it say about only a decade's worth of economic change? Even Karl Marx would have hesitated to suggest that the political superstructure could respond with such alacrity and elasticity to a change in the base economic structure. Wagner's Law offers little empirical traction among these three countries.[11] The Czech Republic has the highest per capita gross domestic product (GDP) in the region, yet one of the lowest rates of administrative expansion.[12] Nor does Wagner's Law fare much better if the metric is switched to that of economic growth. While the Polish and Slovak economies grew somewhat more quickly than the Czech one at the beginning of the 1990s, the difference in the rate of state growth far outclassed the economic one. Indeed, looking more broadly at the region casts serious doubt on the hypothesis that state growth follows economic growth. According to available secondary sources, the Bulgarian and Russian administrations grew by 33 and 53 percent at the same time that these countries' economies contracted by 9 and 17 percent.[13] Rapid state expansion seems just as likely in countries in the midst of economic collapse as in those experiencing growth.

Perhaps it is a question of formal institutions: constitutions and legislation. How then to explain the differences in expansion among countries with similar institutions? Poland, the Czech Republic, and Slovakia are all parliamentary democracies.[14] For most of this period, there were no notable differences in legislation governing party finance[15] and the civil service. Until 1997, Poland lacked a civil service law, meaning there were no standard guidelines for hiring and firing state personnel. After 1997, it had not one but two civil service acts within approximately a year. The first, legislated by the postcommunists, was perceived as a political gambit by the following post-Solidarity government and replaced with a new version. The irony, of course, is that this is precisely the kind of maneuvering that civil service legislation is supposed to prevent. Slovakia and the Czech Republic lacked civil service legislation until after 2001.

One tempting institutional explanation is to attribute the Slovak state's expansion to its winning independence in 1993; however, this explanation has two important shortcomings. First, Czechoslovakia was a federal state from 1968 until its dissolution in 1993; thus, the Slovak Republic had had its own state apparatus—republican governments, ministries, and branch offices—since 1968 (Hendrych 1993, 45–47). Second, the timing of Slovak expansion suggests that party political factors were paramount. As Figure 1.1 shows, the lion's share of expansion took place not in the first years after independence but later, in a concentrated spike from 1996 to 1997. This spike coincided with a blatantly self-serving "reform of the public administration" undertaken by the governing political machine of Vladimír Mečiar, which is detailed in Chapter 4. That the Czech and Slovak Republics were part of the same federal state until very recently is, in fact, analytically advantageous because it allows one to control almost perfectly for formal institutional factors as rival hypotheses.

A third potential cause of state expansion in postcommunist Eastern Europe is the project of joining the European Union (EU). Some have argued that the need to implement EU law has led to the expansion of the state bureaucracy (Nunberg 1998; 2000; Torres-Bartyzel and Kacprowicz 1999). Chapter 4 deals intensively with the role of the EU in postcommunist state-building. I argue there that while the EU's influence was certainly present (particularly at the end of the 1990s), it was also strongly shaped by domestic party politics. Thus while much of the conventional wisdom expected the EU to bring institutional convergence in Eastern Europe, considerable institutional variation resulted from how the opportunities and demands of EU enlargement were refracted through the lens of party system type. In countries with less robust and less institutionalized competition, EU accession often served as a cover for governments to undertake patronage-enhancing "reforms" that did little to add real state capacity. This finding also underscores the importance of periodizing the EU's relationship with Eastern Europe. Until the European Commission began formal evaluations of the applicant states in 1997, the EU was more of a promise than an institutional constraint, yet the signs of dramatic bureaucratic growth in Eastern Europe were evident immediately after 1989. Underscoring the limits of EU influence, Eastern European governments were just as likely to look to Americans like Jeffrey Sachs when undertaking macroeconomic reform or to countries like Chile for policy templates when reforming the pension system.

Finally, one might point to differences in political culture. Herbert Kitschelt (1999), for example, has argued that Poland and the former Czechoslovakia long belonged to different bureaucratic traditions before the communist era, that these differences carried through communism, and that they have reemerged in postcommunist politics. Such an argument allows for national differences in state expansion. It suffers, however, from two problems. First, even if there were differences in bureaucratic culture in these countries prior to World War II, it is a grave underestimation of the influence of communism in Eastern Europe to argue that political and social differences from before the interwar period simply reemerged after 1989. The Soviet state was a coherent, comprehensive, and revolutionary model of administration that was imposed with uniformity across Eastern Europe. It was calculated to uproot and replace the national political cultures with which it came into contact (Gross 1989; Jowitt 1992). What then were the mechanisms that sustained national bureaucratic culture during the Leninist revolution? Second, the national bureaucratic hypothesis stumbles empirically when it comes to the postcommunist period. In Chapter 5, I focus on local-level bureaucracies in Poland, the Czech Republic, and Slovakia—a comparison that allows me to stand the bureaucratic and party competition hypotheses directly up against each other. The evidence provided by this comparison runs counter to the predictions of the bureaucratic tradition explanation.

A PARTY SYSTEMS EXPLANATION

Rather than economic transition, institutional difference, European integration, or political culture, my argument finds a party political logic in the expansion of postcommunist state bureaucracies. However, my formulation of this argument differs from Martin Shefter's, who has argued that where democratic politics precedes the consolidation of state bureaucracies patronage politics is the rule. In looking at the contemporary new democracies, especially the postcommunist ones, it is apparent that Shefter's insight is at once very appropriate *and* too sweeping. There are many cases where patronage predominates but also a number where it does not. State administrations in new democracies may be *predisposed* to patronage politics, but they are not *predestined* to it. Where robust and institutionalized party competition has developed, the legacies of demobilized societies and delegitimized states have not sufficed to produce patronage politics. We need a theory that can explain both the cases where patronage has led to runaway state-building and those where it has not.

The theory proposed here has three elements:

1. Demobilized societies
2. Delegitimized states
3. The logic of party system competition

Focusing on the social context and historical sequencing of democratization and state-building, the first two elements follow Shefter's take on state development in the postcommunist new democracies. The third represents a pluralist view of the relationship between parties and the state. Though the focus here is on the postcommunist context in which the core country-studies are embedded, the path of state-building will be greatly complicated wherever publics are disengaged from politics, trust in public institutions is low, and party competition is not robust and institutionalized. The cross-national comparison in Chapter 7 shows how these factors play out in the new democracies of Latin America, Africa, and Asia.

Demobilized Societies

In demobilized societies, it is difficult to build and maintain party organizations on the basis of mass membership, which forces parties to rely instead on activists and popular leaders who can organize successful election campaigns. The absence of political participation by the general public gives government parties a motive to attract and hold on to these crucial political supporters, and patronage is the key to attracting them.[16]

The distinction between externally and internally mobilized parties is helpful for understanding patronage-based party-building. Internally mobilized parties are those "founded by elites who occupy positions within the prevailing regime and who undertake to mobilize a popular following behind themselves in an effort either to gain control of the government or to secure their hold over it" (Shefter 1994, 30). They are, in short, the insider parties. In Russia, such parties are referred to as "parties of power" (partii vlast'i). Internally mobilized parties use access to state resources, in particular to state employment, as a means of patronage in the process of party-building. Of course, these state resources need not be restricted to patronage appointments. They can include stripping the state of its financial assets, corruption, and so on. Externally mobilized parties, in contrast, are "established by outsiders who did not hold positions within the prevailing regime and who organize a mass following either in an effort to gain entry into the political system for themselves and their supporters or in an effort to overthrow that system" (30). Because they do not have access to state patronage, externally mobilized parties must use ideological and solidary appeals to attract a following. The demobilization of society in postcommunist countries gives government parties a motive to use patronage because it is exceedingly difficult to generate externally mobilized parties.

One might well ask, were not the dissident movements like Poland's Solidarity, whose members fought the Communist Party at great personal cost and little hope of victory throughout the 1980s, externally mobilized? The answer is yes, they were—but with two important caveats. Their ability to externally mobilize supporters effectively ended in 1989, and they were movements, not parties. Ironically, the total collapse of the communist regimes in Poland, the Czech Republic, and Slovakia in 1989 sealed the fate of the dissident movements that overthrew them. Without the communist enemy, these informally organized dissident movements collapsed entirely, riven by internal conflicts and spawning new, constantly subdividing factions. Solidarity was the most dramatic example of this failure to translate the shared experience of opposition into organizational capital, but the same process occurred with the Czech Civic Forum (OF) and the Slovak Public Against Violence (VPN), all of which had been eliminated or totally weakened by 1991.

As for the difficulty of generating new externally mobilized parties, the communist regimes' suppression of civil society and attempts to force participation in a Party-defined public sphere ingrained a suspicion of political participation in Eastern European societies (Rose 1995; Howard 2003).[17] As Ken Jowitt has described the culture of political nonengagement under communism, "The Party's political monopoly and punitive relation to the population produced a 'ghetto' political culture in Eastern Europe. The population at large viewed the political realm as something dangerous, something to avoid. Political involvement meant trouble. Regime-coerced political activity (not participation) sustained and heightened the population's psychological and political estrangement" (1992, 288). The appeal of slogans such as the Czech Civic Forum's "Parties are for [Communist] party members; the Civic Forum is for all" captured the public's ambivalence toward parties after 1989 (quoted in Rose, Mishler, and Haerpfer 1998, 155).[18] In the New Democracies Barometer (NDB) survey initiated by Richard Rose, only 5 percent of respondents voiced trust in political parties, the lowest score of any public institution, while 50 percent were skeptical, and 45 percent voiced outright distrust.[19] Party identification is far lower than in Western Europe (Rose 1995, 20–24), with electors "much more likely to be able to name a party they would *never* vote for than a party that they identify with" (Rose, Mishler, and Haerpfer 1998, 157).

The number of Poles who are members of a political party has been estimated at no higher than 1.5 percent of the electorate; the comparable figures for the Czech Republic and Slovakia are 6.4 and 3.1 percent (Szczerbiak 2001, 111–12). Party membership figures in Western Europe are around 9 percent.[20] As a result of their small memberships, most parties cannot maintain organizations on the basis of membership dues; therefore, state jobs are used to keep party organizers available for party work. Lacking strong ideological or programmatic ties to voters, party organizations are unusually top-heavy, depending on a small core of popular personalities and party activists to win votes. Satisfying this "internal constituency" and their hangers-on, again through access to state resources, is essential to winning votes at election time (Geddes 1994, 40–41).[21]

If postcommunist electorates have been deaf to external mobilization, the activists and leadership of a great many parties have also demonstrated a weak commitment to programmatic ideals and a proclivity for political opportunism. The half-life of political parties in new democracies like those of Eastern Europe is much shorter than in established democracies, which increases politicians' uncertainty about the future. If their party enters future elections weakened by the defection of a popular leader—or even if the party no longer exists at all—their careers could easily be cut short. The uncertainty of a career in electoral politics increases the allure of one in the state administration, which provides greater insulation from the vicissitudes of electoral competition.

Although conventional wisdom holds that public sector salaries in Eastern Europe are too low for state jobs to be attractive, this is only partially the case. It is true that, overall, public sector salaries—particularly those of nurses and teachers, who make up much of total public employment—are low, but those of state administrative officials in Poland, the Czech Republic, and Slovakia have been quite attractive in relative terms. In Poland, for example, the average central-level administrative official's salary was 44 percent higher than the general average in 1998, and in Slovakia it was twice as high (*Statistical Yearbook of the Republic of Poland* 1999; Plenipotentiary 1999). State officials also may have opportunities for rent-seeking. In countries where economic transition has brought high unemployment rates, the attractiveness of such jobs should not be underestimated.

Finally, the legacy of social demobilization also influences the process of party-building in deeper ways. The culture of political nonparticipation keeps civil society underdeveloped. There are too few civil society organizations serving as public watchdogs and checks on the exercise of state power, and those that do exist are often too weak to matter (Bartkowski 1996). The underdevelopment of civil society reduces the risks of strategies based on the distribution of patronage. Political parties are less likely to be exposed for appropriating public resources for their own benefit, especially if they are careful to avoid blatant abuses of power.

Delegitimized and Unconsolidated States

The second feature the postcommunist democracies share is the delegitimization of the administrative apparatus of the state as the Soviet system disintegrated.[22] As noted earlier, until only very recently most of Eastern Europe lacked civil service legislation, which meant that there were no formal safeguards against patronage. But even beyond these regulatory loopholes, there was a more important legitimacy crisis of the state, which provided government parties the means to use the administration as a source of patronage. Tainted by the communist past, state bureaucrats were in an extremely disadvantageous position after 1989. They could not credibly propose a program of reform that would maintain their positions. At the same time, the revolutionary regime change gave elected politicians extraordinary license to reform the state.

After 1989, the public tended to see administrative officials as remnants of the *nomenklatura* system—or, as one Polish phrase had it, the *"mierni ale wierni"* (mediocre but loyal) (Letowski 1993, 5, 9; Vidláková 1993, 70–71). Aside from the lingering resentment of the privileges formerly accorded to the *nomenklatura,* the public remembered the widespread corruption and informal connections needed to get things done (Rose, Mishler, and Haepfer 1998, 124–25). These associations still color public perceptions. Brym and Gimpelson's observation that "Russians' dislike of their state bureaucracy is so strong that they are ready to attribute to it almost all sins imaginable" (2004, 94) holds for the rest of postcommunist Eastern Europe as well. In the NDB III's questions about trust in fifteen public institutions, the category "civil servants" evoked more skepticism (61 percent of respondents) than any other institution except for the media—with 28 percent voicing outright distrust and only 11 percent trust (Rose, Mishler, and Haepfer 1998, 154).[23] More broadly, 1989 represented the collapse of a "hollowed out," posttotalitarian state, which had long since lost its sense of historical mission and which was staffed by officials no longer sure of their own place (Linz and Stepan 1996, 48–49).

Besides the infelicitous incentives inclining party politicians to engage in short-term thinking in questions of staffing the state administration, party activists and leadership in postcommunist politics also lack experience in public administration—with the partial exception of former Communist Party members. As field interviews indicated, when the anticommunist coalitions came to power in the early 1990s, their first task was to replace "red" officials wherever possible. In their view, it was necessary to remove these officials and replace them with others who had anticommunist credentials. Beyond such credentials, most politicians had an ill-formed idea of what bureaucratic professionalism entails.[24] Needless to say, this vision of public administration reform is not a firm base on which to build bureaucratic autonomy (Shefter 1994, 59).

The Logic of Party Competition

The postcommunist legacies of demobilized societies and delegitimized states are necessary, but not sufficient, conditions to produce patronage-led state-building. Robust and institutionalized party competition determines whether the predisposition to patronage politics becomes the practice of patronage politics. As noted earlier, the pluralist view argues that elections discipline governing parties by allowing voters to punish or reward them.[25] Two important assumptions lie behind the pluralists' faith in the disciplining power of elections, however. First, the mechanism of vertical accountability depends crucially on party system institutionalization, especially in new democracies.[26] Underinstitutionalization means that rather than choosing among a manageable number of familiar and relatively stable parties, voters are faced with too many party choices, many of them new, unfamiliar, and having uncertain prospects. A variety of measures of institutionalization have been proposed.[27] In this book underinstitutionalized party systems represent those characterized by extreme multipartism (high fractionalization),[28] unstable party orga-

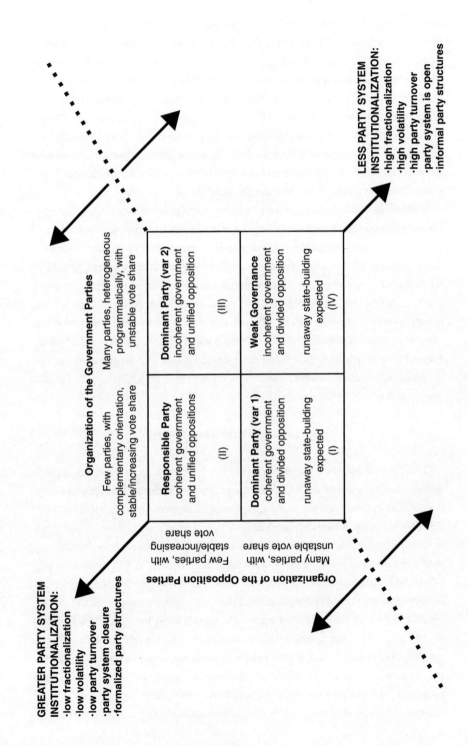

GREATER PARTY SYSTEM INSTITUTIONALIZATION:
- low fractionalization
- low volatility
- low party turnover
- party system closure
- formalized party structures

Organization of the Government Parties

Few parties, with complementary orientation, stable/increasing vote share

Many parties, heterogeneous programmatically, with unstable vote share

Organization of the Opposition Parties

Few parties, with stable/increasing vote share

Many parties, with unstable vote share

Responsible Party
coherent government and unified oppositions

(II)

Dominant Party (var 1)
coherent government and divided opposition

runaway state-building expected

(I)

Dominant Party (var 2)
incoherent government and unified opposition

(III)

Weak Governance
incoherent government and divided opposition

runaway state-building expected

(IV)

LESS PARTY SYSTEM INSTITUTIONALIZATION:
- high fractionalization
- high volatility
- high party turnover
- party system is open
- informal party structures

nization (high volatility and high party turnover),[29] unfamiliar patterns of coalition-building (low party system closure), and parties lacking formalized internal structures.[30] Chapter 2 specifies how these variables can be operationalized and measured. The second assumption, as basic as it may seem, is the absence of dominance: no party enjoys overwhelming organizational advantages over the rest.[31]

If party competition is to constrain patronage, it must produce *both* coherent governments *and* credible oppositions. The party system variables of institutionalization and dominance set the parameters for the relationship between government and opposition, which I refer to as the logic of governance (see Figure 1.2).

The usual story about state-building in new democracies holds that the sequencing of party competition and bureaucratic formation is sufficient for explaining the emergence of patronage politics. I argue instead that another step is necessary to produce patronage politics: in the absence of party system institutionalization, party competition is not sufficiently robust to generate vertical accountability. Applying the pluralist view to new democracies without considering the variable of party system institutionalization leads to a conundrum: there is electoral competition, but it often does not give voters levers over government behavior by presenting them with party alternatives. Problematically for new democracies, however, the pluralist view assumes competition between established, programmatically distinct, and relatively fixed parties, which have medium to long time horizons. Because new party systems are in most cases not yet developed, these are not safe assumptions. Instead of stability, there is fluidity, and parties' time horizons are short. Instead of internally coherent and programmatically defined parties, one finds heterogeneous coalitions. Instead of predictable coalition-building, one finds marriages of convenience. As a result, both government formation and opposition are as unpredictable to voters as they are to social scientists. Competition fails to constrain government behavior.

The less institutionalized the party system, the more difficult it is to generate vertical accountability. Extreme underinstitutionalization favors the creation of incoherent governments and less-than-credible oppositions, which I term the weak-governance logic (box IV). The organization of both the government and the opposition blocs reflects the fact that the party system contains too many parties, which are organizationally unstable and have unfamiliar coalition-building preferences. It is difficult to build governments of programmatically compatible parties; instead the tendency is to cobble together big, heterogeneous coalitions, with pat-

Fig. 1.2. (opposite) Party System Institutionalization and the Logic of Governance

ronage as the emollient smoothing over programmatic differences.[32] The general instability of party organizations shortens the time horizons of government coalition members; they are more likely to capture organizational advantages from state patronage than in systems where, having more stable vote shares, parties feel less need to create such party-building advantages. Absent reliable information on parties' coalitional preferences, voters are unsure what kind of government a vote for a particular party will produce. Multipartism, party instability, and unclear coalition preferences also weaken the ability of the opposition to present itself as a credible alternative to the government.

In the weak-governance logic, patronage is maximized but not monopolized by a large number of small government parties. The larger the government, the more difficult it is for voters to monitor patronage-seeking by individual parties within it, creating an incentive for each party to engage in patronage from which it alone profits but the costs of which (in voter disapproval) are shared out across the coalition. Because government majorities are too tenuous to risk radical intervention in the administration, systematic purges are unusual. Without a civil service code, hiring is easy, however. The result is localized and uncoordinated interventions, which are difficult to monitor but which steadily add up. In Western Europe, perhaps the best example is the French Third Republic (1875–1940), which was a swirl of weak governments, numerous parties, and wide-ranging patronage (Thomson 1969, 96–103, 109–115; Shefter 1994, 57).[33]

It is not uncommon for democratic transition to give rise to dominant parties. Dominance creates a degree of overall institutionalization since the dominant party controls a large and relatively stable vote share and tends to set the terms for government formation, but it is an uneven and incomplete kind of institutionalization, producing a different logic of governance. The rest of the party system is left under-institutionalized, composed of small, unstable, and unpredictable parties. Reflecting this uneven development, aggregate measures of party system institutionalization will fall between those of the weak-governance and responsible-party logics.[34] Such systems tend to produce either an overweening government and an ineffectual opposition (the dominant-party, variant 1 logic of governance) or an ineffectual government and an intransigent opposition (dominant-party, variant 2).

When the government includes a dominant party and the opposition are too divided to provide a credible alternative (variant 1), then the government parties can be expected to monopolize and maximize patronage. Intervention in the administration takes the form of purges, ousting officials unsympathetic to the political machine and affecting the entire administration potentially down to the lowest levels. Variant 2 of the dominant-party logic occurs if the party machine loses an election, which in free elections is always a possibility. The party machine, now in the opposition, is able to block the new government's policies while that government faces the problem of uniting its many heterogeneous parties to attack the accumulated advantages of the machine. Given their history of rivalry, each of the new government parties fears that administrative reforms will benefit the other coalition members more than itself. The result is preservation of the status quo: no new expansion but no significant rollback of the former government's policies. With administrative reform effectively blocked, it is unlikely that the switch from dominant-party (variant 1) to dominant-party (variant 2) will result in a significant improvement in the professionalism and capacity of the state administration. Because it leaves both a power vacuum in the government and a strong party in the opposition, this trajectory of party system development seems inherently unstable over the long term.[35]

The post–World War II Italian party system, with its dominant Christian Democratic party, is a good example of the dominant-party (variant 1) logic. At the center of each of Italy's many governments stood the Christian Democrats, who were able to pick parties as needed from the "opposition" to build patronage-based majorities (Tarrow 1977; Arian and Barnes 1974). Until recently, Mexico's party system was one of the most stable dominant-party arrangements on record, with the Institutional Revolutionary Party (PRI) monopolizing both elected and appointed public office from the 1920s until the mid-1990s (Craig and Cornelius 1995). Under Putin's leadership, Russia seems to be moving toward the dominant-party (variant 1) model (Lynch 2005; Meyers 2004; Mydans 2004).[36] Croatia after the death of the nationalist leader Franjo Tudjman is a good example of a dominant-party (variant 2) system; the formerly dominant Croatian Democratic Union (HDZ) lost the 2000 elections to a broad and heterogeneous coalition of opposition parties.

Finally, when party systems exhibit increasing institutionalization and no party is dominant, the conditions are there for vertical accountability—the responsible-party logic of governance. Absent extreme multipartism, governments can be formed from a small number of programmatically compatible parties, and patronage is not needed to build and maintain a majority. Voters are less likely to dilute their vote among many opposition parties, enhancing the opposition's credibility. Increasing stability of party organization means parties can survive without being in government. Familiar patterns of coalition-building allow voters to better predict how their vote will affect the composition of the government. Typically, responsible-party systems are characterized by bipolarity, meaning that party competition is anchored by two major parties. There may be additional parties, but these define themselves vis-à-vis the anchors' positions on a unidimensional policy spectrum. Given the sequencing of party-building and state consolidation, it is naïve to expect that competition can ever eliminate patronage, but the opposition is able to minimize this patronage by threatening to make it an issue in future elections. Britain's "majoritarian model"—with competition anchored by the Conservative and Labor parties—typifies the bipolar logic of competition (Powell 1989; Epstein 1980). Germany's pattern of Social Democrats vs. Christian Democrats also fits the bill.[37] Both systems are noted for their lack of patronage (Shefter 1994, 42–53).

As Chapter 2 describes in detail, the organizational strength of parties depicted in Figure 1.2 depends on the stability of their electorate, the clarity of their programmatic definition, their degree of internal homogeneity, and the stability of their leadership. These are not organizational resources that depend on the ability of parties to engage in external or internal mobilization. They do depend in large part on the shape of underlying cleavage structures in society, however. If these cleavage structures do not simplify into a left-right bipolar issue space, then party electorates are less stable, programmatic definitions are less coherent, and political elites are divided in more ways—all of which leads to internal heterogeneity and weakly organized party structures. As noted earlier, my argument assumes that governing parties are predisposed to raid the state for patronage in all new democracies with unconsolidated state administrations. The main control on this tendency is the ability of the opposition to discipline them for doing so.

The differing logics of party competition can be mapped onto the politics of state-building. Runaway state-building—rapid expansion in the size of the state administration without a commensurate increase in its professionalism and effectiveness—occurs when the opposition parties cannot effectively constrain the government. It occurs in political systems that fall into weak-governance or dominant-party (variant 1) types. Runaway state-building is not associated with responsible-party systems. While the political deadlock of dominant-party (variant 2) systems should arrest the patronage-led expansion of their state administrations, it also precludes any meaningful increase in the effectiveness of the state administration as a result of toppling the old party machine.

This simple typology captures a wide range of party systems in new democracies. Poland, the Czech Republic, and Slovakia before and after 1998 provide examples of each logic. In Slovakia between 1992 and 1998, a powerful party machine entrenched itself while the opposition parties remained fragmented and unstable. With the fall of the Mečiar political machine in 1998, Slovak party politics quickly switched to the dominant-party (variant 2) type. In Poland's fragmented system, the formation of governments still depends on the entry and exit of new, organizationally unstable parties who must form large, internally divided coalitions; here,

the multiplicity of weak parties precludes the formation of responsible governments that can deliver on their electoral promises and live to survive the next elections. Last, Czech party competition quickly developed into the responsible-party
type. Czech politics is not immune from patronage and corruption, but because
there are a few strong parties competing with each other for power—parties whose
defined programs and stable constituencies give them the organizational where-
withal to survive between elections without being in the government—democratic
pluralism allows for a credible opposition that voters can use to discipline the government and constrain patronage.

HOW PATRONAGE AFFECTS STATE EFFECTIVENESS

The final task of this chapter is to show how the logic of party competition
affects the organization and effectiveness of the state administration. In countries
where democratic regime change necessitates a radical reorientation and reconstruction of the state, at least two contradictory modes of legitimation are at work
in the development of the state administration. Each mode leads to a different institutional outcome regarding the effectiveness of the state administration. The first
mode of legitimation is patrimonialism, which in postcommunist states, is merely
the continuation of the status quo, with all its pathologies. The second mode of legitimation is legal-rationalism, which leads to bureaucratic administration in the
Weberian sense of the word (Weber 1978, 956–1005).[38] Peter Evans and James Rauch's
(1999; 2000) research on the developing world convincingly demonstrates that legal-
rational state administrations are more effective and have higher long-term economic growth rates than patrimonial ones, or as they write, "Weberianness" matters (1999, 760). However, just because it is more effective, the legal-rational state is
far from being the "natural" endpoint toward which state-building inevitably
moves. Either outcome—patrimonialism or Weberian legal-rationalism—is possible in new democracies with unconsolidated state administrations, for each mode
of legitimation is identified with a different and competing set of interests. The
logic of party competition determines the relative strength of these interests and,
hence, which will prevail. The first set of interests represents those of the personnel of the state administration themselves and the second, those of the elected
politicians. Because they generate more patronage in the administration, party systems of both the weak-governance and dominant-party types tip the advantage
away from administrative personnel and toward politicians, stalling bureaucratization and hamstringing state effectiveness.

This view of the state is Weberian, but unlike much of Weberian theorizing, it is microlevel, or microinstitutional because it focuses on the incentives of individual administrators and party politicians (Solnick 1998). The argument here has two steps. First, legal-rational bureaucratization is a developmental path that state administrators prefer to follow. Second, government parties seeking patronage in the state can knock state administrations off this path, enforcing a patrimonial dynamic of state legitimization. In short, this argument assumes a rivalry between the administrative class and the political class. State administrators prefer to insulate themselves from patronage politics in order to maximize control over their own careers and their access to the state's organizational resources; their strategy for doing so is to find legitimacy in legal-rational authority (Weber 1978; Silberman 1993; Piatonni 2001). Administrators strive to define themselves as policy professionals, and the administrations they are part of as legal-rational bureaucracies. There is a self-interested calculation behind this choice, one that depends on an individual's long-term expectations about the strategy's future benefits. Patronage politics, which is most pervasive in weak-governance and dominant-party systems, introduces uncertainty into this calculation.

If a change in the political winds seems likely, and if such a change could adversely affect the administrator's future as a professional bureaucrat, why invest the time and effort in the slow strategy of professionalization? Why not ingratiate oneself with the party or parties of power and hope for quick advancement—even if it means surrendering control over one's career path? This choice represents the patrimonial mode because it depends on personalist ties to party benefactors; loyalty is not to the office but to the benefactor and is based on the exchange of favors (Weber 1978, 1006–69). The guiding principles of this form of administration are personal discretion, informal relations, and ad hoc rules. Thus, and this is the second grounding assumption here, the other class of actors in this model, the politicians, intervene opportunistically and self-interestedly in the state administration, driven by the search for patronage resources. This strategy preserves many of the key aspects of the Leninist model of the state, which in its posttotalitarian phase had settled into patrimonialism (Linz and Stepan 1996, 247–52; Jowitt 1992, 139–51).

Now that the microlevel incentives of administrators and party politicians have been laid out, what are the institutional features of the patrimonial and legal-rational states in this model? In Eastern Europe the starting point for state-building after the democratic revolutions of 1989 was the communist-era state, which after years of ideological decay was a rickety "posttotalitarian" structure held together by personalist ties and patrimonialism (Linz and Stepan 1996, 249–52; Kennedy and Bialecki 1989). Initially, the Leninist model of the state had been charismatic, not patrimonial (Jowitt 1992, 127–39). It had been born in revolution and charged with the task of spreading that revolution to the rest of the globe. It had a compelling ideology, and when that ideology could not command the allegiance and obedience of the officialdom, leaders like Lenin and Stalin freely substituted raw force and terror. With de-Stalinization, however, the Leninist state left its charismatic stage, and instead used patrimonialism to legitimate its authority. Because the Communist Party could not sustain its rule by force alone, it used a combination of patronage and forced dependency to build support, or at least acceptance (Fish 1995). For the political elite, which included state officials, loyalty to the Communist Party was ensured through a system of institutionalized privileges, the so-called *nomenklatura* system.

What were the defining institutional features of the Leninist patrimonial state, which was the starting point for postcommunist state-building?[39] The first was the fusion of the Communist Party and the state administration. Through the *nomenklatura* system, the Communist Party carefully vetted applicants to positions in the administration and used these offices as rewards for the party faithful. Second, with the weakening of the ideological core of Leninism, the state was increasingly marked by personalism and corruption. In Weberian terms, corruption signifies the absence of a clear separation of the office and the office-holder; the former is a source of personal enrichment for the latter. Third, the patrimonial posttotalitarian state administration lacked an ethic of professionalism; rather than reflecting policy expertise and the primacy of rules, administrative decisions were noted for their arbitrariness and instrumentality.[40] Fourth, career paths in the state administration were unpredictable. Even though it was unlikely that an official would be fired, advancement in the bureaucracy depended as much on political qualifications as professional ones.

Institutionally, the legal-rational mode of administrative organization is the reverse image of the patrimonial one (Weber 1978, 1028–31). First, the political autonomy of the state administration is strictly observed. Second, office and office-holder are separated, which means official corruption is minimal. Third, professionalism is the basis of authority: the transformation of the administrative role means a new principle of selection into and promotion within the administrative apparatus. That principle becomes the accumulation of knowledge, and more importantly, the accumulation of knowledge that can be measured (Silberman 1993, 5). This produces the fourth institutional feature, predictable career paths. As Silberman puts it, "The officeholder now be[comes] accountable to a set of formal organizational rules that c[an] be observed and regulated rather than to the informal and unregulated rules governing patron-client relations"(1993, 4).

Finally, bureaucratization is a process, one that gathers momentum over time and spreads from one organizational context to others. Once a critical mass of professional administrators is in place, the impulses of rule-based impersonalism, autonomy, professionalism, and the accumulation of measurable knowledge and experience will shape the institutional environment of the administration, transforming it from patrimonial apparatus to Weberian bureaucracy. This state bureaucracy will become more complex, more routinized, more effective, and more indispensable (Weber 1978, 987–89). If the administration can clear the developmental hurdle posed by patronage politics, it will in time become a valuable asset for the government, an effective and professional tool for the governing parties to deliver on their campaign promises. As it becomes institutionalized, bipolar party competition moves toward this admirable state of affairs, which some political scientists have referred to as "responsible-party" government (Shefter 1994; Goodnow 1900). The problem with this rosy scenario, of course, is that it requires a long-term political calculation, and politicians in a new and not-yet-stable democracy may be very unsure about the long-term prospects of their parties. Patronage and patrimonial administration is the surer route to short-term survival, which is, needless to say, the prerequisite for long-term survival.

My interviews with individual state administrators in Poland, Slovakia, and the Czech Republic reveal impulses toward professionalism, autonomy, and efficiency within state administrations. If allowed to develop uninterrupted, these impulses would eventually form the basis for bureaucratic rationalization. Officials with these impulses were often weak politically, however. In weak-governance or dominant-party systems that routinely throw up pressures for intervention in the administrative apparatus, these impulses do not develop uninterrupted. A critical mass of professional administrators never forms, and the state administration remains mired in the patrimonial mode. The failure to bureaucratize in turn reinforces the tendency for patronage politics: an ineffective administration makes it hard for the governing parties to deliver on programmatic campaign proposals, reinforcing the voters' disillusionment, which again increases the parties' reliance on the critical party activists and popular leaders who can win elections and whose own loyalty rests on the informal *quid pro quo* of patronage politics.

In the Czech Republic—where responsible-party competition has meant that patronage is less prevalent and less sweeping—the state administration has begun to develop the features of legal-rational, bureaucratic organization. In both Poland's weak-governance system and Slovakia's dominant-party system, by contrast, the inability of party competition to constrain the parties of government has created frequent patronage-seeking interventions in the state administration that have retarded, and even derailed, the process of bureaucratization.

Some readers may object that I have idealized the virtues of bureaucracy while overlooking its faults. The field of organization theory has recently embraced concepts such as "new public management," which argues that bureaucracy is overly rigid, too resistant to change, and too isolated from society (Hood 1991; Boston 1991; Barzelay 1992).[41] My argument that postcommunist states need to become more bureaucratic may at first seem misguided given that specialists in public administration say Western state institutions need to become less bureaucratic.

What this objection fails to realize, however, is that states in Eastern Europe and states in the West are at very different stages of development, and what is appropriate for one may be inappropriate, even damaging, for the other (Evans and Rauch 1999; 2000). Introducing greater flexibility in hiring and firing personnel, upsetting traditional career paths, breaking down the divisions between administrators and social or political interests may all be good ideas in a state administration where the boundaries between politicians and the state, the individual and the office, are well established and where the primacy of impersonal, legal-rationalism over patrimonial and personalized administration is assumed. Where these boundaries and modes of social action are not well established—as in the delegitimized state administrations of postcommunist Eastern Europe—the introduction of such reforms is more likely to reinforce patronage than to allow these states to leapfrog bureaucracy and land at a more effective form of state administration. The drawbacks of bureaucracy—its insistence on rigid rules, isolation from outside interests, resistance to radical policy change—are problems the majority of Eastern European states would be lucky to have.

CONCLUSION

I am using this theoretical framework to probe the tangled relationship between party-building and state-building in the new democracies of postcommunist Poland, the Czech Republic, and Slovakia. Democratization before state consolidation is the necessary, but not sufficient, condition for runaway state-building. The logic of party competition is the decisive factor. Unconsolidated states may be predisposed to runaway state-building in new democracies, but they are certainly not doomed to it. If the party system stabilizes into the responsible-party logic—with a few, stable, well-organized parties that can mutually police each other—patronage politics can be reined in, and state-building can produce more effective, less expansive states. This is what has occurred in the Czech Republic and what so far has failed to occur in either Poland or Slovakia. The words "so far" are important, for both party system formation and state-building are open-ended processes. One of the chief advantages of the theory here is that it can also be used to explain change in new democracies with unconsolidated states: when and if their party systems develop robust, bipolar competition, their state administrations will begin the transformation from patrimonialism to Weberian bureaucracy.

CHAPTER TWO

Constraining Government Patronage

Different Logics of Party Competition

In modernizing society "building the state" means in part the
creation of an effective bureaucracy, but more importantly the
establishment of an effective party system capable of structuring
the participation of new groups in politics.

Samuel Huntington (1968, 401)

Robust and institutionalized party competition is critical if new democracies
with unconsolidated states are to constrain patronage politics and avoid runaway
state-building. The state-building trajectories of postcommunist countries have
diverged widely, and this divergence traces back to the logic of party competition.
Illustrating this process, this chapter shows how the Slovak, Czech, and Polish
national-level party systems quickly developed different logics of party competition
after the fall of communism.[1] In short, this chapter is about parties and party competition; it provides the concepts and empirical categories that underpin the analysis of state development in the rest of the book.

Slovakia's machine politics and Poland's failure to build stable parties in either
the government or the opposition were both catalysts for runaway state-building.
In contrast, the ability of the Czech party system to generate strong government
and opposition led to genuine checking and balancing between these two party
camps, and that restrained the tendency that it and other countries across the region have toward patronage politics. In the Slovak system, a dominant-party logic
emerged, with one party enjoying decisive organizational and resource advantages.

The Czech Republic saw the emergence of responsible-party competition: well-organized parties, the conservative Civic Democratic Party (ODS) and the Czech Social Democratic Party (ČSSD), anchored the party system. In Poland the system was characterized by a failure to consolidate around either one or two parties; rather, in a logic of fragmentation, the political space was filled with many smaller, less organized parties that banded together in unpredictable and untransparent electoral alliances. Both weak-governance and dominant-party systems muddy the choices that elections offer to voters—dividing the protest vote against a corrupt government (as was typical in Slovakia) and hiding individual party accountability behind the front of a big coalition government (as was typical in Poland)—so that the general dislike of political corruption described in Chapter 1 does not generate government accountability. In the broader picture, the emergence of three such different logics of party competition in these countries was the result of historical factors, in particular of nationalist and religious-secular cleavages present in both Poland and Slovakia but largely absent in the Czech Republic.

This chapter comprises three sections. The first presents quick sketches of Polish, Czech, and Slovak parties' starting points, which were quite similar. The second section systematizes the distinction between the three logics of party competition—dominant-party, weak-governance, and responsible-party—by introducing a more precise conceptualization of these categories along with empirical measures to accompany them. The third section applies these measures to Poland, the Czech Republic, and Slovakia during the 1990s. Each of the country descriptions starts with an overview of the main political actors and developments, followed by a systematic comparison of indicators of party system competition and institutionalization, and concludes with a brief encapsulation of how the ability (or failure) of party competition to constrain government patronage affected the course of state-building—setting the stage for the next chapter's focused analysis of patronage and state-building.

THE POLITICAL STARTING POINTS

Although, in 1989, party systems looked almost identical across Eastern Europe, by 1992 they had already begun to diverge radically in Poland, the Czech Republic, and Slovakia. The first parliamentary elections were contests between anticommunist umbrella groups and former (or, in some cases, still) Communist Parties. As is typical in democratizing systems, the first free elections were "founding elections," in which voters chose not between different policy programs or cultural agendas but simply between the remnants of the old regime and the representatives of the new (Bogdanor 1990; White 1990; Wightman 1990). The euphoria of regime change acted as a substitute for party organization in the opposition political groupings. The anticommunist blocs that contested these elections were not true political parties with clear distinctions between leaders, members, voters, and sympathizers. In fact, the very notion of party politics was suspect, evoking memories of the Communists. In the Czech Republic, for example, the anticommunist umbrella group Civic Forum (OF) ran a campaign marked by self-mockery, irony, and willful amateurism: "Having long endured a politics imposed from above, full of insufferably wooden rhetoric, elaborate ceremony, and self-important men in cheap suits and slicked-back hair, they decided the only antidote was to make this campaign into a carnival" (Horn 1990, 11). These founding elections were dominated by personalities like Václav Havel and Lech Wałęsa—whose authority derived from their "moral" qualifications—not by party programs. Decisions about the distribution of power and influence among the leadership were governed by informal, often invisible, and usually short-lived agreements.

As is typically the case with founding elections, the veneer of unity was short-lived. Once the old regime was gone, the glue that held together the opposition camp disappeared.[2] New and divergent logics of party competition began to take shape. Between 1989 and 1992, the mold of party competition was set for these countries, at least for the rest of the 1990s. Slovakia fell into dominant-party politics, Poland into the weak-governance logic, and the Czech Republic moved quickly toward a responsible-party system.

Once the anticommunist umbrella parties broke apart, unresolved nationalist and religious-secular cleavages in Slovak and Polish society prevented the emergence of responsible-party competition based on a left-right, social democratic–conservative cleavage such as developed in the Czech Republic (Bútorová and Bútora 1995; Krause 2000a; Kusý 1998; Wightman 1995). In Slovakia, the nationalist-secessionist issue quickly came to trump all others. That nationalism should have risen to prominence in Slovakia was not surprising. It was surprising, however, that so many of Slovakia's political elites should have misjudged the importance of this issue, arguing instead for some continued form of federation with the Czechs in the critical period from 1991 to 1992.[3] As a result of this misstep, Slovakia's nationalist parties, in particular Mečiar's Movement for a Democratic Slovakia (HZDS), were able to present themselves as the true defenders of Slovak interests, parlaying nationalism into party dominance for the better part of the 1990s.

In Poland, nationalism did not take the form of secessionism; but, as other scholars have shown, a nationalist-religious cleavage bisected the socioeconomic dimension of party competition (Carpenter 2002; Kitschelt et al. 1999; Wiatr 1999; Zarycki

2000). As Kitschelt and others write in their exhaustive study of postcommunist party systems, "In addition to a first factor that pits socio-economic protectionists against market liberals in ways similar to those found in the Czech Republic, Poland displays a rather strong second factor that rallies secular and libertarian cosmopolitans, on one side, and religious, authoritarian nationalists on the other" (1999, 231). Thus, among Polish "conservatives" one found both neoliberals like Mazowiecki and Balcerowicz and labor union leaders like Wałęsa. The resulting confusion of party identity was best summed up by one of the interviewees in my field research, a local politician in Cracow, who described the difference between her conservative Freedom Union (UW) party and its national-level coalition partner, the Electoral Action Solidarity (AWS):

> It's funny because both parties call themselves liberals, but, in fact, we have much different understandings of the term. Speaking about UW, we are economic liberals. That means we think taxes should be low, government should not be intrusive, in short, that the government should merely create the conditions for the individual to make their own economic decisions. The "liberalism" of AWS consists of nationalism and religiosity. In economic terms, AWS are socialists. In their economic policies, they always seem to favor plans that allow for massive intervention by the state. For example, in terms of economic development strategy, we would like to bring business to Cracow by creating easy conditions for investors and merchants to come to the city and do business. AWS, on the other hand, are suspicious of outside investors. They want to be able to pick and choose who is allowed to come.

The Polish "left" has a similar, though less extreme, split personality. The postcommunist Democratic Left Alliance (SLD) contains market-oriented Europhiles like President Aleksander Kwaśniewski and the economist Grzegorz Kołodko as well as hardline stalwarts suspicious of the market and the West and associated with Leszek Miller's wing of the party. To further complicate matters, sharp geographical cleavages remain in Poland from its historical partition into Russian, Prussian, and Austrian zones (Zarycki 2000; Jałowiecki 1999). This geographical particularism makes the task of building unified party structures at the national level even harder.

By contrast, the Czech Republic lacked divisive religious and nationalist cleavages, and party competition there quickly formed in an issue space divided between left and right (Brokl and Mansfeldová 1999; Kitschelt et al. 1999, 226–30; Markowski 1997). Even parties like the Christian Democratic-People's Party (KDU-ČSL)— whose name suggests a religious-nationalist dimension rather than a socioeconomic one—in practice defined themselves as "quite distinctly market-liberal" (Kitschelt et al. 1999, 227). In this bipolar issue space, nationalist and religiously

defined parties were relegated to the status of niche players. The most clearly nationalist party in the Czech Republic, the Republican Party (SPR-RSČ), suffered increasing marginality over the course of the 1990s.[4]

The demise of the umbrella coalitions that had unseated the Communists in
1989—the Civic Forum in the Czech Republic, Public Against Violence in Slovakia,
and Solidarity in Poland—set these three party systems on very different paths. To
be systematic about comparing these party system trajectories, however, a more
precise conceptualization of the logic of party competition and corresponding measures are needed.

CONCEPTUALIZING THE LOGIC OF PARTY COMPETITION

As noted in Chapter 1, the essential difference between these trajectories concerns the relationship between parties of government and parties of opposition. In
weak-governance systems, such as Poland's, both government and opposition parties are weak, fragmented, and underinstitutionalized. In dominant-party systems
like Slovakia's, one party dominates and the rest are weak; the former's dominance
rests on its organizational advantages relative to an opposition that is as fragmented
and underinstitutionalized as its counterpart in a weak-governance system. Depending on the point in time at which one observes a dominant-party system, one
finds either an overweening government and an ineffectual opposition (variant 1) or
an ineffectual government and an intransigent opposition (variant 2). Finally, in a
responsible-party system, such as the Czech one, one finds that both government
and opposition parties are strong and well organized.

Categorizing new democracies within this schema depends on a cluster of attributes, including the coherence of the government, the fractiousness of the opposition, and the organizational stability of the parties composing both. In the case of
the Czech Republic, Poland, and Slovakia these attributes are described in the de-
scriptive studies in this and the following chapters. They can also be captured more
succinctly, using the fractionalization index of the government and opposition blocs
as a measure (see Table 2.1). This measure is simply a modified version of Laakso-
Taagepera's index of the number of "effective parties," so that,

$$\text{Government or Opposition Fractionalization} = \frac{1}{\Sigma p_i^2}$$

where p_i is the fraction of parliamentary seats in the overall government or opposition bloc won by the i-th government or opposition party.[5]

The weak-governance logic would be characterized by high fractionalization indexes for both government and opposition.

As described in Chapter 1, the party system parameters determining which logic of governance obtains are the robustness and degree of institutionalization of party competition. Though developed largely with reference to American and Western European parties, the literature on comparative party systems offers a wealth of conceptual distinctions and empirical measures for these variables. However, importing measures developed with reference to the West without adapting them to the peculiarities of new democracies, especially postcommunist ones, is dangerous and can lead to distorted and misleading results. There is, however, also the danger of ignoring these measures. There are several conceptual distinctions from the broader literature on parties that can be adapted to reflect the idiosyncrasies of democratizing party systems. Of particular use are the five dimensions listed below, with their corresponding empirical measures shown in parentheses:

1. Dominance (vote differential)
2. Number of parties (fractionalization index)
3. Electoral volatility (volatility index)
4. Party system closure (Mair's composite index [1997])
5. Internal party organization (centralization, leadership, programmatic definition, degree of internal homogeneity)

As illustrated in Figure 1.2, the measures of party system competitiveness and institutionalization describe the party system parameters that determine which logic of governance obtains.

The first indicator, dominance, refers to the electoral strength of the largest party or electoral coalition relative to the next most popular alternative. It can be measured as the difference in vote share between these two entities (Sartori 1976, 193). The greater the vote differential, the less the governing party has to fear the possibility of losing future elections and the greater its dominance over the opposition. Dominant-party systems sustain high vote differentials over time. In weak-governance and responsible-party systems, the vote differential is low; in responsible-party systems the vote difference between two largest parties and the rest is considerable, whereas in weak-governance systems it is not.[6]

Having a large number of parties leads to overall fractionalization, a cardinal feature of weak-governance party systems. Low levels of fractionalization characterize responsible-party systems because competition is dominated by a few organizationally rooted parties who can survive outside of government. The dominant-party system falls between these two types: in variant 1, the opposition parties are more fragmented than in responsible-party systems, but the government parties are coherent and well-organized. In variant 2, the situation is reversed.[7]

Typically, fragmentation is operationalized using the Laakso-Taagepera index of the number of "effective parties" (Laakso and Taagepera 1979, 4):

$$\text{Number of effective parties} = \frac{1}{\Sigma p_i^2}$$

where p_i is the fraction of seats won by the i-th party.

In established party systems, it is straightforward to compute this index, but in underinstitutionalized party systems it can be difficult to tell what counts as a party. Does an electoral committee of several small political groupings that band together before the elections in order to pass a minimum threshold for representation count as one party? My indicator of fragmentation considers such a grouping as several parties, not as one. This operationalization accords most clearly with the logic of my hypothesis: robust party competition constrains patronage politics by providing voters with real choices in elections. The more these choices are between heterogeneous coalitions lacking a clear uniting position, the less meaningful the choice presented to the voter. Once in parliament, such coalitions tend not to behave as one party. Therefore, I use the postelection allocation of parliamentary seats to the political groupings within these electoral alliances to compute fractionalization.[8]

Electoral volatility is a compact, easily comparable measure of the degree of party system stability (Toole 2000, 441). In volatile systems, parties lack stable support bases, and their vote shares fluctuate sharply from one election to the next.[9] This can happen through both the disappearance or marginalization of unsuccessful parties and the appearance of new, initially popular parties. Volatility shapes the time horizons of government coalition members. In highly volatile systems coalition members are more likely to try to capture organizational advantages from state patronage than in systems where, due to having more stable vote shares, parties feel less need to create party-building advantages through intervention in the process of state-building. High volatility also makes it difficult to create oppositions capable of constraining the government. The ever-present doubt as to the future viability of opposition parties weakens their credibility as an alternative to the government. Weak-governance systems and dominant-party (both variant 1 and 2) systems are characterized by high volatility, and responsible-party systems by low volatility.

Fourth, party system closure is a conceptual category developed by Peter Mair (1997) to mark when competition among parties settles into stable patterns of government formation and opposition behavior. Open systems are unstable and offer few cues to voters on the formation of governments after the election. In closed systems, familiar patterns of party behavior make government formation predictable given a certain set of election results. Underlying this distinction are three dimensions capturing the degree of party system closure. Openness on each dimension yields the weak-governance logic and closure the responsible-party one. Incomplete closure—party systems that are closed in some respects but not others—favors a dominant-party logic of governance.

The first aspect of party system closure is "alternation of government," which refers to when, how, and to what degree the party composition of the government changes when it alternates.[10] In closed systems, government alternations are regular—occurring after, not between, elections—and wholesale, producing either complete or no change in government composition. In open systems, alternations are partial, with the coalition containing both new parties and old ones from the previous government. They also are as likely to occur between elections as after them: government alternations between elections remove politics from the influence of voters. A third possibility is irregular but wholesale alternation. This is the pattern in the dominant-party logic: because of the bitter divide between the political machine and the underorganized opposition, alternations are wholesale. Absent a loyal opposition, votes of no-confidence are common and alternations between elections more likely.

The second dimension concerns the predictability of "governing formulas" for building government coalitions. If familiar combinations of parties make up government coalitions, the system is closed. If innovative party combinations are acceptable as governing coalitions, the system is open. Innovative governing formulas also characterize the dominant-party logic, given the opposition parties' "my enemy's enemy is my friend" coalitional principle.

Finally how open is "access to government"? Are some parties permanently excluded? In open systems, the instability of governing coalitions means that coalition-makers are willing to overlook programmatic differences with outsider parties if they can furnish the requisite votes to make a government. The same is true in the dominant-party logic, as the opposition's underorganization allows space for newly generated parties; there is not full openness, however, because many alliances across the government-opposition divide are unthinkable. In closed systems, outsider parties are excluded.

The above measures of institutionalization have focused on the structural features of party systems. The different character of the Czech, Slovak, and Polish systems is evident even at this structural-level analysis, but to follow through the logic of the conceptual categories and to lay the ground for exporting them to other contexts, it is necessary to examine the internal dynamics of party organization across countries. In a weak-governance system, all the parties that matter will have weak internal organization. In dominant-party systems, the political machine will have strong internal organization, but the opposition parties will not. Finally, in the responsible-party system, the few parties that dominate competition for government all will have strong internal organization.

Organizationally speaking, strong parties are characterized by centralization, stable leadership, programmatic definition, and internal homogeneity.[11] Weak parties lack these attributes and, in Eastern Europe, usually tend toward decentralized, even confederal, structures; a proclivity toward leadership struggles; differing ideological agendas; and internal heterogeneity.[12] I do not consider electoral strength to be a feature of internal party organization. To understand that electoral strength does not translate into organizational strength, one need only consider the fate of the Civic Forum, which took power from the Czech Communist Party in the first free elections in 1990. With 50 percent of the popular vote and 64 percent of the seats in the National Council, the great umbrella group that was the Civic Forum disintegrated within a year of the elections and ceased to exist as an organization.

MAKING SENSE OF PARTY COMPETITION

The Polish, Czech, and Slovak party systems began to take different trajectories as early as 1992. The conceptual distinctions developed above chart this divergence clearly. Over the course of the 1990s, there were four elections for the Czech Republic and Slovakia and three for Poland.[13] As other scholars have noted, even this relatively small number of elections has produced surprisingly clear patterns of party system differentiation (Toole 2000, 442).

Tables 2.1 and 2.2 summarize the important points of difference between Polish, Czech, and Slovak party system development. Table 2.1 shows over-time trends in vote differential, fractionalization, volatility, party system closure, and the internal organization of the main parties. Table 2.2 shows the number and character of government alternations. It highlights regular alternations—that is, those that followed elections—and irregular alternations, such as those following the collapse or restructuring of a government. There was a far higher degree of government instability in Slovakia and Poland. Table 2.1 also shows the separate government and opposition fractionalization indexes over time; for example, Slovakia's switch from dominant-party (variant 1) to dominant-party (variant 2) politics in 1998 greatly increased its government fractionalization index and decreased its opposition one.

TABLE 2.I.
Party Politics Compared (1990–2000)

	Poland	Slovakia	Czech Republic
PARTY SYSTEM MEASURES:			
Vote Differential			
• 1st Election	0.3%	10.1%	36.3%
• 2nd Election	4.9%	22.5%	15.7%
• 3rd Election	6.7%	24.6%	3.2%
• 4th Election	—	0.7%	4.6%
Fractionalization			
• 1st Election	10.8	5.1	2.2
• 2nd Election	6.2	3.2	4.9
• 3rd Election	9.9	4.7	4.1
• 4th Election	—	9.7	3.7
Volatility			
• 1st Election	—	—	—
• 2nd Election	34.5%	51.9%	67.3%
• 3rd Election	54.2%	37.3%	28.7%
• 4th Election	—	55.1%	17.5%
Party System Closure	Open:	Semi-Open:	Closed:
	1. Irregular and partial alternation	1. Irregular and wholesale alternation	1. Regular and wholesale alternation
	2. Unpredictable governing formulas	2. Unpredictable governing formulas	2. Predictable governing formulas
	3. Access to government open	3. Access to government semi-open	3. Access to government closed
Internal Organization of Parties	• Government parties unorganized	• Government parties organized	• Government parties organized
	• Opposition parties unorganized	• Opposition parties unorganized	• Opposition parties organized
LOGIC OF GOVERNANCE MEASURES:			
Government Bloc Fractionalization			
• 1st Election	6.7[a]	2.5	1.0
• 2nd Election	3.5	1.0	1.8
• 3rd Election	6.8	1.7	1.9
• 4th Election	—	6.2	1.0
Opposition Bloc Fractionalization			
• 1st Election	6.1	3.2	2.6
• 2nd Election	3.1[b]	3.9	4.3
• 3rd Election	3.5	5.4	2.3
• 4th Election	—	1.6	3.0

SOURCES: See Appendix 4.

NOTE: The table covers all the elections from 1990 to 2000. These were 1990, 1992, 1996, and 1998 for the Czech Republic; 1990, 1992, 1994, and 1998 for Slovakia; and 1991, 1993, and 1997 for Poland.

[a] The extreme fluidity of government coalitions between 1991 and 1993 makes this difficult to calculate precisely. I counted the seat shares of all parties that received cabinet posts in the Bielecki and Suchocka governments in order to make this calculation. The rest were classified as opposition.

[b] This measurement greatly understates the fractiousness of the Polish opposition bloc in 1993 since most opposition parties failed to gain seats in parliament and so are not counted in the opposition fractionalization index.

Dominant-Party Politics in Slovakia

The development of the Slovak party system in the 1990s was sharply periodized (Krause 2003; Bútora et al. 1999).[14] In the first period, from 1992 to 1998, the logic of competition was dominant-party (variant 1); one party, Mečiar's Movement for a Democratic Slovakia (HZDS), enjoyed overwhelming organizational and institutional advantages over a fragmented and wavering opposition (Haughton 2001; Fish 1999). In the second period, from 1998 on, the logic was dominant-party (variant 2): Mečiar's machine was overthrown, and the fragmented former opposition parties formed a shaky governing coalition. The post-Mečiar government comprised eight parties that shared little in common programmatically other than their opposition to Mečiar. Comparing the character of state-building under both party system types throws the impact of party competition on state-building into sharp relief.

In the first period, a nationalist political machine faced a fluid, weakly organized, and internally divided group of opposition parties. As shown in Table 2.1, between 1992 and 1998, HZDS maintained a 20-plus percentage point advantage on its closest rival in parliamentary elections. Worse still, the opposition parties were inconsistent in their opposition, often cooperating with HZDS to gain short-term political advantages. Since the Slovak opposition did not pose a credible threat of alternation to HZDS in elections, it had little incentive to restrain its use of patronage. In short, the Slovak party system failed to generate accountability because it did not offer voters meaningful choices at election time. There were too many parties in the opposition for voters to coordinate on any one or group of them to punish the government, and the constant turnover of these parties meant that there was little information from which to predict their future behavior. But what made the opposition parties so weak?

Even in the first free elections in 1990, a nationalist theme was evident in Slovak politics.[15] The Slovak Nationalist Party (SNS), which won 11 percent of the vote but which was excluded from government, had openly called for Slovak autonomy in its campaign. The more moderately nationalist Christian Democratic Party (KDH) had polled around 20 percent. Ironically, the future nationalist strongman of Slovak politics, Prime Minister Vladimír Mečiar, was at this time a moderate member of Public Against Violence (VPN) who "emphasized the danger of KDH's and SNS's separatism" (Darski 1991). By the end of 1990, however, Mečiar's rhetoric underwent an abrupt change, now calling for the "liberation" of Slovakia from Czech domination.[16] This development precipitated a leadership struggle within the VPN, the fall of Mečiar's government, and the subsequent disintegration of the VPN.

TABLE 2.2.
A Chronology of Governments and Opposition (1990–2000)

	1990	1991	1992	1993	1994
Czech Republic	ELECTION: 1 Gov't party 3 Opp'n party	→	ELECTION: Wholesale Alternation (full recomposition) 4 Gov't parties 5 Opp'n parties	→	→
Slovakia	ELECTION: 4 Gov't parties 4 Opp'n parties	*GOV'T FALLS: Wholesale Alternation (no recomposition) 4 Gov't parties 6 Opp'n parties*	ELECTION: Wholesale Alternation (full recomposition) 1 Gov't party 5 Opp'n parties	→	*GOV'T FALLS: Wholesale Alternation (full recomposition)* 3 Gov't parties 4 Opp'n parties ELECTION: Wholesale Alternation (full recomposition) 3 Gov't parties 9 Opp'n parties
Poland	ELECTION: Shifting coalition of gov't parties *GOV'T FALLS: Partial Alternation Shifting coalition of gov't parties*	ELECTION: Partial Alternation Shifting coalition of gov't parties	*GOV'T FALLS: Partial Alternation Unable to form a gov't GOV'T FALLS: Partial Alternation 8 main Gov't parties 21 Opp'n parties*	ELECTION: Wholesale Alternation (full recomposition) 6 Gov't parties 6 Opp'n parties	→

NOTE: Wholesale alternation means complete or no change in the party composition of government. These possibilities are noted as either "full recomposition" or "no recomposition." Irregular alternations (those following the collapse or restructuring of a government) are indicated in italics.

In the next major elections, which occurred in 1992, the Slovak political scene was polarized between the nationalists, the leading party being Mečiar's newly founded HZDS, and the all rest—the dissidents, the neoliberals, the postcommunists, the ethnic Hungarians, and the Christian Democrats. These elections set the mold for Slovak politics until the present day, which is still polarized between

1995	1996	1997	1998	1999	2000
→	ELECTION: Wholesale Alternation (no recomposition) 3 Gov't parties 3 Opp'n parties	→	ELECTION: Wholesale Alternation (full recomposition) 1 Gov't party 4 Opp'n parties	→	→
→	→	→	ELECTION: Wholesale Alternation (full recomposition) 8 Gov't parties 2 Opp'n parties	→	→
GOV'T FALLS: Wholesale Alternation (no recomposition) 6 Gov't parties 6 Opp'n parties	*GOV'T FALLS: Wholesale Alternation (no recomposition) 6 Gov't parties 6 Opp'n parties*	ELECTION: Wholesale Alternation (full recomposition) 11 Gov't parties 8 Opp'n parties	→	→	*GOV'T RE-ORGANIZATION: Partial Alternation 10 Gov't parties 9 Opp'n parties*

Mečiar's clique and the rest. As one political observer noted, "The long-term dividing line in Slovakia leads neither between the left and the right, nor between the liberals and the conservatives, but, since Vladimír Mečiar came to power, simply between the ruling coalition and the opposition" (Kusý 1998, 45). HZDS won 49.3 percent of the seats in the national parliament, forming a government with the even more nationalist SNS. The addition of a nationalist, postcommunist splinter party, the Slovak Worker's Party (ZRS), to the nationalist coalition allowed HZDS to form another government after the 1994 elections.

Nationalism and the personal charisma of Mečiar, not the party's vague policy program, were the factors on which HZDS built its initial dominance; however, its mass appeal began to decline after Slovakia's independence in 1993 (Krause 2000). Rather than consolidate its support through programmatic redefinition, it sought to use its control over the machinery of government to maintain its position through patronage, particularly in the privatization process (Haughton 2001). As HZDS consolidated, the Slovak opposition parties underwent continuing fragmentation, their popular appeal tarnished by the memory of their ambivalence toward Slovak independence between 1990 and 1992. In 1994, the opposition parties succeeded in bringing down the HZDS government with a vote of no-confidence; however, their success was short-lived, as HZDS swept back into power in new elections held five months later. From this point on, HZDS ruled in coalition with two very junior and compliant nationalist parties, SNS and the short-lived ZRS, who shared in the spoils of patronage. HZDS regarded the 1994 no-confidence vote as an act of betrayal that served to justify its colonization of the state apparatus after its return to power in the elections later that year.

The Slovak opposition finally toppled the Mečiar government in 1998, ushering in the period of dominant-party (variant 2) politics. Ironically, HZDS was undone by its own dominance; in a bid to disqualify a number of the opposition parties, it changed the electoral law just four months before the 1998 election to require *all* parties, even those in electoral alliances, to win 5 percent of the vote for parliamentary representation (Lebovič 1999).[17] This move had the unintended effect of forcing the opposition parties to cooperate at last and form a single party—whose name, the Party of the Democratic Coalition (SDK), betrayed its quasi-party character. Although HZDS won more votes than any other party in the election, it was unable to form a government, having eliminated all potential coalition partners by forcing the opposition to unite.

Instead, the SDK formed a government that faithfully reflected its own ad hoc and heterogeneous character. The SDK consisted of five parties of greatly different programs and constituencies: the conservative, confessional Christian Democratic Movement (KDH), the liberal Democratic Party (DS), the conservative, nationalist Democratic Union (DU), the Social Democratic Party of Slovakia (SDSS), and finally the environmentalist Slovak Green Party (ZS). The government formed after the election was a grand coalition of the SDK, with its different member parties, the post-Communist Party of the Democratic Left (SDL'), the Party of the Hungarian Coalition (SMK), and another newly formed party vehicle the Association for Civic Understanding (SOP). Although in 1998 HZDS finally lost its control of the government, it has remained the top vote-getter since. It has also constituted an intransigent opposition in the parliament, using referenda and votes of no-confidence to destabilize the government.

The distinguishing feature between variant 1 and variant 2 dominant-party systems is the vote differential and whether the dominant machine is in government or not. In terms of volatility, fractionalization, government closure, and party organization, the two variants are indistinguishable—though, of course, they are distinguishable from responsible-party and weak-governance systems.

In the period of dominant-party (variant 1) politics, HZDS had on average a 23.5 percent electoral advantage over its nearest competitor. In the period from HZDS's fall in 1998, the biggest opposition party actually had a *smaller* vote share than HZDS, for a vote differential of −0.7 percent. Because dominant-party systems combine elements of the weak-governance system (a divided and unstable opposition) and the responsible-party system (well-organized government parties), one would expect the Slovak system to fall somewhere between the Czech and Polish ones in terms of fractionalization and volatility. And Slovakia's average fractionalization score of 5.8 does stand between Poland's 9.0 and the Czech Republic's 4.2. However, Slovakia has approximately the same high level of electoral volatility as Poland, a volatility that showed little sign of decreasing over time in either country.[18] Though HZDS voters remained faithful, the opposition parties stole votes from each other in each election.

Slovakia's party system was more closed than Poland's but less so than in the Czech Republic. Like Poland, government alternation was irregular, with two out of six alternations coming between elections (in 1991 and 1994; see Table 2.2). Unlike Poland, however, these alternations were wholesale rather than partial: in both cases, they were precipitated by deep enmity between HZDS and the other parties. Second, the sharp dividing line between the nationalist-populist parties grouped around Mečiar's HZDS and the rest of the political spectrum made for governing formulas that were at once unpredictable and familiar. They were familiar because most parties would not form a coalition with HZDS but unpredictable insofar as there was no clear governing formula for building a government coalition, aside from not allying with HZDS. In the early 1990s, the opposition coalition consisted of Public Against Violence, the Christian Democratic Movement, and the Democratic Party. In 1994, the composition of the opposition coalition had shifted, now including the postcommunists, the nationalist Democratic Union, and the Christian Democratic Movement. The year 1998 saw another change in the anti-Mečiar coalition, which now formally included three newcomers: the Party of the Democratic Coalition (SDK), the Movement for Civic Understanding, and the Hungarian SMK. The inclusion of the Hungarian party in the anti-Mečiar coalition—despite the Hungarians' pariah status in Slovak politics—illustrated that, on the last criterion of party system closure, access to power was open.

Consider, finally, the internal organization of the major Slovak parties. Since its founding in 1991, HZDS has exhibited by far the greatest organizational centralization and stability of leadership of any Slovak party (Haughton 2001). As one scholar of Slovak political parties wrote of HZDS, "In Slovakia a single party, the Movement for a Democratic Slovakia, . . . was more organized and more centralized than any other, with more electoral incentives and parliamentary seats, and its elites and supporters showed the least appreciation for accountability of any major party" (Krause 2000, 172). Much of the party's centralization is the result of Mečiar's charismatic leadership. He was known for his several-hour tirades delivered to enthralled audiences in soccer stadiums outside Bratislava (Fish 1999). More importantly, he was personally credited with the standing up for Slovak interests and winning independence from the Czechs in 1992. So far he has easily put down all challenges to his party leadership.

In terms of internal heterogeneity and programmatic definition, HZDS's organizational advantages were less commanding, but when one considers the other Slovak parties, it becomes clear that HZDS enjoyed superiority even in these areas. HZDS's program was always a mixture of nationalism and economic populism, two themes that also defined the programs of its junior coalition partners, the Slovak National Party and the Slovak Workers' Party (Bútora et al. 1999). Within these admittedly broad parameters, the HZDS-led government was remarkably consistent in terms of policy. Its opposition to European integration, its long-running political battle with the ethnic Hungarian minority, its attempted rehabilitation of the collaborationist Slovak government during World War II,[19] its criticism of rapid privatization, and its insistence on following a Slovak "third way" of economic transition all fit into a coherent world view that the Slovak voting public certainly understood and that party scholars such as Kitschelt consider a stable and distinct programmatic type (Kitschelt 1992). Certainly, HZDS's nationalist-populism constituted a more coherent programmatic identity than its political rival the SDK could claim for itself, but I will return to this point shortly.

HZDS showed a great deal less internal heterogeneity than the main Slovak opposition party, the SDK. At the formal level, HZDS has always been a single, integrated party, not a confederation of different movements, political groupings, and labor unions—as have been AWS and SLD in Poland. Moreover, as the sociologist Gil Eyal documents in his study of Czech and Slovak elites in the early 1990s, those in the HZDS leadership were drawn from a relatively homogenous social group— Slovakia's former-Communist "aristocracy," a class formed by an industrial lobby of managers of formerly state-owned enterprises and a cultural elite of former Communist historians and writers (1997, 159–202). As Eyal argues, given Slovakia's small size, this former Communist aristocracy is a tightly knit circle with shared interests and a shared world view.

In comparison to HZDS, the Slovak opposition parties looked hopelessly unorganized. Emblematic among them is the SDK, which overturned the long-reigning Mečiar government in 1998. As mentioned, the SDK was formed several months before the 1998 elections in response to the Mečiar government's attempt to disqualify the opposition by barring electoral committees from the election. Although legally it was a single party, in practice it was an umbrella group of five parties established in the early 1990s, the Christian Democratic Movement (KDH), the Social Democratic Party, the Green Party, the Democratic Union, and the Democratic Party. After the election, the SDK in effect dissolved back into these constituent groupings. More recently, the SDK's leader, Prime Minister Mikuláš Dzurinda attempted unsuccessfully to centralize the organization of the party by creating a new party called SDKÚ.

In addition to its decentralized structure, the SDK suffered from leadership disputes. Dzurinda founded the SDK after leaving the KDH because he had lost a leadership battle with KDH's longtime leader Jan Čarnogurský (Bútora et al. 1999). This history greatly complicated Dzurinda's relationship to the KDH. His leadership of the various factions of the SDK looked most like a never-ending struggle to mediate between these factions' contrary impulses. Dzurinda's role as leader was not made any easier by the absence of a programmatic vision for the SDK. As the list of its constituent parties suggests, the SDK was not a party with a defined program beyond overturning Mečiar.

Finally, those in the SDK leadership were quite heterogeneous in terms of their background. In the KDH, Green Party, and Democratic Party, one could speak of a camp dominated by former dissidents. The SDL', on the other hand, were drawn largely from former Communist Party officials, toward whom former dissidents would understandably feel a certain ambivalence. Finally, the more nationalist Democratic Union primarily comprised former members of HZDS who had broken with Mečiar in 1994. In short, not only did the membership of the SDK come from very different groups, it came from groups with histories of mutual antagonism.

Party intervention in the administration in Slovakia produced a quite different pattern of expansion than in Poland. If in Poland the successful official's maxim was "You can't be no one's" (Matys 2001), in Slovakia under Mečiar it was "You can't be the wrong person's." To be on the wrong side of the party line after a change of government often meant replacement, even for those low in the ranks. Unlike the Polish governments' ad hoc and incremental interventions in the administration, the Mečiar governments' were systematic and concentrated.

After the election of the first HZDS government in 1992, "purges took place throughout the state administration and media; officials at all levels were frequently replaced by political supporters, regardless of whether they possessed the necessary professional qualifications" (Fisher 1994d, 10). Under the second HZDS government of 1994–1998, the use of patronage expanded. After the election, the government devoted an all-night parliamentary session to purging every major post in the state. But its most radical gambit was the "reform of the public administration" in 1996–1997 (analyzed in detail in Chapter 4). Announced as a decentralization of the administration, it doubled the number of district-level state offices and added a new regional level to the state administration, expanding the territorial administration by more than ten thousand positions. As this territorial administration was being restructured, so-called action committees sifted through the lower ranks to replace opposition sympathizers with government loyalists (Krivý 1998, 59; Falt'an and Krivý 1999). The reform also redrew boundaries to create pro-government voting districts.

When HZDS was not in government, it was still the largest parliamentary party and blocked attempts by the former opposition to reverse its colonization of the state. Under the two non-Mečiar governments of March-October 1994 and 1998 on, a very different relationship between the ruling parties and the state administration obtained. As the data in Figure 1.1 show, there was only a moderate personnel growth in 1994 and a small decline after 1998. Attempts by these governments to replace HZDS appointees met with overwhelming opposition from Mečiar's supporters. After a handful of top officials, such as the chairman of the Supreme Auditing Office, were replaced by the 1994 government, several thousand HZDS supporters demonstrated in Bratislava. Weighing in at the time, Mečiar admitted that the number of officials in question was not large but promised retribution (Fisher 1994d, 11). After 1998, the SDK-led government encountered similar opposition. Its most public failure, however, was its inability to push through a carefully planned revision of Mečiar's public administration reform. Unable to hold together its parliamentary majority and facing withering opposition from HZDS, the government accepted a face-saving reform that left the Mečiar reform's boundaries and institutions unchanged (Kunder 2001; Vagovič 2001).

The Fragmented Polish Party System

Since the collapse of the Solidarity movement, the Polish party system has remained underinstitutionalized, generating unstable governments and fractious oppositions. As Frances Millard has observed, Poland experienced not just one but a "whole series of 'founding elections'" after the fall of communism (1999, 77). Each national election in Poland produced a major shift in both the organization of individual parties and the organization of the party system as a whole. As a result, both the government and the opposition parties were fluid, weakly organized, and fragmented. This made for large and unwieldy government coalitions that, in the absence of programmatic agreement among their members, were held together by sharing out the spoils of patronage. Moreover, the large number of parties in the government coalitions made it difficult for voters to assign blame to any individual government party, creating an incentive for each party to free-ride, to use its access to the state for patronage from which it alone would benefit while the costs in voter disapproval were spread across the whole coalition. Facing this logic, each government party had an incentive to seek patronage. In short, party competition in Poland offered voters few levers to hold governing parties accountable. This turbulent party system generated eight governments between 1990 and 2000, plus one provisional government that failed to gain a parliamentary majority and one major reshuffling in 2000. Six of these failed to endure to the end of their scheduled term of office.[20] Although a "cultural" divide has remained between post-Solidarity and postcommunist political groupings, the programmatic differences are often as great within these camps as between them. Over the course of the 1990s, both camps underwent major reconfigurations and reversals of fortune.

Several main events contributed to the development of Poland's postcommunist party politics. The first, partially free elections in 1989 overturned the Communist Party's political hegemony.[21] The second, and now fully free, elections in 1991 precipitated the disintegration of Solidarity and the fragmentation of the party system.[22] The fragmentation produced by the Solidarity movement's demise was exacerbated by an electoral law based on pure proportional representation, which the 1990 government had adopted. With no minimum threshold for parliamentary representation, 29 parties entered parliament in the 1991 elections; none won more than 12 percent of the vote. This led to razor-thin and unpredictable government majorities, with three changes of government in seven months.[23]

The 1993 elections were a second watershed moment in Poland's postcommunist political development, for they brought two unexpected and, to many Poles, traumatic developments. First, the former Communists returned to government, having reorganized the Communist Party into the Social Democracy of Poland (SdRP) party and gathered together the heterogeneous parties of the left in a sprawling 30-plus-member electoral grouping called the Democratic Left Alliance (SLD).[24] Second, the overwhelming majority of Solidarity's successor parties failed to win enough votes to be represented in parliament. One of the last acts of the previous post-Solidarity government had been to overhaul the electoral law, imposing minimum thresholds for parliamentary representation.[25] Although these changes were intended to reduce the number of parties in parliament, the fragmented and uncooperative post-Solidarity parties had hardly expected to play a part in the plan.[26] Only two of them, Lech Wałęsa's Non-Party Bloc to Support Reform (BBWR) and the Democratic Union (UD), passed the threshold.[27] All of the other post-Solidarity parties failed to meet the electoral threshold. Together, these parties had polled 33.6 percent of the vote (Millard 1999, 89). In terms of the overall vote, the 1993 elections presented the staggering spectacle of 35.1 percent of votes being wasted on parties that failed to win seats in parliament.[28]

As such, the 1993 elections were a particularly extreme example of the failure of Polish party competition to provide levers for voters to influence public policy and government behavior. A good third of the parties competing in the elections were not viable candidates for government or even for opposition. During the three SLD-led governments from 1993 to 1997, a critical mass of the opposition functioned outside of the parliament. Moreover, during that period, the SLD-led governments were internally divided, as attested to by the premature collapse of two of them in a parliament that did not even include their bitterest critics. Despite their numbers in parliament, the SLD were not a coherent and forceful government in large part due to the hostility directed at them as former Communists (Boduszyński 1997; Wesołowski 2000). In constructing its government majority, the SLD had formed a coalition with the Polish Peasants' Party (PSL). The PSL quickly gained a reputation for political opportunism, having formerly identified itself with the post-Solidarity camp. Once in the government, the PSL used its king-maker status to extract major concessions from the SLD both in terms of agricultural subsidies for its constituents and patronage positions for its members (Kulesza 1994; Czubiński 2000, 377–378).

The 1997 elections saw another reorganization of the party system with the reconstitution of a post-Solidarity coalition as an umbrella group called Electoral Action Solidarity (AWS). Beneath the surface, AWS was another version of the anticommunist electoral coalition of the 1989–1992 period, not a party: in all it contained 36 different political groupings (Toole 2000, 447). In fact, the parliament looked in 1997 more like it did in 1991 than in 1993; the plethora of squabbling post-Solidarity parties that had been excluded in 1993 had returned. AWS formed a shaky government with the Freedom Union party (UW), which left the government in 2000.

Finally, the 2001 parliamentary elections produced another realignment of the Polish party system, as the government parties of the AWS failed to meet the minimum threshold for representation in parliament. Again there were shades of the 1993 elections. The 2001 elections also saw the appearance of five new parliamentary parties, three of which had not existed a year prior. One of these parties, Self-Defense (SO), was clearly a party of the antisystem type, its leader having gained prominence by calling for a peasant rebellion and organizing road blockades across the country. The 2001 elections produced another postcommunist government.

Table 2.1 puts these developments into comparative perspective using the measures of party system institutionalization. Throughout this turbulence, no party possessed a significant electoral advantage, as the average vote differential of 4 percent indicates. On the positive side, the low vote differential prevented the kind of dominant-party politics that emerged in Slovakia; however, this differential reflected not robust competition but the general weakness of parties across the board and the extreme, even anarchic, distribution of political power. After breaking down the SLD and AWS electoral alliances into their constituent parties and other groupings, the Polish party system had an average fractionalization score of 9.0 "effective" parties during the 1990–1998 period. Not only is this score more than twice that of the Czech Republic or Slovakia, it is also remarkably high in broader comparative terms. In Linz and Stepan's survey of party fractionalization in 41 democracies from 1979 to 1989, Poland had the highest score of all. France and Germany, European countries of comparable size and ethnic homogeneity, had fractionalization scores of 3.2 during the 1980s, and as Linz and Stepan point out, Poland has "substantially more parties than any existing democracy in the world with ten years' duration" (1996, 275–77).

The Polish party system was also extremely volatile, and this volatility shows no signs of abating. On average, some parties saw an aggregate gain in vote share of as much as 44.3 percent from one election to the next, while other parties saw loss of vote share of equal magnitude. Poland's system was twice as volatile as the Czech one, and in broader terms it was off the charts.[29] By comparison, the highest recorded volatility in Europe—Weimar Germany from 1919 to 1920—was 32.1 percent. The average for the advanced industrial democracies was 9 percent between 1948 and 1977 (Mainwaring 1996, 374).

The Polish party system was also the least "closed" of the three. First, government alternation was irregular and often partial. Four out of eight alternations of
government were partial (in 1990, 1991, 1992, and 2000).[30] Five out of the eight alternations occurred between elections (in 1990, 1992, 1995, 1996, and 2000). Second,
Poland showed the greatest innovation in governing formulas during this period. In
1990, the entry, exit, and internal reorganization of parties in the Mazowiecki and
Bielecki governments was so frequent that it is not possible count them all in Table
2.2. After 1993, the governing formula appeared to be simpler, as the field of possible government coalitions reduced to the SLD together with the PSL and AWS together with the liberal-minded Freedom Union (UW). As noted earlier, however,
appearances were misleading because the coalition of AWS-UW was more in the
nature of an umbrella group than an alliance of two parties. Finally, as in Slovakia,
new parties were generated relatively easily because access to power was open.

Finally, there is the internal organization of the government parties to consider.
AWS was often criticized for its lack of programmatic definition, and given its organization, it is little wonder. There were at least four major, sometimes mutually
antagonistic, programmatic orientations within AWS.[31] There was a syndicalist orientation associated with the Solidarity trade union, a nationalist orientation, a conservative Catholic orientation, and even a liberal-conservative orientation (Smolar
1998). In the 1997 elections, the party leadership did not even try to reconcile these
different elements into a single vision. Instead, they attempted to turn the election
into a referendum on decommunization. As one political observer wrote of the 1997
campaign, "Both major blocs mobilized around slogans that were of a moral and
historical rather than an economic or social character" (Smolar 1998, 129). *The Economist* wrote after the 1997 election that AWS "embodies not so much a vision of the
future as an appetite for justice," which is to say, a desire to rid Poland of the former Communists (quoted in Smolar 1998, 130).

In terms of leadership, AWS underwent protracted struggles throughout its career. The organization was founded by the leader of the Solidarity trade union, Marian Krzaklewski, in 1996. As a leader, Krzaklewski preferred to exercise influence
from behind the scenes. He selected a relatively unknown political figure, Jerzy
Buzek, to be prime minister after AWS's 1997 victory. Buzek soon emerged as a
more popular politician than Krzaklewski himself, however. This led to a long-
running leadership struggle. In addition, there were struggles between Krzaklewski
and the heads of many of AWS's member parties and movements. Krzaklewski
wanted to turn AWS from an electoral confederation into a single political party in
order to stabilize it and make it more competitive. These plans ran into fierce opposition from the nationalist, conservative Catholic, and liberal factions. After his

unsuccessful run for the presidency in 2000, Krzaklewski lost this struggle definitively, and the AWS leadership adopted an even more confederal organizational structure.

The postcommunist electoral committee SLD was stronger organizationally than AWS but was weak compared to similar parties such as the Czech Social Democrats. During its 1993–1997 term in government, the SLD was not a classical political party but a coalition of several parties, social groups, "non-party" candidates, and the All-Nation Trade Union (OPZZ) (Wesołowski 2000, 134). As the Polish scholar of political parties Włodzimierz Wesołowski wrote, "The [SLD] is in fact a conglomeration existing only thanks to history and the fact that it functions in the unfriendly environment of post-Solidarity parties" (quoted in Boduszyński 1997, 51).

Both the leadership and membership of the SLD were quite heterogeneous. On the one hand, there was a very large group of former Communist Party members, who joined the SLD to defend themselves against the decommunization campaigns of the more extreme post-Solidarity parties (Wesołowski 2000; Boduszyński 1997). On the other hand, the SLD also attracted a lot of younger politicians who were not active politically before 1989 and who have now vaulted into the SLD leadership. This younger generation tended to see itself as a Polish version of Tony Blair's Labour Party—secular, pro-European, and progressive. To much of the older generation, this kind of vision was anathema. Both the leadership of the party and its programmatic definition reflected the tension between these two groups. There were two leadership figures in the SLD: the country's current president, Aleksander Kwaśniewski, who represents the young moderates, and the party's official leader, Leszek Miller, a former apparatchik of the older generation. Both men were politically astute enough to soften their differences, but those differences were evident. In the 1990s, the SLD was better organized than the post-Solidarity camp, but it was still more a movement than a party. In time, the younger generation of leadership will predominate, but since its founding, the SLD has constantly struggled to unite its different elements.

Poland's recurring problem of how to produce a coherent government led to a pattern of inconsistent, ad hoc interventions in the administration by the many political groupings in each of its governments. In one characterization, these groupings were "institutional nomads [who] take over institutions or create institutions for the sake of expediency, use them and abandon them" (Kamiński and Kurczewska, quoted in Ganev 2001, 398). Unlike Slovakia, no one party ever monopolized patronage. The effect of Poland's overly competitive party system on the state administration was nicely summarized by Jan Pastwa, head of the Polish Civil Service under the AWS government: "Once there was the mono-party nomenklatura. Now, a multi-party nomenklatura has appeared. Each party tries to gain as many positions possible for its people" (quoted in Bogusz, Macieja, and Wojtkowska 2000). Pastwa's was only the latest in a long series of such assessments. From the period of the first Solidarity governments (1991–1993), "Since the time of the accession to power of the Solidarity camp, this is our third cabinet, and once again we have new people who are even less prepared to govern. Once more they are replacing even less important officials in the ministry, governors, heads of department of various state institutions. Changes are most often based on political criteria; the personnel merry-go-round continues, and there is even less place in it for stability and professionalism" (quoted in Letowski 1993, 2).[32] Under the postcommunist governments of 1993–1997, a new wave of patronage interventions in the administration prompted the resignation of the government's plenipotentiary for public administration reform, Michał Kulesza, who wrote in an open letter to the prime minister, "The *nomenklatura* model of administration was the characteristic trait of the whole PRL [communist] era; Minister Strąk [the head of the state administration (PSL)] has in the course of a few months recreated this model" (Kulesza 1994).[33]

In the ongoing crisis of keeping the coalition together, there was little oversight of how parties acted in their ministerial fiefdoms and no coherent direction for state reform (Taras 1993, 14, 20–21). Unlike Slovakia, it was difficult to fire people from the Polish state (governments were not strong enough to risk that kind of intervention), but in the absence of civil service regulations, it was not difficult to hire them. As Figure 1.1 shows, the effect was additive: the state administration grew steadily regardless of who was in government.

The Bipolar Czech Party System

Unlike Poland and Slovakia, the Czech system presented voters with a manageable number of familiar parties who engaged in predictable coalition formation—which produced both coherent, organizationally stable governments and credible, organizationally stable oppositions. It was a responsible-party system. Facing a credible opposition, and hence the possibility of being turned out of office, the Czech governing parties limited patronage politics. There was continuity of party organization in the midst of change of government. In Poland, by contrast, change of government was typically accompanied by change of party organization. In another difference from both Poland and Slovakia, alternation of government occurred only after elections in the Czech Republic, not between them.

Since the early 1990s, the Czech system has been anchored by two major parties, the conservative Civic Democratic Party (ODS) and the Social Democratic Party (ČSSD). There are smaller parties such as the Christian Democrats (KDU-ČSL) and the Union of Freedom (US) on the right and the Communists (KSČM) on the left, but these have failed to dislodge ODS and ČSSD from their positions of prominence. Moreover, as Brokl and Mansfeldová point out, the smaller parties in the Czech system align neatly on this bipolar spectrum of ODS and ČSSD (1999, 210). With the exception of the Communists, these parties have served in the government but as decidedly junior partners. In general, these parties have either failed or banded together in electoral blocs, which, it is necessary to emphasize, are far smaller and more manageable than their Polish or Slovak equivalents. Over time, the party system has simplified—the majority of the smaller parties have been eliminated and attempts to create new ones have ended in failure.

Unlike Poland or Slovakia, the Czech party system quickly developed robust and stable party competition based on a clearly distinguishable left-right, socioeconomically based issue space (Kitschelt et al. 1999). In the 1990 elections, the anticommunist umbrella group Civic Forum (OF) won a near majority of the popular vote. Its antipolitical party philosophy was best summed up in its campaign slogan: "Parties are for party members. Civic Forum is for everybody" (quoted in Carnahan and Corley 1992, 123). As it turned out, Civic Forum was not for everybody. As early as 1991, the government finance minister Václav Klaus broke away from OF, founding the Civic Democratic Party (ODS) and taking much of the OF membership with him. Klaus's party embraced, even epitomized, the neo-liberal agenda of rapid privatization and market reform.[34] A number of other parties emerged from Civic Forum, but they also tended to be self-labeled political parties rather than the assortment of social movements, politicized trade unions, and shifting electoral alliances typical in Poland and Slovakia (Orenstein 2001, 83). On the conservative side, parties included the Civic Democratic Alliance (ODA) and the KDU-ČSL. Both joined the ODS-led governments in 1992 and 1996 but lived in ODS's shadow.[35]

After ODS, the most notable successor party to Civic Forum was ČSSD, which after 1992 emerged as the fastest growing party in the Czech Republic. ČSSD defined itself as an alternative to ODS's vision of neoliberal economic reform. Although still weak in the 1992 elections, from 1993 on the opposition Social Democrats were the fastest-growing party in Czech politics. The increasingly competitive nature of the party system was evident in the election results. In 1992, ODS enjoyed a 15 percent lead on its closest competitor in parliamentary elections; by 1996, this lead had shrunk to 3 percentage points, and in 1998 it trailed the Social Democrats by 4 percent.[36] In the ČSSD, Czech voters had a clear and credible alternative to the conservative government of ODS. During this period, ODS also remained strong electorally, however, with roughly 30 percent of the vote. ODS governed in coalition with a few junior parties from 1992 to 1997. As the initial glow of Czech economic reform began to wear off, ČSSD gained steadily in strength in the parliament. An economic crisis coupled with a party financing scandal resulted in the fall of Klaus's government in 1997. After the following elections, ČSSD formed a minority government, which ODS—now the second largest parliamentary party—officially tolerated.

Table 2.1 puts the Czech party system's defining features in comparative perspective. The average vote differential in the Czech system was 7.8 percent, less than Slovakia's and just slightly more than Poland's. In fact, this average overstates the degree of dominance since ODS's initial electoral advantage of roughly 15 percent in the 1992 elections shrank to 4 percent and then disappeared entirely in the following two elections. The Czech system had half the electoral volatility of its Polish and Slovak counterparts and, reflecting the process of party system institutionalization, this volatility decreased rapidly over time. This combination of low vote differential and low volatility reflected robust competition: two stable parties— whose organizational strength enabled them to survive outside of government, allowing them to focus on the medium-to-long term—competed at rough parity in elections. In Poland, in contrast, the vote differential was low, but the extreme dispersion of power and high volatility made for anarchy. In terms of fractionalization and party turnover, the Czech system's 4.2 "effective" parties put it in line with Western European party systems (Linz and Stepan 1996, 277).[37]

How did the Czech Republic compare with Poland and Slovakia in terms of party system closure during this period? First, there were fewer governments in the Czech Republic than in Poland and Slovakia (four as opposed to six and eight), and unlike Poland and Slovakia, each alternation of government took place after elections, never between them (see Table 2.2).[38] Alternations were wholesale, which also fits the pattern of closed competition.[39] Second, the governing formulas of Czech politics were familiar. Until 1998, governments were led by ODS in coalition with the Christian Democrats (KDU-ČSL) and Civic Democratic Alliance (ODA) as junior members. In that time, the opposition consisted most notably of the Social Democrats, the Communist Party, and the Republican Party. It was always understood, however, that the Communists and the Republicans were not coalition material; in short, access to government in the Czech party system was closed. The exclusion of the Communists was all the more remarkable given that they were one of the top three parties in terms of election numbers and that their left-wing views would seem to make them natural partners for the Social Democrats.

In comparison with Poland and Slovakia, the Czech party system showed a more even distribution of organizational capacity among the major parties, and that organizational capacity was of a high level. Both ODS and ČSSD exhibited centralized organization from their founding in 1991 (Krause 2000; Kopecký 1995). The insistence on centralized structures and internal discipline sprang from the personal frustration of both party founders, Václav Klaus (ODS) and Miloš Zeman (ČSSD), with Civic Forum. They had led opposing factions within OF, and both had decried the group's ineffectiveness as a result of its refusal to impose a hierarchy of leadership. In 1991, at a time when the majority of Polish and Slovak parties were still in the mode of antipolitics, refusing even to call themselves parties, in the Czech Republic two new party leaders had broken with the major postcommunist umbrella group and were self-consciously building conventional party organizations. Klaus took Margaret Thatcher's Conservative Party as his model, and Miloš Zeman styled the Czech Social Democrats after their German and Scandinavian counterparts.[40]

In both ČSSD and ODS, centralized party organization went hand in hand with a strong leader who exercised a high degree of personal control over the party. A Czech scholar of party systems wrote in 1995 that ODS had become the "party of just one man" (Kopecký 1995, 528). Certainly, there were shades of charismatic authority in Klaus's leadership of ODS. Klaus presented himself as a no-nonsense economist with all the answers, an expert often invited to lecture in the West on the Czech success story that he had created (Eyal 1997, 89–158). It would be a mistake to overdraw Klaus's charisma, however. His glow of omniscience was fading as early as 1995. Moreover, that charisma was based on a deep faith in the science of management, which facilitated rather than impeded the building of a modern party organization for ODS. As Kopecký notes, despite Klaus's enormous personal influence, ODS had been moving since 1991 "towards [being] a complex, routinized, and institutionalized electoral organization" (1995, 528). Klaus's tenure as leader has been stable since the party's founding.[41] While not as strong as Klaus's, Miloš Zeman's leadership of ČSSD was also very stable throughout the 1990s. Zeman's authority stemmed from his achievement in building ČSSD from a small parliamentary faction in 1991 to the most popular party in the country by 1998. Zeman's position as party chief was never formally challenged in that time, though in 2000 he voluntarily stepped down.

In terms of programmatic definition and internal heterogeneity, ODS and ČSSD stood out from the majority of Polish and Slovak parties. Both parties' programs were based primarily on economic and social issues—not on national, religious, ethnic, or regional identity or attitudes toward democracy. They espoused distinct economic positions that placed them on different ends of the conventional left-right spectrum (Kopecký 1995; Kitschelt 1992). ODS favored liberal, pro-business policies and a minimal economic role for the state, whereas ČSSD proposed a greater role for the state in the economy and in the promotion of social equity. Because these were centralized parties, one did not find a diversity of programmatic schemes within either of them. They were also relatively homogenous in terms of their leadership. The ODS hierarchy was drawn predominantly from the class of mid-level managers and officials in the previous regime who were not members of the Communist Party and who owed their jobs to their technical competency (Eyal 1997, 95). For example, Klaus came from a middle-level position in a government-funded economic research institute. ODS members took great pains to distinguish themselves from the dissident politicians.[42] ČSSD's leadership combined a large number of mid-level professionals from before 1989—though a higher percentage of them had Communist Party pasts—with younger politicians. Like ODS, ČSSD eschewed the label of dissident politics and counted few former dissidents in its ranks.

With fewer turnovers of government, there were fewer opportunities for administrative reshufflings, and the Czech administration experienced considerable autonomy from patronage politics.[43] When governments changed, administrative turnover was limited to the top leadership of the ministries. As Figure 1.1 and Table 1.1 show, the Czech Republic saw much less growth in the size of the administration but ranked higher in terms of both effectiveness and gains in effectiveness. In his recent study of the Czech Republic and Slovakia, Kevin Krause undertakes a comprehensive review of government party influence on state institutions. Although, as Krause notes, there were instances of patronage-seeking, "most political institutions in the Czech Republic behaved in a manner consistent with horizontal accountability. The frequency of accountability violations among political institutions remained low and their scope remained relatively small. Furthermore, most of the Czech Republic's accountability violations prompted formal investigation and sanction" (2000b, 72). This description conforms to my prediction about responsible-party systems; namely, the timing of party-building and state consolidation in the Czech Republic—as in the rest of the region—generated pressures for patronage, but unlike the rest of the region, the existence of a credible opposition and predictable patterns of government formation constrained those pressures.

The government crisis of 1997, because it was precipitated by a party financing scandal around ODS,[44] at first might seem to indicate the failure of party competition. However, the existence of a viable opposition party enabled voters to punish ODS in the 1998 elections, electing ČSSD. ČSSD's minority government was made possible by the so-called Opposition Agreement between ČSSD and ODS, which granted ODS a number of parliamentary positions (but no ministerial portfolios) and the right to consult on major political decisions in exchange for not initiating no-confidence votes. Though viewed by some Czech critics as an "unholy alliance," in reality the Opposition Agreement allowed the formation of a programmatically coherent minority government while preserving a credible opposition.[45] It also prevented the kind of postelection administrative purge in Slovakia and shuffle in Poland, thereby insulating the administration. Finally, the Opposition Agreement brought about a further simplification of the party system, as four smaller parties combined in order to challenge ODS and ČSSD. In the 2002 elections, when their vote share allowed them to do so, ČSSD jettisoned ODS. The end result of the 1997 crisis, then, was to deepen the bipolar character of the party system.

CONCLUSION

The differences in the logic of party competition revealed in this analysis point to the absence of robust competition in Poland and Slovakia. In both countries, party competition gave voters little leverage to punish patronage-seeking government parties. The choices offered in elections were difficult to assess, and the eventual coalitional outcome, given a certain set of returns, was even more difficult to foresee. In an environment already predisposed to patronage politics, there was little to check governing parties from abusing their position of power. It is not that Czech politicians were any "cleaner" than their postcommunist counterparts, only that they operated within a different system of constraints. Even if elections in these countries were not primarily fought over the issue of patronage politics but instead over more bread and butter issues such as social policy or the state of the economy, the ability of the party system to simplify political alternatives to a few major parties has the effect of making government formation more predictable and regular, thereby allowing party competition to check patronage politics. In a disorderly and unpredictable party system, parties have short time horizons, which makes them more likely to take the patronage and run. Also, the difficulty of building parliamentary majorities gives them a weapon to demand patronage concessions from the government. In a dominant-party system there is no one to prevent the government parties from overstepping their bounds.

Because of their differing logics of party competition, the Polish, Czech, and Slovak party systems generated greatly differing patronage shocks to their respective national state administrations as those administrations were in the process of re-definition. The most damaging patronage shocks were generated by Slovakia's dominant-party politics. Unchecked by a credible opposition, the government parties were able to make far-reaching and relatively frequent interventions in the state administration. Poland's weak-governance system—with its revolving governments and musical chairs coalitions—threw up the most frequent shocks to administrative development, but the absence of any one dominant party meant that these interventions were less far-reaching. Finally, the Czech system's more orderly and less frequent change of government insulated its national state administration from patronage interventions of the same frequency and scale as in Poland and Slovakia.

CHAPTER THREE

The Runaway State-Building Phenomenon

Patronage Politics and Bureaucratic Rationalization

A fundamental characteristic of the process of the transformation of the public administration [in Poland] is the systematic growth in employment . . . Surprisingly, this gigantic growth in the central administration has occurred in a period of transition to the free market—a transition which has been accompanied by a well-developed privatization process, a radical decrease in the public sector's share of the economy, and official support for the ideas of subsidiarity and civil society. Equally surprisingly, successive changes of the government coalition have not affected this tendency in the least.

> *Witold Kieżun (2000)*

The extensive fragmentation of local (territorial) policy has caused a substantial increase in the expenses for public administration, i.e. *too large a public administration, in comparison with too small a state.*

> *Plenipotentiary for the Reform of the Public Administration,*
> *Government of Slovakia (1999, 13, emphasis added)*

During the campaign for Poland's 1997 parliamentary elections, Marian Krzaklewski, the leader of the Solidarity trade union, promised some 4,000 of his key supporters positions in the state administration if elected. Krzaklewski's promise was surprising not for its substance but for its brazen articulation of an open secret of Poland's new democratic politics—the prevalence of party patronage. The hall-

mark of Polish patronage is incrementalism; Krzaklewski's coalition was not powerful enough to turn out the old government's appointees from the state administration and was content to add its coterie to the existing state administration, transferring political battles to the administration as new and old appointees vied with
each other for influence.

A different pattern of patronage characterized Slovakia for most of the 1990s.
The emblematic moment was Slovakia's 1994 elections, in which the party of
Vladimír Mečiar won a sweeping victory. As the fragmented opposition looked on,
Mečiar's Movement for a Democratic Slovakia (HZDS) devoted its first day in government to a round-the-clock parliamentary session that purged the top-level state
posts of its perceived political enemies and instated its own supporters. Over the
course of the next year, the party extended this purge down through the lower ranks
of the state administration, through the regional and district offices (Falt'an and
Krivý 1999). The Mečiar government's restructuring of the state administration also
involved expanding it—creating new regional and district offices—in order to maximize the patronage positions it could distribute (see Chapter 4).

These episodes highlight a fundamental problem facing democratizing countries: under what conditions may new democracies tame patronage and undertake
much-needed reforms of the state? What are the costs to state capacity if they fail
and patronage goes unchecked? This chapter explores how the logic of party competition shaped both the size and capacity of the Polish, Czech, and Slovak state administrations during the democratic transition.

Drawing together multiple data sources, some of them previously unpublished,
provides a variety of measures of the size and cumulative expansion of the state administration.[1] As noted in Chapter 1, the state is an expansive concept and scholars
have defined it in different ways: since my concern is for the influence of patronage
on the administrative core of the state, the primary measure of state size will be the
number of personnel in the national-level state administration—the central ministries and offices together with their territorial administration. I do, however, also
include data on salaries, administrative expenditures, and government spending
more generally. The second part of the chapter presents field interviews with state
officials, politicians, and policy experts from 1999 to 2001. These interviews illustrate
the difficulties of creating a professional, autonomous, meritocratic bureaucracy
out of the administrative apparatus of the Leninist state. They also show, on an individual level, the presence of patronage politics in the state administration. Together with the data on state personnel, the interviews depict Polish and Slovak administrations that, following the transition to democracy, rapidly expanded in size

but not effectiveness. In the Czech Republic, the interviews present a picture of emergent bureaucratic autonomy and professionalization.

THE GROWTH OF THE STATE

How much have the Polish, Czech, and Slovak state administrations expanded in the transition to democracy? How attractive are positions in the state administration as a means for parties to reward their internal constituencies? How does the growth of the state administration compare to other areas of the state?

In analyzing paths of state-building, the most important comparative dimensions are the *rate* and *scale* of expansion. How quickly do state administrations grow during democratic transitions, in what are often conditions of imperfect party competition? The rate and scale of expansion can be measured using official statistics on the size of the state in terms of number of personnel and public expenditure. As noted in Chapter 1, however, ensuring the cross-national comparability of statistics on so broad a concept as the state is difficult. Because the state administration is a more focused concept and because it constitutes the vital common core across various definitions of the state, it facilitates meaningful cross-national comparisons.[2]

As the Chapter 2 shows, party competition can differ considerably in still-forming party systems and in ways that create varying degrees of opportunity for governing parties to extract patronage from the administration and use state-building to gain party-building advantages. Different party system types structure this patronage politics differently. In weak-governance party systems such as Poland's, government instability combined with the pressure to hold together large, heterogeneous coalitions generates frequent opportunities for patronage extraction. Given the fragility of their coalitions, however, governments are unlikely to attempt radical patronage interventions in the administration; they avoid purging the appointees of previous governments. Thus, patronage leads to incremental, localized expansion of the administration, with government alternation bringing no reversals of earlier personnel build-ups. To quote Kamiński and Kurczewska's apt description once again, this is patronage driven by "institutional nomads [who] take over institutions or create institutions for the sake of expediency, use them and abandon them" (quoted in Ganev 2001, 398). In dominant-party systems such as Slovakia's, the state expands rapidly if the political machine is in government and stops in place if it is not. In variant 1 of the dominant-party logic, patronage is maximized, and the purge is the typical mode of intervention in the administration: given the governing parties' electoral strengths, they can exclude other parties from patron-

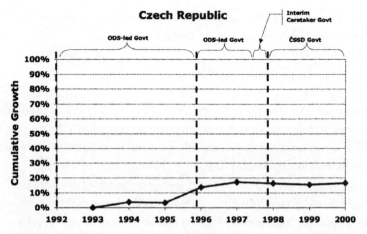

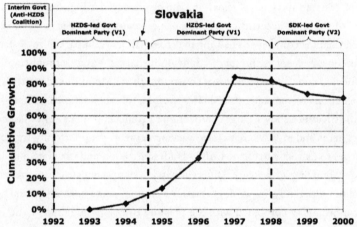

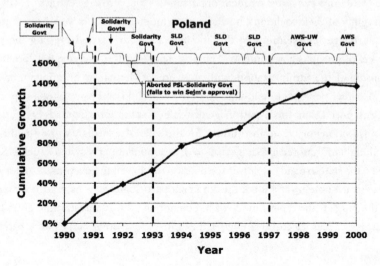

age, replacing unsympathetic officials down to the lowest levels. If the dominant machine loses an election (variant 2 of the dominant-party logic), the result is gridlock between the new government and the political machine now sitting in the opposition. The new government is too internally divided to reverse the former government's administrative build-up, and the political machine constitutes an intransigent opposition, blocking change and posing the threat of a no-confidence vote. Responsible-party systems such as the Czech one generate fewer changes of government than weak-governance systems. Unlike dominant-party systems, the lower vote differential between the government and opposition constrains the government parties from engaging in self-serving administrative reorganizations that could hurt them in future elections.

When aligned against data on the cumulative growth in the number of state administrative personnel, as in Figure 3.1, the pattern of government alternation in Poland, the Czech Republic, and Slovakia conforms closely to the logic outlined above.[3] First, both Slovakia and Poland saw a very dramatic increase in the number of state administrative personnel. Between 1993 and 2000, the Slovak state administration expanded by 71 percent and the Polish one by 55 percent.[4] If 1990 is taken as the baseline, the Polish state administration has more than doubled during the transition to democracy, with an increase of 137 percent.[5] The number of central state officials in Poland—excluding those in the provincial administration—tripled over that period.[6] Increase of this magnitude in so short a space of time is nothing short of extraordinary (Schiavo-Campo, de Tommaso, and Mukherjee 1997), even compared to other postcommunist states, namely the Czech Republic, which grew by only 16 percent from 1993 to 2000.[7] Moreover, Poland and Slovakia's more rapid growth was not matched by any appreciable gains in state capacity, as evidenced by the World Bank's "government effectiveness" indicators cited in Chapter 1 or by the interviews presented in the second part of this chapter.[8]

Figure 3.1 also indicates how the pace of administrative expansion varies over time, in particular over changes in government. The dotted vertical lines in the figure represent national parliamentary elections, and the brackets running along the top of each graph represent each of the different governments.[9] As would be expected for a responsible-party system with few changes of government and a small vote differential between the main government and opposition parties, the pace of administrative expansion in the Czech Republic does not vary under different governments. With the threat of alternation posed by an organized opposition

Fig. 3.1. (opposite) Cumulative Expansion and Government Stability

and the longer time horizons provided by low electoral volatility, the government is more constrained in using state-building as a source of party advantage.

As the graph for Slovakia shows, the pace of state expansion differs considerably in a dominant-party system. In Slovakia, the expansion of personnel is very rapid and concentrated entirely in the periods of dominant-party (variant 1) competition. The period of greatest expansion (1995–1997) coincided with Mečiar's second coming in Slovak politics. Mečiar's first HZDS government lost a vote of no-confidence in 1994 only to return to power several months later with a thirst for revenge (see Chapter 2). This was the period of all-night parliamentary sections devoted to removing opposition sympathizers from state agencies and posts. It was also when HZDS's so-called action committees systematically went through the state's territorial administration (the regional and district offices) purging them of personnel considered unsympathetic to HZDS and replacing them with party loyalists.[10] It was also the period in which Mečiar's government undertook a wide-scale institutional overhaul of the state administration, redrawing the administrative map to include twice as many district offices and a new layer of regional administration, both of which could be filled with party supporters (see Chapter 4).

The pace of expansion came to an abrupt halt when Mečiar's HZDS, despite receiving a plurality, failed to win enough votes in the 1998 elections to form a government, and the party system switched from variant 1 to variant 2 of dominant-party politics. Figure 3.1 shows that the state administration even contracted somewhat after 1998. However, the small decrease in the size of the administration after 1998 testifies to HZDS's ability to block efforts to reverse its administrative policies from 1992 to 1998. As described in Chapter 2, attempts to replace HZDS-era appointees from the administration were met with heavy protest. In parliament, HZDS spearheaded successive initiatives to hold referenda on pre-term elections, constantly destabilizing a government that never enjoyed enthusiastic popular support. The biggest failure of the Party of the Democratic Coalition (SDK)–led government to turn back HZDS's self-serving administrative policies was its aborted reform of the public administration (see Chapter 4). This is what one would expect in a dominant-party (variant 2) system.

Last, Figure 3.1 shows that Poland's weak-governance party system generated eight governments from 1990 to 2000,[11] over which time the state administration expanded by a relatively constant increment regardless of which government was in power. That much of the government turnover occurred between elections only further removed governmental politics from the influence of voters. Marian Krzaklewski may have been the one to publicly promise his party's internal constituency 4,000 positions in the administration, but each government has engaged in the same behavior. Each had to maintain a slim majority built from an unstable and shifting array of party allies, who were in a good position to press for material advantages for their support. In terms of the pace of administrative expansion, there is not the same periodicity of state expansion as in Slovakia and not the same constraint as in the Czech Republic. Not surprisingly, the political discourse of both the right and the left has criticized the government parties for filling the state with party faithful (Kulesza 1994; Hirsz 1998; "Internal Bickering" 2003).

If governing parties in Slovakia's dominant-party system sought party-building advantages through purges and rapid, systemic expansion, in Poland's weak-governance system patronage was the "reform-driven" type. This patronage is reform-driven not because it solves some policy problem but because reform is the pretext for political intervention in the state-building process. Reform is, after all, a good way to shake up the state administration, establish new offices, and create some posts to satisfy a government coalition partner. Unlike dominant-party patronage, the reform-driven sort often occurs between elections rather than immediately after them. Because these reforms are not punitive purges and because the governing parties lack the political strength to antagonize the opposition parties, who have their own supporters in the state administration, the result of such reform is additive. Instead of purging officials from the old political order, it adds more officials.

This dynamic of incrementalism and localized expansion on many fronts is apparent in Polish state-building since 1989. The operating budgets and very existence of state offices in postcommunist Poland have been open to negotiation and renegotiation on a yearly basis. Moreover, key decision-making power over budgets and offices has lain with the parliamentary deputies, not with the state administration itself. State ministries are subject to multiple reorganizations and new offices appear with vaguely specified mandates, which quite often overlap with those already existing offices. As one Polish commentator wrote, "The following process is the rule: first, a modest office is established, and afterwards, its expenditures swell from year to year. In the first year, the expenditures are not great, going only for the construction of the new office. In the next year, expenditures grow at a lightning pace. As a rule, after two or three years some MPs come to the conclusion that this rapid expansion has provided opportunities for the abuse of public funds. So, the expenditures of that institution are curtailed drastically. Then, after a year, maybe two years, the expenditures begin to grow once again, though now at a less conspicuous pace" (Jędrzejewska 1999).

A notable example of the redundancy and duplication of offices that come with Poland's brand of state-building was the creation of a new central ministry concerned with regional development little over a year after decentralization had created regional parliaments entrusted with exactly that task. Thus, shortly after creating an extensive network of regional parliaments, the Electoral Action Solidarity (AWS) government effectively relieved those parliaments of their most important policy task (Paradowska 2000). The first minister appointed to the Ministry of Regional Development was Jerzy Kropiwnicki, an influential and well-connected politician in one of the restive but indispensable parties of the then AWS government's majority coalition, the Christian Nationalist Party (ZChN).

In a weak-governance system, where government majorities are slim, it is especially difficult to reverse earlier administrative expansions. The Polish state grew steadily through the 1990s in large part because it was so difficult to close old offices. For example, the 1998 decentralization entailed the closure of some 33 prefectural administrations (voivodships), which sparked a wave of loud protests from their employees and political patrons.[12] Under pressure, the government promised that these officials would qualify for jobs in the new decentralized administration (the new voivodships and district administrations). It is also costly to retrench the administration. In 1997, for example, the government of Poland undertook to transform a number of big central ministries and offices. The reform consisted in part of creating eight new offices at a cost of 10.8 million zloty (approximately $2.7 million). Two of these offices were created from scratch, and the rest were essentially reorganized from existing central offices and ministries. Closing old offices cost almost as much as creating new ones, about 9.5 million zloty, or $2.4 million (Jędrzejewska 1999). Thus, creating new offices is doubly expensive—not only because it adds to the wage bill of the state administration but also because a bigger wage bill drains financial resources the government might otherwise use to streamline unnecessary state offices. In Poland, the pressure to create new positions as a source of patronage combined with the difficulty of eliminating old has led to a constant upward creep in the overall number of personnel. The Polish governments' difficulty in closing old offices stands in sharp contrast with the situation in Slovakia under Mečiar, where HZDS's dominance allowed it to make sweeping changes to the state administration.[13]

Salaries

If the rapid expansion of the Polish and Slovak state administrations in the democratic transition is driven by government parties' thirst for patronage, then how attractive are state administrative positions as a means for rewarding these parties' internal constituencies? As I argue in Chapter 1, the general suspicion of party politics common in postauthoritarian societies—and in particular the posttotalitarian societies of Eastern Europe—means that parties have weak connections to voters. The internal constituency of popular personalities and party organizers become unusually important to a party's electoral success (Geddes 1990, 40–41). In the volatile party systems of both Poland and Slovakia, for example, the names of and alliances between parties have changed radically over time, but the cast of political figures and personalities has remained surprisingly familiar. Providing access to state posts for these figures and their coterie helps to ensure their support and availability at election time. Small membership numbers also mean that parties have few resources to employ organizers and activists; therefore, state jobs are a means for keeping these organizers available for party work.

All of this assumes, however, that state administrative positions are attractive, and the conception in the West is that state salaries in Eastern Europe are abysmally low. As I discovered in my field interviews, this conventional wisdom has two problems for the countries in this study. First, although it is true that those who work in the educational system, the health care system, and the police are underpaid, the positions in the state administration itself have been very well paid relative to the economy as a whole. Second, as the Polish political scientist Antoni Kamiński has observed, the conventional wisdom is based on inappropriate comparisons: lining state salaries up against, as is often done, those in Western multinational companies (which are out of the range of most of the labor force) rather than against the typical job in a still-developing economy with high unemployment (which is the more realistic alternative for most people).[14]

The appropriate comparison for assessing the value of state administrative positions is to compare the average salary of those positions with the average salary in the overall Polish, Czech, and Slovak economies (see Figure 3.2).[15] According to the data, the average wages in the Polish national state administration are well above those prevailing in the general economy. In real terms, the latter rose only marginally for most of the 1990s, whereas between 1990 and 1999, the salaries of central-state officials approximately doubled.[16] The salaries of central state bureaucrats were 44 percent higher than the average citizen's in 1999. Slovakia's wage statistics paint a similar picture. Interestingly, however, there was a sharp spike in the state administration's wages between 1995 and 1997, the same period of the dramatic increases in personnel following Mečiar's return to government and his subsequent "reform" of the state administration. Not only was the central bureaucrat's salary considerably higher than the average salary in absolute terms, its rate of growth was higher too.[17] As in the other two cases, the wages of the Czech national-level bureaucrat outpaced considerably the average salary in the general economy.[18]

Despite its limitations vis-à-vis the state administration, the conventional wis-

Poland

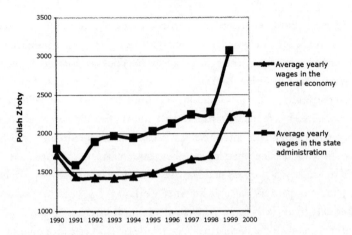

Czech Republic

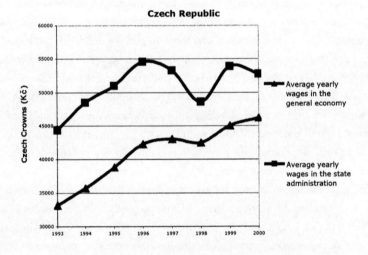

Slovakia

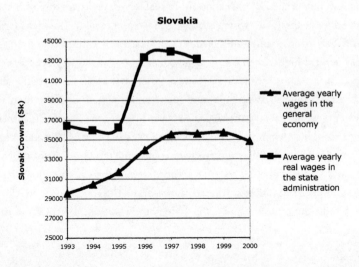

dom that public salaries are too low in postcommunist countries is, however, quite accurate for much of the rest of the state. Consider the example of welfare policy, which was one of the largest sectors of the state under communism and which has remained largely state-owned since 1989: whereas the state administrations of Slovakia and Poland have mushroomed since the fall of communism, the number of welfare state personnel has been flat, even declining, and the salaries of those personnel have either failed or just managed to keep up with wages in the rest of the economy.[19] As noted in Chapter 1, patronage in the welfare state is harder to manage than in the administration. First, the *nomenklatura* system was less extensive in this sector under communism. Second, being a doctor, nurse, or teacher requires professional, measurable qualifications that being an "administrator" does not. As any nurse or teacher in Eastern Europe will attest, these jobs are not political plums. As Table 3.1 shows, this sector of the state has lagged far behind the administrative sector in terms of expansion.

Table 3.1 indicates the cumulative growth of personnel in the sectors of education and health care and social work in the period from 1990 to 1997, as well as the average wage in those sectors compared to the prevailing average wage in the overall economy. For the most part, the numbers of personnel have been declining in all three countries, and wages are lower than average. Personnel and wage figures for the national-level state administrations for all three countries demonstrate that in each the number of personnel is expanding (very rapidly in Slovakia and Poland) and their salaries have stayed ahead, sometimes far ahead, of the overall average wage. The difference between state administration and welfare services is stark. Since the shortest link between political parties and the state is in the administration and since positions in the administration pay considerably more, it should not be a surprise that the administration has grown more quickly than the welfare state—and, in some sense, at its expense.[20]

In sum, salaries in the Polish, Czech, and Slovak state administrations have more than kept up with the rest of the economy. These are attractive jobs in economies where the average wage is considerably lower, and unemployment rates are high.[21]

The Economic Footprint of Runaway State-Building

In my description so far, runaway state-building has meant an expansionist administration in personnel, not a growing government budget deficit; after all, as

Fig. 3.2. (opposite) Average Real Wages in the National-Level State Administration and the General Economy (in 1990 National Currencies). See Appendix 2 for sources

TABLE 3.1.

A Comparison of Personnel Growth and Salaries in the State Administration and Selected Sectors of the Welfare State (1990–1997)

	Education		Health Care and Social Work		National-Level State Administration	
	Change in the Total Number Employed between 1990 and 1997	Ratio of Average Wages in Sector to Average Wage in Overall Economy (1997)	Change in the Total Number Employed between 1990 and 1997	Ratio of Average Wages in Sector to Average Wage in Overall Economy (1997)	Change in the Total Number Employed between 1990 and 1997	Ratio of Average Wages in Sector to Average Wage in Overall Economy (1997)
Poland	−20.6%	0.92	+7.1%	0.82	+117.3%	1.35
Czech Republic	−5.8	0.88	−23.1	0.90	+17.24	1.16
Slovakia	−5.9	0.86	−7.2	0.93	+84.5	2.02

SOURCES: Author's calculations using data on the number and salaries of those employed in education and health care and social work. Personnel sources from Poland: *Statistical Yearbook of the Republic of Poland* (1992, 98: 1998, 123); Czech Republic: *Statistical Yearbook of the Czech Republic* (2000, 294); Slovakia: *Statistical Yearbook of the Slovak Republic* (1994, 142: 1998, 186). Salaries sources from Poland: *Statistical Yearbook of the Republic of Poland* (1992, 190; 1998, 151); Czech Republic: *Statistical Yearbook of the Czech Republic* (2000, 295); Slovakia: *Statistical Yearbook of the Slovak Republic* (1994, 148; 1998, 192). For the data on the number and salaries of state personnel and the average wage in the overall economy, see Appendixes 2 and 3.

NOTE: Since, for the Czech Republic and Slovakia, there are no data on the number of personnel in the national-level state administration available from before 1993, the time period being compared for those cases in the sixth column is 1993–1997.

noted in Chapter 1, these kinds of economic indicators are the result of a much broader set of causal factors than patronage politics. That said, patronage is a causal factor; therefore, it would seem plausible that a similar, albeit less distinct, pattern should be visible when comparing these broader measures in Poland, Slovakia, and the Czech Republic. The natural question, then, is whether patronage politics has left any discernible economic footprint in Poland and Slovakia. Have their states grown in economic as well as personnel terms in the 1990s, and if so, does the pattern of expansion match that in the number of personnel?

One can look, of course, at a number of economic indicators to measure the size of the state in economic terms. The usual problems beset statistical cross-national comparisons such as these: different methodologies of collection, different time spans for which data are available, and the fact that ministry-level data are unavailable for the Czech Republic and Slovakia. Fortunately, however, there are Organization for Economic Cooperation and Development (OECD) statistics available for Poland, Slovakia, and the Czech Republic as newly admitted members of the OECD.

Overall government consumption is a statistic that captures the size of the public sector in economic terms. Obviously, the problem with overall government consumption as an indicator is that it comprises much more than just state administration. It includes expenditure on all of the types of personnel—firefighters, soldiers, prison guards, employees of state-owned enterprises, welfare providers, and so on—that fit only imperfectly within the realm of patronage politics.[22] It has the considerable advantage, however, of being collected by the OECD using a consistent methodology—which makes it ideal for cross-national comparison.

As Figure 3.3 shows, the outlines of the economic picture show a relatively good fit with those in the state administration. The public sector has been growing steadily in Poland since the 1990s. In Slovakia, its growth has been more precipitous, with the highest growth rates coinciding with the HZDS government from 1994 to 1998. In contrast, the public sector has been decreasing (albeit slowly) in the Czech Republic. To give a sense of how large a portion of gross national product (GNP) government spending constituted, it was highest in Slovakia, at 56.3 percent. The next highest percentage was in Poland, at 43.3 percent, and government spending constituted 40.6 percent of GNP in the Czech Republic (OECD 1999).[23] Thus, for the time period from 1993 on, the rank ordering of the countries fits the pattern visible in the national-level state administration (see Figure 1.1).

Finally, there are more detailed data available on the Polish state administration, though not, unfortunately, for the Czech Republic and Slovakia. Table 3.2 presents a more detailed picture of the Polish national state administration, charting the ex-

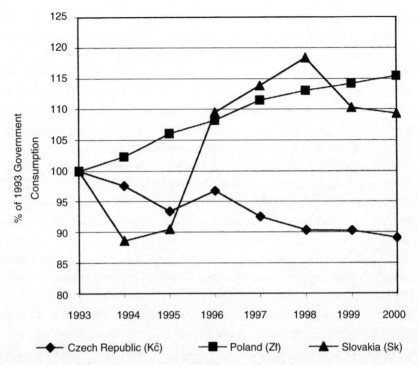

Fig. 3.3. Cumulative Change in Government Consumption (in 1998 National Currencies). From author's calculations using figures on "Real Public Consumption Expenditure" from *OECD Economic Outlook* 70 (2002): 85, III, II5

penditure of just the central ministries and offices from 1993 to 1999. As the table indicates, these expenditures have been increasing at an average clip of 10.2 percent per year during this period—sometimes by as much as 18 percent per year.[24] Cumulatively, these expenditures increased by approximately 77 percent between 1993 and 1999. This pace of growth matches the personnel growth evident in the state administration.

Taken together, this evidence challenges the view that the transition to market capitalism has meant a smaller state. While it is true that the state's share of the economy may be decreasing in relative terms—as a result of privatization and private sector growth—in actual terms it has been increasing throughout the 1990s. Moreover, among the three countries in question, the rates of increase in state spending correspond to those of administrative personnel. The rate of increase in Poland and Slovakia is markedly higher than in the Czech Republic.

Some commentators have used per capita comparisons with Western European countries to downplay the trend toward state expansion in the new democracies of

TABLE 3.2.
*Expenditures of the Central Ministries and Offices of the
Polish State Administration (1993–1999)*

Year	Expenditures (in 1,000s of Zł.)	Real Change over Previous Year
1993	210,650	—
1994	283,500	1.8%
1995	394,600	8.9
1996	549,221	16.1
1997	729,642	15.6
1998	824,097	1
1999	1,055,227	18

SOURCE: Polish Ministry of Finance, as quoted in Jędrzejewska (1999)

Eastern Europe, but per capita terms make for bad comparisons in analyzing postcommunist state-building and patronage politics. For example, Nunberg and Barbone (1999) argue using 1992 figures that the Polish state is still far smaller than Western European ones. "Despite serious comparability problems, international comparisons strongly suggest that in the aggregate, Poland's government is not overstaffed" (20). The per capita ratio of Poland's national state administration was 2.6 bureaucrats per thousand citizens in 1992, when Nunberg and Barbone made their assessment. Just six years later, the ratio had nearly doubled to 4.3 bureaucrats per thousand. If Poland was not overstaffed in 1992, was it in 1998? How much of an increase would it take to be overstaffed in per capita terms?[25] This example points out the difficulties with such per capita comparisons. What are the "right" ratios? What are legitimate comparisons? Comparisons with Western Europe are dubious because they forget that Western European states are several times wealthier than the most developed of their Eastern European brethren. The implied counterfactual is thus something of a straw man: if Poland had the same number of bureaucrats per capita as France at its present level of economic development, that would signify runaway state-building on a miraculous scale. The most legitimate comparisons are *among* postcommunist state administrations. Such comparisons rule out many obvious confounding variables and capitalize on the fact that the simultaneous regime change in 1989 provides a common baseline for comparing both the scale and rapidity of expansion.

FROM PATRIMONIAL ADMINISTRATION
TO WEBERIAN BUREAUCRACY?

Does the overnight expansion of the democratizing state administration correspond to greater state capacity? To what extent do the Polish, Czech, and Slovak state administrations exhibit the organizational traits of Weberian bureaucracy after ten years of democratic politics? Or do the characteristic traits of patrimonial administration that defined the states of Eastern Europe at the time of their collapse in 1989 still predominate? As noted in Chapter 1, either mode of administrative organization is possible in new democracies with unconsolidated states. Just because Weberian administrations are more effective and lead to better long-term economic outcomes than patrimonial ones does not guarantee that state-building will produce Weberian states (Evans and Rauch 1999; 2000). Although state officials would, ideally, prefer to define themselves as policy professionals or bureaucrats, rather than as the current political favorites (often a short-term proposition), frequent and sweeping political intervention in the state-building process adversely influences the payoffs to this strategy. The character of political intervention in the state administration has differed considerably in Poland, the Czech Republic, and Slovakia; now, the task is to characterize the actual organizational practice of the state administrations in these countries. Between 1999 and 2001, I conducted three rounds of field interviews with state officials, politicians, and policy experts in each country. These interviews serve as a measure of the effectiveness of the state administration and as further evidence of the pervasive presence of patronage politics in postcommunist state development.[26]

Chapter 1 notes the core features of Weberian bureaucracy and contrasts these with the features of patrimonial administration found in the posttotalitarian state. The interview questions (see Table 3.3) tap into these core attributes, offering an index of "Weberianness" against which to measure state administrations. First, Weberian bureaucracy is premised on political autonomy, whereas patrimonial administration fuses the political and administrative spheres. Second, Weberian states separate the office from the office holder, minimizing corruption; patrimonial states do not. Third, Weberian states allow for stable predictable career paths, while in patrimonial administrations, political favor determines rank, and officials' careers rest on the fortunes of their political patrons. The lack of career predictability disrupts bureaucratization because it prevents the development of an institutional memory stored and transmitted by career staffers in the state bureaucracy. Practically, this means that the state is forever reinventing the wheel not only when policy problems arise but simply in its day-to-day operations. Fourth, whereas patrimonial administrations lack an ethic of professionalism, in Weberian bureaucracy, officials define themselves as policy professionals, deriving their authority from legal-rationalism and measurable expertise.

The interviews also included two questions to measure the capacity and effectiveness of the state administration directly. The first asked respondents to assess the effectiveness of the administration in implementing policy (see Question 5 in Table 3.3). The second, which asked whether the respondent believed the state administration to be the "right" size, assesses the degree to which state expansion corresponds to state capacity. The underlying assumption is that if patronage is rampant, the state will seem too big for the quality of administration and services it delivers. Of course, the state might seem too big for reasons other than patronage. If, however, a state scores poorly on the other measures (autonomy, corruption, meritocracy, professionalism, and effectiveness), then the addition of state sprawl to the list further suggests that Weberian bureaucratization is not occurring.

The two issues with which all interview research must deal are measurement validity and representativeness. Unfortunately, research on state capacity and patronage politics presents difficult problems on both scores. To best address the dilemmas of validity and representativeness, I conducted open-ended interviews using a combination snowball/quota sampling technique.

The first and most obvious validity issue is how can one be sure that respondents talk accurately and truthfully about issues like patronage? In getting officials to speak candidly about their experience in the state administration, it was necessary to win their trust, and for this personal recommendations and long, open-ended interviews were necessary.[27] It was also necessary to guarantee anonymity to the respondents.[28] Simply contacting officials at their place of work and reading them a list of survey questions would not have broken the trust barrier; it seems self-evident that the potential for superficial and even invalid measures is great in large-N surveys of corruption. How to tap informed opinion based on personal experience with the state administration—as opposed to the widespread disappointment of the public with the state—was the second validity issue posed by this research. A random survey of the Polish, Czech, and Slovak populations will not tap this kind of informed opinion. Instead, it is necessary to build an interview sample of state officials, politicians, and policy experts.

This leads to the second consideration of interview research, representativeness: how representative is this sample of assessments of the Polish, Czech, and Slovak state administrations? Are there biases in the choice of respondents, such as including too many officials at the central level or respondents of a particular political stripe? Normally, survey research solves this problem through random sampling, but for this research that was impractical. First, approaching officials through a personal recommendation was often the first step to winning their trust. Second, government ministries do not allow academics to draw up an interview list of officials randomly drawn from their ranks. In order to put together a representative sample, I conducted interviews with people at all of the various levels of state organization:

TABLE 3.3.

Interview Responses: *Toward a Weberian Bureaucracy?*

Question	Czech Republic		Poland		Slovakia	
	% of Respondents	Number of Respondents	% of Respondents	Number of Respondents	% of Respondents	Number of Respondents
1. How secure do you feel state administrative personnel are from inappropriate pressure from political parties?						
• Secure enough	84.6	22	21.4	6	11.1	2
• Not secure enough	15.4	4	78.6	22	88.9	16
2. In your opinion, has the problem of administrative corruption improved, worsened, or stayed about the same compared with the situation in the early 1990s?						
• Improved	40	6	11.8	2	18.2	2
• Unchanged	60	9	82.4	14	81.8	9
• Worsened	0	0	5.9	1	0	0
3. Do you believe that there are stable, predictable career paths in the state administration?						
• Yes	68.8	11	7.7	1	6.7	1
• No	31.2	5	92.3	12	93.3	14

	%	n	%	n	%	n
4. Do you consider the majority of state administrative personnel to be sufficiently professional?						
• Yes	27.8	5	0	0	7.1	1
• Still not professional enough but improving	61.1	11	55.6	10	7.1	1
• Neither professional enough nor improving	11.1	2	44.4	8	85.7	12
5. Do you consider the state administration to be effective and capable in carrying out its tasks?						
• Yes, sufficiently so	75	15	4.8	1	7.1	1
• Not sufficiently so	25	5	95.2	20	92.9	13
6. Do you believe the state administration to be . . .						
• too big?	31.3	5	75	15	100	7
• the "right" size?	50	8	25	5	0	0
• too small?	18.8	3	0	0	0	0

central, regional, district, and local.[29] Second, I conducted interviews with state officials, elected politicians, and domestic experts (academics, journalists, and staff at relevant nongovernmental organizations [NGOs]) so that I would not just have the administrators' view of their own organization. Within the category of elected politicians, I endeavored to be as representative of the whole political spectrum as possible, interviewing both the left wing and right, Christian Democrats and nationalists. Finally, I conducted interviews in both English and Polish, Czech, and Slovak. This last consideration was important in making sure that my sample was not biased toward more Westernized respondents.

In order to aggregate and analyze the interviews by country, I coded them according to the questions in Table 3.3. Because not all of the interviews could be definitively coded in these terms, and because not every person in the sample could answer each question based on their personal experience, the sample sizes reported in the table are less than the total interviews conducted. Choosing to err on the side of caution, I have left those interviews that could not be easily and unambiguously coded out of the aggregate analysis rather than trying to shoehorn them into the coding categories. Because this sample was not drawn randomly, I have chosen not to use the conventional statistical apparatus of confidence intervals and so on to analyze the results.

A clear and relatively stable pattern emerged from these interviews, as Table 3.3 shows. The Czech Republic stood out as the most bureaucratically developed administration. Over the course of the democratic transition, the Czech administration has become more professional, stable, and internally cohesive, largely because it has not been subject to the same degree of political intervention as the Polish and Slovak ones. For the most part, the latter two countries cluster at the other end of the spectrum, that of posttotalitarian patrimonialism. They emerge from the interviews as state administrations in turmoil or, more kindly, ongoing redefinition.[30] Slovakia's administration is still struggling with the legacy of Mečiar. Poland's is still seeking internal cohesiveness and stability.

The Interviews

There was a sizable difference between perceptions of administrative autonomy in the Czech Republic—with its high degree of autonomy—and Slovakia and Poland, with their low degrees of autonomy (see Table 3.3).[31] The wording of the first question is broad, however; "inappropriate pressure from political parties" may mean different things in Poland and Slovakia. Judging by the full responses of my interlocutors, this seems to have been the case. In Slovakia, such pressure included sweeping and punitive intervention, especially under the various Mečiar governments, from 1992 to 1998. In Poland it was relatively rare to hear of specific cases of administrators losing their jobs because of politics, but in Slovakia that incidence was common.

In the course of my interviews in Slovakia, I talked with a number of officials who worked, or who had worked, in the Ministry of Foreign Affairs (MFA). One official, who at the time of the interview had left the foreign ministry to work for a foreign policy NGO, related the following account of personnel change in the MFA after Mečiar's return to power following the 1994 elections: "HZDS had organized 'hiring campaigns' for new officials even before the elections. Then, after the elections, they brought these political recruits into the MFA using them to replace the people there, especially those not sympathetic to HZDS. These old officials were forced to leave for having 'collaborated' with the former government."

Another respondent, who at the time of the interview had migrated from his job at the foreign ministry to the Office of the Government, described the patronage politics in Slovakia as "naïve," that is, based as much on the urge for revenge as on gaining political advantage. Across Slovakia, respondents stated that under HZDS's governments, the replacement of state officials had extended far down into the ranks of the administration, often below the upper mid-level positions of, say, office director.[32] As the interviewees pointed out, the result of such intervention was to demoralize administrators and severely set back any kind of institutional learning.

On the surface, the Polish interviews sound similar to the Slovak ones: politics is rampant in the administration. The basic view of the Polish state administration was most directly articulated in an interview with an official in the local-level state administration: "You have to know that in Poland [state] offices are political units. The managers in our city office are political too, and sometimes they are not good managers."

The character of political intervention in Poland is different from that in Slovakia, however. First, party influence there does not take the form of purges but rather occurs in waves of administrative recruitment that follow political cycles and that are poorly integrated into the existing administration. One former Polish state official, who had worked in the Chancellery of the Prime Minister argued that the state administration reflected political changes: "The development of this office in the 1990s has been chaotic and, I think, very typical for these last ten years. This office reflects the see-saw development of the political system. You have to bear in mind that every four years we change our government entirely, and in the early 1990s it was every two years. The result of these radical changes in the composition of the government is that each new government brings in a new wave of administrative staff who are completely inexperienced and who need the help of the old staff."

Second, unlike the very direct nature of Slovakia's party interventions, the Polish respondents described political influence as operating behind the scenes by blurring administrative-political boundaries rather than by overstepping them. To quote from the same interview, "Officially, the political cabinet and the rest of the office are separate. In practice, however, the separation between the political staff and the rest of the office is not nearly so clear as it appears on paper. The political cabinet works very closely with certain departments in the office and, so, comes to exercise a lot of influence in those departments. Because such relationships are formed, the political cabinet makes recommendations regarding the hiring and promotion of the non-political staff. This is a very, very popular practice. The political cabinet have a lot of influence, often the most influence."

Third, the result of this more subtle party influence in Poland is to produce overlapping, blurred political allegiances rather than the clear separation into pro- versus anti-Mečiar camps evident in Slovakia. According to a mid-level official in one of the Polish central state offices, "In the current situation, administration officials too often see stabilizing their position as their first task. As a result, they often try to cultivate good relationships with *all* the political parties. This way they can make their own jobs more secure, but for the state [as a whole], this is a very dangerous tendency because it interferes with them doing their job. For most officials, the problem is not that they will lose their positions after a change of government, though this is indeed a problem for some. The problem is rather that, they have become entirely ensconced in these political networks in order to stabilize their positions."

In the Czech interviews, none of the respondents who felt that the state administration was not sufficiently secure from party influence were actually state administrators. Two were academics, and one was an NGO employee. Despite my best attempts to probe deeply in my interviews with Czech state officials, the closest my interlocutors came to expressing the opinion that party influence extended into the state administration was that this had been the case in the early 1990s. For example, an official in one of the central ministries stated, "In the early 1990s, recruitment was chaotic. How did people enter the ministry? Some came on their own. The others were deliveries from other ministries and the political parties, of course. There was a very unusual recruitment based on networks of friends. It was sort of a client system: a known dissident now in the ministry hires five of his friends. This sort of thing no longer happens, though." He went on to describe the combination of seniority and qualifications that now governs personnel policy in that ministry.

Administrative corruption is a topic that has received considerable attention from others, especially NGOs like Transparency International (1996–2000). My survey handles the question somewhat differently, however (see Question 2). First, I addressed the question explicitly at state officials, politicians, and experts on administration; in contrast, Transparency International's surveys are drawn from businesspeople and country residents. Second, my wording stresses relative change in the degree of corruption over time, not the absolute level as in the Transparency International surveys. For my argument, the important fact is change in the level of corruption, or in Weberian terms, the emergence of separate public and private roles for state officials (Silberman 1993, 4). Even if the level of corruption is high compared to other countries, if respondents answer that the situation has been improving since the beginning of the 1990s, it would constitute evidence of the routinization of bureaucratic norms.

My respondents were not on the whole very sanguine on this score. In all three countries, a majority of respondents answered that the problem of administrative corruption had not improved since the early 1990s.[33] The Czech respondents were more likely to see improvement, but the following response from a high-ranking official in a central ministry, which was emblematic, suggests that this difference should not be pushed too far: "I am pretty sure that at the height of privatization, corruption could have been immense, though I don't have personal knowledge of any particular cases. I think that generally the situation with regard to corruption has improved since then. I would say that the problem of corruption here is not too much bigger than in some EU countries."

The aggregate results of my survey do not differ markedly from those of Transparency International—despite the differences in wording and sampling. There are not huge differences among the countries, but their ranking relative to each other—with the Czech Republic scoring best followed by Poland and then Slovakia—corresponds to the Transparency International's (1996–2000) ordering. In sum, it is hard to discern the glimmerings of bureaucratization in any of these countries in terms of corruption; in this area anyway, they fall closer to the posttotalitarian administrative apparatus type.

My third survey category sought to capture the degree to which a position in the state administration represented a stable and predictable career path (Question 3). In a bureaucratic organization, an administrator can reasonably predict where he or she will be ten or twenty years down the line based on a combination of seniority and qualifications. In an administration of the patrimonial type, career paths are unpredictable and unstable, as political patronage can vault a newcomer to the head of an office and topple a career official in the process.[34]

In Poland, all but one respondent told me that administrative career paths were not stable and predictable. First, there was not the sense that the best administrators could work their way to the top by the established routes of seniority and professional qualifications. Second, there was the commonly expressed view that stability and predictability were lacking; as another official told me, "I worked in the Interior Ministry for seven years [after 1990], and I felt that my career had the same low level of stability as if I had been in business—but without the salary I would have earned in business. Many of the decisions that you take in the state administration are quite political, and thus they have the potential to rebound against you. The government is now trying to establish some criteria for promotion in the state administration that would make the job more stable and less political. But there are still ways to get around these criteria and regulations." Surprisingly, the one dissenting view among the Polish respondents regarding the stability and predictability of careers in the state administration came from a political advisor at the Interior Ministry, a position which is explicitly a *political* appointment.

In the Czech Republic, a majority of respondents told me that the state administration offered stable and predictable career paths. One of my Czech interviews was with a highly placed official in the Czech MFA, who had been recruited to the ministry for his foreign language skills in the early 1990s. As he told me, he had vaulted almost immediately to a top position in the ministry, ahead of many senior officials; he added, however, that the era of such careers was over: "In the early 1990s, ministers brought people with them who they knew. The rationale was: 'I'm going to take over the ministry.' There was a lot of turnover because of the revolution. My own case could not have happened in a Western country, to get to the top of the MFA in five years. But even here [in the Czech state], this is now changing. It was only possible to have a career like mine before 1998. Now, there is a system in place in our ministry that bases advancement on seniority and qualifications."[35]

According to a number of younger, mid-level officials I interviewed in the Czech Republic, the greater stability of career paths relative to the private sector as well as the opportunities for advancement were the reasons why they had entered the state administration.

As one might expect given the results of the first question, stable career paths were not often noted by the Slovak respondents. In Slovakia, however, even among officials who themselves had had bad experiences under the HZDS governments, there was the belief that without continued political interruptions career paths would emerge in time. As one state official told me: "There are starting to be career paths. There are *some* people who stay in the administration, who have studied at Comenius [University in Bratislava], have gone into the MFA, have gone abroad and come back. But even these officials still have to think ahead to what will happen after the next election. In time, however, this will be less and less important, I think. The dust will settle. I think we need one or two more elections to settle down, unless HZDS and SNS[36] win. Then all bets are off." As this quote clearly illustrates, administrators see their world in terms of incremental organizational improvement, gradual accretion of expertise and experience, and increasing predictability as bureaucratic norms become entrenched; they also understand the threat to this process posed by patronage politics.

Fourth, I coded the interview sample for the perceived degree of professionalism in the state administration (Question 4). In addition to technical skills, I use this question to capture the emergence of an identity of the administrator as a policy professional, that is, as possessing a certain status as a result of holding the office. With this status comes a core loyalty to the office and pride for being part of a group of other such professionals, regardless of their political stripe. Overall, the results of the interview coding on this criterion showed a somewhat different grouping of the countries. The differences between Poland and the Czech Republic were not as great. Slovakia remained an underperformer, though, with only a small fraction of the respondents seeing any trend toward administrative professionalism.[37]

In Poland, it was a common refrain that, while professionalization was occurring at the individual level, the overall level was still not high enough. A typical expression of this view comes from a former top-level official in one of the central offices:

> My biggest success in my first year as Director-General [of the office], the thing I rate most highly, was that to a degree I found a way to create a common platform for all the various groups within the office—especially the older and newer staff. (I mean by this the groups hired under earlier governments.) They began to communicate and work together. We started, I think, to create a core group with loyalty to the state, to the office. But for this to grow will take time. You must remember, we are very young politically. I think it will take another ten years to develop, and then new governments will begin to expect that the old staff are professional and will do their job regardless of which party is governing.

In my interviews with Czech administrators, the majority of respondents saw either increasing professionalism or even full-blown professionalism, indicating a sense of pride in their qualifications and their office. The response from a mid-level official with a law degree working in an office dealing with legal harmonization for EU integration is a good illustration: "Even though the salary is relatively low, I think a lot of people would like a job in this office, but it's not easy to get in since you need to know foreign languages and to be a lawyer. Because we are dealing with new things, you don't need as many people with Czech experience. I myself would like to stay in the state. I like the work, and the job has good prospects for the future. For a lawyer, this is a good job, possibly a springboard to working in the EU Commission after the country joins the EU." One might point out, of course, that this respondent is in a different position than the typical Czech official, that the work is somehow more exciting and demanding because it deals with the EU. Yet even among Czech officials far removed from the EU or Prague, a similar sense of professional pride and identity emerged from the interviews—even as far as a remote Czech town in the eastern part of the country where I interviewed the director of a Labor Office (Úřad práce).

A much smaller portion of respondents in Slovakia saw the emergence of professionalism in the state administration. An upper-level official in one of the central offices sharply contrasted the degree of professionalism between the Slovak and Czech state administrations: "In Slovakia, we don't have a tradition of statehood, and you can feel it when you look at the administration. After independence [in 1993], the state suddenly needed people; there were lots of spaces. How to fill them? The most important criteria were party loyalties and connections. These were not experts or professionals, but people brought in from the provinces. This is the basic difference between the Czechs and us: our state-building took place in the absence of a replacement elite in waiting."

The one exception to this negative rating of the administrative professionalism among my Slovak interviews was in an interview conducted with a mid-level official at the Slovak central bank (Národná banka Slovenska) in Bratislava: "I've worked at the bank since 1996, and I feel that the people working here are professionals. Most people are about 30 years old and either came here from the banking sector or from the universities. Outside of the bank, I can feel a change in the atmosphere, can see the lobbying around, say, the construction of a new building or a new factory. But here, in the bank we are independent of politics."

Before generalizing from this example, it is important to recognize, as this official acknowledges herself, that the situation of the central bank is unusual among Slovak state institutions. There are, in fact, historical reasons why it should be so. The central bank is formally independent of politics. More importantly, its head is appointed by the president of the country rather than the government. Given that Slovakia's president for most of the 1990s, Michal Kováč, was locked in a bitter struggle with the governing HZDS party machine, it is not surprising that Kováč tried to use his appointment powers to keep the bank independent of HZDS's influence. Moreover, the central bank is one of the only Slovak state institutions to have been built entirely from scratch beginning in 1993, which to a large extent has shielded it from penetration by old networks of party-affiliated officialdom.[38] Thus, the central bank seems to have benefited from institutional late development.

On the final two coding criteria, the respondents in my survey also showed considerable separation along country lines, with the now familiar grouping of the Czech Republic at one pole and Poland and Slovakia at the other (see Questions 5 and 6). Whereas the previous questions sought to capture individual aspects of the state administration's organizational culture, these last two questions sought to capture a picture of how the respondents viewed the state administration as a whole. Inevitably, they are phrased somewhat bluntly and are coded along a limited range of responses, but the results are suggestive.

First, I coded the interviews for the respondents' assessments of the effectiveness and capability of the state administration in carrying out its tasks (Question 5). A clear divergence emerged between the countries. Both Poland and Slovakia received almost unanimously poor ratings of the state administration's capacity and effectiveness. In Poland, the response from a career bureaucrat in the Supreme Audit Office (NIK), was typical for the naysayers: "On the one hand, it is obvious that the state administration functions more effectively now than it did before 1989. On the other hand, it's also obvious that in the period after 1989, it hasn't gained in effectiveness proportionate to its growth in numbers, particularly the number of officials. That's obvious too. The state is obviously not as effective as it should be." In Slovakia, one official compared the situation at his ministry, the MFA, with his experience dealing with counterparts in the Hungarian state: "It's amazing to see how far ahead of us they are, how knowledgeable and prepared they are. When you compare it with the situation here, it's like you're looking at a Western country."[39]

By contrast, a clear majority of my Czech respondents felt that the state administration was sufficiently capable and effective. In the Czech interviews, there was not the tendency, evident in both Slovakia and Poland, to criticize one's own office and then characterize these deficiencies as typical of the system as a whole. If anything, there was the opposite tendency: officials often ranked their own state administrative office or ministry as better than the rest. For example, an official in the Ministry of Education told me apropos of the possibility of decentralization: "It may happen that the newly elected politicians in the regions will not be sufficiently experienced in the administration of schools. I think there is a consensus in this country that our educational system works quite well and, as a result, doesn't need to be changed. By changing this system, the reform risks damaging it."

Another official, a veteran administrator in the parliamentary research institute, expressed scorn for the idea that EU harmonization would improve the Czech administration. She cited the example of regional policy as evidence of the Czech state's effectiveness: "Until now, our regional policy was not done according to the EU model. Instead, it was done through state aids, this is, through the Ministries—Agriculture and Economy mainly. If you ask me, the EU's regional policy is nonsense. I don't see any good results, except perhaps Ireland. The regions that were receiving support in the 1970s are the ones receiving support today. The creation of new regional agencies and institutions—just to please the EU—will only lead to over-bureaucratization."[40]

Last, I coded my interview respondents in terms of their perception of the size of the state administration in comparison with their own idealized conception of the appropriate size (Question 6). At first glance, this question would seem problematic. It would seem that this question might better capture the political views of the respondents than their assessment of the size of the state. Namely, left-oriented respondents would presumably favor a larger role for state action and, therefore, would be more likely to describe the state administration as too small. Conservatives would be biased in exactly the opposite direction. A certain amount of this bias was evident in my interviews, but surprisingly little. Conservatives did tend to attach greater importance to the issue of state size than left-oriented respondents, but in Poland and Slovakia an overwhelming majority responded that the state administration was too big. For example, a former regional governor in Poland, who was appointed by the postcommunist government, maintained: "The structures of the state have become overbuilt. For example, the structures created by decentralization cost more than the tasks that they are to perform. I read recently of a district office that receives 24 million zloty from the central government to keep up the roads in its district, but the office itself requires 17 million zloty to pay its personnel. That means 7 million go to the roads and 17 million to salaries. This example is typical."

In Slovakia, respondents were unanimous in describing the state administration as too big. Many pointed to the expansion of the state administration under Mečiar in the mid-1990s.[41]

In contrast, in the Czech Republic, a minority of respondents described the state administration as too large. About half felt that it was the "right" size, and a few argued that it was too small. The typical Czech response resembled the following interview quote from a highly placed individual in one of the central ministries: "If you read today's paper, there is an article that the Czech state has become too bureaucratic, that the number of officials in the state administration has increased by I don't know what percent for the last five years. I do not think that's the point. The truth is that when we're a country in the EU, the number of officials in the state will probably increase again. The point is whether the officials we have now are all in the right places, that is, where they're required." A number of the Czech respondents argued that the state was not big enough, that more personnel were needed to perform an increasingly demanding set of tasks.

To summarize, two main conclusions stand out from these interview data. First, there is a clear pattern in the interviews, dividing the Czech Republic, in which the emergence of bureaucratic practice can be discerned, from Poland and Slovakia, where patrimonial practices continue to predominate. This division was clearly evident along the dimensions of administrative autonomy, the stability of career paths, state effectiveness, and state size. It was less clear along the dimensions of corruption—where all three countries performed poorly—and professionalism, where Poland aligned more closely to the Czech Republic and Slovakia was the outlier. One of the necessary conditions for bureaucratization is that the state administration have sufficient autonomy from patronage politics. My interviews indicate that both Poland and Slovakia fail to meet the minimum threshold of administrative autonomy. Indeed, the interviews provide strong evidence of widespread patronage politics in the Polish and Slovak state administrations. Second, this analysis should serve as a caution that even in the Czech Republic, one can still only speak of bureaucratization, not of bureaucracy. Many of the Czech respondents noted just how recently their state administration was in deep flux. At this point in time, one can only discern the first stages of Weberian bureaucracy in the Czech Republic.

A Ministry Case Study: Foreign Affairs

Several of my interviews were conducted with officials and former officials at the Ministry for Foreign Affairs (MFA) in each country. These interviews were particularly insightful because they presented comparable case studies of how the state developed in the democratic transition.[42] As the following cases show, the development of the Slovak, Czech, and Polish MFAs reflect again the strong influence of the logic of party competition on state development.

The first years after independence represent a period of upheaval at the Slovak MFA. Before the break-up of Czechoslovakia, many of the officials who would later work at the Slovak foreign ministry worked in the Federal Ministry of Foreign Affairs, which had branches in both the Czech and Slovak Republics. In addition to the personnel working in the Slovak branch of the ministry, a large number of ethnically Slovak officials who were working in Prague returned to positions at the Slovak ministry. Even with this base to start from, however, there was a scramble to build up the Slovak foreign ministry. The first two years of independence (1993–1995) were a very unsettled period in the ministry—as they were in the Czech foreign ministry. In addition to the task of setting up republican ministries, there was also the problem of decommunization, which had been going on since 1990. In the Ministry of Foreign Affairs, many of the senior officials had been trained in Moscow, and their past raised doubts about their loyalty to the newly independent state.

The result of this upheaval was the influx of large numbers of officials into a ministry whose hierarchies and conventions were undergoing a radical reordering. Three broad groups predominated in the first two years. Two of these consisted of political newcomers, people who swept in on the tails of the 1989 revolution and who could be divided into subgroups. The first arrivals were usually young people politically connected with the new regime, who had taken one-year degrees in diplomacy abroad, most often in Vienna or Bonn. After this first wave, there came the graduates of newly established courses in diplomacy at Slovak universities. According to my interview respondents, these early rapid training programs were quite lax, especially the Slovak diplomas. The third group consisted of Soviet-era career diplomats who had not been placed highly enough in the former regime to be replaced outright; these were people in their diplomatic prime, in their forties and fifties and with actual experience but the wrong political credentials. Each group viewed the others with suspicion and a feeling of outright rivalry. Needless to say, this was not a state bureaucracy with a coherent corporate identity, pride in its professional qualifications, and a shared sense of purpose. It was an uneasy amalgam of three mutually suspicious camps.

Political connections were very important for selection into the foreign ministry throughout the 1990s. Until 1992, the most important means of recruitment was the network of dissidents and "democrats" based around the Public Against Violence (VPN). Beginning with Mečiar's break from VPN in 1991, the political tide began to turn. Mečiar's new HZDS party openly recruited new state officials from its supporters. In the case of the Ministry for Foreign Affairs, HZDS organized "hiring campaigns" for new diplomats even before the national parliamentary elections in 1992 and 1994. One could go to a HZDS office and apply to join the foreign ministry after the elections. In 1994, after HZDS did in fact win the election, these recruits were used to replace the party's perceived enemies in the foreign ministry (i.e. appointees affiliated with the dissident network).

The Mečiar purges meant the replacement of most of the recently arrived diplomats with diplomas from one-year programs in foreign relations. A lot of the older generation, Moscow-trained diplomats joined the HZDS and reemerged in positions of power within the ministry. Most replacement occurred among upper- and middle-level positions, such as section heads and department heads. By 1996, there was not a single section chief left at the foreign ministry who was not a member of one of the government parties. Lower-level officials were not as likely to lose their jobs, but even there it was known to happen.

Two of my respondents had worked formerly in a small foreign policy research institute within the MFA in the early 1990s. They were Slovaks in their twenties and thirties who had come to the MFA after 1989 after finishing degrees or lectureships at the university. After the 1994 elections, the chief of this unit, also one of the younger generation officials, was fired. It proved easy to remove him despite his employment contract; the new minister simply changed the qualifications for the post he occupied. The old chief lacked the new qualifications, but they matched the résumé of the already-picked replacement.

At first, most of the research unit's regular staff remained. After a new head of the unit was named, however, the regular staff also turned over almost entirely. The new director was from the opposite pole of the political and experiential spectrum from his staff. He was a Moscow-trained, former-Communist official of retirement age who viewed the younger staff with suspicion. It was at about this time that Slovak foreign policy underwent a pronounced turn from Western Europe and the United States and toward Russia. The new director introduced this new foreign policy line at the research institute, against the inclinations of the staff.

A few of the staff left because they found it too difficult to work with the new director. The rest decided to write to the minister in protest against the replacement of their former manager. In their letter, they argued that the new chief was openly anti-NATO, that he had written articles criticizing Slovakia's integration with the EU, and that his Communist past would hurt him in dealing with the West. The choice of such a head for their unit went against the government's avowed goal of EU and NATO integration. When the minister received the letter, rather than reconsidering his appointment, he fired the rest of the unit. The new director then hired replacements. In politics, all advantages are temporary, however. When the HZDS-led government was defeated in the 1998 elections, the pendulum swung back the other way at the Slovak MFA. The new government invited all of the purged officials back to the unit.

The story of the Slovak MFA illustrates the quandary of state-building in a dominant-party system. First, it reveals a state administration that ebbs and flows on the tides of electoral politics. Here, there is no sense of career bureaucrats who serve Slovak foreign policy regardless of who is in government. Second, it shows how demotivating the organizational culture of the Slovak state bureaucracy is. Of the former employees at the research unit who were invited to return to the state after HZDS left the government, only one took up the offer. For the others, it was difficult to return to a career in which the future is always uncertain.[43] Without the capacity to retain dedicated and trained bureaucrats, it is very difficult for the Slovak state to be effective.

As in Slovakia, the Czech MFA underwent massive reorganization in the early 1990s. According to a respondent who had worked in the Czech MFA since 1994, a full 80 percent of the communist-era diplomats was forced out of the ministry after 1989. "It was necessary," as he put it, "to clean house." Czechoslovakia's communist regime had been considerably stricter than say Poland or Hungary's, and the secret police (StB) had very carefully vetted any employee in so sensitive a ministry as Foreign Affairs. Because it was necessary to preserve some institutional memory, a few of the more experienced pre-1989 officials were allowed to stay on, but only after passing a special lustration.

The result of this massive purge was an influx of new officials and the dissolution of organizational hierarchies. As in Slovakia, three groups predominated in the MFA of the early 1990s: former Communist officials, young graduates of one- or two-year courses in diplomacy, and friends or connections of political dissidents. None of them got along particularly well with the others. It was possible in this kind of environment to make extraordinary careers, to enter the MFA with little or no knowledge of foreign relations but rather on the strength of knowing a certain foreign language, having spent time abroad, or having some kind of personal connection with someone at the ministry and, after a short time, to find oneself at the top of the ministry managing officials with years of diplomatic experience.[44] This environment allowed large scope for personal clientelism and party patronage. The process of recruiting new officials was, as one respondent put it, "very unusual." In contrast to Slovakia, there were no recruitment campaigns by political parties before general elections. There were no formal or informal codes in the Czech MFA that would have been able to prevent such recruitment from happening, however. In the absence of typical career paths after 1989, such new arrivals could rise straight to the top of the ministry. As in Slovakia and Poland, the political connections became important even for mid-level positions such as department director. In short, the organizational culture and practice of the MFA bureaucracy did not differ noticeably from those of Slovakia and Poland.

By 1996, however, the free-for-all within the state bureaucracy had begun to disappear in the Czech MFA. By 2000, it had vanished entirely. What did this mean concretely, in terms of the organizational culture and practice of the ministry's bureaucracy? First, it meant the development of a code of rules that took the form of an internal operational handbook. Second, it meant the formalization of the process of recruitment. The internal code the ministry adopted in 1996 established routes of entry into the MFA. Third, the end of free-for-all organization meant the establishment of career trajectories in the bureaucracy, ending the era of extraordinary careers without moving up through the ranks.

These reforms took place because the MFA bureaucracy was able to develop without political interference around election cycles. After the 1998 parliamentary elections, in which the ODS government was replaced by ČSSD, there was no purge of the MFA. The new minister, Jan Kavan, brought a team of political advisors from his party. Some of the deputy ministers were changed as well, but the changes stopped there, at the highest level of leadership. There was certainly nothing like the scale of replacements that occurred in Slovakia in 1994 and then to a lesser degree in 1998, or even in the Czech Republic in the early 1990s.

Surprisingly enough, some in the Czech MFA were critical of the government's proposed plan for the adoption of a law on the civil service, a proposal which was strongly urged by the European Union. On deeper consideration, however, this is not really so surprising. In fact, it shows how far the MFA has come to developing its own internal conventions about bureaucratic organization and autonomy from outside political interference. The Czech MFA has come up with its own internal code and views attempts at regulation by the government as outside intrusion. It is not simply that the Czech foreign service likes to have things its own way. Its members fear the reintroduction of party politics into the recruitment and promotion processes in the MFA bureaucracy.

The Polish MFA has not suffered from the same cycle of purging that still occurs in Slovakia. The problem is rather that successive governments create new departments and external offices alongside the old, either because they do not trust the old officials or because they want to reward their own supporters. Not surprisingly, the new offices do not work well with the old, and foreign policy becomes a turf battle between several competing offices. A good example was the decision of the Polish government to create a special Committee for European Integration (KIE) separate from the Ministry of Foreign Affairs. This decision led to an internally contradictory foreign policy toward the European Union, resulting, most disastrously, in the failure to qualify for considerable monetary aid from the EU (Bielecki 1998; "Czarnecki bez teki" 1998).

When, in 1997, the fractious AWS-UW coalition came to power, nowhere were differences among the coalition members more evident than in policy concerning the European Union. AWS had a pragmatic, liberal core that accepted EU integration as the best long-range strategy for Poland's interests. It also had a nationalist wing with an unpragmatic and uncompromising understanding of Poland's national interests. To the nationalist and religious-conservative parties in AWS a supranational EU state was anathema; the more radical among them saw it as German power under a new guise.[45] The nationalists and religious conservative in AWS were not about to surrender EU foreign policy to one of the coalition's liberal pragmatists.

The government appointed Ryszard Czarnecki, a prominent member of the nationalist-religious conservative ZChN party and an open critic of the European Union, as head of the KIE. It was a good political move in terms of holding AWS together, but a very poor diplomatic move in terms of advancing Poland's accession to the EU. In addition to his antipathy to the EU, Czarnecki had little experience in public administration and diplomacy. If Czarnecki had been able to draw on a capable and experienced staff, this appointment might not have been so damaging, but according to my respondents, he was not able to do that either. In fact, the culture in the KIE described to me was one of patronage and organizational disarray.

One respondent, a former MFA official, had been appointed by the AWS government to establish and then lead a section within the KIE in 1998. He was an outside expert with no political contacts to the KIE's leadership. After his appointment, he drew up a report laying out the goals for his new section and calculating the necessary resources, staff and materiel. He waited three months for a response. Despite repeated phone calls and memos concerning the office he was supposed to set up, none of the KIE hierarchy paid any attention to him. He was given a "cell phone and a handsome salary and that was that." The problem was that he had no political avenues to the office's decision-makers. He resigned after three months because he was petrified by the thought that someone would ask him several months down the road what progress his office had made. Meanwhile the KIE was growing in size by leaps and bounds. In 1998, it employed about 200. In 2001, at the time of the interview, the staff had grown to over 300. According to my respondent, this sizable office lacked any sort of internal communication and was run in a way best described as "byzantine."

The very founding of the KIE exemplified the kind of duplication of offices characteristic of state-building in a weak-governance party system—with its proclivity for multiple, localized, and uncoordinated intervention in the state administration by the many members of the governing coalition. The government also had a third major office dealing with the EU in the Chancellery of the Government, the Office of the Chief Negotiator for EU Integration. The separation of the office of the KIE from the office of the negotiator made little sense from an organizational point of view. But more damaging than the duplication was the tension between the two offices. The KIE was headed by the euroskeptic Czarnecki, whereas the Office of the Chief Negotiator was the europhilic Jan Kułakowski. The antagonism between the two offices escalated to a major public row, widely covered in the newspapers in the summer of 1998, with each office accusing the other of betraying Poland's national interests. Moreover, the EU was frustrated at dealing with conflicting signals from two noncooperative offices. In the end, the Czarnecki episode proved an embarrassment to the AWS government. After the EU revealed that Poland had failed to qualify for a sizable amount of PHARE funding because of poorly designed project proposals, Czarnecki was dismissed.[46]

CONCLUSION

Patronage politics has a very adverse impact on state development in new democracies. A variety of data show that the explosive growth of administrative personnel in Poland and Slovakia was not accompanied by an organizational transformation of those states. In a process of runaway state-building, these states grew without becoming more professional, effective, or autonomous. Only in the Czech case, and after a rocky start, has the state administration been allowed the autonomy and stability to begin to develop its own internal regulations and professional code; a bureaucratic model has begun to replace the patrimonial apparatus inherited from the communist model of the state. Although the progress of bureaucratization has been the most tepid where political intervention in the state administration has been greatest, the word "bureaucratization" deserves special emphasis. Even the Czech state administration does not yet fully constitute a bureaucracy in the Weberian sense of the word. That will take time yet.

CHAPTER FOUR

Remaking the Regions

The Europeanization of the State or Domestic Politics as Usual?

In response to the observation that several postcommunist states have rapidly expanded during the 1990s, some might argue that international factors, in particular European Union (EU) enlargement, are at work, not the attendant difficulties of democratization. As Charles Tilly's observation that "states make war and war makes states" suggests, the international dimension has always played an important role in state-building. Of course, EU enlargement is not about war; it is about the requirements of accession, which include the capacity to implement EU regulations. On one level, the influence of the EU is undeniable. It has put administration and regulation on the agenda for Eastern European governments. But how much control does the EU exert over state-building once these items are on the agenda? What are the limits of EU conditionality? Can the EU's preferences explain variation in state-building in Eastern Europe? This chapter uses a comparison of one policy area, regional governance reform, to answer these questions.

Across Eastern Europe, one of the first acts of democratically elected governments after the 1989 revolution was to abolish institutions of regional government, which were seen as tools of Communist Party influence. By the mid-1990s, however, a number of domestic policy experts began to argue that the elimination of regional institutions had been ill-conceived and that some intermediate level of governance between the central and local levels was necessary (Gilowska 2000a; Koral 2000; Gorzelak and Jałowiecki 1999; Chancellery 1998; Plenipotentiary 1999; and Illner 1999). Regional decentralization soon appeared on the government agenda. For scholars of state-building, decentralization is a natural frame of reference for cross-national comparison since, as noted earlier, how national governments handle decentralization gets to the heart of the relationship between party competition and state-building. Do governments truly devolve power, or do "decentralizing reforms" create new public offices that depend heavily on central government resources and so, in essence, extend the influence—and patronage—of the center to the provinces? Regional state reform is also a good indicator of the influence of the EU on state-building in Eastern Europe because the EU has exerted direct and long-standing pressure for decentralization there.[1] Given its timing and context, regional governance reform[2] in Eastern Europe would seem to fit within a larger process of Europeanization that a number of scholars have argued is increasingly shaping state-building in this region's new democracies (Grabbe 2003; Jacoby 1999).[3]

Noting the unprecedented power asymmetries between the EU and Eastern European states, this Europeanization thesis predicts institutional convergence in Eastern Europe (Grabbe 2003). The EU exercises the powerful instrument of conditionality through the requirement that the candidate countries implement the *acquis communautaire* prior to accession. Through such policies as administrative twinning—that is, partnering Eastern European officials with counterparts in Western Europe—the EU, it can be argued, socializes Eastern European political elites to embrace European policy norms.[4] This process of cognitive-sociological convergence has been vividly, if ruefully, described by a Czech politician who complained of "the political, intellectual and economic elite who are Euro-corrupted, funded by Euro-grants, Euro-funds and Euro-programs."[5] Indeed, given the power asymmetries of EU enlargement, Europeanizing pressures toward policy convergence are, it is argued, stronger in Eastern Europe than in both the rest of the EU and in earlier rounds of expansion (Grabbe 2003, 4–6).

While fully recognizing these power asymmetries, other scholars have begun to point out the limits of Europeanization in actual practice. Several have used regional governance reform as a policy case for testing the Europeanization thesis because the incentives for compliance are so great (Hughes, Sasse, and Gordon 2003; Marek and Baun 2002; Yoder 2003). Since regional policy is one of the biggest avenues for development aid in the EU, the incentives to conform to EU policy templates in this area would seem particularly great. As these analyses have suggested, however, the practice of regional governance reform in Eastern Europe has proven much more elastic than the Europeanization hypothesis's prediction of convergence would suggest. While persuasively showing the limits of conditionality over such reform, these skeptics of Europeanization have been less successful, though, in advancing a parsimonious and generalizable explanation of what does drive the undeniable and far-reaching reforms that are currently reshaping Eastern European institutions.

The logic of party competition can explain both the timing and varying content of this aspect of state-building in Eastern Europe. What both the proponents and the skeptics of the Europeanization thesis fail to recognize is that regional state reform holds its own rewards from a purely domestic political point of view, that is, quite apart from the incentives and sanctions presented by the EU. These rewards account both for the enthusiasm with which certain Eastern European governments undertook regional governance reform and for the widely varying outcomes of these reforms. The most important factor determining institutional outcomes is the coalitional politics of the government that enacts it, which in turn directly reflects the logics of party competition described in Chapter 2. The Europeanization hypothesis is correct insofar as it maintains that regional state reform is not a purely domestic political story. The EU is essential to the wave of state restructuring currently reshaping regional politics in Eastern European countries because, by advancing its own regional agenda, it opened up a critical juncture for reform. The variation in outcomes suggests the EU's limited success in using conditionality to implement this agenda, however. The EU was a factor in the growth of postcommunist states, though not necessarily in the positive sense that much of the literature on Europeanization assumes: it figured as a useful pretext for reforms that allowed domestic political forces, in particular governing party coalitions, to shape regional state institutions in their own interests.

Poland, the Czech Republic, and Slovakia make for a good comparison because each has undertaken to reform its regional state institutions and because the particular domestic political configuration in each led to a different variant of reform.[6] The time frame of the comparison will be from the signing of the first European Agreements in 1991, which formalized the relationship between Eastern European states and the EU, until the legislation of basic regional governance reform, which took place at different times in different countries.

Reduced to its most basic elements, the story of regional reform in these three countries is as follows. In Slovakia, regional reform occurred in two stages. In the first, under Vladimír Mečiar, a logic of dominant-party (variant 1) competition led to a policy of administrative deconcentration that actually centralized power in the hands of the government and the Mečiar-led party machine that dominated it.[7] A second, post-Mečiar reform foundered as a divided and unwieldy government found it could not push through a meaningful reform and maintain its fragile majority (dominant-party variant 2). In Poland's weak-governance party system, reform did bring regional devolution but, because the government was composed of a large and unruly coalition, coalitional politics led to a kind of runaway decentralization in which the government bought votes for its reform by inflating the number of subnational units. In the responsible-party competition of the Czech Republic, the concern with economic costs of decentralization produced a reform that achieved regional devolution but that, unlike Poland's, was fundamentally a rationalization of the territorial apparatus of the state. Czech regional reform was framed as an economic question, as a choice between big and small government, reflecting the country's essentially bipolar party competition of Social Democrats versus conservatives.

First I present the benefits and drawbacks of the Europeanization argument for understanding the dynamics of regional state-building in Eastern Europe. Afterward, I specify and compare the differing coalitional logics in Poland, the Czech Republic, and Slovakia and then show how they shaped regional state reform in each country.

EUROPEANIZATION AND ITS LIMITS

The Europeanization view of Eastern European institutional development contends that the asymmetry of power between the EU and the Eastern European countries creates strong convergence toward EU policy models and institutions. Given the special circumstances of the EU's enlargement into Eastern Europe, it even predicts a greater degree of policy convergence in the formerly communist countries than has occurred within the countries of Western Europe (Grabbe 2003, 4; Huges, Sasse, and Gordon 2003, 11–15). At least three reasons are commonly cited. First, there is the unprecedented speed of adjustment, with the Eastern European countries being required to adopt and implement EU policy frameworks *prior to accession*.[8] Second, as a result of the postcommunist transition, the Eastern European countries are more open to EU regulatory models: with fundamental structural changes already under way, it is argued, there is less "institutional resistance." Third, the EU's institutional agenda is broader, more ambitious, and hence more ambiguous in Eastern Europe than in previous enlargements. It is harder to determine when accession criteria have been met, and this ambiguity gives "the EU a license to involve itself in domestic policy-making to a degree unprecedented in the current member-states" (Grabbe 2003, 5).

Perhaps the strongest evidence for the Europeanization hypothesis is that of the timing of regional state reform in Eastern Europe. Put simply, it was a no-starter until EU integration put it on the agenda (Yoder 2003, 268; Hughes, Sasse, and Gordon 2003, 26). From strikingly similar institutional starting points, Poland, the Czech Republic, and Slovakia undertook regional state reform only after 1994, when the European Commission took over the enlargement process, assuming responsibility for screening each applicant country's regulatory framework and negotiating the terms of accession with its government. Thus concrete action began only after a long period in the early 1990s that had generated much talk about regionalization but few concrete results. From the point of view of regionalization, the early 1990s were a setback. When the anticommunist political coalitions captured power in 1989, they viewed the territorial administration as an instrument of Communist Party control, and one of their first acts was to abolish the regional self-governments outright.[9] In Poland, the regional level was centralized under the national government; district administration was eliminated; and elected institutions at both levels were eliminated. In Slovakia and the Czech Republic, the regional level institutions were abolished, and the district level was centralized under the national government; elected district councils were dissolved.

Although some political elites began to float proposals for restoring regional-level self-government as early as 1991, no such institutions were put into place.[10] The Czech constitution even mandated the creation of new regional governments in 1993, but the government ignored this provision for most of the 1990s. It was only with the acceleration of EU integration—and the European Commission's promotion of a European regional vision—that regional state reform appeared on the Polish, Czech, and Slovak governments' agenda. Thus, European integration motivated the regional reforms, even though the Commission's influence over the course of this reform proved to be quite limited.

The Europeanization thesis makes much of conditionality and the basic power asymmetry in the Eastern European governments' relationship with the Commission during the accession process. Beyond the negative incentive that ignoring the *acquis*'s regional policy precepts would have precluded EU membership, the Eastern European governments had much to gain materially from adapting to EU norms. The financial incentives included pre-accession regional assistance such as the PHARE-STRUDER program, which in 1993 made 80 million ECU available for a pilot project in regional policy in Poland. The Czech Republic has received about 40 billion Czech crowns in EU assistance since 1990 (Šafaříková 2003). More importantly, there is the incentive to gain access to the EU's regional policy expenditures, which amount to as much as a third of the EU's overall budget. More than 90 percent of this regional policy expenditure occurs through the structural funds, under whose economic criteria almost all of the Eastern European regions can expect, as EU members, to qualify for funding—provided, of course, that they meet the administrative criteria for implementation.[11] The EU's Agenda 2000 foresaw 38 billion ECU in structural funds assistance to the applicant states between 2000 and 2006 (Kirchner 1999, 211–12).

Attaining these benefits depends on meeting a raft of formal criteria and informal, though hardly imagined, expectations of the European Commission. As the Association Agreements of 1991, and later the Copenhagen declaration, made clear, joining the European club would entail adoption of specific political and economic institutions, including the unprecedented requirement that the applicants be capable of implementing its imposing body of regulation, the *acquis communautaire,* prior to accession. Chapter 21 of the *acquis* covers regional policy, setting out criteria for putting together, financing, and implementing regional development projects (Kirchner 1999, 211). Thus, regional reform mattered first of all because, as a chapter in the *acquis,* the administration of regional policy had to be tackled in some form in order to join the EU. By requiring the adoption of particular regulations and then publicly monitoring their implementation, EU conditionality "led to a perception among key actors in the CEECs [Central and East European candidate countries] that the Commission was attempting to foist an EU 'model' of regionalisation on them" (Hughes, Sasse, and Gordon 2003, 7). For example, the Commission's 1997 opinion, which stated that "the Czech Republic lack[ed] an independent regional development policy" and noted the absence of elected institutions between the national and local levels, was a public rebuke that elicited consternation among the country's political and media elites (Marek and Braun 2003, 899). The Commission again criticized the applicant countries in its Agenda 2000 as lacking "suitable infrastructures for regional policies, due to small or non-existent budgets, poorly developed instruments, skeletal administrations" (quoted in Kirchner 1999, 212).

Chapter 21 of the *acquis* requires a host of administrative and legal changes for implementing the EU's regional policy. These include mechanisms for interministerial communication; capacity for multiyear programming; capacity for monitoring and implementing policy; the adoption of a national development plan; and the adoption of the EU's Nomenclature des Unités Territoriales Statistiques (NUTS)[12] for structural funds implementation.[13] Beyond the technical details of the *acquis,* stood a more consequential expectation, which in Marek and Braun's formulation, was a "regional policy not just *for* the regions, but *by* them as well" (2003, 898). The idea behind this "partnership principle" was participation by regional-level actors in making regional policy. Thus, the Commission strongly urged the Eastern European governments to create elected regional institutions with financial and legal autonomy (Brusis 1999, 1–2; Yoder 2003, 268; Hughes, Sasse, and Gordon 2003; Marek and Braun 2003).

The Europeanization thesis has come under considerable criticism by scholars looking at the course of institutional and policy development on the ground. First, a number of scholars have pointed out that as detailed and challenging as the accession requirements appear, in practice they allowed considerable leeway for institutional variation. Hughes, Sasse, and Gordon write that regional policy is a "thin area of the *acquis* with sparse and ambiguous regulations [and national governments have a] great deal of power to decide the institutional framework and means of implementation" (2003, 28). To avoid the appearance of interference, the Commission publicly maintained that it was for national governments to decide which institutional arrangements best suited them (9–10).[14] Indeed, as a look at the EU member countries makes clear, there are any number of models of subnational government—from thoroughly decentralized to unitary—that are compatible with the *acquis*. A second set of criticisms challenges the assumption that the EU is a unitary actor with fixed goals toward which the instrument of conditionality is exercised. Internal divisions and inconsistencies within the institutions of the EU have often diluted the leverage of conditionality (Hughes, Sasse, and Gordon 2003). A third set of criticisms of the Europeanization thesis emphasizes the role of historical legacies and regionalist traditions in society (Yoder 2003).[15]

A final set of criticisms emphasizes domestic politics. As Hughes, Sasse, and Gordon write of regional reform in Eastern Europe, "On balance, it seems that domestic political considerations, informed by historical experiences and legacies, seem to have played a more important role than the influence of EU conditionality" (2003, 27). As penetrating as their analysis of the limitations of EU conditionality is, however, the skeptics of convergence do not provide a framework that can explain when and how domestic political considerations are important.[16] The absence of such an explanation is all the more conspicuous given that major institutional changes are occurring at the regional level, even if they do not accord with the convergence predicted by the Europeanization hypothesis. Linking the European and domestic political dimensions of regional state reform in Eastern Europe, I argue that European integration provided domestic governing coalitions a useful justification for restructuring regional-level institutions, but the flexibility of the EU's concept of regionalization allowed for wide-ranging interpretations of this project. In each country, the interpretation of regionalization was carefully adapted to the political needs of the governing coalition. In Slovakia under Mečiar, it meant a centralizing deconcentration of power. Later, under the Party of the Democratic Coalition (SDK) government it meant cosmetic decentralization. In Poland under a fragmented post-Solidarity coalition, it meant inflationary devolution. In the Czech Republic under what was essentially bipolar competition, it meant devolution coupled with rationalization of existing structures. In this diversity of outcomes, the limits of an EU-centered explanation of postcommunist state-building are apparent.

THE LOGIC OF COALITIONAL POLITICS

The differing outcomes of regional state reform in Poland, Slovakia, and the Czech Republic reflected the different coalitional logic of the government that enacted the reform in each. The parameters of coalitional politics were set by the differing logics of party competition anatomized in Chapter 2. This section compares the particular coalitional logic of each government at the time of reform.

In all three countries, the political class have always been much more interested in regional state reform than the general public, who were concerned with (to them) more relevant issues like health care.[17] Re-creating and restructuring regional institutions offers political parties both a convenient rationale and a potent tool for tailoring state institutions to their advantage. The governing coalitions that legislate these reforms are in a position to determine the boundaries of regions (and tailor them to the geography of their own electoral support), the staffing of new regional administration (and use them as patronage), and to gain access to the resources at these new institutions' disposal (resources which would become considerable with the advent of EU structural funds).[18] In short, regional reform matters to politicians because it offers opportunities to facilitate party-building in a postcommunist political environment that, so far, has proven less-than-fertile ground for building stable party organizations. Regional reforms were very often worded in such expansive terms as "remaking the state" (Chancellery 1998, 5–11). The more radical the remaking of the state, the more room for tailoring outcomes to the government parties' advantage.

Table 4.1 uses a few simple measures to encapsulate the differences in the domestic political conditions for reform in each country. As noted in Chapter 2, electoral volatility set the time horizons of government coalition members over the course of the 1990s. In highly volatile systems, coalition members are more likely to try to capture organizational advantages from institutional reforms like regional decentralization than in systems where, due to having more stable vote shares, parties feel less need to create party-building advantages through state reforms. Table 4.1 also contains two other indicators from Chapter 2, vote differential and government concentration, which capture the coalitional logic at the moment of reform enactment. Since the analysis here is of a single event, the enactment of regional reform, I calculate vote differential using only the last election before reform en-

TABLE 4.1.
Coalitional Dynamic of Government Undertaking Reform

Reform Attempt	Trend of Party System Development	Electoral Volatility (1990–2000)	Vote Differential Between Biggest Government Party and Biggest Opposition Party at the Time of Enactment	Government Concentration at the Time of Enactment
Slovakia's 1st Reform (1996)	Political machine vs. fragmented opposition (1992–1998)	46.2% High	24.6% High	*Highly Concentrated:* Three-party coalition, dominated by HZDS with two nationalist junior partners
Slovakia's 2nd Reform (2001)	Fragmented government vs. entrenched opposition (after 1998)		–0.7% Low	*Highly Diffuse:* Eight-party coalition of programmatically heterogeneous parties
Poland (1998)	Parties are many, small, short-lived; governments are heterogeneous and unstable	44.3% High	6.7% Low	*Highly Diffuse:* Umbrella coalition "Electoral Action Solidarity" (comprising 30-plus political groups) in coalition with Freedom Union
Czech Republic (1997–1998)	Bipolar competition, programmatic parties; coherent, stable government with orderly alternation	23.1% Low	4.6% Low	*Highly Concentrated:* Single-party minority government under the Social Democratic Party (ČSSD)

SOURCES: Author's calculations of electoral volatility and vote differential using election results published by the Center for the Study of Public Policy at the University of Strathclyde, www.cspp.strath.ac.uk/index.html?catalog20_0.html

actment. This indicator provides a good measure of the threat of alternation posed to the government by the opposition: the higher the vote differential, the more commanding the advantage of the government and the more easily it can shape regional reform to its own advantage. The next indicator, the "concentration" of government, refers to how many actors—parties and other political groupings—are contained within the government coalition and how diverse they are programmatically. The less concentrated the government coalition, the more fragile its majority and the greater the pressure to keep its various elements together using patronage. Diffuse governments also have a greater number of members among whom patronage needs to be shared out.

At the time of reform enactment, it is crucial how vote differential and government concentration interact. In Slovakia under Mečiar, a large vote differential combined with highly concentrated government was a recipe for regional reform that maximized political benefits for one dominant political actor. As one would expect in a dominant-party (variant 1) system, Mečiar's "reform" was, in essence, a policy of deconcentration that centralized power at the same time that it created patronage by expanding institutional structures. Poland's weak-governance party system, by contrast, combined a small vote differential with highly diffuse government, resulting in a version of regional reform that maximized political benefits but shared them out among a wide range of political actors. Unlike Slovakia, Poland's reform did devolve power from the central government, but it unnecessarily expanded the units of subnational governance in order to buy support from a wide coalition of political interests. In the end, no party increased its advantages over the others, but the original technocratic and efficiency goals of decentralization were sharply diluted. The backdrop in both countries was one of chronic electoral volatility, which shortened governing parties' time horizons and increased the allure of regional reform that could further party-building goals. In the Czech Republic's responsible-party system, where reform was undertaken against a background of much lower electoral volatility, the coalitional politics at the time of reform combined concentrated government with low vote differential—a much more favorable constellation of factors. This constellation meant (1) longer time horizons among the parties, (2) a more competitive party system and more accountable government, and (3) less need to dilute the programmatic intentions of the government to win acceptance from a wide coalition of interests.

The political backdrop leading up to Poland's 1997 regional reform was one of electoral volatility, party fragmentation, and unpredictable coalition formation. The Electoral Action Solidarity (AWS)–Freedom Union (UW) government that initiated the reform was a coalition with a slim majority which contained some 30-plus parties and other political groupings of often opposing programmes. The weakness of the Polish government meant that all parties were able to extract political benefits from reform. The result was a greatly expanded subnational administration.

The development of the Slovak party system in the 1990s was sharply periodized, and because the country tackled regional reform in both periods, comparing them highlights the impact of coalitional politics on regional reform. Throughout the 1990s, the one constant in Slovak party politics was high volatility, as Table 4.1 demonstrates. In both periods, parties had short time horizons and were tempted to use state administrative reforms to create party-building advantages. In the first period (dominant-party variant 1), high vote differential and concentrated government led to a "reform" that was a thinly disguised means of aggrandizing Mečiar's Movement for a Democratic Slovakia (HZDS) party while weakening the opposition. Power was centralized, and new subnational units became a source of patronage for HZDS supporters. In the second period (dominant-party variant 2), there was a very low vote differential and low government concentration, essentially the same situation as in Poland. Also as in Poland, the government found it necessary to try to bridge many diverse interests in order to pass any reform and did so through diluting the reform's original technocratic intentions. The divided Slovak coalition tried unsuccessfully to replace Mečiar's regional structures with a more democratic and rational system of regional self-government (Plenipotentiary 1999).

The political background and the coalitional politics at the time of reform in the Czech Republic differed considerably from those in Slovakia and Poland. Facing lower electoral volatility, Czech parties had longer time horizons than Slovak or Polish ones. With a more stable support base, the main government parties, Civic Democratic Party (ODS) and Czech Social Democratic Party (ČSSD) were less tempted to enact self-serving institutional reforms in the attempt to further party-building. Unlike Slovakia under Mečiar, the vote differential was low at the time of reform: the Social Democrats in 1998 were not a dominant machine lording over a weak opposition. Unlike Poland, it was not an unwieldy coalition of many disparate interests whom government reformers needed to buy off. Instead, the Czech government consisted of a single party that was closely checked by an opposition party that was sufficiently organized to prevent the government party from capturing reform for its own ends.

DIFFERENT VERSIONS OF REGIONAL REFORM

With the domestic political conditions in place, this section turns to a comparison of the genesis, implementation, and institutional consequences of regional reform in Poland, the Czech Republic, and Slovakia.

Slovak "Reform": Strengthening the Party Machine

The first round of Slovak regional reform took place in 1996 and was the culmination of HZDS's political revenge on the opposition parties after their short-lived victory in toppling the first HZDS government. A small group of reformers loosely affiliated with the political opposition had been advocating regional decentralization since the early 1990s. To the initial surprise of this group, the HZDS-led government announced its intention to take up the issue of regional reform. However, rather than understanding this program in terms of devolving power to elected regional parliaments, as the opposition had, the Mečiar government decided to create regional prefectures, which it would appoint directly. It also expanded the number of districts (*okresy*) in the country, which would function as administrative units below the regional level. Though strongly resisted by the opposition parties, Mečiar's government had a parliamentary majority and refused to make concessions.

Political-electoral considerations of HZDS and its coalition partners dictated the shape of Slovakia's version of regional reform. First, the government parties needlessly expanded the territorial administration in order to reward their supporters with appointments. This expansion is depicted in Figure 4.1, which maps the boundaries of Slovakia's public administration before and after 1996. The reform created eight regional-level offices appointed by the government and expanded the number of district offices, also appointed by the government, from 38 to 79 (Falt'an and Krivý 1999, 107). Thus, the policy added one new layer of state bureaucracy and doubled the extant bureaucracy at the district level.[19] Slovakia is a small country, and if the addition of eight regions was questionable, the addition of eight regions accompanied by a two-fold expansion of its districts was excessive. These additional levels expanded the territorial administration by roughly ten thousand positions.[20] As part of this reform, a number of policy areas were further centralized; for example, the appointment of provincial education officials became the prerogative of the Ministry of Interior rather than, as previously, the Ministry of Education.

Unfortunately, there is no systematic documentation of the exact numbers involved, but it is common knowledge in Slovakia that the staffing opportunities created by the reform provided HZDS and its partners with the opportunity to colonize the state bureaucracy. To quote a description of this period in a volume on public administration reform in Eastern Europe: "The current policy of recruiting personnel, not only for top posts in the new regional and district levels of administration, fits into a more general political and clientelistic style of holding power—what is more, it prefers candidates to hold similar views to those of the ruling parties" (Falt'an and Krivý 1999, 110).

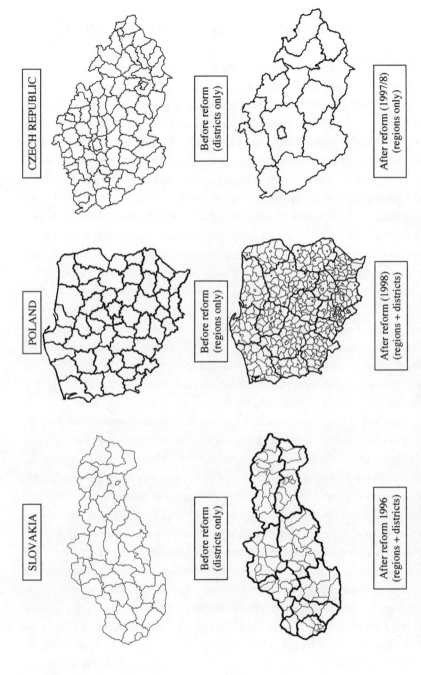

CZECH REPUBLIC

POLAND

SLOVAKIA

Before reform
(districts only)

Before reform
(regions only)

Before reform
(districts only)

After reform (1997/8)
(regions only)

After reform (1998)
(regions + districts)

After reform 1996
(regions + districts)

Fig. 4.1. Maps of the Slovak, Polish, and Czech Public Administrations Before and After Reform

There is even evidence of the government parties' penetration of the state bureaucracy by those parties' own admission. An internal HZDS document entitled "The Main Tasks of HZDS" was leaked to the press in 1996. It recommended that "HZDS should work to strengthen its position within Slovak society by continuing to reshuffle personnel within the state administration and diplomatic corps" (Krivý 1998, 59). Even the HZDS leadership's statements confirmed the party's attempt to recruit its supporters into the state bureaucracy: "Asked whether the HZDS knows that state administration employees are being approached and asked to join the parties of the government coalition in order to secure their remaining in the state administration, the HZDS deputy chairman [Marian Huska, then the vice-chairman of parliament] replied: 'Yes, the governing parties are expanding their membership base in this way, whether anyone likes it or not'" (Krause 2000b, 38).

The second way the reform benefited the government parties was in the redrawing of district boundaries: "Apart from strengthening the position of Mečiar's party in state administration, in connection with the establishment of new regions and districts, the recently introduced division has some other partisan connections. The new territorial-administrative division of the Slovak Republic has significantly multiplied the number of districts in which the HZDS achieves electoral success, so that they now outnumber the districts in which support for HZDS is low. Under the previous administrative structure, this was not the case" (Falt'an and Krivý 1999, 115). The gerrymandering of district boundaries was especially pronounced in Slovakia's ethnic Hungarian areas, where the new boundaries minimized the Hungarians' voting power. Ethnic Hungarian parties have traditionally formed the best organized opposition to HZDS, and these areas were their strongholds.

Because of the major shift in Slovakia's political scene in 1998, there is a postscript to this story. The Mečiar government fell and was replaced by a large, heterogeneous coalition of former opposition parties. Having suffered from the patronage politics of the first regional reform and having campaigned on a pro-EU platform, the new government reopened the issue of regional reform. The circle who had advocated regional reform in the early 1990s now came into its own: Viktor Nižňanský led a team of experts who, over the course of two years, developed a meticulous blueprint for decentralizing the administration.

In August 2001, the government proposed Nižňanský's plan in parliament. It quickly became apparent that the government did not have sufficient votes even among its own coalition to pass Nižňanský's proposal (Kunder 2001). Several parties feared that they would not compete successfully in regional-level elections (Vagovič 2001). More problematic still, HZDS, which had won the plurality of votes in the 1998 elections, strongly opposed changes to the regional structures it had created in

1996. HZDS proved very successful in transforming the intent of Nižňanský's plan through a series of parliamentary amendments, which a number of government parties ended up supporting—reflecting the divided and unpredictable nature of government coalitions in dominant-party (variant 2) systems. In the parliamentary voting, only the Christian Democratic Movement (KDH) and Party of the Hungarian Coalition (SMK) voted for the government proposal. The main government parties—the Party of the Democratic Left (SDL'), Association for Civic Understanding (SOP), and many of the deputies from SDK—voted with the opposition HZDS against the key points of the government's plan. Where Nižňanský's proposal had called for new regional boundaries, drawn to match EU criteria, the enacted legislation retained the old, gerrymandered lines. Where Nižňanský had called for liquidating the old government-appointed district and regional offices, the enacted version retained them. Essentially, all the second round of regional state reform accomplished was to add a new level of regional governance institutions, whose powers and sources of funding were left largely unspecified and who would have to compete with the state's territorial administration (Vagovič 2001; Kunder 2001). Nižňanský resigned his post, loudly criticizing the legislation (Hríb 2001).

In all, Slovakia's experience with regional reform highlights the primacy of domestic party politics over the influence of the EU in the process of state-building. Although the EU put the regional issue on the agenda, it exercised very little control over how it played out. In the first iteration, Mečiar's government co-opted the idea of regional reform to solidify its hold on power and weaken the opposition. It was a classic case of institution-building in a machine-style party system: one party was able to capture the reform project to increase its patronage resources and to exclude other parties from this state-derived patronage. The second iteration of regional reform occurred only after the domestic political situation changed, and the character of that reform—a watered-down, face-saving measure by a government unable to rally its coalition partners—reflected the dominant-party (variant 2) coalitional logic of the post-Mečiar political order.

Poland's Reform: Something for Everyone

Devolution was the chosen instrument of regional reform in Poland. Against reformers' original intentions, however, Poland's regional reform increased the size of the public administration as a whole while introducing new ambiguities and competitive dynamics between the state administration and elected officials (Koral 2001, 51; Sepioł 2000).[21] The administrative boundaries before and after Poland's decentralization are illustrated in Figure 4.1. Before 1998, the administrative map of the country consisted of the central government, 49 governmental[22] regions, and elected local governments. After the reform, the administrative map contained the central government, 16 regions with separate governmental and elected administrations, and 373 elected district governments.[23] Local governments were left unchanged. In all, the reorganization created 324 new units of subnational state administration. It also established 324 elected subnational governments, amounting to 12,469 new positions (*Statistical Yearbook of the Republic of Poland* 1999, 358).

The first thing to notice about this reform, then, was a massive increase in the size of the public administration. In the commotion of reorganization, roughly fifty thousand positions were either created or reassigned (*Statistical Yearbook of the Republic of Poland* 1999; 2000). The new elected regional and district councils provided a means to build party organizations at the subnational level. Throughout the 1990s, Polish parties had very weak subnational organizations because of insufficient financial resources.[24] The district and regional councils would be salaried posts, providing parties new resources to build up subnational organizations. Moreover, the extensive influence of political parties over the selection and promotion of administrative staff meant that the 1998 reorganization was a bonanza for parties at all levels of government. The central government parties had a free hand to radically "reorganize" the governmental regional administrations, as they consolidated staff from 49 offices to 16. In each of the new regional and district elected councils, the victorious party or party coalition was in a position to set up its own administration. Thus, the opportunities for patronage were bountiful, and they were enjoyed by all parties—or at least those parties that could win elections at any of the now four levels of government. An examination of the process leading up to reform enactment shows how that inflation of the public administration occurred.

The leitmotif running through this process is one in which a fragile coalition of government reformers—led by Plenipotentiary for Public Administration Reform Michał Kulesza—attempts to bring reluctant coalition partners on board, and buy off opposing parties, in order to win a parliamentary majority to enact reform while the political conditions are still favorable. The list of parties co-opted in this fashion included virtually the entire parliamentary spectrum. From the fractious government coalition, it included the Christian Nationalists and manifold groups within the post-Solidarity AWS. It even included the opposition Democratic Left Alliance (SLD) and Peasants' Party (PSL). In this political horse-trading, each party got a little piece of the spoils. The result differed sharply from the Slovak one, where the benefits went to the dominant political machine rather than being shared. It also reflects the instability and fluidity of the Polish party system, which makes it difficult to form coherent governments and for those governments to build majorities for enacting policy.

A review of the stages of reform, from proposal to parliamentary enactment, illustrates this dynamic. The first question facing the reformers was the number of regions (*kraje*) to be established. Policy experts who had been working on this problem since the early 1990s agreed that the ideal number of regions was 12. Their criteria were the following: fitness for receiving outside funds (especially EU structural funds), economic self-sufficiency, diversified industrial profile, cohesive infrastructure, culture, the presence of an academic center, the presence of a hub city. The more politically popular alternative, however, was 15 to 17 regions. Despite lobbying within the coalition for more regions, Kulesza prevailed initially, and the government's proposal to the parliament envisioned 12 regions.

Once the reform passed from Kulesza's experts to the political arena, however, the inflation of units and personnel began—as well as the dilution of the policy's original intent. The opposition PSL and SLD rejected the government's number because it encroached on their organizational advantages in the regions (especially in the case of the PSL) and because it was seen as a way of undercutting the government tactically (in the case of the SLD). It soon became apparent that even within the government coalition there were many who wanted more than 12 regions; the government could not count on a majority within its own coalition (Kerlin 2001, 16). Kulesza's team decided to make concessions in order to get the reform passed.[25] First, they agreed that the reduction of the number of regions would not force those already employed in the regional administrations out of their jobs if their region was abolished. Instead of the 12 regions originally proposed, they settled for 16.

The *powiat*, or district, also became an important bargaining chip in the passage of Polish regional reform. The district was a unit of government that had existed since before the first partition in 1795 and later in the interwar Polish Republic, but the Communists abolished it in 1975. In the minds of the technocrats designing the 1998 reform, regions—not districts—were the most important element of decentralization because regions were seen to further EU accession. In the parliamentary negotiations, however, districts became a major element of decentralization, and a new inflationary spiral began. Initially, the expert opinion prepared by the Ministry of Finance proposed 150 districts, which, it argued, would yield economically viable units capable of efficiently delivering public services. The government team proposed a so-called 5–10–50 formula for drawing district boundaries—meaning that each district would comprise at least five municipalities (*gminy*), have at least ten thousand inhabitants in the district seat, and have an overall population of at least fifty thousand. From the original 150 districts, the political process drove the number up to 373, including 71 that did not fulfill the 5–10–50 formula. The finance ministry team objected and drew up a list of districts that should not be created because they would be unviable economically and administratively (Kerlin 2001, 14).

By now, however, political considerations were more important than techno-cratic ones. Kulesza wanted to push through decentralization as quickly as possible, before the political situation changed. The conviction that speed was paramount came from Kulesza's personal experience under the post-Solidarity governments of the early 1990s. At that time, Kulesza and others had worked out a plan for decen-tralization only to see it die a quick, mostly unnoticed, death when the SLD-PSL coalition took power in 1993. To avoid a repetition of this experience, Kulesza de-cided to make concessions in order to get support in the parliamentary voting.

First, he courted local politicians, who were eager to form small districts under their control, not only for the new offices and posts that would be created but also because they believed the new districts would be the conduits for central govern-ment funds. According to the reformers' plans for fiscal decentralization, smaller districts would not mean more money from the national budget at the local level, but the mental habits of a long-centralized system of public finances were deeply ingrained. This local lobbying was directed toward the respective national MP. The government reformers used districts as coinage to buy the votes of recalcitrant members for the reform as a whole. As one parliamentarian confessed about this process: "There are also too many counties [districts] because we succumbed to blackmail so representatives would support the reform. We bought representatives. If a representative was not in favor of the reform—was going to vote against it—we gave them a county in their region in exchange for their vote. Representatives would say they would not vote in favor of the reform unless they were given a county in their region . . . It was a compromise—a worse solution for the reform in exchange for the reform to happen at all."[26]

The reform's proponents also accommodated disgruntled interests in cities that had served as regional seats in the former 49 regions. These cities wanted to keep their status as gatekeepers between the provinces and the central government. To buy off this group, the reformers introduced an amendment conferring district sta-tus on larger cities—in addition to their status as municipalities. As one parlia-mentarian noted, "We also knew that allowing the creation of cities with county status was not sensible. Here again we succumbed to blackmail. We had to give in to the demands of former provincial capitals for county status" (quoted in Kerlin 2001, 15).

Although regional reform radically changed the Polish political map, early indi-cations suggest that, in the best case, it has not ameliorated problems of subnational governance and, in the worst case, it has exacerbated them (Sepioł 2000; Koral 2000; Kieżun 2000, 3–12). The general public's opinion of regional decentralization a year after the fact was more critical than approving. According to one survey, only 17 percent of Poles rated the reform as an improvement on the previous system ("Naj-gorzej ze zdrowiem" 2000). The first major problem with the reform was that no decentralization of public finances accompanied that of offices and policy tasks, leading to severe budget problems for the new subnational governments. Second, the reform did not clearly divide tasks and powers between the subnational self-governments and the branch administration of the central state, the detrimental effects of which were perhaps clearest in the field of social policy (Tyrański 1999; Kerlin 2002). Even while noting the difficulties of evaluating the 1998 decentralization policy so soon after its implementation, the Polish public finance expert Zyta Gilow-ska made this critical assessment: "The new units of territorial self-government are weak, and the central government has not gotten any stronger . . . It seems that the opinion as to the weakening of public power during this stage of the transformation is justified. The real course of reform has been rather a process of chaotic scattering [of offices and tasks] than of coherent decentralization" (2000a, 37).

Czech Regional Reform: Social Democrats versus Conservatives

If Slovak regional reform brought deconcentration and expansion, while Poland's variant meant devolution and expansion, the Czech reform brought devolution with consolidation—that is, without politically fueled state expansion. The regional reform debate in the Czech Republic was framed in essentially economic terms. The main actors in the debate were the Social Democrats (ČSSD) led by Mi-loš Zeman and the conservative Civic Democratic Party (ODS) led by Václav Klaus, both well-organized, programmatically defined parties. ČSSD supported decentralization, arguing that regional self-governments are better able to frame regionally tailored economic policies and thus create faster rates of growth. ODS opposed regional governments as leading to creeping state interventionism in the economy and runaway state expansion, arguing that decentralization would lead to the "atomization" of the state, that it would tie the central government's hand in economic policy-making, and that the loss of control over regional budgets would lead to inflation (Korecký 2000; Mlynář 1994; "Nové kraje" 2000; Marek and Braun 2003, 899). As Klaus remarked in 1996, "After having successfully abolished regions in 1990, do we really want a new regional bureaucracy?" (quoted in Beckman 1999).

The coalitional logic of regional reform was thus very different from that of Slovakia and Poland. Neither ODS nor ČSSD ever had enough of an upper hand to impose its own self-serving solution, as in Slovakia. However, each party was able to form strong enough governments that it did need not to scramble to buy off a host of other parties to enact its policies, as happened in Poland.[27] Instead, regional reform was a battleground between two entrenched political rivals, each of which had the organizational strength to survive without being in government. To the observer, the politics of Czech regional reform often resembled gridlock, and the eventual version of decentralization was very much a political compromise.

The Czech constitution had mandated the creation of regional governments since 1993, but the ODS government had thrown up obstacles to implementing the mandate. The first skirmish came in 1993, when the Office for Legislation and Public Administration made two proposals concerning the reform of the state administration, the first calling for thirteen regions and the second for eight. The proposals envisioned elections to new regional parliaments in 1995. Though the government coalition had agreed to approve legislation for setting up regional structures no later than 1994, ODS offered a counterproposal that it knew would be unacceptable to the other parties. Another counterproposal to create nine regions by one of the other government parties came close to passing but was blocked by ODS (Korecký 2000). This gridlock began to ease after the 1996 elections, which saw greatly increased support for ČSSD and an erosion of ODS's position. A coalition for regional decentralization led by ČSSD formed over the issue of creating regional parliaments. ODS remained opposed. On December 3, 1997, the parliament took the initiative and passed a constitutional act creating 14 new regions, arguing that decentralization could not be postponed any longer.

What had changed to make such a breakthrough possible? It was, quite simply, the alternation of government, attendant on the rapid decline of ODS's political fortunes. As noted in Chapter 2, the party had undergone a corruption scandal in the fall of 1997, which resulted in Klaus's resignation as prime minister and the departure of a number of the party's MPs to the newly established Freedom Union (US). ODS's fall from power ended in a vote of no-confidence and the installation of a caretaker government from January to June 1998, when fresh elections brought the Social Democrats to the government. Thus, regional reform happened at a moment of political crisis, not because of EU pressure. Even in its weakened state, however, ODS was able to serve as an effective opposition party, constraining the new Social Democratic government from pushing through a regional state reform to its own political advantage.[28] It was able keep regional reform less sweeping than the Social Democrats would have liked, even if it could no longer block it.

In its final version, Czech regional reform was a compromise between, on the one hand, ČSSD's vision of region-led economic development and expanded political participation and, on the other hand, ODS's fears of an expansionist state bureaucracy.[29] This reform achieved real devolution of power but not, as in Poland, at the cost of unnecessary expansion. As Figure 4.1 shows, the policy established 14 regional parliaments in the Czech Republic, consisting of 685 elected positions and exercising as yet vaguely defined powers in education, culture, and regional policy. Because ODS feared that granting the regional governments too much discretion would invite expansionary fiscal policies, the public finance system remained quite centralized. To address conservatives' fears that decentralization would swell the size of the public administration, the reform abolished 76 government-appointed district administrations effective in 2002.[30] As a further concession to the avowedly Euroskeptic ODS, the Czech regional boundaries were drawn differently than the NUTS 2 used in EU regional policy; this had the effect of preserving the central government's control over the implementation of structural funds programs.[31] Not simply façade institutions for satisfying EU criteria, however, the new regional self-governments have fundamentally changed the institutional apparatus of the territorial administration, having taken over a whole set of tasks from the system of state-appointed district offices that they replaced.

What is most striking is that decentralization did not expand the Czech public administration. A comparison of all the "before and after" maps in Figure 4.1 shows that the Czech regional reform was the only one that simplified the administrative map rather than complicating it. This reflects the coalitional logic of the Czech party system, which prevented reform being captured as a source of patronage. The political opposition was strong enough to constrain the government that enacted the reform, and the government was sufficiently cohesive that it did not need to buy off other parties to build a parliamentary majority.

CONCLUSION

The substance of regional state reform varied across Poland, the Czech Republic, and Slovakia in ways that illustrate the limits of Europeanization and the impact of domestic political considerations. The coalitional politics faced by the government undertaking regional reform have been the primary factor shaping institutional outcomes.

In Slovakia, regional reform led, ironically enough, to centralization. In Poland, real devolution occurred but only at the cost of dramatically expanding the state apparatus rather than simplifying and streamlining it. In both cases, political parties were the real beneficiaries of reform, but there was a marked difference in terms of how the spoils of reform were shared among parties. The political benefits of Slovakia's version of public administration reform flowed chiefly to HZDS, the party that had executed it. In Poland, no one party wholly controlled the shape of regional reform, and no one party enjoyed its benefits. Only the Czech Republic managed to avoid a patronage-dominated regional reform, achieving devolution without runaway expansion. It did so because the Czech party system allowed for the formation of strong governments and a credible opposition.

Contrary to the institutional convergence predicted by the Europeanization hypothesis, the demands of EU enlargement can produce very different state-building outcomes in the postcommunist states. These differing outcomes reflect how EU incentives and pressures are refracted through the lens of domestic party politics. In the absence of robust party competition, government parties often use the EU as cover for patronage-enhancing "reforms."

There remains, of course, the question of how well this argument about regional-level state-building applies to other policy areas. Can one discern the same combination of political opportunism and policy unpredictability in other areas of Eastern European states' harmonization with the *acquis communautaire?* Should the lackluster results of the Europeanization hypothesis in the area of regional governance reform cast doubt on the applicability of this hypothesis across the board? This analysis does offer one clear lesson: the presence of the EU does not guarantee any one particular outcome to state-building. Since the limits of conditionality are clear even in this area of exceptional EU leverage, one may harbor very legitimate doubts about how well the new resources that the EU makes available to Eastern European governments will be used. Given the apparent limits of conditionality, there is no guarantee that these resources will not be used as a new reservoir for patronage and party-building advantage. Already, there have been more than a few scandals regarding the use of EU funds in Eastern Europe. In addition to all of the limits to EU conditionality that become apparent in examining an area like regional decentralization, its greatest limitation has not yet been considered here at all. Namely, once the Eastern European states accede to the EU, the European Commission's extraordinary leverage disappears (Moravcsik and Vachudova 2003). It may be that the Commission's decisive opportunity to mold the course of state-building in Eastern Europe is rapidly drawing to a close.

CHAPTER FIVE

Local Control

Local Parties and Local State Administrations

I have to say that for the whole first term of its government, in fact for the whole post-1989 period . . . the average local government was run by the local people, meaning that political orientations didn't count. After all, there still weren't political parties. To this day, a party system hasn't been built in the countryside.

Piotr Buczkowski, former Chairman of the Polish National Congress of Self-Governments (quoted in Sochacka and Krasko 1996, 100)

Neither on the left, nor on the right.

Campaign slogan of the party Our Capital in Warsaw's 1994 local government election (quoted in Matałowska 1994)

A battery of evidence implicates patronage politics as the driving force behind the extraordinary expansion and lackluster performance of the Polish and Slovak states. This combination of symptoms is typical not just for much of the postcommunist region, but for democratizing countries around the world where underdeveloped party competition fails to hold government parties in check. One issue that has remained at the periphery of this analysis so far is political culture: how can one be sure that the observed differences between Polish, Slovak, and Czech statebuilding are not the result of different administrative traditions rather than party competition? Herbert Kitschelt (1999) has argued that the countries of Eastern Europe developed three different types of state during the communist period: "bureaucratic-authoritarian," "national-accommodative," and "patrimonial." With its less doctrinaire Communist Party and greater cultural freedom, the Polish state was an example of the national-accommodative type. Czechoslovakia, by contrast, was a bureaucratic-authoritarian state from the time of the Soviet invasion in 1968, which systematically ousted "nationalist" Communists and reformers from positions of political authority.[1] Kitschelt uses these differing administrative cultures to explain democratization in the postcommunist era. Though he does not use them to explain postcommunist state-building, it seems a natural extension of his argument—an extension that would posit a competing explanation to the one offered here.[2] A cultural explanation of this sort might argue that national administrative cultures developed differently under the Communists and that these differences determined the course of both postcommunist party-building and state-building. In short, national administrative culture would be a confounding variable. It is the task of this chapter to control for this potential confound. To do so, I use a comparison of municipal government administrations to control for differences in national administrative culture. The evidence this comparison provides suggests the limited explanatory power of national administrative traditions in these countries and reaffirms the crucial role of party competition in shaping state-building.

Without denying that national differences did exist in Eastern Europe under communism,[3] unduly emphasizing them risks ignoring the universal and lasting features of the Leninist model of the state as it was imposed across Eastern Europe (Gross 1989; Jowitt 1992). Under communism, far more united these states than differentiated them: the state's monopoly of public life, the ubiquitous *nomenklatura* system, the hollowing out of the ideological core of the communist officialdom and its concomitant corruption, all these features led to the two defining features of postcommunist politics that are the necessary requisites for runaway state-building, demobilized societies and delegitimized states. The somewhat greater national feelings of the Polish Communist Party compared with the Czechoslovak one do not meaningfully alter the more fundamental legacy of the Leninist state.

This chapter is about who controls local state administrations, patronage-seeking political parties or administrators themselves. It is also about local control in the sense that it is built around a comparison that controls for the potentially confounding variable of national administrative culture: comparing local- and national-level state-building within Poland, the Czech Republic, and Slovakia shows that the incidence of runaway state-building cannot be predicted simply by national administrative culture.[4] By law, local governments in each country enjoyed considerable autonomy from the national government. They were responsible for hiring local personnel, and fixed tax-sharing formulas with the central government gave them their own fiscal resources.[5] Therefore, since local party systems in each country were predominantly of the weak-governance type, the party competition framework would predict runaway state-building at the local level in all three. Conversely, the national administrative culture hypothesis would predict the same pattern of state-building at the local level in each as obtained at the national-level: rapid growth in Poland and Slovakia, constrained growth in the Czech Republic. The growth of local state administrations does not fit the national administrative culture hypothesis. Both the Polish and the Czech local government administrations grew rapidly in the transition to democracy, while the Slovak ones—for reasons that had to do with the country's dominant-party politics on the national level—actually contracted.

The logic of case selection behind this local-level comparison is opposite that in the previous chapters. In those chapters, the differences in national-level state-building in Poland, Slovakia, and the Czech Republic represented the result of differences in their national-level party system development. By the logic of Mill's method of difference (Copi 1961, 355–72), I was able to exploit the similarities between these countries to rule out alternative explanations for their divergent state-building outcomes. The case selection logic of this chapter is Mill's method of agreement. In order to test the national administrative culture explanation against my own, the following cases differ in terms of their administrative culture but are similar in terms of the logic of party competition at the local level. If the national administrative culture hypothesis is correct, Poland, the Czech Republic, and Slovakia should have different patterns of local-level state-building. The contrary finding that, in fact, they do not differ in this respect would not be compatible with administrative culture hypothesis; such a finding would, however, be perfectly consonant with the party competition framework.

As will become clear, the political baseline for local-level state-building in Slovakia differed considerably from that in Poland and the Czech Republic. The national governments of Mečiar's Movement for a Democratic Slovakia (HZDS) treated local governments as political rivals, starving them of financial resources, encroaching on their decision-making, and appropriating their resources for national-level patronage politics. Methodologically speaking, it is not possible to look at local state-building in Slovakia separately from the national government and national-level party system—as it is in the Czech Republic and Poland. Substantively speaking, however, that the logic of party competition structures the mode of state-building only underlines the overarching argument. What the local-level analysis loses from these methodological considerations, the analysis of the national level gains; the predatory practices of the HZDS governments vis-à-vis local governments strengthen the characterization of Slovak national politics as belonging to the dominant-party type.

In order to be clear about the units of analysis, a few definitional clarifications are necessary. This chapter focuses on local units of government.[6] Each of these governments is responsible for establishing, hiring, firing, and funding its own administrative units and agencies, which I collectively refer to as the local administration. Each unit of elected local government has its own associated network of parties, electoral committees, and social movements which compete for office and which collectively form local party systems, one for each government unit. Elected local governments were established in all three countries in 1990, immediately after the 1989 revolutions. By local state administration, I mean the administrative positions appointed by elected local governments. Thus, these administrative personnel are separate from the national state administration in Chapters 3, as well as from the regional- and district-level personnel of Chapter 4.

Organizationally, this chapter is divided into two parts. The first half compares the logic of local party competition in Poland, Slovakia, and the Czech Republic, showing why these localities are best classified as weak-governance party systems. The second half then describes the development of local state institutions in each of the cases, focusing on how much they have expanded.

THE LOGIC OF PARTY COMPETITION AT THE LOCAL LEVEL

Across the multiplicity of local-level party systems in Poland, the Czech Republic, and Slovakia, local politics is characterized by personalism, fractionalization, volatility, open rather than closed competition, and weakly developed party structures. In these party systems, political notables form alliances of convenience with other relevant political actors regardless of their political program. Even in the case of the best organized national parties, the resources of the national-level party organization are too small to effectively fund, monitor, and control its local branches. Consequently, local party leaders are largely unconstrained by the national party program, national party alliances, and national party rule, and they often behave very differently than the national-level party organization (Szczerbiak 1999b, 532). Moreover, there are often significant regional differences, so that parties indomitable in one locality may be nonexistent in a neighboring region.

At least one scholar has explicitly compared the local politics in 1990s Poland to party politics in the pre-Hamiltonian United States, both being "a swirling confusion of interests, issues, leaders, opinions, shifting factions or faction-like formations, and loose alignments, marked by extremes of particularism and localism" (Grabowski 1996, 250). A Czech sociologist described local politics in his country as follows: "The system of political parties (with the exception of the Communist Party) was new, unstable, and poorly differentiated. Parties were not profiled, and they differed more in names than in programs, which were unspecific and overlapping . . . Except for urban centers, the voters' choice was based more on the personalities of candidates than on party allegiance . . . Besides the national parties, many unusual political subjects entered the local political scene in many municipalities—individual independent candidates, social organizations, and coalitions representing all possible combinations of the above subjects" (Illner 1998, 60).

Slovak political analysts have had an equally difficult time in discerning a party pattern in their country's local election results, as evinced in the Slovak politic scientist Grigorij Mesežnikov's dry summation of the 1998 elections: "Because of the heterogeneous composition of local coalitions, and the fairly large differences between the populations of individual municipalities, it is difficult to evaluate the election results (of mayors and local councilors) in terms of the success or failure of individual political parties" (1999, 32–33). This small sampling of scholarly accounts paints a picture of local party systems that accords well with the weak-governance type.[7]

The underinstitutionalization of local politics stands out very clearly when one compares party politics from town to town in Poland, Slovakia, and the Czech Republic. The further removed from the national level, the stronger the role of voters' personal identification with candidates becomes. This favors independent candidates over party-backed ones. Thus, local elections are dominated by independent candidates and the temporary, umbrella-style electoral alliances these candidates often form at election time. The conditions of muddled electoral competition between underinstitutionalized election teams, not conventional political parties, lead to fluid government formation. The more local the situation, the more unpredictable government formation is.

Background Conditions: Social Demobilization and Party Fragmentation

The beginning point and enduring quandary for party-building, including that at the local level, in Eastern Europe is a demobilized society in which political labels and political participation are anathema (see Chapter 1). Demobilized society is a poor basis on which to build stable party organizations, and the 1990s witnessed the ongoing fragmentation of the local party scene. As the broad-based anticommunist movements of the 1989 revolution—Solidarity, Civic Forum, and Public

Against Violence—broke down, so too did the local committees associated with them.

One measure of the political demobilization of society at the local level is the rate of voter turnout in local elections, and the figures on turnout suggest a gradual demobilization of local society.[8] Across Eastern Europe, these rates have been steadily declining throughout the 1990s. Except for Poland, the trend was for high turnouts in the first local elections in 1990, as part of the general euphoria accompanying the revolutions of 1989. As the euphoria cooled, voting participation fell off sharply. In the Czech Republic's 1990 local elections, participation was 73.5 percent.[9] In 1994, it fell to 62.3 percent. For the local elections in 1998 it was only 46.7 percent. By comparison, turnout in Poland's local elections has been disappointing from the very beginning. In 1990, it was 42 percent. By 1994, Polish turnout had fallen even further to only 34 percent. The 1998 Polish elections saw an increase to 45 percent turnout; that increase was not due, however, to increased interest in local government but instead reflected the bundling of local elections with those for the newly established regional and district governments (Zarycki 1999). That the turnout for elections for two brand-new, much-trumpeted levels of government was only 45 percent was in fact a sign of public apathy. Finally, the Slovak participation rate has generally followed the Czech and Polish trend of gradual decline, falling from 63.8 percent in 1990 to 54 percent in 1998. Thus, by the end of the 1990s, each country had converged to an unimpressive local election turnout somewhere in the mid-forties to mid-fifties.

Another sign of the demobilization of local society was the antipolitics ethos of the local politicians. As the chairman of the Cracow Citizens' Committee told a panel of scholars on local government in 1991: "I must say, I am not a fan of parties in general. This is because, to me party means, first, party discipline to which I would have to submit, in many cases against my beliefs. Besides, . . . I prefer to vote for individual persons, not parties" (quoted in Grabowski 1996, 235). As one Polish social scientist summarized the findings of a study conducted of the 1990 local elections in one medium-sized town, "The formation of new subjects of local power was something in which the wider community showed little interest. All of this undoubtedly weighed on the character of local events, and the friction and conflicts. Local politics came to be seen as dominated by personal bias, individual ambitions and conflicts of narrow interests irrelevant to the community at large. They rarely assumed the form of serious disputes about programmes affecting the most important problems of the local community" (Bukowski 1996, 160).

In many ways, the same script played out at the local level of each of these countries as occurred nationally. During the 1989 revolution, there was a spontaneous flowering of organizational activity directed against communist rule. Though concentrated in the cities, this flurry of political organization reached down to the smaller towns as well: Solidarity, Civic Forum, and Public Against Violence had both local and national organizations. The local organizations were even less institutionalized than the amorphous national bodies, however, and when the national bodies broke apart soon after the first fully free parliamentary elections, the local organizations lost their primary link with party politics as such. Ties between national and local party organizations loosened, and a withdrawal from the political world outside the borders of a given town began. Viewed from the national level, the situation a decade after the 1989 revolutions is one of the failure of the national party system to link itself to the local level. Seen from the local perspective, the situation is one of an established model of notable-style politics and unpredictable government making (Grabowski 1996).

It is hardly surprising, given the chaos of its national-level party system, that Poland's local party systems should also fit the weak-governance type. It is difficult for national party offices to establish a local-level network if the foundations of the national-level party itself are shifting. Even without the problems of social demobilization, Poland's local parties were disadvantaged by the lack of stable national parties with which to build institutional linkages. In a parallel development to the rise and fall of Solidarity at the national level, Poland witnessed the explosive growth and then total disappearance of a nationwide network of local Citizens' Committees (Komitety Obywatelskie) between April 1989—during the campaign for the country's first partially free elections—and October 1991, just after the first fully free elections of that month (Grabowski 1996; Kubik 1994). Solidarity's well-developed local political network disappeared overnight, and nothing similar replaced it.

The Czech Republic and Slovakia—then part of the federal Czechoslovakia—began the 1990s with local political organizations relatively underdeveloped in comparison to Poland. Neither had a history of grassroots organizing such as Poland's Solidarity movement. On the contrary, Czechoslovakia ranked among the most hardline communist regimes of Eastern Europe (alongside East Germany) as an enduring legacy of the 1968 Soviet invasion. Until the break-up of the Czechoslovak federal state in 1993, the legal basis for local government developed in tandem in the Czech Republic and Slovakia. The federal parliament laid out the framework for local government in both republics in July 1990, and supporting legislation followed in the separate republican parliaments (Illner 1999, 82–83). Though both countries had quiescent civil societies during the communist regime—especially in comparison to Poland—that quiescence was greater in Slovakia than in the Czech Republic (Suruszka 1996): before 1989, the "anti-politics" espoused by Czech opposition groups such as Charter 77 had, like that in Poland, contained an element of local autonomy and local organization (Illner 1998, 52–53). This provided the impetus for the speedy establishment of local government legislation in both halves of the federation after 1989.

The Independents' Advantage

An analysis of the first three rounds of local elections (in 1990, 1994, and 1998) since the 1989 revolution brings the underinstitutionalization of the Polish, Czech, and Slovak local-level party systems sharply into focus. Candidates backed by national-level political parties fared poorly, while independent and local party candidates, who typically did not distinguish themselves programmatically, did consistently well. These were not elections that presented voters with clear choices between political parties with differentiated programs and stable organizational resources—the prerequisites for responsible-party competition of the kind that constrains governing coalitions and holds them accountable to voters.

The very act of gathering local election results in Poland, the Czech Republic, and Slovakia during the 1990s indicates the disordered nature of local party systems. There is very little continuity among the electoral groupings contesting these elections—both geographically, from town to town, and temporally, from election to election. The most complete electoral statistics are available for the Czech Republic (*Statistical Yearbook of the Czech Republic* 1995; 1999). The Slovak electoral commission has not been as forthcoming about local election results, but it has published the seat shares of each of the parties and electoral groupings (*Statistical Yearbook of the Slovak Republic* 1995; 1999). Statistics on local election results are by far hardest to come by for Poland. The Polish local elections of 1990 were animated by the struggle between the anticommunist Citizens' Committees and the Communist successor parties, which simplified the political spectrum and enabled the categorization of electoral groupings across municipalities. By the time of the second local elections in June 1994, the Citizens' Committees had fragmented into hundreds of unconnected, programmatically diverse local groupings. Faced with this reality, the Polish electoral commission did not even attempt to publish a national breakdown of aggregate seats shares of the parties in the local councils (Szczerbiak 1999a, 81). Unfortunately, the situation for the 1998 elections in Poland is not much better. As of this writing, the State Election Commission still had not officially published the results on its Web site, but some aggregate figures were published in the regional newspapers (Szczerbiak 1999a).

If the available results for the 1990, 1994, and 1998 elections are pooled across municipalities, it is possible to roughly gauge the strength of national political parties—with their more clearly defined programs and superior organizational resources—relative to local party and independent candidates.[10] Over the course of the 1990s, national-level parties claimed only 47.4 percent of seats in local elections in the Czech Republic, and still fewer (41.3 percent) in Poland. This figure was higher, approximately 74.7 percent, in Slovakia, but even that number indicated a sizable presence for local parties and independents.[11] In the Czech Republic, the majority of competitors to national party candidates are not local parties but independents, candidates without any party institutional backing whatever. In the Czech Republic, independents have on average won 46.8 percent of local seats, and in Slovakia they have won 14.2 percent. After 1990, the Polish statistics do not allow for distinctions between independents and local candidates, but almost certainly the success rate of independents there approaches the Czech figure.[12] The difficulties posed by varying degrees of statistical completeness notwithstanding, the local election results clearly indicate, first, that national parties are responsible for only a small share of the local-level councilors and, second, the prominence of independent candidates.

The success of independent candidates—and the concomitant poor showing of national-level parties—in local elections cannot be attributed to the electoral systems. The majority of seats were allocated under proportional representation (PR) rules, which in general favor political parties over individual candidates.[13] That individual candidates did so well in PR systems is only further testament to the weak organizational basis of political parties at the local level.

If anything, these statistics may actually overstate the influence of national parties because many of the candidates winning seats from a certain party's electoral list were not actual members of that party. National-level parties often sponsored candidates who were not officially members. Gauging the extent of this phenomenon is difficult, again, because statistics are scarce. There are, however, data on this issue for the Czech 1994 elections (*Statistical Yearbook of the Czech Republic* 1995, 600). On average, one half of the national parties' candidates in local elections were not members of the party but independents with party sponsorship[14]—further evidence of the weak influence of national parties at the local level.

No aggregate level results have been published for the 1994 Polish local elections. One can, however, put together a picture of what happened from the accounts of regional academics and journalists. The Polish political scientist Paweł Świaniewicz (1996) undertook a study to assess the role of political parties in mobilizing candidates and voters in the elections by interviewing 183 candidates in 12 municipalities and reviewing campaign documents and meetings. His assessment underscores the general features of local politics that I have laid out here. Świaniewicz describes a

local political scene with evident social cleavages but without the organized political expression of those cleavages, or to put it more simply, with politics but not political parties. It is worth quoting him at length on the nature of local party systems:

> Parties were almost invisible in the local election campaign. This was not very sur-
> prising in small municipalities with a simple majority system of voting. In rural areas
> people often vote for individuals, and not for parties or programmes in general. Most
> candidates thought that admitting any political preference would spoil rather than im-
> prove their chance of winning. A telling example drawn from my survey concerns two
> candidates who both belonged to political parties but stressed very strongly that it had
> no relationship to their election programmes and would not have any influence on
> their future activity in the local council.
>
> But more surprisingly, for an outside observer, it was also very difficult to find any
> trace of party activity in larger cities with proportional electoral systems. Obviously,
> candidates needed to organized in groups, but they tried to avoid any party labels and
> used local names instead. In most cases a well-informed voter could quite easily rec-
> ognize which party was hidden behind the name of which "local committee," but it
> was considered safer to do without a party name.
>
> The typology of the parties presented above may certainly be surprising for many ob-
> servers of the Polish political scene and even offensive for others. Is BBWR, a move-
> ment created by [Lech] Wałęsa, similar in its economic preferences to the leftist (post-
> communist) governing coalition? Are ZChN and PC really close to UW, despite the
> official hostility between those parties' elites? (1996, 741)

This description of parties hiding behind local committees captures a crucial element of local politics in all of these countries: local party systems frustrate rather
than facilitate accountable government. Parties are important in recruiting, organizing, and mobilizing elites, but not in guiding voters at the polls. As Świaniewicz
succinctly puts it, "Politics does matter but it is hidden from the public" (1996, 742).
In weak-governance party systems such as these, no credible opposition checks the
governing coalition, so party competition does not constrain these coalitions from
using the local state administration as a source of patronage.

Underinstitutionalization

Stable party organization is a second requisite for responsible-party competition.
By and large, local party organizations in all three countries have remained ad hoc
and underinstitutionalized, which can be seen by comparing the major parties and

a party possessing a well-institutionalized local apparatus. Across the region, every country provides at least one notable example of the latter type of party, the Communist successor party.

Immediately after 1989, the anticommunist social movements often worried that the Communist successor parties and their former satellites would have an overwhelming organizational advantage in free elections.[15] This was because these groups had inherited most of their assets and infrastructure from a time when every town had had its own party office, with staff, equipment, and other resources. Today, the reorganized Czech Communist Party (KSČM) alone has almost as many local party organizations as the rest of the major political parties combined, with a local party organization in each municipality.[16] The Christian Democratic People's Party (KDU-ČSL), a former satellite party,[17] has the second most party organizations in the Czech Republic, with one in approximately every third municipality. The Civic Democratic Party (ODS) and Czech Social Democratic Party (ČSSD) have only a fifth as many local organizations as the Communists. In Poland, the local organizational network of the Democratic Left Alliance (SLD) and the former satellite Polish Peasant Party (PSL) dwarfs that of their post-Solidarity rivals. According to one study of local party organization in Poland, PSL maintains party structures in 79 percent of Polish municipalities (Szczerbiak 1999, quoted in Lewis 2000, 105). In contrast, the Freedom Union (UW) maintained party organizations in only 13 percent of municipalities.

By the last available reckoning, Slovakia's SDL' (Party of the Democratic Left) maintained 2,000 local organizations, an impressive figure given that the country has approximately 2,700 municipalities. Interestingly, however, the dominant HZDS, along with its junior coalition partner the Slovak Nationalist Party (SNS), was able to build up comparable local party networks. Indeed, the local organizations of HZDS actually outnumbered those of the SDL'. The size of these parties' local apparatus owed a great deal to the dominant-party position enjoyed by their national leadership from 1992 to 1998, which was able to fund larger party organizations on both the national and the local levels as a result of its control of the central state.[18] This evidence further confirms that the dominant-party logic of Slovakia's national-level party system strongly influenced its local politics, making it more difficult to separate local state-building from national state-building than in Poland and the Czech Republic.

Government Formation

It should come as little surprise that building local government majorities should prove largely unpredictable and that both party ideology and programmatic differences are more or less irrelevant at the local level. As is often the case in the untidy world of local politics, information about the process of government making is difficult to gather. The Czech Republic offers the most extensive data, Poland and Slovakia considerably less.

The Czech political scientists Aleš Kroupa and Tomáš Kostelecký (1996) offer one of the most detailed studies of local politics in the Czech Republic. They collected data about the pre-electoral coalitions of local party organizations in the Czech Republic's 1990 local elections. They then analyzed this data to see how similar the behavior of local party branches was to that of the national party organizations with which they were associated. For each of the main national parties in the elections, Kroupa and Kostelecký looked at the number of coalitions its local branches formed with the local branches of other national parties in the campaign before the elections. They counted the instances when the parties' local branches formed coalitions with (1) the local branches of national-level party allies, (2) independent candidates or associations of independent candidates, or (3) the local branches of national-level party opponents. For almost all parties, the local branches showed themselves equally likely to form a coalition with an independent or national opponent as with a national ally. In a number of cases, local parties were even *more* likely to form coalitions with national opponents. As Kroupa and Kostelecký write, "For the smallest category of municipality, these right-left or otherwise programmatically inconsistent coalitions were even more frequent than coalitions between parties with a similar political orientation" (1996, 110).

Unfortunately, a similar analysis of government-making at the beginning of the 1990s is not possible for Slovakia and Poland. In Slovakia, the data have not been collected systematically. In Poland, the reality is too messy to even begin collecting such data. In both countries, however, the scholarly consensus is that building local governments in Poland and Slovakia is certainly not any less chaotic and unpredictable than in the Czech Republic (Krivý 1999). The example of Warsaw would suggest that, if anything, it is more chaotic in Poland. After the 1994 local elections, it took three months for the parties to agree on a mayor for the city (Świaniewicz 1996, 735).

As this survey of local politics has shown, municipal party systems were weak-governance systems in Poland, the Czech Republic, and Slovakia. Party competition did not give voters the levers to generate coherent governments and credible oppositions, which in democratizing systems with unconsolidated states, opens the door for patronage-fueled state-building. Because the dominance of Mečiar's HZDS extended down from the national level to the local one, local party competition in Slovakia was more institutionalized and more party-based than in Poland

and the Czech Republic. Even in Slovakia, however, local politics was still less institutionalized than at the national level.

LOCAL-LEVEL STATE-BUILDING

I encountered local-level patronage politics in my first interview with a public official in a Polish municipality. This person worked in the city government's office for the promotion of the local economy, whose main task is to attract foreign investors by promoting the city in trade forums and putting together promotional literature. According to my interviewee, even the activity and staff of this office, seemingly far removed from local political issues, changed radically after the city's change of government in 1998. The chief of the office was replaced with a close friend of the new city mayor. Within a year, about one-third of the office's staff had left or been fired, and the outside contractors from whom the office commissioned brochures had been changed.

The second part of this chapter will trace the consequences of fragmentation in local party systems for the development of the local state administrations tied to those party systems. Does one find the pattern of runaway state-building that the theory would predict for such party systems? The state-building outcomes predicted by the party competition framework conform well to the actual outcomes, while the predictions of the national administrative culture argument find little support. As expected given their weak-governance local party systems, Poland and the Czech Republic both experienced dramatic expansion of their municipal administrations. Contrary to my initial expectations, municipal administrations actually contracted in Slovakia during the same period. On closer inspection, however, it turns out that Slovakia's contracting local administration is the exception that proves the rule: it reflects the logic of dominant-party politics at the national level. The critical difference was Mečiar's HZDS. In HZDS Slovakia had a powerful national-level political machine that sought to monopolize the available patronage resources from state-building. It also had a political system that placed almost all political levers in the hands of the national government. It was very easy for Mečiar's machine to starve local governments of resources—resources that were used instead to fuel state expansion at the national level. In short, the national-local distinction was considerably more blurry in Slovakia than in Poland and the Czech Republic.

To measure and compare the growth of the local state as a whole across countries, the empirical analysis focuses on personnel and budgets. The number of administrative personnel in local state administration, at least in Poland and the Czech Republic, saw rates of expansion of similar magnitude to the national-level expansion described in earlier chapters. Particularly in the Czech Republic, this personnel expansion was accompanied by an expansion in the number of municipalities. The budgets of local governments—their degree of independence from the central state budget and, of course, their size—also reflect the logic of party competition.

Personnel

In all three countries, local governments were given a free hand in the appointment of personnel to their local administrations. Local-level administrative positions were not covered by the regulations for hiring and firing personnel, which, weak and belated though they were, existed for the national-level state administration by the end of the 1990s.[19] As early as the 1989 Round Table negotiations in Poland, Solidarity activists sought to minimize legal constraints on the new local governments, explicitly including constraints on the hiring and firing of staff (Kisiel and Taebel 1994, 55). The autonomy of Polish municipalities was guaranteed by the expansively worded provision in the law that "the scope of activity [of municipal governments] shall embrace all public matters of local significance that are not reserved by law for other units" (quoted in Kisiel and Taebel 1994, 55). After all, anticommunist activists in the early 1990s saw creating autonomous local governments as a way to dismantle the communist state.

As with the national-level state, the best, most comparable measure of administrative expansion is the number of personnel.[20] In both Poland and the Czech Republic the number of personnel employed in local governments' administrations grew impressively in the 1990s. In Poland, the local-level administrations expanded by 58 percent between 1990 and 1999. In the Czech Republic, they grew by 56 percent from 1993 to 1999.[21] These growth rates are comparable with the dramatic expansion of national-level administrations described in Chapter 1; the two cases of runaway state-building there, Poland and Slovakia, experienced expansion rates of 48.4 and 71.2 percent, respectively.

The Czech figures run counter to the predictions of the national administrative culture hypothesis. While the national-level Czech state grew by a modest 15.4 percent between 1993 and 1999, the local-level Czech state increased by 56.2 percent. This contrast between the national and local levels simply does not accord with the view that the Czechs avoided runaway state-building because they had a more developed administrative culture than the Poles and the Slovaks. If this truly were the case, the Czech rate of expansion should have been about the same at the local and the national levels. Furthermore, the Czech Republic should not have led the others in the expansion of state personnel at the local level, as it did between 1993 and 1999. The disparity between the expansion of the Czechs' local- and national-level administrations does accord very well, however, with the party competition argument proposed here. Namely, runaway state-building occurs when party competition is not robust and therefore does not constrain patronage politics. The bipolar competition at the national-level Czech party system was not matched by any such pattern in the country's local party systems. Poland's similarly disordered and fragmented local party systems also did little to constrain municipal government patronage, so its municipal administrations dramatically expanded as well.

If the trends in the Czech and Polish systems fit the theory's prediction that runaway state-building will occur in weak-governance party systems, the data for Slovakia's local state administration raise questions. There, the number of local state personnel actually decreased between 1993 and 1999, by 17.7 percent. Slovakia's local-level party competition is, as the first part of this chapter shows, somewhat more institutionalized and party-based than in the Czech Republic and Poland, but these are differences of degree, not of kind. Why then has there been such a different outcome—a reduction in the size of the local administration? It is the consequence of Slovakia's dominant-party logic of competition at the national level: the development of local state institutions is closely dependent on the national-level government.

Mečiar's HZDS machine always had an antagonistic relationship with local governments in Slovakia. In part, this antipathy stemmed from the suspicion that local government was the cradle of the political opposition, the shelter to which the opposition could return after setbacks at the national level. In part, the antagonism stemmed from the fact that HZDS's patronage policies at the national level hurt local governments. First, these policies were funded indirectly by local governments, who had to forgo financial resources they might otherwise have had. Second, the expansion of the national-level administration was a threat to the autonomy of local government.[22] Interviews in the field made clear that local-level politicians and activists regarded the contraction of local administrations as a problem, not an accomplishment. Far from crediting this contraction to responsible-party competition in town and city councils, they blamed it on a hostile national government.

Slovakia's local administrations could not grow because the national political machine gave them ever smaller financial resources with which to operate. Before moving to the public finance data, however, it is worth considering one other measure of administrative expansion at the local level.

The Number of Local Governments

After 1989, local state institutions also grew in terms of the total number of local administrations. Especially in the early 1990s, and especially in the Czech Republic, the number of municipalities multiplied rapidly. The process occurred as suburbs and small towns seceded from administrative centers and incorporated themselves as autonomous municipalities. Each new municipality would, of course, need its own local government—council, mayor, and municipal administration. As the Czech sociologist Michal Illner (1998) has noted, this process was one of unco-ordinated fragmentation, not institutional design or comprehensive reform. The decision to constitute a new municipality was taken solely by the inhabitants of a particular locality, not as part of some government plan for state reform or admin-istrative decentralization, such as that described in Chapter 4. It was idiosyncratic, individual, and according to Illner, often ill-advised.

Again, the Czech Republic experienced the greatest rate of growth, with a roughly 50 percent increase in the number of municipalities in just ten years.[23] Poland's rate of increase was a more modest 17.3 percent.[24] The lion's share of the increase in localities occurred between 1989 and 1992. In the Czech Republic, the number of municipalities increased by 40 percent between 1989 and 1991. Statistics for Slovakia are not readily available for comparison, though according to com-mentators, a similar dynamic of local fragmentation occurred there during the early 1990s (Bryson and Cornia 2000, 510).

Viewing these developments from the point of view of the efficient provision of public services, academics and policy analysts regarded the swelling ranks of local governments with concern. They pointed out that many of the new localities were too small, too poor, and too inexperienced to provide basic services such as trash collection, schooling, and so on. As a result, the new governments usually turned back to the neighboring towns, from which they had seceded, to provide these ser-vices. In terms of public services, then, local administrations were less effective af-ter this expansion than they should have been. The difference was that now there was a bigger local state administration. As Michal Illner puts it, "Criteria of eco-nomic and organizational rationality seldom played a role in such decisions [as the one to secede and establish a new municipality]" (1998, 54).

The Financial Resources of Municipal Governments

What are the financial resources that can fund this kind of rapid expansion of lo-cal institutions? A large portion of local governments' budgetary resources take the form of earmarked grants from the central state. As they have limited discretion in using these revenues, local politicians are less able to use them for patronage. Local governments have other budgetary revenues that are beyond national-level over-sight, however. These are tax-sharing revenues, which constitute a certain percent-age of the personal income and corporate taxes collected in each locality's territory.

Unlike state grants and subsidies, tax-sharing revenues can be used as each local government sees fit. In all three countries, the tax-sharing revenues comprise the largest tax revenue source for local governments. Tax-sharing revenues for local governments fluctuate between 40 to 60 percent of total tax revenues (Kameničková 2000, 4; Kňažko 2000, 3).[25] Because tax-sharing revenues are the biggest source of local tax revenues and because local governments exercise the greatest amount of discretion with this item of their budgets, I focus first on the dynamics of tax-sharing in order to explain the similar development of local state institutions in Poland and the Czech Republic, as well as the very different development in Slovakia.

A comparison of tax-sharing between Poland and the Czech Republic, on the one hand, and Slovakia, on the other, makes clear why the number of personnel in the local state administration has declined in Slovakia and why it has grown in the other two countries. In all three countries, the mechanics of tax-sharing have been essentially the same since 1989. Personal income and corporate taxes are collected centrally in a national budget, and then a certain percentage of those taxes is transferred back to the municipalities and districts in which they were collected. The percentage given to local governments is determined by the national-level parliament and is the same for each locality. Clearly, the advantages in this system are weighted decisively toward the central government, and away from local governments. That said, several factors can make tax-sharing more or less advantageous to local governments. First, of course, is how high the fixed percentage going to localities is set. Second is the degree of stability of tax-sharing criteria over time. If these criteria fluctuate on a yearly basis, long-term budgeting becomes very difficult (if not impossible), and the financial footing of local governments is precarious.

Tax-sharing arrangements between the central and municipal governments were least favorable, if not outright deleterious, in Slovakia. In 1993, Slovak localities received 70 percent of personal income taxes collected within their respective borders; in 1999, they received 19 percent; the localities share of corporate income taxes declined from 5.87 percent in 1994 to 4.04 percent in 1999 (Kňažko 2000). Moreover, the tax-sharing rates have varied every year in Slovakia, for both the income and the corporate taxes. Even as the ratio determining the division of tax revenues between the central government and localities has tipped toward the central government's advantage, the relative size of tax revenues in local budgets has increased from 38.4 percent in 1995 to 42.5 percent in 1999 (Kňažko 2000). In short, local governments have become increasingly reliant on a source of revenue over which they have no control and which has been dwindling in size. Faced with an unpredictable, declining tax base, it is not surprising that local governments in Slovakia have not been able to support increases in the size of local administration.

Tax-sharing arrangements have been both stable and generous in the Czech Republic and quite favorable in Poland as well. In both cases the tax-sharing ratio between central and local governments has been stable over time. From 1990 to 1994, local governments' share of personal income tax in the Czech Republic was 70 percent. While that percentage fell to 50 percent in 1995, this reduction was compensated for by an increased share of the more important revenues from corporate taxes—from 4.61 to 20 percent; as a result, overall tax revenues for localities were not adversely affected by the change (Kameničková 2000, 4). In Poland, the tax-sharing rates have been stable since 1990, with 27.2 percent of personal income tax revenues and 5 percent of corporate tax revenues (Chancellery 1998, 19). Thus, tax-sharing rates are more favorable to local governments in the Czech Republic and Poland than they are in Slovakia, particularly in the Czech Republic. By 1999, Czech and Polish municipalities were receiving 50 and 27.2 percent of personal income tax respectively, whereas the Slovak rate was 19 percent. The corresponding figures for corporate tax rates were 20 percent for the Czech Republic, 5 percent for Poland, and 4.04 percent for Slovakia.

To put it bluntly, Czech local governments have had the most money since 1989. At $521 per person, they have had the highest per capita expenditures of the three countries. Poland's have been the next largest at $330 per person. Slovak local governments have been cash-starved by comparison, with expenditures of only $119 per person.[26] Local state institutions have not grown in Slovakia because they are very dependent on a hostile national government. Tax-sharing arrangements provide a good window onto the predatory tactics of a machine-style, national government vis-à-vis the local level. These practices have severely reduced the capacity for patronage-fueled expansion of the local state in Slovakia, even though the character of local party systems in Slovakia would predict such expansion.[27] According to these figures, Czech local governments enjoyed a more favorable situation than Polish ones, which may account for the greater rate of expansion of Czech local administration since 1993.

CONCLUSION

In Poland and the Czech Republic the development of local state administrations largely conforms to what one would expect in weak-governance local party systems. The differences in party organization and party competition that were evident at the national level between Poland, Slovakia, and the Czech Republic fade away when one looks at local-level politics. The analysis of local-level state-building shows little difference between Poland and the Czech Republic. Using the logic of

Mill's method of agreement, then, one can rule out the alternative hypothesis of national administrative culture as an explanation for the observed differences in local-level state-building.

At first glance, Slovakia appears to be a troublesome case because its local state administration decreased in size between 1990 and 1998. Was this outcome the result of a distinctive administrative culture? Given my interviews in the field and the picture of Slovak politics that has emerged over the last chapters, I am confident that the answer is no. Slovakia's local administration declined in ways consistent with my runaway state-building hypothesis—though not, admittedly, because of the logic of local party competition. It declined because of the logic of national party competition, and in Slovakia during the 1990s, national politics was more important than local politics. Mečiar's governments starved local governments of funding in order to maximize their own patronage extraction. This outcome only emphasizes the power of the national-level political machine that dominated Slovak politics under Mečiar. Ultimately, then, Slovakia is the exception that proves the rule and strengthens the party competition framework advanced here: the logic of party competition at Slovakia's national level determined the path of state-building at its local level.

CHAPTER SIX

A Runaway Welfare State?

Postcommunist Welfare Politics

One of the most striking contrasts between Polish and Czech social policy is the extent to which the greater centralization and efficiency of state administration in the Czech Republic facilitated the pursuit of its transitional social strategy. Poland decentralized most social-welfare functions in 1990, placing them under the authority of local governments rather than in the local branch of state administration. While this may have been good for Polish democracy, it had tragic results for social-service provision.

Mitchell Orenstein (1996, 20)

Fashioning a Weberian bureaucracy from a posttotalitarian, patrimonial administration has been a major challenge for the new democracies of Eastern Europe. Poland and Slovakia exhibit swelling administrative apparatuses and stalled bureaucratization, whereas there is more measured growth and incipient bureaucratization in the Czech Republic. Examining the administration, the heart of the state, reveals that the party competition model fits with these cases of democratic transition quite well. But how well does this model fit the rest of the state, in particular the welfare state, which has traditionally been and still remains one of the largest areas of public employment and public expenditure in Eastern Europe? This chapter is devoted to testing the applicability of my argument about party competition and state-building to the welfare state, in particular health care and pensions.

Extending the analysis to the welfare state offers two important benefits. First, since welfare policy is one of the most concrete and most visible "outputs" of the state, it is, at least in the eyes of the general public, the measure of state effectiveness that really matters. Do the state's welfare outputs live up to the benefits to which the public are legally entitled? Although the postcommunist welfare states of Eastern Europe are legally defined in universalistic terms, in practice there is considerable variation in the extent to which governments honor these commitments.[1] This variation is clearest in the area of health care: although Polish, Czech, and Slovak citizens are legally entitled to free health care, in both Poland and Slovakia, patients typically have to make under-the-table in order to get treatment, especially for more involved procedures. Second, welfare politics is another arena in which to study the relationship between party competition and the capacity for governments to undertake and see through reform measures affecting the state. Why was the Czech Republic able both to reform its health care and pension systems earlier and to close off the inevitable loopholes that appeared and carry through the reform? Why was Poland unable to correct obvious flaws and clamp down on rampant abuse in its social insurance system even after expenditures in this area reached crisis proportions?[2] The logic of party competition matters to how welfare states perform. Countries with responsible-party systems have less of a gap between welfare entitlements and actual welfare outputs; furthermore, these countries' governments tend to undertake necessary, though painful, reforms earlier and carry them through more consistently.

What would the party competition model predict for the reconstruction of unconsolidated welfare states in times of extraordinary license for reform and dysfunctional party competition? Since previous chapters have highlighted the role of political patronage, one might expect runaway state-building to take the form of personnel expansion, high salaries, and political intervention in the hiring and firing of personnel. This, after all, is what happened with the administration. Recalling Table 3.1, however, it would initially seem that the party competition framework has little to say about the development of welfare states in the transition to democracy. The number and salaries of welfare personnel have been stagnant, even declining in the 1990s. By and large, these have not been attractive patronage positions.[3]

The superficial differences between the development of the state administration and the welfare state mask deeper, more fundamental similarities—similarities that link directly to the quality of government generated by party competition. The first fundamental similarity is the resilience of the welfare state in the transition to democracy, despite the lower salaries and stable personnel numbers. Like the state administration, the overweening and outmoded welfare state inherited from the communist regime was, at the beginning of the transition, largely expected to be scaled down and rationalized. In more recent years, these expectations have been revised, as the actual trends in welfare state politics in many postcommunist countries have been of resilience and even, in some areas, expansion.[4] Why has the number of welfare state personnel been so resilient, even in the face of serious declines in their salaries? Why does the welfare sector maintain high levels of employment at low levels of pay?

Second, although the number of welfare providers has been rather stable, countries like Poland have seen explosive growth of welfare expenditures, including under-the-table expenditures. That these expenditures were so high for countries of such comparatively limited resources meant that they constituted an ongoing fiscal crisis. Tax revenues were at around half of GDP across much of Eastern Europe, largely in order to sustain social expenditures (Charlton, McKinnon, and Konopielko 1998, 1415).

Third, as in the state administration, there are few signs of the emergence of a distinction between the office and the officeholder in countries where government instability or lack of interest has delayed welfare reforms. Because the wages of doctors and nurses are low, petty corruption between welfare providers and welfare clients—a pervasive trait of the communist-era welfare state—persisted and even deepened during the democratic and economic transition. Rather than raise the wages of personnel, governments turned a blind eye to petty corruption, tolerating a system of overemployment at low wages.

There are, then, both underlying similarities and compelling reasons for extending the party competition framework to the development of the welfare state. It gives us another measure of state capacity: does the state honor its welfare commitments? Or does the state fall back on a kind of "fictitious universalism," preserving nominally free benefits for which under-the-table payments are necessary? Moreover, with some adjustment of the dependent variable—focusing instead on the timing and quality of reform—it is clear that the logic of party competition strongly influences the outcome of welfare state-building. To put the question more concretely, would Poland's welfare state have developed differently in the 1990s if Poland had had a party system like the Czech one? Viewed in this light, the overarching argument about the link between party system development and state-building is relevant and useful. There is a relationship between the logic of party system competition and the development of the Polish, Czech, and Slovak welfare states in the 1990s. To show this influence, this chapter will test the following propositions:

1. Because responsible-party systems generate more coherent, stable governments and more credible oppositions, governments in such systems undertake necessary and fundamental welfare reforms earlier than those of weak-governance and dominant-party systems.

2. For the same reasons, governments in responsible-party systems are better able to implement those reforms once undertaken, correcting for unforeseen contingencies and carrying through the initial reform plan.

3. In countries with responsible-party systems, the gap between legal welfare entitlements and actual welfare benefits will be smaller than in countries with weak-governance or dominant-party systems.

This conceptualization of state performance is true to the spirit of runaway state-building: states that fail to undertake necessary reforms, fail to rationalize high personnel levels, and do not deliver on their legal commitments are states that are too large for the services they render. Before moving to the chapter's empirical sections, a quick word on the assumptions behind these propositions is necessary.

The first assumption is that governments are, in general, apprehensive about undertaking fundamental welfare state reforms because these reforms are politically unpopular with segments of the electorate who benefit under the status quo (Nelson 2001). Paul Pierson (1994) has very cogently laid out the argument why it is easy to expand welfare states but exceedingly difficult to retrench or reform them. It requires a stable and sure government majority to undertake a policy that directly—and in the short term probably negatively—impacts the economic situation of what may be a sizable number of voters. This dilemma is particularly acute in societies in transition. Even before the collapse of communism, scholars had termed these "premature welfare states" (Kornai 1992).[5] Though many of the communist state's welfare services did not then match those in the West, there was free health care, free education, guaranteed housing, extensive disability benefits, and generous pensions. All of these things were state-guaranteed, and the expectation that they remain so is shared by much of the public today (Mandelbaum 1997).

The second assumption is that welfare reform is a particularly administration-intensive reform. As Joan Nelson writes, "The intrinsic character of social-sector reforms poses political obstacles . . . Initial [macroeconomic] liberalization [such as Poland's "shock therapy"] entails dismantling controls and subsidies. Such measures are politically controversial, but they are not complex administratively . . . Social-sector reforms, like most institutional changes, are inherently slower and more complex. They demand the cooperation of far more agencies and groups within and outside of government, and they take months or years to put into effect.

Multiple actors mean many potential veto players; lengthy implementation means multiple veto opportunities" (2001, 236–37).

As the following case studies of health care and pensions show, poor administrative implementation led to inequities in policy application, wasteful use of resources, and subpar outcomes in Poland's weak-governance system and Slovakia's dominant-party one. To initiate and sustain welfare reform, governments need to be stable, programmatically coherent, have medium- to long-term time horizons and face a credible opposition. As the previous chapters have shown, the different logics of party competition produce these qualities in different proportions and different combinations.

Institutionalized party systems with robust competition are best able to provide these conditions. With less electoral volatility, parties have longer time horizons to initiate reforms whose eventual benefits may come in the medium to long term. With less internal heterogeneity and less frequent turnover, governments face fewer internal veto players and are more stable. Finally, the existence of a well-organized and credible opposition provides an impetus for the government to be responsive to the electorate, correcting obvious policy failures and undertaking reforms that will strengthen their electoral prospects in the medium to long term. The existence of a credible opposition also lessens the chance that "reforms" are captured by particularistic interest groups close to the government. These conditions—difficult to achieve even in consolidated democracies—have been described by the Polish economist and sometime government minister Jerzy Hausner as follows: "Under a democratic system, ruling elites frequently change during the reform as the government and opposition alternate roles. It follows that the actual implementation of the reform calls for a majority far above that which is necessary to put through even the most difficult short-term projects. I call this kind of majority a strategic majority: a long-lived, non-opportunistic one, capable of effecting a profound structural change" (2001, 232). Hausner was lamenting the absence of such conditions in Poland, which he knew quite well from his experience with the country's pension reform.

Of the three party systems, the responsible-party Czech one provided the best conditions to establish a coherent organizational direction and administrative follow-through for restructuring the postcommunist welfare state. The Czech Republic undertook reforms early, corrected them over time, and did the best job of meeting its legal commitments to universalistic benefits. As one would expect when party competition is anchored by programmatically defined parties, alternation of government produced adjustments to welfare policy. Left-leaning governments expanded welfare policies when they were in power, and conservative governments scaled them back. Governments of both stripes had the cohesiveness to push through reforms without needing to water them down in an attempt to hold together a majority coalition.

Weak-governance systems such as Poland's produce governments that delay welfare reforms, implement them inconsistently once initiated, and tend not to meet their legal commitments to universalistic benefits. High electoral volatility means that governing parties have short time horizons, making them unwilling to risk changing the status quo through welfare reforms whose eventual benefits they may not survive to see. The greater government heterogeneity in weak-governance party systems virtually ensures that the governing coalition will include members with core constituencies wedded to elements of the current welfare system: in Poland, these were the labor unions, who were important members of both the post-Solidarity and postcommunist coalitions. Because necessary reforms are delayed in these political conditions, an informal or, semiprivatized, welfare sector develops in parallel to the official one (Kochanowicz 1997). Those who can afford it pay for welfare services—under the table. Not only do overall welfare expenditures tend to be expansive in such conditions, they are essentially beyond administrative and, ultimately, government control. Consequently, party programs and government alternation have only marginal impact on welfare state development: regardless of whether the left or the right is in power, the welfare state expands. The one advantage of weak-governance party systems is that the fragility of government majorities makes it less likely that particularized welfare advantages will be institutionalized by special interests close to government parties, as can happen in dominant-party systems.

While, in theory, the electoral advantages of the dominant party provide it with the kind of cushion that allow it to contemplate policies such as welfare reform that bring electoral rewards only in the long term, in practice this advantage tends to work the other way in dominant-party systems. For the dominant party, there is a smaller risk attached to welfare reforms, but there is also a smaller reward. In the responsible-party system, successful welfare reform may redound to the government party later down the road in what is, after all, a competitive party system; in contrast, dominant-party governments feel little impulse to reform in the absence of a credible opposition. Moreover, party competition in dominant systems tends not to revolve around policy programs and socioeconomic issues like welfare reform. Thus, dominant-party systems such as Slovakia's also tend to delay welfare state reforms. If undertaken at all, these reforms are also implemented inconsistently and inequitably. The problem of "fictitious universalism" is most extreme given the absence of an opposition and an impulse to reform. The corruption and decline in professionalism of welfare state personnel will probably be worse, and the system will be left to limp along without needed reforms, which have little to offer the dominant-party machine. The main difference from the welfare policy in the weak-governance party system is that the absence of a political opposition opens the door to interest groups connected to the government to create and institutionalize welfare advantages.

Empirically, this chapter has an ambitious agenda, to compare developments in the social security and health care systems of Poland, the Czech Republic, and Slovakia. In the first part, I discuss the historical background of welfare politics in these countries. This discussion sets the stage for an overview comparison of the three countries, followed by a close analysis of health care and pension policy.

DELEGITIMIZED WELFARE STATES AND DEMOBILIZED WELFARE PUBLICS

In the case of the state administration, there can be little doubt that the basic preconditions for runaway state-building—delegitimized states and demobilized societies—obtained. Under communism, the state administration had been colonized by the Communist Party through the *nomenklatura* system. After forty plus years of communism, society distrusted politics in general and did not draw fine distinctions between politicians and the state administration that served them. Thus, newly forming political parties had both the means (extraordinary license for reform) and the motive (finding party-building resources in societies that had withdrawn from politics) to combine the reorganization of the state's administrative apparatus with patronage politics.

Did these same conditions obtain in welfare politics? The answer is yes, but with some qualification necessary. There was one important difference between welfare and administrative politics from the outset. Namely, the communist-era welfare state was considerably more popular before and after the 1989 revolution than the state administrative apparatus. It had numerous problems and critics in its day, but its defining feature of universal, nominally free benefits is remembered nostalgically today by much of the population (Connor 1997). The word *nominal* is, of course, critical here. Though benefits were in principle free and universal, they were of low quality and often one had to make informal payments to obtain services. With social security, the strongly redistributive design of the pension system guaranteed high income-replacement rates regardless of individual contributions. Thus, the first legacy of the communist welfare system is the enduring attachment to the idea of free, or at least nominally free, services and generous benefits.

The communist welfare state's popular principles were not the same thing as legitimacy, however, especially since the reality of welfare provision and the principles differed so completely. The convention of under-the-table payments for nominally free benefits had two important implications for post-1989 welfare developments. First, because no one other than bribe-takers liked this reality, politicians had extraordinary license for welfare reform, at least initially. Second, the habit of going around the rules to get what one needed—of colluding with low-level welfare personnel against the system as a whole—was another form of withdrawal from public responsibility by postcommunist society, analogous to the withdrawal from party politics. Of course, the legacy of demobilized societies also functioned in its direct sense by making it difficult to build parliamentary coalitions for welfare reform. What postcommunist politics has tended to generate instead are narrow interest groups fighting for their own entitlements, say, a railway workers' union that lobbies to retain its own preferential pension category. Postcommunist civil society has had little difficulty generating coalitions for such sectorally concentrated, politically targeted welfare policies (Hausner 2001; 1994).

The characteristic feature of unreformed, runaway welfare states in Eastern Europe is "fictitious universalism," the first indicator of which is pervasive collusion in the provision of state welfare benefits—ubiquitous, informal payments for nominally free services that the government tolerates but does not officially acknowledge.[6] The beneficiaries of collusion are welfare service providers, poorly paid but usually organized and electorally important interest groups—for example, doctors' associations—without whose acquiescence the government would face a political crisis. By tolerating collusive welfare provision governments buy the acquiescence, if not actual support, of these key interest groups (Kochanowicz 1997; Cain and Surdej 1999). The best example of such collusion is the Slovak and Polish government's tolerance of doctors taking bribes from patients to perform nominally free procedures. If the doctors had, in fact, to live on their official salaries alone, the health care system would grind to a halt. The result of such collusion is gaps in policy implementation that give rise to de facto particularistic and inequitable policies (Lewis 2000). The social security system and disability pensions, in particular, provide a good example of this phenomenon. In the absence of effective administrative regulation, the multitude of different pension categories—each with its particular benefits—opens the door for collusion. The lax control of disability pensions in Poland led to an explosion in the number of such claims virtually overnight.

The second feature of "fictitious universalism" is the persistence of policy loopholes and implementation gaps that undermine the ability of the state to live up to the social safety net's ultimate purpose, assisting the most needy. The development of pension policy in Poland is a good example. To buy the acquiescence of its trade union core for its shock therapy economic program, the Solidarity governments of the early 1990s loosened eligibility requirements for early retirement and expanded retirement benefits (Hausner 2001, 213). These policies quickly led to an explosion in both the number of pensioners and state expenditure on their pensions, a development that benefited certain classes of pensioners and imperiled the whole social security system. The following postcommunist governments found it very difficult to correct the course of the Polish pension system.

The following sections will present case-study comparisons of the social security and health care systems in Poland, the Czech Republic, and Slovakia. Social security policy has the advantage of being the best area of welfare policy in which to quantify expenditure growth because pension benefits are accounted for on the books—even if there may be collusion in qualifying for them. The same certainly cannot be said of the health care system. Because so many of the procedures performed are accounted for off the books—which, of course, is not to say that they are free—the aggregate expenditure numbers are suspect. Perversely, the more collusion goes on, the smaller the health care system will look in terms of official expenditures. The obvious drawback, then, is that health care systems are harder to compare in terms of expansion. However, there is a hidden virtue for the argument advanced here: health care offers the best window on collusion. For both policies, the metric for comparing these three countries will be the timing of reform, the success of implementation, and the ability of the state to meet its legal commitments to universalism.

HEALTH CARE

This section first presents the broad picture of state performance in the arena of health care, in terms of aggregate expenditures, level of corruption, and public satisfaction. Official health care expenditures are of roughly the same level in these three countries, but there are sharp differences in terms of both the degree of petty corruption and overall public satisfaction with the quality of health care. In the Czech Republic, under-the-table payments for nominally free benefits are rare; such is not the case in Poland and Slovakia. This accounts for the higher levels of public satisfaction with the health care system in the Czech Republic. The second part of this section compares the ability of each country's governments to initiate and see through necessary reforms to the system. Where the Polish and Slovak governments delayed tackling health care for most of the 1990s, the Czech government radically reformed the system in the beginning of the 1990s. Czech governments also proved more consistent and capable in seeing through the implementation of health care reforms.

Although the World Health Organization's more recent estimates of health care expenditures as a percent of gross domestic product (GDP) put only a percentage point of difference among Poland, the Czech Republic, and Slovakia, looking over time reveals sharper contrasts between these countries' health care systems (see Figure 6.1).[7] Despite the very moderate expansion of the Czech state administration in the transition to democracy, it had the greatest expansion in health care spending from 1990 levels among these three countries. Between 1990 and 1993, Czech health care expenditures rose by two percentage points of GDP, though after this point they remained constant for the rest of the 1990s. In Poland, on the other hand, the initial spike of health care expenditure after 1990 was less extreme, and since 1991, expenditures as a percentage of GDP have actually declined slightly. In Slovakia, the overall trend has been more volatile. The initial increase in expenditures was more gradual than in the Czech Republic and Poland, but there was a second sharp spike from 1995 to 1997 (under the second Movement for a Democratic Slovakia [HZDS] government) followed by a steady decline in expenditure from 1997 onward.

The apparent profligacy of the Czech state health care system was, paradoxically, a sign of the success of the governments' health reforms. Unlike both Poland and Slovakia, the Czech health care reforms after 1989 largely succeeded in monetizing health care—that is, eliminating informal, collusive arrangements between health care providers and patients—a step that provides the foundations for policy rationalization and increasing effectiveness. Moreover, the "profligacy" of the Czech health care system is, indeed, only apparent. Because official health care expenditures cannot account for the existence of widespread informal payments, expenditure accounting in Poland and Slovakia presents an incomplete, even distorted, picture of reality. The more prevalent collusion is, the less expansive the state health care system will appear in the official statistics, and it may well be that combined formal and informal expenditures outpace those in the Czech Republic.

Two independent research projects conducted in the region confirm that the practice of making informal payments for nominally free procedures is prevalent in Poland and Slovakia but rare in the Czech Republic (see Table 6.1). Maureen Lewis of the World Bank has carried out the most thorough cross-national study of collusion in Eastern European health care systems, using public opinion surveys to estimate the frequency of informal payments across countries.[8] Unfortunately, Lewis's study does not include the Czech Republic, but another study by the World

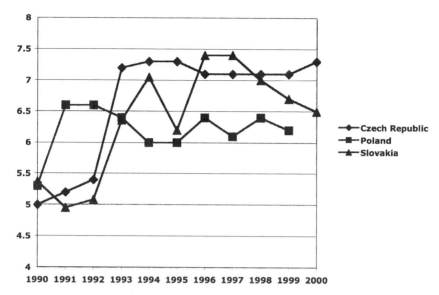

Fig. 6.1. Official Health Care Expenditures as a Percentage of GDP. From World Health Organization's *Health for All Database,* http://hfadb.who.dk/hfa/

Health Organization, which provides a related measure of collusion by ranking 191 countries in terms of their fairness, does.[9] Poland and Slovakia ranked at the top of a cross-national comparison of the frequency of informal payments in the health care sector. A staggering 78 percent of health care visits in Poland were financed through informal payments.[10] Moreover, time-series data for Poland indicate that the scope of informal payments has been growing since 1989: "In Poland, real household expenditures [on health care] climbed almost fivefold between 1990 and 1997, despite the fact that free health care is enshrined in the country's constitution and private options are few" (Lewis 2000, 18).[11] Slovakia polled somewhat lower in terms of the incidence of bribes, at 60 percent.[12] The fairness ranking provided by the World Health Organization awards the Czech Republic the highest ranking in Eastern Europe, even ahead of Slovenia. Poland ranks twice as far down the list. While not entirely absent, under-the-table payments for medical services are significantly lower in the Czech Republic.[13]

Reflecting the gap between legal welfare entitlements and actual welfare benefits—a gap filled by informal payments—the public's evaluation of the health care system is lower in Poland than in the Czech Republic, the two countries for which comparable survey data are available. As Table 6.2 indicates, only 19.6 percent of Czechs expressed dissatisfaction with their health care system in a 2002 poll,

TABLE 6.1.
Prevalence of Informal Payments for Health Care in Selected Countries

Country	Frequency of Informal Payments for Health Care	Ranking on WHO's "Fairness Index" (1 = most fair, 191 = least fair)
Armenia	91%	—
Poland	78	150
Azerbaijan	78	—
Kyrgyz Republic	75	—
Russia	74	185
Moldova	70	—
Tajikistan	66	—
Slovakia	60	88
Latvia	31	—
Bulgaria	21	—
Slovenia	—	82
Czech Republic	—	71
United States	—	54
France	—	26
Germany	—	6

SOURCE: Lewis (2000: 18); WHO (2001)

compared with 47.7 percent of Poles. Although the time frame for comparison is only one year, almost twice as many Poles (39 percent) were likely to have seen deterioration in the quality of health care as Czechs (22.9 percent).[14]

In comparison with Poland and Slovakia, then, the Czech welfare state has done far more to close the gap between legal welfare entitlements and actual benefits in the health care sector. The Czech welfare state's higher health care spending is a sign of monetizing the system, of eliminating "fictitious universalism." A second standard by which to evaluate welfare state development in Eastern Europe is in terms of the willingness and capacity of governments to undertake and see through welfare reform. The following sections trace this story through each country, linking the success or failure of the reform effort to the parameters for government action set by the differing logics of party competition.

Czech Health Care: Early Reform, Consistent Implementation

Of these three countries, the Czech Republic implemented health care reforms the earliest and most consistently. According to a recent survey of the Czech health care system: "A dense network of general practitioners, hospital and ambulatory services, maternity care and generous distribution of drugs and medical aids, all

TABLE 6.2.
Public Satisfaction with the Health Care System in the Czech Republic and Poland
(December 2002)

Overall, how satisfied or dissatisfied are you with the health care system in your country?

	Very to fairly satisfied	Neither satisfied nor dissatisfied	Fairly to very dissatisfied
Czech Republic	40.5%	37.5%	19.6%
Poland	25.4	23.0	47.7

In your opinion, has the quality of health care in your country in the last year . . .

	Strongly to moderately improved	Stayed the same	Moderately to strongly deteriorated
Czech Republic	20.8%	47.4%	22.9%
Poland	9.7	44.8	39.0

SOURCE: Central European Opinion Research Group (2002)
NOTES: n = 1,051 for the Czech Republic, n = 986 for Poland

funded by public resources, provides wide health coverage. This has helped to achieve a remarkable improvement in the health status of the population since the early years of transition, at a pace unmatched in the region with the exception of Slovenia" (OECD 2003, 71). It was the only country to successfully establish a system of health care insurance funds that consistently met their financial obligations, competed with each other for patients, and provided benefits without the need for informal payments (Vepřek et al. 2000); in contrast, Slovakia's health care insurance funds did not meet their financial obligations, and in Poland, health care insurance funds were introduced in 1998–99 only to be dismantled by the next government. The Czech reform was filled, it is true, with design mistakes that helped fuel the initial spike in aggregate expenditures. It should be emphasized, however, that reforming the communist-era health care system is a massive task, and it seems unrealistic to expect complete success immediately. The initial loopholes in the reform have largely been addressed over time. The precondition for the Czech Republic's reform success was the strength of its party competition, which generated governments with enough organizational coherence and stability to undertake a sustained reform effort.

The first step toward reforming the Czech health care system after 1989 was to dismantle the territorially organized administration of the communist system, decentralizing and privatizing the network. In 1991, the regional and district organization of hospitals and clinics was abolished. Smaller facilities such as clinics and small hospitals, which constituted the majority of hospitals and clinics, were transferred to municipalities and districts, becoming legally and financially independent of the Ministry of Health (Marrée and Groenewegen 1997, 59). These changes removed direct state influence from the staffing and budgeting decisions of hospitals and clinics. They also spurred the development of the physical network of the health care system, with the number of units expanding from 142 state-owned facilities in 1989 to 24,500 in 1998 (OECD 2003, 79). Privatization also increased the number of doctors working in private practice, which now includes about 60 percent of physicians (OECD 2003, 80). Establishing a viable private health care sector is important because it helps eliminate the kind of quasi-private, or corrupt, practices that emerge in a partially reformed or unreformed health care system.

The second step of Czech health care reform was the 1992 establishment of a fee-for-service system financed by third-party payers, newly created insurance funds. This step effectively separated health care funding from supply. The first insurance fund was the General Health Insurance Company (GHIC), which was operationally autonomous of the central government. In the first year of its operation, GHIC was funded by the Ministry of Finance and from the state budget (Marrée and Groenewegen 1997, 61). Beginning in January 1993, however, GHIC's financial dependence on the state ceased, as it began to collect premiums directly from those it ensured. The working population pays premiums in the form of a payroll tax, which is supplemented by their employers. The rest of the population is covered by the state, so that the system offers universal coverage of basic hospital and physician services. The reform also provided for private health insurance funds to operate alongside GHIC. Like GHIC, the private health funds were financed through the same payroll taxes and employer contributions, with the state making contributions for the rest of the population. People were free to choose among the funds; each guaranteed the same basic benefits, so that competition would occur on the basis of providing extra services such as limited dental care. The health funds were intended to act as third-party payers, negotiating contracts with hospitals, clinics, and private doctors on behalf of their insured. The state provided the framework for this negotiation in the form of a so-called points system.[15]

It soon became clear that there were mistakes in the Czech reform plan. Doctors overestimated the time spent on procedures by as much as two times (Massaro et. al 1994), and the number of procedures claimed jumped dramatically. There was little incentive for either patients or doctors to economize. Health care spending rose much more dramatically in the Czech Republic than in Poland or Slovakia as a result. In inflation-adjusted terms, it jumped by almost 40 percent in the year following the introduction of the reform (Marrée and Groenewegen 1997, 64). There were too many health funds, and competition among them was clearly not keeping costs down.

There was an important benefit to the reform, though: it introduced transparent and full-cost accounting—largely eliminating the need for informal payments—while at the same time preserving universal access. Equally important, the Czech government acted quickly to "reform the reform," preserving its basic principles but tightening loopholes in the system. In 1994, it passed amending legislation that introduced budgetary caps and readjusted compensation mechanisms for doctors to cut down overbilling. This legislation also standardized the benefits packages among funds. Again in 1997, the legislative basis for the health care system was amended, with adjustments to payment and financing mechanisms that preserved universal access and public financing (OECD 2003, 81–82). Over time, a number of less successful insurance funds exited, and their patients transferred to GHIC without disruption to their health care.[16]

From a comparative perspective, then, the Czech health care reforms were a considerable success. First, they provided for a consistent and high level of public financing. "Health care expenditures have grown at a smoother pace than the institutional turmoil might have implied. Somewhat surprisingly, the Czech Republic demonstrates the lowest annual variance of its health expenditures as a percentage of GDP among *all* OECD countries since 1995" (OECD 2003, 82, emphasis added). The ability to fully, publicly, and consistently fund what is, after all, a formally public health care system is the sign of a state that is meeting its welfare obligations. In contrast, OECD figures for Poland show that public expenditures on health as a percentage of total public expenditures have dropped from around 90 percent in 1990 to as low as 65 percent in 1997 (83). The corresponding statistic for the Czech Republic is over 90 percent throughout the 1990s. Second, the Czech system has low corruption and high fairness since under-the-table payments are a rarity. Finally, the reform was undertaken early, and its institutions were preserved and improved over time.

The reason that the Czech health care reforms achieved relative success was that the Czech political system provided stable governments interested in more than just the short term and balanced by a credible opposition, which kept the government responsive to the electorate. The first phase of Czech welfare reform reflected the market-oriented principles of Václav Klaus's Civic Democratic Party (ODS), most notably, the idea of cost competition among private health insurance funds. As the problems in this reform became apparent and as the pressure from the growing Social Democratic party to maintain social protections in the economic transition became stronger, the ODS governments chose to correct the reform mistakes "social democratically"—that is, through greater government regulation—rather than neoliberally, through more deregulation (Rueschemeyer and Wolchik 1999). For example, the government used its role in managing financing negotiations between health insurance funds and health providers to regulate and contain prices (OECD 2003, 85). The stability of the Czech governments was the prerequisite for reform consistency over time.

Polish Health Care: Late Reform, Inconsistent Implementation

In addition to its ubiquitous under-the-table payments for nominally free procedures, the notable characteristic of the health care system in postcommunist Poland was the absence of any major reforms until 1999. The governments tinkered around the edges of the system, but the essence of the system changed little from the pre-1989 period (Nelson 2001). The system was (under)funded through the national budget (hence, through general taxation), rather than through third-party payers.[17] Public financing of the system was volatile and declined throughout the 1990s, with informal financing left to take up the slack. Informal payments became so widespread that the Ministry of Health felt compelled to issue a formal letter prohibiting "the charging of any patient entitled to state health care," but as area expert Frances Millard noted, "the letter appeared to make little difference" (1995, 183). Whereas the state health network was quickly privatized in the Czech Republic, in Poland the state continued to own and operate the majority of hospitals and clinics. A small network of private clinics existed, but it constituted an insignificant portion of the health care sector as a whole. The official salaries of health care personnel were risibly low, but unofficially they were often much higher. As the Polish political scientist Jacek Kochanowicz wrote in a 1997 article,

> In the public health care system, reforms are opposed by lobbies of highly placed bosses of Poland's clinics and hospital wards. The existing system allows them to realize high incomes through private practice, often executed on the premises of public health care institutions. Since they control patients' access to public medical facilities, which are in short supply, not surprisingly they do not lack private patients. As for the lower-level medical personnel, such as nurses, they also find accommodation within the existing system due to private, untaxed payments from patients searching for better care. In both cases, the monopoly of ill-functioning and partly corrupt state institutions is only slightly affected by the emerging private sector, which mostly serves the more affluent members of society. (1997, 1446)

In short, Poland's weak-governance party system was incapable of producing governments with sufficient stability and coherence to attempt reform: governments avoided risking their fragile majorities on a difficult reform like health care and tolerated widespread collusion (Millard 1995). When reform was finally initiated in

1999, it was implemented disastrously—so disastrously, in fact, that the reform was essentially repealed in 2003 and the institutions it had established were abolished.

The inertia of the Polish health care system made 1999's major reform led by the post-Solidarity Electoral Action Solidarity (AWS) all the more surprising. As already described, this was a sprawling, internally divided government—not, at first glance, the type one would expect to be able to rationalize and provide coherent direction for the ailing health care system. As it turned out, the AWS government's reform of the health care system was very similar to its reform of regional governance (see Chapter 6). It was a plan that originated with, and was developed by, teams of policy experts; that was envisioned as a comprehensive rather than incremental reform; and that was eviscerated by political parties once it entered the parliamentary arena.

The basic principles of the reform were to introduce competition into the health care system which, it was hoped, would improve the quality of care and rationalize prices (Włodarczyk 1999). To this end, the original reformers envisioned establishing a number of health care insurance funds (*kasy chorych*), which patients could choose among and which could negotiate directly with hospitals and clinics about the prices for procedures—much like the system in the Czech Republic. Such a system makes sense on two conditions: if patients can choose their funds and the funds compete against each other. The actual enacted reform prevented either condition from happening. Funds were defined on a regional (that is, territorial) basis, meaning patients could not choose a fund in a different region. With no incentive to compete for patients, funds had little incentive to compete with each other to provide the best services for a given price (Włodarczyk 2000; Tymowska 2000).

Establishing the funds on a regional, territorial basis reflected the kind of political compromise necessary within a government coalition as large and heterogeneous as AWS. Because government reformers perceived their window of opportunity for reform to be short, they linked health care reform to the regional decentralization reform described in Chapter 4. Linking the reforms seemed the more sure path to their passage, rather than waiting to attempt each consecutively.[18] Thus the health care reform established the health insurance funds as regional political institutions, managed by boards appointed by the newly established regional parliaments described in Chapter 4. With their large budgets and political importance, the fund boards became the subject of intense party interest, filled not with medical experts but with the politically connected (Walewski 1999; Fandrejewska-Tomczyk 2000; Jelonkiewicz 2000; Filinson, Chmielewski, and Niklas 2003, 396). This solution, which shared out state power among the host of small, often regionally centered, parties in the government coalition also made political sense in

Poland's fragmented party system. The AWS-led government's reform decentralized the state's health care monopoly in Poland—sharing out control of the state's resources among a bunch of political parties—but it did not eliminate the monopoly.

The reform also largely removed the health care system from central government control, which had negative consequences for both funding and the quality of care. When in the Czech Republic, the inevitable initial reform mistakes became apparent, the central government was able to tighten regulation and close loopholes. One way it did so was by supervising negotiations between the health insurance funds and the service providers. In Poland, decentralization made this impossible: as one analyst put it, the regional health insurance funds operated as "independent princedoms" (Golinowska 2001, 11). Many of the regional insurance funds proved unable to manage their budgets and quickly ran into debt, prompting the wry observation that the best time of year to get sick in Poland is the beginning of the year, before the regional health insurance funds have used up their budgeted allotment (Jelonkiewicz 2000).[19] Disparities in treatment and access also emerged between regions, undermining the promise of universalism (Czerwińska 2002). Heavily indebted, poorly functioning, and widely unpopular, the health care insurance funds were dissolved in 2002 by the next government, which was led by the Democratic Left Alliance (SLD).[20] As one Polish expert noted, the health care funds' "only advantage is that they have *begun* to be governed by economic calculations—however ineptly—and have imposed these criteria on both public and non-public health care centers" (Hubert Izdebski, quoted in Czerwińska 2002, emphasis added).

More than ten years after the transition from communism began, the system has only begun to be rationalized; the gap between legal entitlements and actual benefits remains; and real reform has yet to be undertaken. Reform came late and then did not survive a change of government.

Slovak Health Reform: A Squandered Opportunity

To many Slovaks, the near-death experience of Slovakia's president Rudolf Schuster in 2000 seemed emblematic of the decline of the Slovak health care system. The president checked into one of the country's top hospitals for a routine operation. This procedure was performed poorly, and the president's wound became infected. His condition became so bad that a priest was called to administer the last rites. After he was given several hours left to live, it was decided to evacuate him by helicopter to Vienna for an emergency operation. The Viennese doctors were able to rescue him, and he eventually recuperated. That even the head of state should receive such poor treatment seemed to illustrate how far the health care system had fallen.

The Slovak health care system makes for an illuminating comparison with the Czech one because both countries began 1992 with the same health care system. The elections that year dissolved the federal state and set Slovakia on the trajectory of dominant-party politics, after which the trajectories of the Slovak and Czech health care systems began to diverge (Demes 1997). The difference was one of reform implementation. Where the Czech governments adjusted financing and regulatory mechanisms to guarantee the universal benefits promised in the original reform, the Slovak governments under Mečiar neglected the system, and the post-Mečiar coalition after 1998 talked much of reform but accomplished little. The basic problems remain the same as at the beginning of the transition: shortages of needed supplies like prescription drugs, low salaries for medical professionals, and the extensive use of informal payments to contract medical services. As one expert report on Slovak health care put it, it is a system "dominated by high overemployment, low effectiveness, and a high level of abuse of the system" (Zajac and Pažitný 2001, 503). Thus, although the Slovak government inherited the same institutions for financing health care as in the Czech Republic, the state found itself chronically unable to meet its financial commitments. The result was a deteriorating level of care, clientelistic lobbying for scarce state funds, and political cronyism (Zajac and Pažitný 2001; Demeš 1997; Demeš et al. 1998).

On paper, the financing of health care in the Slovak system resembles the Czech one. Namely, services and facilities are in theory no longer funded directly from the national state budget, as they were in the communist period. In 1993, a General Health Insurance Fund (GHIF) was established, which served as a social insurance fund covering the whole population. All employees and employers contributed jointly to the fund according to their wages. The state was responsible for making contributions to the fund on behalf of the non-working population, for example, children, pensioners, and the unemployed. In January 1995, private health insurance companies were permitted to operate alongside the GHIF, the idea being to introduce some competition among the different funds. As in the Czech Republic, health care providers were to be compensated according to a points system for services provided; the value of each point would be determined by the state. The health insurance funds would then act as third-party financers, compensating health care providers according to the number of points they had provided. The elements of financing were basically the same as in the Czech Republic.

In practice, however, the system has not worked as billed (Lawson and Nemec 2003). First, the state has consistently been unable to meet its obligations to cover the nonworking population through its contributions to the GHIF. In 1994, the state's contribution was only 80 percent of the necessary amount to cover the non-working population (Marrée and Groenewegen 1997, 73). As a result, GHIF was unable to recompense health care providers fully. It was estimated that GHIF's reimbursement to hospitals was 60 to 85 percent of their real costs (73). Consequently, the Slovak system became increasingly cash-strapped and, with extensive political intervention by parliament, the financing criteria less transparent (Lawson and Nemec 2003, 227). As Figure 6.1 shows, the uncertain funding was reflected in much more volatile health care expenditures. The result has been ever more murky financing, with the state transferring its obligations to the private sector, a growing informational problem as no central registry of the insured has been established, and mounting debt problems among Slovak hospitals (Demes et al. 1998; "Minister zdravotníctva" 2001).

Since the early 1990s, there have been no systematic attempts to correct the implementation gaps in the health care system, just tinkering around the edges. As one study noted in comparing the statements of both the Mečiar and post-Mečiar governments with the actual situation on the ground,

> Taken together the governmental statements identify the main aims of the first decade after transition as improving efficiency, equity and the provider-patient relationship. But in practice, such aims have not been consistently realized, and by 2002 the Slovak system, and especially the hospital and insurance sectors, were heavily indebted. In addition, several crucial and chronic weaknesses remained. Specifically, these were low economic efficiency, a lack of evidence-based decisions, low relative pay and the attendant labor-retention problems, overlarge drugs bills and insufficiently effectively managed capital programs, and a general underdevelopment of preventive medicine. (Lawson and Nemec 2003, 230)

As one would expect in a dominant-party (variant 1) system, the Mečiar governments were not interested in reform. Though the anti-Mečiar coalition in government since 1998 has talked a lot about reform, it has been too divided internally to undertake one—as one would expect in a dominant-party (variant 2) system. As the president of the Association of Health Care Funds stated in an interview: "There is a lot of talk about transformation, but little is done. On the one hand, the [health] ministry maintains that transformation is at hand; on the other hand, it preserves the status quo in the form of minimum wages and has no motivation to take rationalizing measures" (quoted in Velecký and Biehunek 2001). An indifferent party machine and a fragile antimachine coalition have produced the result that one would expect in a dominant-party system, an absence of reform. As in Poland, the result was "fictitious universalism" and enduring inequities in service provision.[21]

SOCIAL SECURITY

Unlike health care, benefits and expenditures from social security are accounted for on the books; thus it provides a clear picture of the variation in public spending.[22] Like health care, however, the social security system proved ungovernable in countries where the absence of robust party competition made for weak governments. Poland, for example, delayed reform until well after the point that the explosion in pension expenditures threatened to undermine the social safety net. As in health care, it proved vulnerable to collusion, people taking advantage of lax administration to fraudulently claim benefits or, as in Slovakia, the legislation of preferential pension categories for "friends of the government." In this section, I first present the overall picture of spending and then move to country case studies on the timing and implementation of reform.

By virtue of a number of similar background features, pensions make for a nice comparison among these three countries. These countries began with a similar pre-1989 pension model and have been undergoing similar demographic trends in the last decade (Andrews and Rashid, 1996). At a very basic level, it was clear what all three countries had to do to reform their pension systems after 1989: they needed to establish a link between an individual's pension contributions and his or her benefits (Cain and Surdej 1999). In the communist era, pensions had been just another form of social redistribution, which is to say that individuals' contributions to the social security system were only very loosely related to their eventual pensions; most people got very generous benefits regardless of their contributions (Fultz 2001).

The variation in the ability of government to control pension spending illustrates again the diversity of state-building outcomes after communism. As Figure 6.2 illustrates, the Polish pension system is clearly in a league of its own: between 1990 and 1994, Poland's pension spending climbed from 8.1 to 15.8 percent of GDP, nearly doubling. Attempts to wrestle these expenditures back down to earth only achieved modest results, with a decline to 14.1 percent of GDP in 1999. This kind of expenditure growth is nothing short of explosive and, as numerous scholars and Polish policy-makers have pointed out, potentially destabilizing for Poland's emerging market economy (Orenstein 1999; Ringold 1999, 43; Cain and Surdej 1999). It occurred because the first Solidarity governments tried to ameliorate the pain of un-

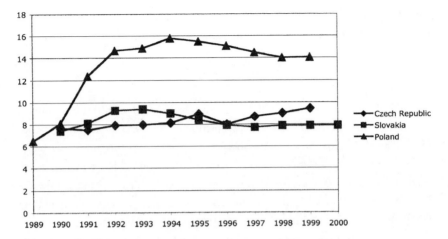

Fig. 6.2. Pension Expenditures as a Percentage of GDP. Czech Republic 1990–1993 figures are from Andrews and Rashid (1996: 31), later figures are the author's calculations using the *Statistical Yearbook of the Czech Republic* (1997 and 2000). Slovakia 1990–1993 figures are from Andrews and Rashid (1996: 31); later figures are the author's calculations using Gonda et al. (2002: 11). Poland 1989–1996 figures are from Cook and Orenstein (1999: 76); later figures are the author's calculations using the *Statistical Yearbook of the Republic of Poland* (2000).

employment by expanding eligibility for early retirement. Workers over a certain age who had been laid off by a restructuring firm automatically qualified for early retirement. Unsurprisingly, the number of pensioners skyrocketed. From 1989 to 1992, the retirement age population grew from 4.8 to 5.06 million people, while the number of people collecting pensions grew from 6.83 to 8.5 million.[23] The average retirement age for men fell to 57 years, although the official age remained 65. Although Poland's high unemployment rate contributed to the explosion, it was not the whole story. Pension benefits were also exceedingly generous: the average pension rose from being 43 percent of the average salary in 1989 to 65 percent in 1995. By way of comparison, in the Czech Republic the average pension declined from 62 percent of the average salary in 1990 to 44 percent in 1995. As rocketing pension expenditures imperiled the rest of the welfare state, the Polish government not only found it difficult to reduce the level of benefits, it increased them. Though the social insurance system was clearly spiraling into crisis—the system's indebtedness rose to 3.2 percent of GDP in 1995—meaningful reforms were delayed until 1998 because of political infighting.

After a sharp increase in expenditures in the early 1990s, Slovakia's pension system now looks better than Poland's in macro terms, but the system's foundations have been deteriorating steadily since 1997. As in Poland, the Slovak pension system bore a greater strain than the Czech one because of its higher unemployment rate, but as in Poland, this did not prompt the government to scale back generous benefits. As a percentage of the average wage, the average pension was increasing after 1990 until it stabilized at around 58 percent in 1995. Though governments ran steadily higher pensions deficits since 1997, they were unable to scale back the more generous pension benefits, and the long-term viability of the current system looks doubtful. In 2000, the system's indebtedness stood at just over 1 percent of GDP.

Of the three countries, the Czech Republic has managed pension politics with relative aplomb. Pension expenditure relative to GDP did not spike sharply in the early 1990s, and it has remained level since then. The pension system has run a small surplus since 1994. Although part of its success was due to its lower unemployment rate, the Czech Republic was virtually alone among the countries of the region in scaling back benefits and tightening eligibility criteria in the early 1990s. This is not to say that the Czech government proved unresponsive to the electorate. Under pressure from the Social Democrats, Klaus's ODS moderated the neoliberal pension reforms that it had originally envisioned.

Poland's Social Security System

Social security spending exploded in Poland because necessary reforms were delayed, and lax administration failed to prevent widespread collusion—that is, fraudulent benefits claims. Polish governments of both the post-Solidarity and postcommunist persuasions used generous social security benefits to buy quiescence from important political groups in order to maintain fragile parliamentary majorities (Hausner 2001; Cain and Surdej 1999). Much of the increase in social security expenditures in Poland in the 1990s resulted from the success of veto players in blocking reforms to the status quo and, to a lesser extent, lobbying for preferential pension conditions. The overrepresentation of unions in the core government parties—the Solidarity Union in AWS and the All-Poland Trade Union (OPZZ) in SLD—posed a difficult internal political obstacle to all reform proposals. Not until 1998, when the system was in full-blown crisis, did the government undertake a more substantive reform to the status quo. This delay is all the more notable given that, as Joan Nelson (2001) has argued, social security reform is one of the few welfare reforms for which there is a clear reform template fostered by international advisory institutions like the World Bank. Poland's 1998 reform, which essentially privatized the pension system, reflected this reform template, but the template was available long before that.

In the early 1990s, the Solidarity governments used generous pension benefits and loosened eligibility criteria to defuse social unrest in the face of mounting un-employment (Cain and Surdej 1999, 148–49). Solidarity was, after all, a trade union at its core, and its leadership's espousal of shock therapy steadily eviscerated the party's social support base. Providing generous pensions to laid-off union members was an attempt to buy breathing space for bigger reforms like macroeconomic shock therapy and privatization. The thinking of the economic reformers at the time was that speed of reform was the primary consideration. The idea was to keep open the window of opportunity for reform as long as possible, even at great cost, because if the reforms were accomplished quickly the costs could be recouped af-ter the economy started to grow again. With the benefit of hindsight, it is clear that the strategy of defusing social unrest through easy pensions was in fact simply a very expensive unemployment policy. Looking back at that period, Leszek Bal-cerowicz, the architect of Poland's shock therapy, has since named "the failure to take on pension reform as the biggest mistake of Poland's first reform government" (quoted in Charlton, McKinnon, and Konopielko 1998, 1416).

It would be unfair, however, to lay all of the blame for Poland's social security problems at the feet of the first Solidarity governments. As the country's weak-governance logic of party competition would lead one to expect, social security ex-penditures mounted regardless of the party constellation in government. Some commentators have argued that it was Solidarity's ambitions to reform pension pol-icy in 1992–93 that finally undid the party's slim governmental majority in 1993 (Orenstein 1999; Ringold 1999). When the alarming trend of pension spending be-came clear, the liberal, reformist wing of the Solidarity leadership had begun float-ing proposals for reform. Saving social security became one of the rallying cries of the postcommunists in the 1993 elections (Hausner 2001).

The experience of the postcommunist SLD governments of 1993–1997 with so-cial security policy was strongly reminiscent of that of their Solidarity predecessors. A rift developed in the SLD over whether to reform or sustain the expanding social security system (Hausner 2001). A smaller clique of liberals favored cutting back be-nefits, tying contributions to benefits, and privatizing the system; a larger base of the rank and file wanted to protect the status quo. In terms of actual policy, social security expenditures and benefits continued to expand. The issue was also com-plicated by the campaign of the Polish Peasant Party to protect agricultural pen-sions that, thanks to their generous benefits and very low contribution rate, were a drag on the system. In 1996, the SLD-led government adopted a limited reform, which consisted of new rules linking pensions to prices instead of the average wage—a far cry from the more radical pension privatization being advocated by economic experts.

In both Poland and Slovakia, lax administration allowed for rampant collusion, which in addition to fueling the expansion of pension expenditures, undermined the fairness of the system. The parties involved in social security collusion are numerous and often operate independently of each other. An incomplete list would include individuals who fraudulently claim disability pensions, individuals who draw pensions and remain employed, and companies (often state-owned) that do not pay the required social security contribution for their employees. The overall effect for public spending is death by a thousand cuts. One form of collusion was the widespread underreporting of earnings (Cain and Surdej 1991, 153). If the management and the workers could agree to nominally report a much lower wage than the actual one, both parties would pay less in payroll taxes. This meant higher wages for the employees, bigger profits for the firm, but dwindling financing for the pension system as a whole.

A second form of collusion was in disability pensions, which constitute a subset of the social security system as a whole (Hoopengardner 2000; Hausner 2001). In a obvious sign of runaway expenditure growth, by the end of the 1990s the volume of spending on disability insurance in Poland climbed to among the highest in Europe, at approximately 3.3 percent of GDP (Hoopengardner 2000, v). Only the Netherlands outspent Poland, at 3.4 percent of GDP. Germany spent only 0.8 percent of GDP on disability pensions and Sweden only 2.4 percent. The number of beneficiaries of disability insurance grew from 9.6 percent of the adult Polish population in 1988 to 14.3 percent in 1996 (17). Disability pensions were serving as a kind of ersatz unemployment insurance during Poland's shock therapy. As a World Bank study of Poland's disability pensions noted, "It seems that there are so many beneficiaries in Poland because of generous treatment of people with the least serious kinds of disabilities, easy eligibility criteria, and lax enforcement" (v). Though it was widely known what was happening, Polish governments preferred to turn a blind eye. Doing so would have meant risking their slim majorities. Until the accumulating problems turn into a full-blown crisis, social security reform is difficult in a weak-governance party system.

Slovakia's Social Security System

The development of Slovakia's social security system has been less explosive than in Poland but less stable than in the Czech Republic. Because the Czech and Slovak systems were entirely identical in terms of benefits, contributions, and eligibility criteria until the revolution in 1989—and largely identical until the breakup of the federation in 1993—the divergence of the two systems over the 1990s makes for a particularly interesting comparison. In the early 1990s, Slovakia was classified by social security experts as one of the region's risk cases (Andrews and Rashid 1996). After 1996, however, the macroeconomic situation stabilized somewhat, which improved the situation of the social security system. There have been no significant reforms to the system, however, and as more recent studies have pointed out, the microlevel fundamentals of the Slovak system are increasingly difficult to sustain (Gonda and Jakoby 2001). As would be expected in a dominant-party system, neither the machine-style governments of HZDS nor the fractious, internally divided governments of the anti-Mečiar parties had the inclination (in the case of the former) or the mandate (in the case of the latter) to carry out a much-needed reform of the system.

From 1990 to 1993, Slovakia's social security system grew at one of the fastest rates in the region—after Poland, of course. By 1993, pension expenditures had grown to 9.4 percent of GDP, from 7.4 percent in 1990 (Andrews and Rashid 1996, 31). According to Andrews and Rashid, the chief reason for this rapid growth was a sharp decline in the number of contributors paying into the system, one of the region's sharpest such declines (7). In large part, this decline was the result of high unemployment, but unemployment was not the whole of the story. Lax administration allowed widespread informal employment, which was also a large factor; Poland, which also saw very high unemployment in this period, did not experience a comparable decline in the number of contributors to the social security system (7). During this period Slovakia also provided comparatively generous pension benefits (1). While the Czech government was trimming social security benefits during this period, the Slovak governments would not risk touching them.

Although an improving employment situation caused overall expenditures to level off in Slovakia in the mid-1990s, the microfundamentals of the social security system have been deteriorating ever since. The current level of benefits look increasingly unsustainable, and the link between an individual's contributions and pension benefits needs to be established. In 2000, the Slovak government was forced to bail out the indebted social security fund with an emergency transfer of SK 7.7 billion, which amounted to about 6 percent of pension expenditures for that year; according to projections, the social security deficit will grow to SK 44.5 billion in 2030 if the system remains in its present form (Gonda and Jakoby 2001, 775–76).

Aspects of Slovakia's social security system bore the strong imprint of dominant-party politics. Under Mečiar, politically connected interest groups gained access to the design and implementation of the pension system, which resulted in pension criteria specially suited to narrow interests. A good example was the development of the pensions of the interior and defense ministries. In the mid-1990s, Mečiar's government allowed these ministries to write their own pension rules. Unsurprisingly, professional soldiers and the police soon commanded very advantageous pension benefits, which they have been loath to give up under subsequent government plans to reform the social security system (Woleková and Radičová 2001, 371–72). The Slovak social security system is, in fact, rife with such special categorizations, which assign people to different pension categories based on often arbitrary criteria. Since the state sets these categories and their eligibility criteria, there is considerable room for awarding special advantages to certain groups regardless of their past contributions to social security. By contrast, the Czechs abolished such special pension categories in 1992 (371).

The Czech Social Security System

The Czech Republic's social security system has been one of the most stable in the region. Systemic reform was undertaken early and followed through consistently, with tighter administration of benefits and less collusion. This made the system more fair and meant that pension expenditure never imperiled the rest of the social safety net, as it did in Poland (and initially in Slovakia). From 1990 to 1998, pension expenditures were level at around 8 percent of GDP. They rose to about 9 percent under the Social Democratic governments after 1998. In contrast to Poland and Slovakia, the Czech governments tightened eligibility criteria and refused to expand benefits during the early stages of the economic transition. In addition to the Czechs' rosier overall picture, the financing of the system has been much more stable as well. Whereas both Poland and Slovakia have consistently run social security deficits, the Czech system has built up a small surplus.

The controlled growth of pension spending in the Czech Republic resulted from the conservative policies of the ODS governments from 1992 through 1997. It was a testament to the strength of its party organization that ODS was able to survive being identified with, and actually carrying out, a plan to cut back on pension benefits. In keeping with their emphasis on market efficiency and individual responsibility, ODS introduced a second tier of private pensions to supplement a universal, flat-rate state pension. The ODS-led governments also managed to push back the retirement age from 60 to 62 years for men and from 53–57 to 57–61 years for women, but the proposal sparked a national strike of 25,000 workers in March 1995. It also produced a large rift in the government coalition, with the Christian Democrats calling for the law's repeal and ODS threatening to expel them from the coalition (Večerník 1996, 199; Orenstein 1996, 18).

The ODS governments found that they could only take their conservative reforms of the pension system so far, as they encountered stiff resistance from the Czech Social Democratic Party (ČSSD). For instance, to encourage the use of the private tier of pensions, they also proposed decreasing the size of the average flat-rate pension in proportion to the average wage from around 45 percent to 35 percent. In the face of opposition from ČSSD, this proposal was withdrawn. Second, because of the political opposition, financing is still on a defined benefit basis rather than a defined contribution one. Finally, as Večerník points out, the effect of the reforms has been to further loosen the link between contributions and earnings—counter to the advice of World Bank advisors (1996, 200).

In the last years of the 1990s, pension spending—as with overall welfare spending—began to increase again in the Czech Republic. This increase is directly linked to the policies of the ČSSD, which formed a new government in 1998. The Social Democrats had campaigned on a program of expanding state assistance to those left behind in the economic transition (Ringold 1999; Rueschemeyer and Wolchik 1999). Does the emergence of greater pension spending in the Czech Republic under the Social Democrats challenge the runaway state-building hypothesis? On the contrary, policy adjustment following government alternation is what one would expect from accountable government. Czech voters felt that ODS's welfare policies were going too far, and the presence of a viable, organized opposition party allowed them to influence government policy. Just as ČSSD forced ODS to rein in many of their welfare reforms in the mid-1990s, so has ODS challenged ČSSD's expansion of welfare policy since 1998.

CONCLUSION

Welfare policy is another indication of state effectiveness: do governments ensure the welfare benefits that the state is legally entitled to provide, or does a kind of "fictitious universalism" prevail? Under what conditions does government undertake reform quickly and see it through consistently, despite the emergence of unforeseen contingencies? If, in the administration, runaway state-building means classic patronage politics—expanding personnel, wages, and political intervention in the guise of "reform"—it has different features in the welfare state: explosive increases in spending (including under-the-table spending), maintaining overemployment at the cost of petty corruption, and an unwillingness by the government to reform the unsustainable level of benefits of the communist-era welfare state. However, as with administrative state-building, there is a pattern to postcommunist welfare state-building that reflects differences in the logic of party competition. Governments in both weak-governance and dominant-party systems are more prone to "fictitious universalism," are slower to initiate welfare reform, and are less consistent in seeing it through than governments in responsible-party systems.

The failure of the Polish state administration to bureaucratize was abundantly evident in the aftermath of its reform of the health care sector in 1998, which created instant upheaval. Amid the general criticism that followed these reforms, even the reforms' defenders blamed the outcome on poor implementation and administration. The failures of bureaucratization in the Polish and Slovak state administrations impeded welfare reform in those countries throughout the 1990s and failed to reduce collusion. In the Czech Republic, however, the relative success of bureaucratization facilitated that country's more controlled and equitable welfare policies. It had a much better record of welfare reform in the 1990s. It arrested expenditure increases early, most notably in the social security system. It largely eliminated corruption in the health care system. In both health care and pensions, the Czech government was able to make difficult reforms early and see them through.

It is important to put the relative failures and successes of these three countries' welfare policies into larger perspective. As a result of their earlier and more successful macroeconomic reforms, their welfare states performed as a group at a much higher level than those of many other formerly communist countries, such as Russia, Romania, and Bulgaria. Yet even among these, the inability of party competition to create stable and coherent government adversely affected welfare outcomes. In Russia, whose politics under Yeltsin resembled the dominant-party (variant 2) logic,[24] the standoff between Yeltsin and the Communists produced a policy vacuum and a failure to reform.[25] In Bulgaria and Romania's weak-governance party systems it was difficult to generate governments strong enough to undertake much needed reforms of the health care system, for example. The link between the development of the party system and that of the welfare state is evident even among these poorer performing countries.

It is tempting, as an outside observer, to see yet another linkage between administrative and welfare state-building. The runaway welfare state is the citizen's revenge—the quid pro quo from the average citizen's point of view for an overweening and underperforming administrative apparatus. Nominally, the citizens retain many of the generous entitlements and benefits of the communist welfare state after the collapse of the communist system. The maintenance of this welfare state is a budgetary albatross around the necks of whichever parties sit in the government. Of course, in the end, it is far from clear which party has the last laugh, the parties in government or the welfare state's clients and collusive welfare providers.

Exporting the Argument

*Party Competition and State Effectiveness
in Other New Democracies*

Though the analysis in this book has leveraged the shared history and unique features of three countries to develop and test a series of hypotheses about state-building, its aim is not only to illuminate Polish, Czech, and Slovak state-building during their democratic transitions. The three causes of runaway state-building—demobilized societies, delegitimized states, and varying logics of party competition—are particularly evident in the postcommunist context, but these are not uncommon features of new democracies in which the introduction or reintroduction of electoral competition has preceded state consolidation. Where levels of trust in public institutions and participation in politics are low, the theory here would predict that the quality of party competition will be of more than usual importance to the development and performance of the state. In such countries, the introduction of democratic party politics may well lead to an expansion of patronage politics.

My intent has been to formulate a clear hypothesis about state-building and democratization and to advance a set of cross-national measures for applying it. The conceptualization and operationalization of party competition and bureaucratization map out a path for extending the research to a greater number of countries. Robust and institutionalized party competition can be distinguished by a discrete set of measurable indicators: low vote differential, a low fractionalization index, low electoral volatility, Peter Mair's composite index of party system closure, and centralized party organization (see Chapter 2). The criteria for empirically measuring the "Weberianness" of state administrations are political autonomy, separation of office and office-holder, predictable career paths, and a sense of administrative professionalism (see Chapter 3). Using these indicators to classify and compare other democratizing countries provides further insight into some of the variables held constant in the comparison of Poland, the Czech Republic, and Slovakia.

How well does a party competition framework travel as an explanation of state-building during democratization? What can it say about the larger universe of countries that have democratized since the 1980s? This chapter expands the hypotheses developed through the close analysis of Poland, the Czech Republic, and Slovakia to include this larger group. This kind of analysis is what Charles Tilly (1984) has called a "huge comparison," so several caveats are in order. Comparing new democracies in Eastern Europe, Latin America, Africa, and Asia in terms of a few variables requires controlling for very significant differences in economic development, ethnic heterogeneity, and basic institutional structure, to name just a few. The multivariate analysis here includes such controls, but there are, no doubt, many other structural factors that could be controlled for. The primary aim is to check whether the cross-national patterns of party competition and state development are consonant with the hypotheses and case-study analysis laid out in the previous chapters. In short, the results should be taken as indicative rather than definitive.[1]

THE DATASET AND THE ANALYSIS

There are, of course, tradeoffs to using a larger sample. Expanding the number of countries does not allow fine-grained measures and attention to the causal mechanisms of patronage politics. Instead, it is necessary to simplify the measures somewhat and to draw on the secondary literature pertaining to other new democracies. The biggest simplification is in finding an impartial, compact, and sensitive indicator of the development of the state administration which has broad cross-national coverage. Unfortunately, no good such measures of patronage exist. In-depth, multi-method country studies, such as those employed in this book, would be ideal, but their coverage is limited, and they are not always easily comparable. As noted in Chapter 1, the practical difficulties of finding comparable cross-national data on the rate of state administrative growth for a large sample of countries essentially rule out the kind of comparison in Chapter 3 (Schiavo-Campo, de Tommaso, and Mukherjee 1997). Faced with these constraints, I have opted to use a measure of the effectiveness and politicization of the state administration. This is Kaufmann, Kraay, and Mastruzzi's indicator of government effectiveness, which "combine[s] into a single grouping responses on the quality of public service provision, the quality of the bureaucracy, the competence of civil servants, the independence of the civil service from political pressures, and the credibility of the government's commitment to policies" (2003, 3). Not only a good composite measure of the effectiveness and politicization of the state administration, "government effectiveness" also has the virtue of being available over time, which allows one to trace how changes in the character of party system affect the development of the state administration.

The universe of cases here comprises the new democracies of Latin America, Asia, Africa, and the rest of postcommunist Eastern Europe. I selected cases from this universe based on the following considerations.[2] First, I only included countries that began democratization in 1980 and later. Countries that democratized earlier already had considerable time to tackle the problem of redefining the state by 1996, the time for which the first of Kaufmann, Kraay, and Mastruzzi's administrative effectiveness measures are available.[3] I looked only at countries that were ranked as at least "partly free" by the Freedom House within this time period and which were classified as either "liberal democracies," "electoral democracies," or "ambiguous" regimes by Larry Diamond in his recent typology of regimes (2002).[4]

The second criterion was to select those countries from within this group for which there existed significant secondary literature on party system development. The literature on party system institutionalization provides a coherent and rigorous set of measures for identifying when party competition is sufficiently developed to produce vertical accountability. Several scholars have, in fact, expanded the scope of Mainwaring and Scully's pioneering analysis of Latin American party systems to those in Asia and Africa. Both Kuenzi and Lambright (2001) and Riedl (2005) have analyzed the degree of institutionalization in African party systems. Stockton (2001), Tan (2004), and Johnson (2002) have compared institutionalization in Asia's new democracies. For Latin America, I use Mainwaring and Scully's edited volume (1995), supplementing it with more recent research on countries whose party systems since underwent important changes, such as Mexico and Peru. Combining this secondary literature on both party system development and government effectiveness allowed me to build the sample of 52 new democracies listed in full in Appendix 5.

The first step in this analysis is to classify party systems as having responsible-party, weak-governance, or dominant-party (variants 1 and 2) logics of competition. The two main criteria for classifying cases here are the degrees of single-party dominance and overall party system institutionalization. In dominant-party (variant 1) systems, a single party sustains a significant electoral advantage, or vote differential, over its competitor parties for at least two election cycles. As a rule of thumb, I characterize a party system as dominant-party (variant 1) if the governing party sustains an electoral advantage of greater than 20 percentage points relative to its nearest competitor over at least two elections.[5] If the governing party enjoys a 20-plus point electoral lead in one election but loses power in the subsequent election,

I do not consider this a dominant-party (variant 1) system. Instances of such huge electoral upsets typically occur in weak-governance systems, which are underinstitutionalized and highly volatile.[6]

Once the vote differential has been considered, the second classification criterion is the degree of party system institutionalization. Party system institutionalization is a more multifaceted phenomenon than can easily be captured by a single measure, especially in new democracies. Electoral volatility is perhaps the best single measure but can miss some patterns of increasing party system coherence and predictability.[7] That is why I supplement my categorization of these emerging party systems by drawing on aggregate indices of party system institutionalization available in the secondary literature, which include volatility as one of their components but are not limited to it.[8] A party system is classified as responsible-party if it has a comparatively low vote differential (below 20 percentage points) and is ranked as institutionalized in the secondary literature. I classify it as a weak-governance system if its vote differential is comparatively low, its volatility is high, and it is considered underinstitutionalized in the secondary literature.[9] Again, a dominant-party (variant 1) system has a high vote differential sustained over at least two elections; generally, it tends to have a higher level of institutionalization than a weak-governance system as a result of the greater organizational resources of the dominant party (see Chapter 2). Unstable configurations in the longer term, dominant-party (variant 2) systems emerge when a dominant government party loses an election and is replaced by a fluid and heterogeneous coalition of the opposition.[10] Unless these new governing coalitions can quickly consolidate themselves, such systems tend to revert to the weak-governance type or else fall back into the dominant-party (variant 1) logic if the old party machine is reelected.

Responsible-party systems can be expected to have the highest government effectiveness scores. Since the governing parties' penetration of the state administration is most concentrated and comprehensive in dominant-party (variant 1) systems, these can be expected to have the worst government effectiveness scores. Weak-governance systems may perform slightly better than the former, but given the coalition incentives faced by their governing parties and the absence of a credible opposition, their performance can be expected to rate significantly below that of the responsible-party type. Finally, since dominant-party (variant 2) systems follow the transition from machine-party rule and since the continued presence of the dominant machine in politics prevents radical reforms to the status quo, these systems should not differ substantially from dominant-party (variant 1) ones in terms of government effectiveness.

Before moving to the multivariate analysis, a quick overview of the distribution of the sample is helpful as a means of orientation. As one might expect for new democracies, the number of responsible-party systems is relatively small. Dominant-party (variant 1) systems are the most numerous, reflecting their over-representation in Africa in particular. Weak-governance systems are the second-most common and are well represented in every region in the sample. Dominant-party (variant 2) systems are the least frequent type in the sample.

The aggregate government effectiveness scores for each party system type conform with the expectations of the theory. Responsible-party systems have significantly higher government effectiveness scores than all other types (0.65 on a scale from −2.5 to 2.5). To put this in context, the Czech Republic and Uruguay are two responsible-party systems that fall very close to this mean score for the group. Dominant-party (variant 1) systems rank lowest (−0.36 on the scale); for most of the 1996–2002 period, Albania was quite close to the mean value for this class of new democracies. With a mean of −0.15, weak-governance systems also score significantly lower in terms of government effectiveness; Brazil is the weak-governance system that falls closest to this mean value.[11] As would be expected for a party system type that is more transitory, there were fewer cases of dominant-party (variant 2) systems, but their mean government effectiveness score was the second from worst at −0.22; the case closest to the mean here was Cape Verde.

Multivariate analysis can take this comparison a step further, allowing tests of the significance of these apparent differences between party systems and incorporating controls for the effects of some of the most obvious structural differences present in a sample of such disparate countries. For example, very large differences in the level of economic development will likely influence the effectiveness of the state; therefore, the multivariate regressions in Table 7.1 include per capita gross domestic product (GDP) in 1996 as a measure of the level of economic development.[12] Likewise, when ethnic heterogeneity increases beyond the comparatively modest scale present in Poland, the Czech Republic, and Slovakia, it may adversely impact state effectiveness. Philip Roeder's (2001) ethnolinguistic fractionalization index, which varies between 0 for a homogenous population and 1 for a maximally heterogeneous one, offers a compact indicator of this variable.[13] As the long-running debate between the advocates of presidentialism and parliamentarism contends, basic institutional differences may also influence government effectiveness; therefore, I include a simple variable on the strength of the parliament in each country.[14] Finally, reflecting a whole range of other structural factors—from political culture to the international environment—regional differences provide a way to probe the theory's exportability. To this end, the lower half of Table 7.1 presents region-specific regression results for the main variables.

Table 7.1 presents the results of a regression analysis on government effectiveness by party system type and incorporates control variables for economic development, ethnic heterogeneity, and presidential versus parliamentary institutions.[15] The lower half of the table breaks the sample down by region to explore if different patterns emerge at this level. Party system type is coded using four dummy variables; therefore, the "missing" party system term in each regression output serves as the comparative baseline for interpreting the coefficients for the other party system terms. For ease of interpretation, that dropped term in most of the models in Table 7.1 is responsible-party type, meaning that the coefficients for weak-governance, dominant-party (variant 1), and dominant-party (variant 2) can be interpreted as the effect of switching from a responsible-party system to any one of these other types.

For example, in Model 1, which looks only at the performance of party system type on government effectiveness, the negative coefficient for the weak-governance term indicates the size of the drop in government effectiveness if a country were to switch from a responsible-party to weak-governance party system: on average, it would mean a drop of 0.696 in its government effectiveness score.[16] As the theoretical predictions developed in Chapter 1 suggest, the adverse impact of switching from a responsible-party system is even greater if that switch is to a dominant-party system, worst of all if to a dominant-party (variant 1) system.

The full model—including all of the party system types and the control variables—is Model 3. The addition of the control variables somewhat reduces the size of the party system coefficients, but they are still substantively strong, statistically significant, and their ranking vis-à-vis government effectiveness unchanged. Somewhat surprisingly, increasing ethnic heterogeneity is associated with increasing government effectiveness, though its coefficient is substantively small and not statistically significant. As expected, higher levels of economic development mean greater government effectiveness. Though it is statistically very strong, the relationship seems modest substantively: a thousand-dollar increase in per capita GDP translates into a 0.1 increase on the government effectiveness scale, which amounts to about 3 percent of the full scale. Last, the regression indicates that, from the point of view of the effectiveness of the state administration, new democracies are better served by parliamentary institutions than presidential ones. Controlling for the big factors that differentiate the disparate countries in the sample does not much affect the coefficients for party system type: responsible-party systems are the best performers, and weak-governance systems maintain a slight edge vis-à-vis dominant-party ones.

Comparing Model 3 with Models 2 and 4 allows for some basic hypothesis testing of the effect of the different party system types. Model 2 can serve as a null hy-

TABLE 7.1.

Regressions of Government Effectiveness on Hypothesized Determinants and Separately By Region

Variable	Whole-Sample Regressions				Sub-Sample Regressions by Region		
	Model 1	Model 2	Model 3	Model 4	Eastern Europe	Latin America	Africa
Responsible Party				.4388229** (.095971)			
Weak Governance	-.6959431** (.1249078)		-.4267813** (.1062832)		-.6120306** (.1307498)	-1.18148** (.2979213)	-.0328595 (.0593549)
Dominant-Party var. 1	-.8033548** (.0890167)		-.4704287** (.0805731)		-.7699821** (.1513642)	-.839601** (.2992951)	-.2203978* (.0994947)
Dominant-Party var. 2	-.7853963** (.1097262)		-.4302407** (.1129245)		-.7689948** (.1408012)	Dropped	.1185586 (.2153366)
Per Capita GDP in 1996		.0001345** (.0000132)	.0001107** (8.17e-06)	.000111** (8.63e-06)	.0001387** (.0000288)	.0000541 (.0000553)	.1185586** (.2153366)
Ethnolinguistic Fractionalization		.0315671 (.1325016)	.105578 (.1325105)	.0888701 (.1433629)	-.2512041** (.0825056)	1.497751** (.4131963)	-.2711559 (.3704415)
Parliamentary System		.190676** (.0630877)	.196772** (.060865)	.193519** (.0639454)	-.0081302 (.0358668)	-.1435716 (.0993116)	.124994 (.1319444)
Constant		-.599804** (.0718098)	-.1995932* (.0882199)	-.6404053** (.0902823)	.2899055* (.1366597)	-.3747124 (.408112)	-.2272115 (.2817336)
R²	.1732	.3606	.4254	.4093	.4397	.5169	.5695
N	200	192	192	192	68	48	58

NOTES: The panel-corrected standard errors are reported in the parentheses. See note 14 for an explanation of the regression technique. I do not include a regional-level regression for Asia because there are not enough Asian country-cases in the sample for meaningful results. This variable is dropped here because there were no dominant-party (variant 2) systems in Latin America in the 1996–2002 time period.

*p < 0.05; **p < 0.01

pothesis stating that there is no difference between the different party systems in terms of government effectiveness.[17] Model 3 constitutes the alternative hypothesis, that the different party systems are not all equal in terms of their impact on government effectiveness. By means of an F-test, the null hypothesis can then be rejected at the 99 percent confidence level: the different party systems are not all equal.[18]

A comparison of Model 2 and Model 4 allows for a second, more fine-grained hypothesis test. Model 2 is again the null: there is no difference between the effect of the various party systems. Model 4 states that the effect of responsible-party systems is systematically different from that of the others as a group.[19] This alternative hypothesis allows a more direct test of the general proposition at the heart of this book, that robust party competition in institutionalized party systems leads to a more effective and less politicized state administration. Again, an F-test comparing the two models easily rejects the null hypothesis in favor of the alternative at the 99 percent confidence level.[20]

The robustness of these results indicates that this theoretical framework can be usefully exported to other new democracies. Party system development has a demonstrable effect on the capacity of state administration to implement government policies in new democracies, even after controlling for macrostructural variables such as economic development, ethnic heterogeneity, and presidential versus parliamentary institutions. In particular, responsible-party systems have significant advantages over their alternatives.

The question remains as to whether there are regional variations underlying the broad patterns presented above. In other words, does this framework do a better job in some regions than others? The other half of Table 7.1 presents the results of running the regression in Model 3 separately by region. In order to probe the regional trends suggested in these regressions more deeply, the following sections comment briefly on the development of party systems and states in the different regions.

Eastern Europe

This region provides a diversity of developmental trajectories for party systems in new democracies. Evolving from a common starting point of weak governance, by 1996 the patterns of party system divergence were becoming clear. This is not to say, of course, that the final contours of party competition were in place by 1996. A number of party systems have transitioned between types since 1996—some, like Russia or Serbia, in a dramatic rupture, others, like Estonia, as a part of a more gradual process of institutionalization. As the regression output for the Eastern Europe column of Table 7.1 shows, the link between the development of robust party competition and the effectiveness of the state administration comes through very clearly in a broader comparison of the region. The party system differences are, if anything, bigger than for the whole sample (Model 3). The ranking of the different party system types is unchanged, and the coefficients are statistically significant. The following descriptions provide a more detailed comparison of the development of the different party system types in the region.

Consider first the responsible-party systems. Besides the Czech Republic, the other party system that fit the responsible-party type for the whole of the period between 1996 and 2002 was Hungary. Hungary's party system closely resembles the Czech Republic in that party competition revolves around a few centralized and programmatically defined political parties, and government alternation is wholesale and regular (Toole 2000). The same main party organizations have anchored the party system since 1990; they align neatly on a left-right issue spectrum; and the patterns of coalition-building among them are familiar to voters. In short, it is a system that generates accountable government by offering voters choice among a manageable number of familiar parties. It is the highest scoring country for the region in terms of government effectiveness, with a score of roughly 1.15. It also is one of the rare states in the region that actually has reduced the size of its bureaucracy in the transition to democracy. As a result of early and consistently implemented reforms, the number of personnel in Hungary's national-level state administration declined by 16 percent between 1993 and 1997 (Nunberg 2000, 280). Its state administration also scores well on the government effectiveness index: with a value of 0.6, it ranks in the top quarter of countries in the sample—just about the same level as the Czech Republic and considerably higher than Poland and Slovakia.[21]

Though its institutionalization process was slower, Estonia also finished this period in the responsible-party category. It made the transition from weak governance to responsible parties in 2000, as its patterns of party competition became more familiar over time and as smaller parties consolidated into larger ones (Kreuzer and Pettai 2003). For most of the 1990s, however, Estonia's party system was volatile and fluid and its governments heterogeneous and short-lived. The increasing institutionalization of the Estonian system was evident in its rapidly declining electoral volatility, which fell from 70.7 percent between the country's first and second elections to 32.4 percent between its third and fourth ones—the latter figure putting it in the same class as Hungary and the Czech Republic. Though Estonia's government effectiveness had been in the upper half of this region's spectrum even in its weak-governance period, its switch to responsible-party competition coincided with a significant gain in its score on this measure.

Not surprisingly, the majority of the region's new democracies have weak-governance party systems, including Latvia, Lithuania, Slovenia, Bulgaria, Romania, Macedonia, Moldova (1996–2001), and, of course, Poland. After the ouster of Slobodan Milosević in 2000, even Serbia joined the list, as Milosević's party was swept away and replaced by an unwieldy coalition of often incompatible opposition groups. The countries in this group are diverse in terms of state development. Romania, Bulgaria, Moldova, and Macedonia rank among the worst in terms of government effectiveness, while Poland, Lithuania, and Latvia are in the upper half of the regional distribution. The top of the weak-governance class, Slovenia, performs at about the level of the Czech Republic. Even with the outlier of Slovenia, the overall pattern of party system type and government effectiveness fits with the theoretical expectations: weak-governance systems as a group perform below responsible-party ones and slightly better than dominant-party ones.

Bulgaria is emblematic of the lowest performing weak-governance systems in the region. As in Romania, the Communist-successor party won the first free elections, and so in a very basic sense, democratization did not initially achieve even the nominal separation of party and state (Ganev 2001). Although Bulgaria's postcommunist government fell as early as 1991, the opposition Union of Democratic Forces (UDF) was a heterogeneous umbrella grouping of different social and political movements. This was a party system with high volatility and frequent, often partial, government alternation—in which to be the main government party meant virtually certain defeat in the next election.[22] Despite what were often quite high vote differentials, governing parties could not sustain them for more than one electoral period, reflecting their lack of dominance. The open and unstable nature of the party system was driven home in 2001when a completely new party, lacking any institutional organization, and based on the popularity of a single figure, the exiled Czar Simeon II, swept the elections, trouncing both the postcommunists and the UDF.

Given its unstable party system, it is not surprising that the available data indicate a runaway Bulgarian state in the 1990s. The number of personnel in the central state ministries and offices doubled in just five years (1990–1995); overall the national-level state administration increased by about 33 percent in the same period (Verheijen 1999, 126). The Bulgarian state administration also received low rankings for effectiveness (Ganev 2001): its 1998 government effectiveness score of −0.97 put it in the lowest third of Kaufmann, Kraay, and Mastruzzi's sample (2002). The combination of rapid expansion and declining government effectiveness scores between

1996 and 1998 suggest patronage-led state-building in Bulgaria. Like Bulgaria, Romania and Moldova saw large swings in the electoral fortunes of the governing parties, rapid cycles of party birth and death, and unfamiliar coalitional formulas. Though comparably detailed data on the Romanian, Moldovan and Macedonian state administrations are not available, the secondary literature indicates a similar, if not more dire, situation to that of Bulgaria (Stan 2002; Barany 1997; Way 2003; Pearson 2002).[23]

Though also characterized by government instability and high electoral volatility, the weak-governance systems of Lithuania, Latvia, Poland, and Slovenia have performed at a comparatively higher level, though not high enough to change the overall relationship between party system type and government effectiveness in the region. Unlike Estonia, Lithuania and Latvia have not seen a significant decline in electoral volatility over time; in Latvia, it has actually been increasing.[24] Slovenia's electoral volatility is only moderately high—around 30 to 40 percent, which is at the low end for the weak-governance category. Nonetheless, its governments have been short-lived and heterogeneous and its volatility shows no sign of declining over time.

Serbia, Albania, Croatia, Russia, Moldova, and Slovakia were dominant-party (variant 1) systems for some or all of the period between 1996 and 2002. Each saw the rise of single parties that far outclassed the organizational and electoral resources of their respective oppositions. This made for high differentials in election results that could be sustained over multiple electoral periods. Under Franjo Tudjman, Croatia's Croatian Democratic Union (HDZ) sustained a 26-plus percent advantage over its nearest competitor; in Sali Berisha's Albania, the advantage was around 35 percent. In marked contrast to the relative stability of the hegemonic parties, the opposition parties in these countries were fluid and unpredictable, making for electoral volatility scores as high as 58 percent in Croatia's 1995 election. Except for Croatia and Slovakia, all of these dominant-party systems ranked in the bottom half of the region in terms of government effectiveness; Croatia and Slovakia were at the median, just on par with the weak-governance systems of Bulgaria but significantly lower than the responsible-party systems.

Two conspicuous shared features stand out among the dominant-party (variant 1) systems. First, each was characterized by a tendency toward the personalization of power by the leader of the dominant party, be it Mečiar in Slovakia, Tudjman in Croatia, Berisha in Albania, or even Vladimir Putin in Russia. Second, each of these leaders was able to exploit unresolved and still resonant nationalist issues. This is not to say that nationalism was absent in weak-governance systems like Poland or

Latvia; in the dominant-party systems, however, the nationalist mantle became associated with one party and one leader.

Finally, this region offers several examples of the dominant-party (variant 2) type. As noted before, this tends to be a transitional configuration as, in the typical case, a dethroned dominant-party either regroups for the next election (Croatia after 2000) or weakens after losing access to its accustomed patronage reservoirs (Slovakia after 1998). In both Croatia and Slovakia, the defeat of the dominant party coincided with a decrease in the government effectiveness score.

Russia's exit from communism, which has been one of the most turbulent in this region, provides a good example of the institutionally based form of dominant-party (variant 2) politics. Under Boris Yeltsin, Russia's party system was extremely underinstitutionalized; aside from a Communist Party that dominated the parliament, this was "floating party system" of ephemeral and extremely underdeveloped political groupings (Rose and Munro 2002). Against this backdrop, Yeltsin's confrontation with the parliament in 1993 drastically concentrated power in the executive. The confrontation between a parliament dominated by the Communist Party and an institutionally powerful president hostile to that party produced a dominant-party (variant 2) system. As others have noted, this period was one of state stagnation, and worse, in Russia (Lynch 2005; Rose and Munro 2002). Russia's government effectiveness score of around -0.5 put it in the bottom ranks among all new democracies. The federal-level state grew very little. Meanwhile in Russia's dysfunctional federalism, subnational administrations—many of them the fiefdoms of subnational party machines—were untethered from central control and exploded in size (Gimpelson and Triesman 2002, 160). The situation in Ukraine paralleled that in Russia, with a gradual increase in the powers of the president being counterbalanced by an uncooperative Communist Party that dominated the parliament; its government effectiveness scores were even lower than Russia's.

Under Putin's further consolidation of power in the office of president, the character of the Russian party system has shifted to dominant-party (variant 1). Putin has much greater popular support than Yeltsin and, unlike Yeltsin, does not face an intransigent parliament.[25] It is a strong indicator of just how great the stagnation of the state administration was in the dominant-party (variant 2) period of Yeltsin that Putin's central imperative has been to rebuild the state. He is building it in just the manner one would expect in a dominant-party (variant 1) system, through directed and systemic interventions, not the gradual and localized accretion of personnel in a weak-governance system like Poland's. Though *some* Russian parties are now building more institutionalized roots, it seems that party competition matters less than ever. Neither of Russia's party systems, under Yeltsin or Putin, generated vertical accountability of government to voters.

Latin America

As a region in which democracy has generally had shallow roots and which underwent a wave of redemocratization in the 1980s, Latin America makes for a natural comparison with postcommunist Eastern Europe. Because of its history of regime change, Latin America's state administrations were not consolidated at the time of this wave of democratization, and most of them had a long history of patronage politics. As in Eastern Europe, the transition to democracy served to further delegitimize an already weak state administration. At the same time, many Latin American party systems remained underinstitutionalized or suffered from dominant-party politics. Reflecting these conditions, the average government effectiveness score among the Latin American countries in this sample was somewhat lower than the mean for Eastern Europe.[26] As indicated in the regional regression in Table 7.1, the intraregional variation in government effectiveness scores conformed to the character of party system development even after including the control variables. While the advantages of responsible-party systems stand out clearly, the effect of weak-governance systems and dominant-party (variant 1) systems is strongly negative—much more negative, in the case of weak-governance systems, than in the sample as a whole. Because there were no examples of dominant-party (variant 2) systems in the period from 1996 to 2002, no coefficient for this category is reported in Table 7.1.

Latin America has an important lesson to offer, namely, that there is no "natural" tendency toward increasing party system institutionalization. As the examples of Venezuela, Peru, and, to a lesser extent, Argentina illustrate, party systems may not only fail to institutionalize (as in Poland), they may under certain circumstances experience strong pressures toward deinstitutionalization. In Venezuela, Peru, and Argentina, economic crisis was the catalyst for the weakening of the party system in the 1990s (Levitsky and Cameron 2003; Burgess and Levitsky 2003).

Chile, Uruguay, and Argentina were responsible-party systems throughout the period, while Mexico shifted to the responsible-party category in 2000.[27] As in the Czech Republic and Hungary, party competition in these countries was anchored by a few parties with clear positions on a left-right, primarily socioeconomic, issue spectrum. Since its return to democracy in 1985, Uruguay's party system has been composed of four principal parties—none of which claims a decisive electoral advantage—and is ranked at the top of Mainwaring and Scully's party system institutionalization index (1995, 17). Chile's gradual transition to democracy from 1988 to 1990 also gave way to a bipolar party system, which was both increasingly competitive and institutionalized over time. Another bipolar system, Argentina, scored somewhat lower than Chile and Uruguay on Mainwaring and Scully's institutionalization index, but still at the high end for the region. Though Argentina's party system was anchored by the Peronist and Radical parties, both of which have historical roots and enduring organization, a significant part of this earlier history is flavored by overly close ties to the state administration. Moreover, there were signs of deinstitutionalization toward the end of the period, precipitated by Argentina's currency crisis in 2001.

A less clear-cut case, Mexico is an example of a party system in which a long decline in party dominance was capped by the emergence of a responsible-party system in the late 1990s. The ruling Institutional Revolutionary Party's (PRI) dominance began to crack in the economic crisis of the early 1980s, as two opposition parties emerged to mount increasingly serious electoral challenges. The PRI lost its majority in Congress in 1997, and by 2000 this party, which had historically claimed overwhelming majorities, was separated from the opposition National Action Party (PAN) by only one seat in Congress. In Mexico's case, it was the long dominance of the PRI and the gradual transition from one-party rule that allowed both opposition and government parties to build a moderate level of institutionalization.[28] Since the mid-1990s, Mexico has functioned as a competitive two- to three-party system with a dominant left-right socioeconomic policy space (Klesner 2001).

With the exception of Argentina after its financial crisis of 2001, each of these countries was located at the upper end of the government effectiveness scale. Although patronage politics is certainly a pronounced feature of some of these countries' politics—notably Argentina and Mexico—relative to the rest of the region, the effectiveness, professionalism, and probity of their state administrations stood out. Mexico's shift from dominant-party to responsible-party politics was marked by an increase in its government effectiveness score, from −0.22 in 1996 to 0.38 in 2000.

Elsewhere in the region, however, party systems were significantly less institutionalized in the 1990s and, as a result, less able to deliver vertical accountability. Indeed, some analysts even spoke of a trend of "reverse institutionalization" (Levitsky and Cameron 2003), which occurred in Alberto Fujimori's Peru, contributed to the rise of Hugo Chavez in Venezuela, and, as mentioned above, was visible to a lesser extent in Argentina after its currency crisis.

There also were the consistently weak-governance systems of Ecuador, Guatemala, Bolivia, and Brazil, in which high volatility and the absence of any dominant party were matched by generally high government instability. Brazil, of course, is one of the paradigmatic cases of a fluid and underinstitutionalized party system, forming the core country study for Mainwaring's elaboration of the type in *Rethinking Party Systems in the Third Wave of Democratization*. Despite its head start as one of the first countries in this sample to democratize, Ecuador has failed to develop a predictable and stable party system. As one scholar noted, the Ecuadorian party system is characterized by extreme multipartism, high volatility, and disillusioned and disengaged voters: its multipartism "is fueled by intense rivalries among career politicians for control over party organization and patronage distribution. Such internal conflicts are resolved frequently by splits and the creation of new parties" (Conaghan 1995, 434–35). With an equivalently low score on Mainwaring and Scully's institutionalization index, Bolivia has experienced high volatility and party turnover since redemocratizing in 1982. To quote one observer, "Parties in Bolivia have been quite permeable ideologically, party loyalty among the political classes has been low, and more often than not the behavior of parties has been driven by access to patronage than by constituting programmatically focused governments" (Gamarra and Malloy 1995, 399). Both Bolivia and Ecuador had consistently low vote differentials in this period, ranging from 5 to 11 percent. Like Bulgaria, Romania, and Moldova, Guatemala saw higher vote differentials, but they were accompanied by government turnovers, as well as by high levels of electoral volatility and party turnover. Generally, these weak-governance systems scored poorly in terms of government effectiveness. Ecuador and Guatemala were at the bottom of the sample for the region. Brazil, the highest scoring of the group, was exactly in the middle for the region.

As in Mexico, Venezuela's party system shifted between 1996 and 2002: it moved from a weak-governance to a dominant-party (variant 1) system. Historically, the country had been considered one of the most institutionalized in the region: from 1973 to the late 1980s, there were only two parties that mattered in Venezuelan politics, the Social Christian Party and the Democratic Action Party. As happened later in Argentina, a deep economic crisis undermined the political order; the first signs of rapid deinstitutionalization appeared in the 1993 elections, as three brand new parties took away roughly half of the traditional parties' electorates. The flight from the traditional parties accelerated in the 1998 elections, with the victory of Hugo Chavez's Patriotic Pole. Exploiting the weakly institutionalized political environment in a fashion reminiscent of Mečiar in Slovakia, Chavez used his personal charisma to build a dominant political machine that by the 2000 elections claimed a 30-plus point advantage over its nearest competitor. As one would expect in the switch to a dominant-party system, Venezuela's government effectiveness score collapsed in this transition, from -0.69 in 1996 to -1.14 in 2002.

Other dominant-party (variant 1) systems in the region included Peru (1996–2000), Paraguay, and Colombia. From 1992 to 2000, Peruvian politics were strongly reminiscent of Russia under Putin. Like Putin, Peruvian president Alberto Fujimori built up a superpresidency in the context of an extremely underinstitutionalized party system.[29] In a bad portent for contemporary Russia, Peru's parties atrophied even more under Fujimori, and his eventual fall led the country back into weak-governance politics (Levitsky and Cameron 2003). Described by Mainwaring and Scully as a "hegemonic party system in transition," Paraguay's politics are still sufficiently dominated by the Colorado Party to place it in the dominant party (variant 1) category. Finally, despite its high rankings on Mainwaring and Scully's party system institutionalization index and well-defined political field—the two major parties are the Liberals and Conservatives—Colombia's Liberals were a dominant party throughout the 1990s, far outstripping the Conservatives in successive elections. Colombia's entrenched dominant-party politics parallels developments in many African countries. All three of these countries fared poorly in terms of government effectiveness, at the bottom end for Latin America.

Africa

Prior to the 1990s most of Africa was nondemocratic, governed by single-party states or military regimes whose leaders were typically supported by either the United States or the USSR as part of their competition for global influence. The events in Eastern Europe in 1989 brought the cold war to an end, and following closely thereafter, more than 30 of Africa's 53 countries underwent a wave of democratization (Gyimah-Boadi 2004). As in both Eastern Europe and Latin America, African state administrations were not, as a rule, consolidated at the time of democratization. The state did not have strong legitimacy given the distorted character of state-building in the period of colonialism, a legacy which was not substantially improved in the general onset of authoritarian rule after decolonization. In short, state administrations in Africa had a deep history of pervasive patronage (Rothchild and Chazan 1988).

At the same time, most political parties in these new democracies were under-institutionalized, and party competition was far from robust.[30] In looking at the development of Africa's new democracies, it is hard not to be struck by the number of dominant-party (variant 1) systems. Unlike Eastern Europe, where the anticommunist coalitions imploded within a couple of years of taking power, in South Africa, for example, the African National Congress (ANC) former opposition coalition has in fact increased its electoral advantage. The ANC's example is more the rule than the exception, as vote differentials are higher in Africa and sustained over longer periods of time than in Eastern Europe or Latin America. Perhaps even more so than in these other regions, the tradition of the state was extremely underdeveloped at the onset of democratic party competition. Certainly, the average state effectiveness score for the region in this sample was lower than in Latin America or Eastern Europe—at −0.267 compared with −0.170 and .002, respectively.

It is all the more notable, given the overrepresentation of dominant-party (variant 1) party systems in this part of the sample, that the general contours of the relationship between party system type and state development bear up in the regional regression for Africa in Table 7.1. First, the coefficients for weak-governance and dominant-party (variant 1) systems are negative, indicating their lower performance than the baseline responsible-party system. Second, as in the sample as a whole, the regression indicates that the adverse effect of the dominant-party (variant 1) type is greater than that of the weak-governance one. Because there are so few examples of these other party system types in the sample, however, the coefficients for them are not statistically significant.

The list of dominant-party (variant 1) systems in Africa is long; it includes Nigeria, Niger, Mali, Zambia, São Tomé and Principe, Djibouti, Seychelles, Malawi, Tanzania, South Africa, Namibia, and Mauritius. Other countries that were dominant-party (variant 1) for at least part of this period include Senegal, Ghana, and Cape Verde. Not surprisingly given the sheer number of countries in this party system category, there were both high- and low-scoring countries in this list in terms of the effectiveness of the state administration.

At the low-scoring end of the scale, one finds countries such as Tanzania, which made its official break from single-party rule in 1992 and whose government effectiveness score ranged from −0.4 to −1.04. The introduction of multipartism has done little to challenge the ruling party of this former single-party state, the Chama cha Mapinduzi (CCM); instead, it has allowed the CCM to disband its supervisory links with labor unions and the army—relics of an earlier era of central planning—and forge closer relationships with the business elite, marking what some observers have called "a return to primordial channels as a basis of political recruitment and gaining support" (Mmuya and Chaligha, quoted in McHenry 2004, 49). Meanwhile, in a dynamic recalling Slovakia under Mečiar, the opposition parties have been in a constant state of flux, unable to cooperate with each other, and suffering from the serial defection of their most popular leaders. The strongest opposition party in the

1995 election virtually collapsed in the next election in 2000, as the governing CCM widened its electoral lead from just under 40 percentage points to almost 60. To quote again from Mmuya and Chilgha, "Although the country is *de jure* a multiparty state, it is indeed a *de facto* single party state" (52).

At the high end of the scale, one finds South Africa, which is considered one of the strongest democracies in the region but whose governing African National Congress (ANC) party faces no credible electoral challenge (Diamond 2002). South Africa's ANC demonstrates how a strongly dominant party need not preclude party system institutionalization and democratic development. Despite the ANC's good record so far, at least one informed observer has noted that the absence of robust competition poses a threat to accountability and state governance in the longer term: "This threat is exemplified by the 1999 ballot, which eroded countervailing power within the system by reducing the key levers of opposition influence, control of two subnational governments, and the ability to block governing party constitutional initiatives in the national legislature" (Friedman 2004, 236). Vertical accountability, an effective and patronage-free state, and single-party dominance probably do not go together in the long term, even in South Africa. Therefore, the South African exception should not be used as a role model for the far more numerous lower-performing dominant-party (variant 1) systems in Africa.

In the period from 1996 to 2002, only one African country in the sample, Mozambique, combined a low vote differential with a high party system institutionalization score.[31] Although I have coded it as a responsible-party system in the analysis, it was not a clear-cut choice. Mozambique emerged from a long civil war in 1992, and the two warring sides, Frelimo and Renamo, quickly transformed themselves into the two leading political parties. Although area-specialists have generally rated the development of the political scene favorably (Mazulo 2004), Mozambique's peace still feels fragile, and Larry Diamond (2002) placed it in his "ambiguous regime" category. Mozambique scored at about the middle of the African countries in the sample in terms of effectiveness. If the peace holds, however, Frelimo and Renamo's history of conflict may prove to be an organizational asset in the long term; just as apartheid forged political loyalties and organizational assets for the ANC in South Africa, the organizational assets from the period of conflict may serve as the basis for building strong internal party organization in Mozambique.

Madagascar and Benin were the lone examples of weak-governance politics. Kuenzi and Lambright (2001) and Riedl (2005) both ranked these countries at the bottom Africa's new democracies in their studies of party system institutionalization. Benin's party system showed some surprisingly close parallels to Poland's; in Benin's 1991 elections, none of the 24 competing parties won a majority, and a large number of those that won seats failed even to make it back into the parliament in the next elections (Kuenzi and Lambright 2001, 450).[32] In Benin, parties are more fluid coalitions of independent candidates than programmatically defined organizations, and coalition formation at the government level reflects this turbulence (Riedl 2005). The effectiveness scores of both Benin and Madagascar varied considerably over time, but on average they were at or just under the median for the region.

Asia

The spread of democracy has been slower and more variegated in Asia than in Eastern Europe and Latin America—and less tilted to the dominant-party logic than in Africa. Of the countries included in the sample here, Taiwan, South Korea, the Philippines, and Thailand began the transition in the mid-1980s to early 1990s, whereas Indonesia's regime change began much more recently, in 1998–1999. The historical and institutional contexts into which democratic competition was set down differed far more from each other than was the case in, for example, post-communist Eastern Europe. While both South Korea and Taiwan developed professional, effective, and relatively politically independent state administrations under authoritarianism—that is, previous to democratization—the Philippine, Thai, and Indonesian states were noted for their pervasive patronage networks prior to democratization (Thompson 1996; Bowornwathana 1997; Tan 2004). Thus, unlike the examples considered above, the Asian new democracies provide leverage for Shefter's argument about the sequencing of democratization and state-building: much of the variation in the effectiveness of the state administration can be explained by the prior consolidation of the state administration.

Unfortunately, there are not enough Asian country cases in the sample for a meaningful regional-level regression analysis. The sample contains five countries—Indonesia (from 2000 to 2002), the Philippines, Thailand, South Korea, and Taiwan—which is fewer than the number of parameters estimated. Case studies remain the best guides for evaluating the hypothesis in the new democracies of Asia.

With the exception of Taiwan, these were all weak-governance systems for the better part of 1996–2002, and they all scored significantly lower than Taiwan in terms of government effectiveness. Recalling again the pattern in Bulgaria and Guatemala, the Philippines has seen broad coalitions elected with large margins only to experience a collapse in their support in the following elections. This makes for very high electoral volatility, rampant party switching, unpredictable coalition formation, and very weak vertical accountability (Montinola 1999). Not surprisingly for such a young democracy, Indonesia's party system also shows signs of underinstitutionalization, including extreme multipartism (some 21 parties were elected to parliament in the elections of 1999), personalism and an absence of clearly defined party programs, a tendency toward internal party factionalization, and weakly defined boundaries between certain parties and the state (Tan 2004).[33] Thailand, whose most recent democratic transition occurred in 1991, was characterized for most of the 1990s by unstable government coalitions, high numbers of parties in parliament, and a lack of vertical accountability (Bowornwathana 1997).[34] In what serves as a nice encapsulation of this book's argument about the effect of weak-governance systems on the state administration, one expert on Thai politics writes:

> For the democratizing Thai polity, the nature of coalition governments is a major obstacle to administrative reform . . . To [the minister], his ministry's plan is his personal masterpiece to strengthen the empire of his ministry. We often see situations of clashes between a coalition of politicians and bureaucrats and another coalition of politicians and bureaucrats who support competing reform proposals. At the end, the survival of the coalition government takes precedence over the reform proposals, which are then dropped or shelved along the way through the complicated bureaucratic decision-making channels. Therefore, after one or two years, the coalition government collapses before the reform plan is passed by parliament. (Bowornwathana 1997)

Reflecting the public frustration generated by such a system—and, perhaps more generally, the possibility that weak-governance systems create the conditions for the emergence of populist demagogues—in 2001 Thailand's party system saw the rapid rise of a new dominant party, the *Thai Rak Thai,* which in the most recent elections enjoyed a 40 point lead over its nearest rival.

Taiwan's path to responsible-party government is reminiscent of Chile's. An authoritarian government managed a gradual transition to democracy, allowing both the hegemonic party and the opposition to build organizational capital over time. For the first decade of democratic government, Taiwan was a dominant-party (variant 1) system, with the hegemonic Nationalist Party (KMT) enjoying a 42 percent advantage over its nearest rival in 1986; however, this differential was steadily declining over time. In 1995, the increasingly robust party competition pushed the system across the threshold of the responsible-party logic; the vote differential was then 12.9 percent, and by 2001 it was just 4.8 percent. The increasing competitiveness of the system was matched by the growing institutionalization of political parties. In his comparative study of party system institutionalization in the region, Asia-specialist Hans Stockton ranks Taiwan just below Latin America's most institutionalized party systems of Costa Rica and Uruguay and just above Argentina (2001). Ranging between 1.0 and 1.68, Taiwan's government effectiveness scores were the highest for the region, and indeed for the sample as a whole.

South Korea would seem to offer a potential caveat to this analysis. South Korea's combination of low party system institutionalization and low vote differential (Stockton 2001) mark it as a weak-governance system, yet it receives relatively high government effectiveness scores. As suggested earlier, the answer to this apparent paradox is the sequencing of state-building and democratization: like Weimar Germany, the Korean administrative question was solved before democratization, so weak-governance did not affect the composition or character of the state bureaucracy (Shefter 1994, 40–41). As the Korean scholar of public administration Young-Pyoung Kim writes,

> As the leading sector of development, the public administration has maintained a high-handed manner toward society. It has been a highly centralized institution which had to take care of a variety of political and social concerns . . . The checks and balances existed inside of the bureaucracy where ministries competed to secure their jurisdictions, rather than in the legislative politics . . . The KCSS [Korean Civil Service System] has been the most dominant elite group in society. In spite of the general corruption of the Korean administrative processes, the recruitment of the KCSS has been based on a very rigid merit system. Formally, it is constructed on the basis of legal-rational authority in the Weberian sense . . . [I]ts policy selection has been rational enough to carry on national industrialization thanks to its professional elite possessing exclusive decision making power. (1997)

Not many new democracies have the good fortune to inherit this kind of state apparatus.

CONCLUSION

In sum, this cross-national analysis reveals strong support for the theoretical framework developed in the previous chapters. There is a clear correspondence between differences in the capacity of the state administration and the logic of party competition. Responsible-party systems score significantly higher on this score than their weak-governance and dominant-party (variants 1 and 2) counterparts. These results hold up after controlling for the very great differences among contemporary new democracies in terms of the level of economic development, degree of ethnic division, and type of political system (presidential or parliamentary). Of necessity for a large-N analysis such as this, much of the interesting variation and information about the mechanisms of patronage-led state building in these new democracies is missed by the multivariate analysis. This analysis, however, demonstrates the wider applicability of the conceptual categories and methodology laid out in the earlier chapters beyond the core cases. Poland, the Czech Republic, and Slovakia exemplify different trajectories of party system and state development; their recent history provides very useful analogies for understanding contemporary new democracies in the wider world.

Conclusion

The research behind this book began as an investigation into how the enlargement of the EU influences state-building in Eastern Europe, but I soon realized that this was the wrong prism through which to view state-building in this region. The project of building a postcommunist state was not only being influenced by the concurrent project of preparing for EU accession but also by the reintroduction of electoral competition and the imperatives of party-building; the latter was having the far more profound influence on the state. As a prominent Polish sociologist told me in one of my first field interviews: "The big problems we face in the state administration are the constant flow of people, the lack of a civil service, the fact that political parties are building their capital using state institutions and money—to co-opt people, to pay people for their support, to get some money for elections. To me, this [process] is very obvious and visible. This is what makes the state weak; it is being used to build party organizations." This theme surfaced again and again as I did more interviews: the most important influence for the new states in Eastern Europe during the transition to democracy was not international, it was domestic, and it was most certainly political.

The process of state-building in postcommunist Eastern Europe has been difficult even among such relatively successful transition countries as Poland, the Czech Republic, and Slovakia. In an ironic twist to the fall of the monolithic and overweening communist states in 1989, the Polish and Slovak state administrations have expanded at truly staggering rates when compared against the expectations of both countries' new democratic leaders, international trends toward smaller states (Schiavo-Campo, de Tommaso, and Mukherjee 1997), and, most significantly, the example of other postcommunist democratizers such as the Czech Republic. As the sociologist I interviewed made clear, patronage-driven expansion makes the state weaker, less Weberian, and less accountable. Not only does this undermine the effectiveness of the state at a time when economic transition puts a premium on the state's capacity to regulate and implement government policy, it undermines the legitimacy of the new democratic order itself.

This is illustrated nowhere more clearly than in Poland, which has undergone a new round of political disintegration. In 2004, the government of the postcommunist Democratic Left Alliance (SLD) fell in a major corruption scandal—the Rywin affair—and, on literally the day after finally fulfilling its dream of entering the EU, the country stood once again without a government.[1] Bringing to mind the collapse of the Polish right described in the previous chapters—first in the form of Solidarity and later as AWS—SLD, which had previously seemed the strongest party in Polish politics, is now in the process of disintegrating. Meanwhile, populist, nationalistic, and antisystem parties are surging, including the Self-Defense (Samoobrona) party and the League of Polish Families (LPR), a nationalist-Catholic party. The current appeal of new, extreme parties such as these is, in large part, based on the fact that they have no history in politics and that, as outsiders, they are untainted by the most recent corruption scandals. While Poland's democracy is not in danger of collapsing any time soon, it is sagging under the weight of public disillusionment.[2] Clearly, voters do not like governments they perceive as corrupt, but when party competition is not robust enough to offer them clear choices and accountability, they withdraw, which only furthers the cycle of patronage politics and voter disillusionment.

If Poland—which is, after all, a success case in relative terms—has found the challenge of state-building so difficult, what does it bode for other countries in which democratization occurs in the context of an unconsolidated state? As Chapter 7 shows, the relationship between party system and state development is relevant in the wider universe of new democracies. We now return to the three countries that have been at the center of this book's analysis to draw out the theoretical and practical implications of the argument. That argument has three main parts:

1. *The sequencing of democratization and state-building matters.* Patronage politics is a limited and manageable problem if democratization occurs *after* the consolidation of the state administration (Shefter 1994). If democratization occurs in the context of an unconsolidated state, it creates strong pressures for patronage politics and a predisposition for runaway state-building. Because democratic leaders have extraordinary license for reform and because the state is associated with the old regime, it is very tempting for governing parties to use state resources for party-building in what often are difficult conditions for popular mobilization.

2. *Sequencing is not destiny.* Democratization in the context of an unconsolidated state does not *necessarily* mean that runaway state-building will occur. The critical factor is party competition. Where party competition is institutionalized and robust—that is, where it creates coherent governments and credible oppositions, both composed of stable, programmatically defined parties with medium-to long-term

time horizons—it allows voters to discipline the governing parties through elections. Robust competition does not simply mean frequent government turnover and the absence of single-party dominance. Too much party competition—perhaps it could be called cut-throat party competition—creates its own problems. It creates pressures to hold together umbrella coalitions of programmatically divergent and often short-sighted parties using patronage; it also reduces government accountability, as individual parties can hide behind the façade of a broad coalition as they seek patronage resources; finally, it fragments the opposition so that voters lack a clear party alternative with which to punish a corrupt government—in essence splitting the protest vote. Robust and institutionalized party competition offers voters familiar parties that behave in predictable ways in forming governments; it requires only the threat of turnover (a low vote differential), not actual turnover, for the opposition to constrain the governing parties' appetite for patronage.

3. *State-building is a process, not an endpoint.* As my interviews with state officials show, there is an instinct for bureaucratization even in state administrations rife with patronage politics. Administrators prefer to define themselves as policy professionals, not as political favorites, because it offers them more career stability. In an era of economic and cultural globalization, administrators in most democratizing countries understand the concept of legal-rationalism. What is necessary for bureaucratization to occur is not the modernization of society—that is, the abandonment of traditional practices—but a certain amount of autonomy from outside political intervention so a critical mass of policy professionals can form. Poland and Slovakia's state administrations can and will become Weberian bureaucracies when their party systems begin to constrain governing parties from intervening in the administration in search of patronage. This last lesson is a hopeful one: while democratization may unleash problematic dynamics in the state, democratic consolidation will tame them.

Three questions spring from this argument about state-building and democratization in Poland, the Czech Republic, and Slovakia. First, what can be done to prevent patronage-fueled state-building in new democracies, and are there institutional mechanisms that might mitigate this phenomenon? Second, how sustainable is runaway state-building over the longer term? Third, what are the implications of this analysis for the study of comparative politics?

CAN THE RIGHT INSTITUTIONS SOLVE
RUNAWAY STATE-BUILDING?

As the interviews in Chapter 3 show, the transformation from postcommunist administrative apparatus to bureaucracy is an internally driven process, the results of which are by no means guaranteed. Given enough political intervention, state officials may never establish legal-rational authority and may instead fall back on political connections, that is, on a patrimonial basis for legitimating their authority. Where officials are given space from politics, however, they have an incentive to define themselves as policy professionals and their organization as a bureaucracy. It is difficult to impose this kind of transformation from the outside through institutional and policy reforms—especially in new democracies whose chief political decision-makers, the party leadership, are less than credible bureaucratic reformers. Yet, as political scientists, it is natural to ask whether there are institutional reforms that can at least ameliorate the syndrome of runaway state-building in democratizing countries.

The key is effecting the political autonomy of the state administration so that its internal proclivity for legal-rationalism can gather momentum—solving what Venelin Ganev has called the "logistical problem" of separating party and state (2001). There are two main approaches to the problem: (1) using constitutional-legal means to strengthen party competition so that it can better constrain the parties of government and (2) using institutional-legal means to safeguard the administration itself. The former include electoral systems design and mechanisms for financing parties publicly. Although these may seem rather blunt and long-term instruments, I am more sanguine about their eventual success compared to bureaucratic reforms.[3] The problem, of course, is that party systems are as much the product of social cleavages as they are of electoral rules (Lipset and Rokan 1967). As described in Chapter 2, Poland and Slovakia's difficulties with party system institutionalization are rooted in the greater salience of national and religious-secular cleavages in their societies, which complicate the task of forming stable parties on a left-right, socioeconomic issue space. The absence of such cleavages in the Czech Republic made it much easier to form stable parties on both the right and the left. Each country was dealt a different hand at the beginning of democratization, and they are not amenable to quick policy fixes.

The problem with the second approach, bureaucratic reforms, is that they require sustained, long-term, and unbiased implementation in order to succeed—precisely the attributes that are lacking in weak-governance and dominant-party systems. Moreover, there is always the danger that such reforms will be captured by patronage-seeking government parties.

To illustrate the lackluster performance of bureaucratic reforms, consider two examples from Poland: civil service codes, which legally establish political protections and career incentive structures for officials, and schools of public administration, which are intended to train new generations of professional bureaucrats.

The Impact of Civil Service Codes

The problem of meritocratic selection and promotion procedures in postcommunist state administration has become more prominent only in the last few years. Much of the credit for raising the issue must go to international organizations active in Eastern Europe, in particular the European Union, which has pressured each of the candidate countries to establish a legally defined civil service code (Kirchner 1999). This has been difficult to accomplish because the major political parties suspect their rivals of tailoring the policy to lock in the positions enjoyed by their appointees and clients in the state administration.

Poland adopted a law on the civil service in 1997 before either the Czech Republic or Slovakia. The law defined certain positions in the state bureaucracy as civil service posts, which would be filled on the basis of specified credentials and written tests. These civil posts would not be political appointments, and their occupants could not be replaced by political nominees. If the objectives of this law sounded pure, its timing was suspicious, coming just months before parliamentary elections that the SLD-led government was widely expected to lose. In the run-up to the elections, the government quick-marched a host of its top officials through the civil service competitions over loud criticism from the opposition parties (Paradowska 2001). When SLD did, in fact, lose the elections, the new AWS-led government repealed the civil service law, replacing it with its own version in 1998. It was not an auspicious beginning for a policy designed to insulate the state bureaucracy from party politics, particularly the kind associated with changes of government (Matys 2001).

The second (1998) law on the civil service designated a number of top posts in the central state administration as civil service positions, whose holders would have to win them in advertised, open competitions.[4] The law also established a system of promotion to the civil service for officials occupying mid- and lower-level posts. It aroused considerable hopes among some state bureaucrats. One bureaucrat in the Ministry of Foreign Affairs noted, "We were very lucky that the law passed in the Sejm. The Ministers protested because they considered that it would tie their hands . . . Politicians of all stripes were criticizing the law. They were afraid they would no longer be able to freely nominate their own people. Taking that step doesn't fit with their mentality" (Matys 2001).

Since its passage, the new civil service code has had unimpressive results, however. Four years after the passage of the second law, the new civil service (*służba cywilna*) consisted of only about 560 people—out of an approximately 110,000 eligible state officials (Paradowska 2001). For most of the administration, the law brought a change in title, not in legal protections or job benefits. Those who did not possess the qualifications to become civil servants became part of the so-called civil corps (*korpus cywilny*). The requirements for joining the civil service (*służba cywilna*) were defined too stringently for most of the current state employees to pass the exams. Moreover, many of the mandated civil service posts have still not been filled with civil servants and are occupied by "acting directors" who may be political appointees and who have none of the job security of civil servants. It may be that the situation will improve with time, but already there is talk of amending the law again (Paradowska 2001). As the eminent Polish journalist Janina Paradowska has written, much of the civil corps are not eager to join the civil service because its advantages are inconsiderable and its dangers are unknown: "Better to have safe membership in the large, virtual civil service (that is, the civil corps) than to put oneself on the front lines. The typical Polish bureaucrat has already passed through more than one storm. Above all, he can see that personnel in the administration are still governed by politicians. What else can a bureaucrat think, even one in an uncertain post, when he sees that it's darkest under the spotlight?" (Paradowska 2001, 24). Paradowska alludes to the poor example of undercutting the civil service law set by the very government that had enacted it. In 2001, the prime minister dismissed the director of the Office of the Committee for European Integration, who was a bona fide civil servant and who occupied a much sought-after post. He replaced her with an appointee who was not a civil servant without calling a competition for the post—both of these actions contravening the civil service code.

The Impact of Administrative Academies

A second means to strengthen the state administration institutionally is through the establishment of schools of public administration. In addition to training public policy professionals, these administrative academies may help create the aura of an elite around their graduates as well as fostering an esprit de corps among those graduates. At the time of my field work, Poland was the only country with an administrative academy, the National School of Public Administration (KSAP). Slovakia used to have such a school, but it was closed down under one of the Mečiar governments (Verheijen 2001, 30).

The Polish government established KSAP in 1991. As Prime Minister Krzysztof Bielecki announced to the students at the academy's opening, "You will be our best representatives, who will build a professional Polish state" (quoted in Matys 2001, 18). The academy was intended to build a cadre of highly trained, select bureaucrats and diplomats to transform the Polish state. As the school's director told me in an interview, KSAP was modeled on L'École Nationale d'Administration.[5] Like the French school, entrance was to be selective and on the basis of exams. Not only was the education to be free, but students at the school received several times the normal national stipend, and housing was free. As in France, the school ranked its students in terms of their performance in classes and exams, so that the highest scorers would get the best state positions after graduation. In return, graduates were bound to work for the state for a minimum of five years ("Raport" 1999; Matys 2001). If any professional career bureaucrats were to emerge in the Polish state, it would be these.

The ambitious initial intentions for KSAP only underscore its limited impact on the culture and organization of the Polish state administration so far.[6] First, there have been too few graduates to make a difference, about 400 over the first ten years ("Raport" 1999). Considering that the central administration alone numbers more than 100,000 officials, this number is largely insignificant. Moreover, these few graduates have been spread scattershot across the state administration, often depending on the largesse of particular politicians to find positions and not the ability of the school to place its graduates where it deemed they would be most effective. As I learned in one interview with a KSAP graduate working in the Supreme Accounting Office (NIK), almost half of that respondent's class had found employment in NIK simply because its director had viewed the school more favorably than had other ministers, who had given them the cold shoulder.

In addition to encountering hostility from other officials, the KSAP graduates discovered the influence of party politics in the state administration and that their own political independence could work against them. One graduate from KSAP described his first contact with the state administration when he began work in it after finishing his degree: "Almost everywhere we [graduates] appeared we became the objects of aggression. Although we were effective and willing to work, we represented a threat to the old cadres. *We didn't have support from anyone because we were not tied to any political party*" (Matys 2001, 18; emphasis added). Other KSAP graduates even came to the conclusion that their school credentials were holding back their careers. One graduate working at the Ministry of Foreign Affairs commented, "KSAP was only an albatross around my neck. I had the feeling that we [KSAP graduates] were being kept on the sidelines. We were set to work, yes sure, but as far as possible from important affairs" (Matys 2001, 19). According to another graduate working in the state administration, "Before the elections in 1993, the staff in my office began to put together files of accusations against their colleagues. They knew that a new management would be coming and would bring its own candidates with them. They wanted to avoid losing their own jobs, so they pointed out others for firing" (Matys 2001, 19). Another graduate of the class of 1993, second in her class, was sent on unpaid vacation after the 1993 elections and her position at the Office of the Council of Ministers filled by an older official associated with the then-ascendant SLD party. She stated, "I don't know if politicians need bureaucrats who aren't tied to anyone . . . Every political party has its own bureaucrats in the administration, and we [KSAP graduates] didn't belong to anyone. That was our chief problem" (Matys 2001, 19). The influence of party politics not only worked against KSAP's graduates on an individual basis but against the school itself, which had been established, after all, by one of the early Solidarity governments. The postcommunist SLD-PSL governments from 1993 to 1997 conspicuously ignored the school.

Finally, the career paths of the graduates of KSAP have not been any more stable or predictable than those of the typical state official. Graduates of the earliest classes have found that they have rarely been assigned to the senior positions in the state, and their career paths since graduation have zigzagged between various state agencies and even the public and private sectors. As described in an article in the Polish press, one of the graduates of the school's first class tracked down seven of his 34 classmates to follow their career paths (Matys 2001). Three of the seven had left the state administration for the private sector. All of them had bounced around from various assignments in the eight years since graduating from KSAP, often vacating posts to make way for politically favored candidates. The reassignments did not have the character of clearly progressing upward to positions of greater responsibility. Reinforcing the impression from this small poll, KSAP published a report in 2001 on the activities and positions of its graduates. One-third of the first class's graduates lacked any information, and so presumably were no longer in the state administration (Matys 2001).

It would be rash to generalize from the Polish experience that institutional-legal reforms of the state administration can never produce bureaucratic rationalization. There are historical examples of powerful political leaders forcibly modernizing state administrations—for example, Turkey under Atatürk or Prussia under Frederick William—though these have typically been examples where state consolidation preceded democratization. In democratizing countries like Poland, the necessity for political leaders to establish a political base through party-building undermines their credibility as bureaucratic reformers. An effective opposition, which is capable of checking and constraining the government, is necessary for establishing such credibility.

These examples reinforce the point that the process of bureaucratization is a cultural shift that occurs quietly and incrementally in the offices and ministries of the state itself, largely outside of official efforts at reform. As Weber originally perceived, the defining characteristic of bureaucracy is a particular rationale for legitimating social action (namely, legal-rationalism), and this rationale works incrementally (through routinization) to gradually change the institutional environment around it. The formal rules and codifications of bureaucracy are secondary to this cultural shift, and absent a change in the underlying culture, merely changing the formal rules will be to little effect.[7]

HOW SUSTAINABLE IS RUNAWAY STATE-BUILDING?

Only another ten years of data will answer the question of sustainability for Poland, Slovakia, and the Czech Republic, but the theory offered here allows for informed speculation. Is it possible that the Polish and Slovak states may outgrow runaway state-building? One could turn the runaway state-building argument on its head and say, "These states already have the numbers. If patronage politics doesn't continue to interfere in the administration, effectiveness will catch up." If this is the case, runaway state-building may seem in the long term like a lag between increases in size and gains in effectiveness, rather than a case of the former without the latter. At some point, of course, it will be impossible for these states to continue growing at their rates in the 1990s. This is a trivial point, though, since it is impossible for any organization or institution to grow in perpetuity at a never-diminishing rate of increase. The concept of runaway state-building is best understood in relative terms, framed by specific comparisons within a certain geographical and historical context. Thus, although it is difficult to imagine the Polish and Slovak state administrations continuing to grow at such a rate and with such lackluster gains in effectiveness as they did in the immediate postcommunist period, the real question is how they will perform relative to responsible-party systems such as the Czech Republic and Hungary in the first decade of EU membership and beyond.

Moreover, as Chapter 7 shows, the problem of runaway state-building can also be viewed in terms of the relative capacity of the state administration under different party system types. It is not inevitable that the Polish and Slovak states will eventually possess state capacity commensurate with their size—again with the neighboring postcommunist states that have different party system types forming the most relevant comparative referent. Even if the rate of expansion slows over time, a state like Slovakia or Poland may never make significant gains in effectiveness if patronage-seeking parties continue to intervene in the state administration. This would constitute a chronic case of runaway state-building.

Another factor that affects the question of sustainability, and that is sure to become more important, is the European Union, of which Poland, the Czech Republic, and Slovakia have been members since May 1, 2004. Will EU membership isolate the state administrations from patronage politics? While the EU's influence is not unlimited, in the short term it introduces a kind of minimum level below which the new member countries cannot fall. For example, pressure from the EU has been important in preventing Mečiar's return to the center of Slovak politics.[8] In the longer term, it is certain to have a salutary effect, as membership increases the prestige of a career in the state and focuses closer scrutiny on the operation of the state administration.

One might also plausibly argue, however, that the EU will only provide governing parties with new resources for patronage. After all, as Chapter 4 shows, the EU's preference for regional government translated into widely divergent institutional outcomes in Poland, the Czech Republic, and Slovakia. As money pours into the new member states of Eastern Europe for regional and economic development, we have to ask if EU membership will provide these states the impetus and resources for strategic policies of the kind that allowed Ireland to climb from Europe's periphery to its technological and economic vanguard, or will Eastern Europe more closely resemble the Greek scenario—prodigious amounts of EU aid money accompanied by relative economic stagnation and a reputation for political clientelism (Papakostas 2001)?[9] The answer will hinge on the effectiveness of the state administration, and as both the variation in state effectiveness among the "old" EU members and Chapter 4's case study of regional governance reform indicate, the task of transposing the *acquis communautaire* will not in itself solve the state-building question.

The theory developed here offers a framework for thinking about how and why postcommunist states may change over time. Highlighting the key variables that shaped state-building in the 1990s allows one to consider how a change in the values of these variables might change outcomes in the next decades. The optimistic implication of the runaway state-building model is this: *if and when party systems stabilize, the character of state-building will change.* As I argue in Chapter 4, state administrations have an incentive to establish their legitimacy in terms of legal-rational authority rather than patrimonial authority. More simply put, administrators would prefer to define themselves as policy professionals than as political favorites, since as professionals they maximize control over their careers, salaries, and work. As political favorites, their control over those things depends on the prevailing, and changeable, political climate. If robust party competition serves to constrain the parties of power from intervening in the administration, then state administrations will begin the process of rationalization and bureaucratization.

With these considerations in mind, what appears to be the logic of party competition in Poland, the Czech Republic, and Slovakia today? Are there indications
that these party systems have changed since the period from 1990 to 2000 analyzed
in the earlier chapters? I will briefly comment on the latest trends in each country,
bearing in mind of course that these observations are fragmentary and impres-
sionistic. With the partial exception of Slovakia, there has been relatively little
change in the logic of party competition.

Slovakia's most recent parliamentary elections of 2002 gave reason to hope that
the dominance of Mečiar's HZDS machine may have finally come to an end, though
what kind of system will replace it is still unresolved. Although HZDS still receives
the most votes in Slovakia, and though a former HZDS speaker of the parliament
is now the country's president, that party no longer polls enough to build a government majority. Initially, it seemed that the anti-Mečiar parties had finally learned
to coordinate their efforts; after the elections, they all resolutely refused to join a
coalition with HZDS or its longtime partner the Slovak National Party (SNS). It appeared that a measure of predictability in the formation of governments was
emerging in Slovakia's party system. A couple of years later, the situation is less
clear. The governing Slovak Democratic and Christian Union (SDKÚ) party is extremely unpopular—the finance minister called it the least popular in Slovak history—and, more surprisingly, there is now open discussion in Slovakia of a pending coalition agreement between the SDKÚ and Mečiar's HZDS before the next
elections (Nicholson 2005). Given that it was the SDKÚ leadership that overthrew
of Mečiar in 1998, this move would signal a return to unpredictable governing formulas and a less-than-credible opposition. Slovakia would move from a dominant-
party (variant 2) system to a weak-governance one. After all, Slovakia's party system is still not oriented around a single left-right, liberal-social democratic cleavage.
A strong nationalist-religious cleavage remains, which imparts an ad hoc and unpredictable quality to coalition-building. Moreover, the party system is still generating new parties that come from nowhere to suddenly capture significant shares of
the vote: two examples are the Smer and the Ano parties.

Poland's recent political developments offer, if anything, evidence that its party
system is becoming even more fragmented. In the 2001 parliamentary elections, the
post-Solidarity end of the party spectrum underwent another seismic shift: the AWS
organization collapsed, and two new right parties emerged in its place, the Law and
Justice Party (PiS) and the Citizens' Platform (PO). Meanwhile, the venerable Freedom Union (UW) failed to win enough votes to gain a seat in parliament. A number of other parties such as the extremist Self-Defense Party (Samoobrona), the religious-nationalist League of Polish Families (LPR), and the left-leaning Union of

Labor (UP) went from obscurity to prominence in the 2001 elections. At the time of this writing, Self-Defense was the number one party in the opinion polls (CBOS 2004). The SLD government collapsed in the "Rywin" corruption scandal in May 2004; a self-styled government of technocrats has been in place since; and the Polish left, in particular the SLD, is imploding.

In the Czech Republic the logic of party competition looks largely unchanged. It remains a responsible-party system anchored around the conservative ODS and the social democratic ČSSD. In the 2002 elections, the ČSSD was returned to power, and the ODS remained the second biggest vote-getter. Unlike Poland and Slovakia, the rest of the party spectrum has undergone further consolidation. Several of the smaller parties, including the Christian Democrats (KDU-ČSL) and Freedom Union (US), formed an electoral alliance, but after a promising start, it seems both to be losing popular support and to have difficulty reconciling its member parties. In fact, the most potentially transformative element currently on the Czech party scene is the Communist Party (KSČM), which has been steadily growing in popularity. So far, no other party has been willing to enter a coalition with the Communists, however. In sum, there have been some changes to the Czech party system with time, but its overall shape looks very much the same today as it did in 1992. There is little reason, therefore, to suspect a significant departure from its favorable state-building trajectory.

REPRESENTATION VERSUS GOVERNANCE

The experience of Eastern Europe is a useful one to frame and test hypotheses about the relationship between state-building and democratization, a topic at the heart of comparative politics. Instead of taking democratization as the thing to be explained, I have used it as a starting point to explore the process of state-building. By isolating the variables that shape the success of state-building in new democracies and by providing means to conceptualize and measure them, the research here encourages and facilitates comparisons with historical patterns of state-building in the West, as well as with ongoing state-building and democratization in Latin America, Africa, and East Asia.

This approach refocuses attention on a major question of comparative politics, the long-standing debate on the relationship between pluralistic party competition and government performance, between representation and governance. By definition, extreme multipartism generates very representative governments, and weak-governance systems, for all their other disadvantages, surely trump responsible-party ones on this criterion. More recently, however, Arend Lijphart has suggested that strong multipartism generates not only better representation but better governance as well. On the one side of this debate are the advocates of majoritarian democracy, which my category of responsible-party competition resembles (Powell 1989; 2000; Huber and Powell 1994). On the other side of the debate stand the critics of the majoritarian model, most notably Arend Lijphart. In *Patterns of Democracy* (1999), Lijphart makes a strong claim that what he calls "consensus democracy" performs better in terms of macroeconomic management and the overall implementation of public policy. Superficially, consensus democracy has many of the characteristics of the weak-governance category in the framework I have presented: multiparty government coalitions, fragmented party systems, and difficulty in undertaking public policy reforms to name just a few. Yet, in Lijphart's analysis of the advanced industrial democracies, these appear to be virtues rather than drawbacks.

This book's analysis of new democracies suggests a more nuanced picture. The difficulty with Lijphart's generalization is that it rests on strong assumptions about the characteristics of political parties in consensus democracy systems. For example, the Swiss, Belgian, and Swedish party systems may appear as fragmented as the Eastern European ones in terms of the number of effective parties. Setting aside, for the sake of argument, the caveat made in Chapter 2 about the danger of counting Eastern European electoral coalitions as parties,[10] the number of effective parties is very high in some West European systems—the number is 9.1 for Belgium, 4.3 for Sweden, and 5.1 for Switzerland, compared with 5.5 for Slovenia and 3.0 for Poland.[11] But simply to count the number of parties in parliament is to miss the more important point. What kind of parties are these? How institutionalized are these party systems? Using electoral volatility as a quick measure of institutionalization, it is clear that the Western European systems are much more stable than their Eastern European counterparts: volatility in the Swiss party system averages 4.7 percent, in Sweden 8.5 percent, and in Belgium 11 percent (Mainwaring 1999, 29). Compare this with 37.6 percent for Slovenia and 55.2 for Poland, very typical values for this region's weak-governance systems.[12] As Chapter 2 demonstrates, fragmentation in Eastern European tends to mean that the party system as a whole changes radically with every election cycle. A small party that fails to make it into the governing coalition may very well not be around in the next election. Alternately, that party may well be a recent offshoot of some now defunct other party, and it may be difficult to distinguish this particular offshoot from other offshoots in terms of their programs. How is the voter to choose among them? In short, what if there are not simply many small parties, but many small, *weak* parties? Another potential problem, of course, is a system consisting of mostly small and weak parties and one large, dominant party, which is for the most part unchecked by the divided opposition—as in Slovakia from 1992 to 1998.

The problem is not simply that Lijphart's categories do not import well to Eastern Europe. Consensus democracy may not import well into newly democratized political systems in general. Given the low payoffs for external mobilization in such systems, parties often depend on being in government to survive. This consideration also has implications for one of the general rules of thumb of the literature on democratization—that two turnovers of government marks the transition from "democratizing regime" to "consolidated democracy." Without questioning the rationale that such turnover is one indication of the absence of single-party dominance, exceedingly frequent government turnover may be an indication of the *weakness* of a new democracy, not its consolidation. Finally, the example of democratizing regimes poses one other challenge to Lijphart's consensus democracy model. This model may work well in democracies with consolidated states, which have defined their autonomy vis-à-vis elected politicians, but as I have argued, in new democracies states are often weak because of their association with the old regime and find it difficult to defend themselves from patronage-seeking parties. As the large-N analysis in Chapter 7 suggests, weak-governance party systems in new democracies suffer from a "government effectiveness penalty"; if that penalty leads to public disillusionment with democracy, it may even outweigh the benefits of those systems' greater representativeness.

The findings here do not, of course, refute Lijphart's argument about forms of democratic governance in the West and advanced industrialized world. However, the comparisons do uncover many of the unstated assumptions lurking in this debate over forms of democracy and government performance. These assumptions are critical variables when the field is broadened to include democratizing countries, offering a valuable reminder that institutions and models that work well for established democracies may, in fact, be a bad idea in other political contexts.

The time span for democratization and state-building in postcommunist Eastern Europe has been very compressed. It is clear, however, that the learning curve for holding elections and running campaigns has been much steeper than the one for reforming the state administration. It is still far too early to pass final judgment on the success or failure of state-building in Eastern Europe. That said, the outlines of this process have already begun to make themselves quite clear, and in many cases those outlines are not what either analysts or even the participants themselves expected.

Appendixes

1. Data on the Number of State Administrative Personnel

This appendix reports the raw data on the number of administrative personnel in the national-level and local-level state administrations.

THE NATIONAL-LEVEL STATE ADMINISTRATION

The data were gathered by the author from the respective national statistical offices of Poland, Slovakia, and the Czech Republic. This section explains how those data were collected and how they were organized for cross-national comparison.

First, I have constructed the data set based on field research at the Czech, Slovak, and Polish national statistical offices in 2000 and again in 2001. In Poland, the statistical office has published these data on a yearly basis in the *Statistical Yearbook of the Republic of Poland* since the beginning of the 1990s. Unfortunately, however, the Czech, Slovak, and former Czechoslovak statistical offices have not published these data, though they do collect them. In order to find comparable data for the Czech and Slovak cases, I went in person to their respective national statistics offices in 2000 and again in 2001. In both offices, I was able to request these specific data after consulting with staff as to which categories most closely matched those used in Poland. That the Czech and Slovak statistical offices had previously both been branches of the Czechoslovak statistical office presented both advantages and disadvantages for my research. The disadvantage was that neither office would furnish data from the period of their postcommunist coexistence, 1990 to 1992. The advantage was that, as a result of their common history, both countries have used the same methodology and classification schema for counting state administrative personnel since 1993—a methodology they inherited from the National Statistical Office of Czechoslovakia.

As noted in Chapter 1, the national-level state administration consists of two parts: the central level and the branch level. The central level includes the ministries and central offices. The branch level consists of the (deconcentrated) branch administration of the central offices and ministries (such things as tax offices, school offices, and statistical offices) and the territorial administration of the central government, which includes the district and regional offices described in Chapter 4. These are summarized in Table A1.1.

TABLE AI.I.
Component Units of the National-Level State Administration

	Poland	Czech Republic	Slovakia
Central Administration	• Ministries and central offices • Foreign service • Labor offices	• Ministries and central offices	• Ministries and central offices
Branch Administration	• Branch administration of central offices	• Branch administration of central offices	• Branch administration of central offices
	• Territorial administration: regional offices (*urzędy wojewódzkie*)	• Territorial administration: district offices (*okresní úřady*)	• Territorial administration: district and regional offices (*okresné & krajské úrady*)

Unfortunately, some differences in the categories used by the respective national statistics offices make it impossible to find completely comparable data; the data for Poland include the staff of embassies and the staff of labor offices, which are not included in the Czech and Slovak data. Fortunately, however, these two categories are not big enough to alter the overall comparison of the growth of the state administration across these cases. The Polish foreign service had 2,298 personnel in 1996 according to Torres-Bartyzel and Kacprowicz (1999, 183)—or about 1.6 percent of the national-level state administration for that year—so subtracting it from the total would not significantly affect the overall picture of the national administration. In the case of the Czech Republic, the labor offices employ about 4,500 officials, and this number only grew by 237 people between 1993 and 1998; therefore leaving out this category does not exclude an important component of administrative growth.

A final methodological issue: what are the limitations and potential biases in the data to be used for this kind of cross-national comparison? I am relying on statistical data on the number of personnel collected by the national government agencies themselves. I have used these figures in order to be as consistent as possible. One might argue that, given their source, these data are politically biased, that governments have an incentive to underreport the employment figures. In reality, however, the statistics reported in each of my cases show an expanding state, in some cases a dramatically expanding state. If there is, in fact, underreporting by state statistical agencies, then the problem of runaway state-building is even greater than the analysis here suggests.

The raw data on the number of personnel are displayed in Table A1.2. More detailed notes on the sources and the data are included in the following section. The final part of this appendix presents the data on the number of local-level personnel.

TABLE AI.2.
National-Level State Administration Compared (Number of Positions)

	1990	1991	1992	1993	1994	1995	1996	1997	1998	1999	2000
Czech Republic											
Central	NA	NA	NA	8,961	8,642	8,519	9,631	10,717	10,583	10,980	11,661
Branch	NA	NA	NA	29,706	31,446	31,431	34,291	34,617	34,377	33,628	33,363
Combined	NA	NA	NA	38,667	40,088	39,950	43,922	45,334	44,960	44,608	45,024
Slovakia											
Central	NA	NA	NA	5,804	5,900	6,262	7,774	7,865	7,951	8,049	NA
Branch	NA	NA	NA	16,319	17,077	18,885	21,568	32,954	32,337	30,381	NA
Combined	NA	NA	NA	22,123	22,977	25,147	29,342	40,819	40,288	38,430	37,880
Poland									_Poland Decentralizes_		
Central	46,062	60,794	68,728	88,561	102,700	110,208	115,503	119,104	126,204	122,361	106,502
Branch	29,167	32,500	36,000	26,800	30,700	31,300	31,286	44,383	45,042	25,474	23,675
Decentralized Units	—	—	—	—	—	—	—	—	—	32,085	48,491
Combined	75,229	93,294	104,728	115,361	133,400	141,508	146,789	163,487	171,246	147,835	130,177
										179,920	178,668

SOURCES AND NOTES ON TABLE AI.2
Poland

The Polish data are taken from the *Statistical Yearbook of the Republic of Poland* (1991–2000), specifically the section entitled "Organization of the State." The data for 1999 and 2000 adjust the branch category of administration to reflect the reassignment of personnel after the country's decentralization, as many of the personnel in the new regional- and district-level self-government administrations were transferred from the old regional offices (*urzędy wojewódzkie*). Thus, the category "Decentralized Units" in Table AI.2 comprises administrative personnel in cities with district status (*miasta na prawach powiatu*) and regional self-governments (*urzędy marszałkowskie*). They are taken from figures provided by the Polish National Statistical Office and reported in the journal *Wspólnota* ("Oficjalne dane" 2000, 11).

Czech Republic

Data were requested by the author from the National Statistical Office of the Czech Republic, August 2001, Prague. In the Czech statistical nomenclature, these positions are called "General State Administration" (*Všeobecná státní správa*).

Slovakia

Data were requested by the author from the National Statistical Office of the Slovak Republic, July 2001, Bratislava. Supplemented by data contained in the "Strategy of Public Administration Reform in the Slovak Republic" (Plenipotentiary 1999).

The Slovak statistics were not compiled as neatly by the statistical office's Infoservis as they were in the Czech Republic. For example, although I was able to get personnel data using the same administrative category of "General State Administration" (in Slovak, *Všeobecná štátna správa*), the data did not distinguish between the central- and branch-level administrations. They only showed the size of the national-level state administration as a whole, with a subgrouping for local-level administration. In order to estimate the size of the branch level, I did the following: First, I used published figures on the size of the central-level administration provided in the "Strategy of Public Administration Reform in the Slovak Republic" (Plenipotentiary 1999, 17). Although these are not the same category of "general state administration," they are the best data available. (These are the figures in the "Central" row for Slovakia in Table AI.2.) Then, in order to estimate the size of the branch-level administration, I started with the total number of general state administration provided by the National Statistical Office and subtracted from it the number of central-level personnel reported by the Plenipotentiary and the number of local-level general state administration reported by the National

TABLE A1.3.

Local-Level State Administration Compared (Number of Positions)

	1990	1991	1992	1993	1994	1995	1996	1997	1998	1999	2000
Czech Republic	NA	NA	NA	38,862	42,817	49,624	51,843	60,818	61,470	60,694	63,627
Slovakia	NA	NA	NA	20,274	21,201	21,748	20,076	18,717	17,531	16,690	16,757
Poland	83,428	77,000	89,400	107,600	134,300	138,523	132,521	141,225	137,292	132,188	NA

SOURCES: Czech Republic.—Data requested by the author from the National Statistical Office of the Czech Republic, August 2001, Prague. As with the data in Table A1.2, these positions are classified as "General State Administration" (*Všeobecná státní správa*). Slovakia.—Data requested by the author from the National Statistical Office of the Slovak Republic, July 2001, Bratislava. As with the data in Table A1.2, these positions are classified as "General State Administration" (*Všeobecná štátna správa*). Poland.—*Statistical Yearbook of the Republic of Poland* (1991–2000), specifically the section of the *Yearbook* entitled "Organization of the State"

Statistical Office. These are the numbers reported in the row "Branch" for Slovakia in Table A1.2. It should be noted that this estimate of the number of branch personnel is higher than that provided by the Plenipotentiary (1999); the reason for this is that the Plenipotentiary's figure includes only the personnel of the regional and district offices, not those of the deconcentrated units of the central offices and ministries; it is, in other words, a more limited category than "general state administration."

The Local-Level State Administration

The data used in Chapter 5 are reported in Table A1.3. These data were also gathered by the author from the respective national statistical offices of Poland, Slovakia, and the Czech Republic.

2. Data on Salaries

This appendix reports the raw data on salaries in the national-level state administration and in the general economy, which are used in Chapter 3. The state-administrative data come from the same sources and use the same administrative units as the personnel data in Appendix 1. (Slovakia is something of an exception, however, as the notes on Table A2.1 explain.) Table A2.1 reports the average monthly salary in nominal national currencies. The data for the state administration distinguish between the central and branch levels—which combined form the national-level state administration. In order to create the overall average for the national-level state administration for the tables and figures in the text, I have calculated weighted averages, weighting the salaries of each level by the number of personnel at that level.

SOURCES AND NOTES ON TABLE A2.1
Czech Republic

The salary data for the state administration were specially requested from the National Czech Statistical Office. The data on the average salary in the overall economy are from the *Statistical Yearbook of the Czech Republic* (various years): these data do not exclude state sector employees in computing the average.

Slovakia

The salary data for the Slovak state administration are not as orderly as those for the Czech Republic and Poland. As they were not readily available at the Slovak National Statistical Office, I have put them together from a variety of sources:

- The salaries in the central state administration were calculated using raw data from the Plenipotentiary for the Reform of the Public Administration (1999). I

TABLE A2.I.
Average Monthly Salaries in the National-Level State Administration and General Economy

	1990	1991	1992	1993	1994	1995	1996	1997	1998	1999	2000
Czech Republic											
Central	NA	NA	NA	9,160	11,682	13,832	15,089	16,017	16,508	18,604	18,937
Branch	NA	NA	NA	7,358	8,715	9,885	11,757	12,376	12,404	13,984	14,150
Economy	3,286	3,792	4,644	5,817	6,894	8,172	9,676	10,691	11,693	—	—
Slovakia											
Central	NA	NA	NA	8,873	10,650	12,017	16,744	18,245	19,914	NA	NA
Branch	NA	NA	NA	5,834	6,316	6,968	8,128	9,518	9,743	10,199	10,450
Economy	NA	NA	NA	5,379	6,294	7,195	8,154	9,051	9,685	10,728	11,715
Poland										*Poland Decentralizes*	
Central	151	235	434	575	757	1,009	1,291	1,575	1,779	2,445	—
Branch	149	208	307	431	537	714	888	1,066	1,221	1,908	—
Economy	144	205	290	390	525	691	874	1,066	1,233	1,697	—

have divided the total expenditures on salaries for the central state administration (Plenipotentiary 1999, 18) by the total number of personnel in the central state administration (Plenipotentiary 1999, 17).

- The data on salaries in the branch administration were provided at the author's request by the Slovak National Statistical Office. Unfortunately, they do not completely overlap in terms of administrative categories with the branch-level data on personnel reported in Appendix 1: they only include employees in the regional (*krajské úrady*) and district offices (*okresné úrady*) and so are more restricted than the branch-level data on the number of personnel, which are based on the broader category of "general state administration" (*Všeobecná štátna správa*). They are, however, the best available data.

- The data on the average salary in the overall economy are from the *Statistical Yearbook of the Slovak Republic* (various years). These data also do not exclude state sector employees in computing the average.

Poland

The Polish data are from the *Statistical Yearbook of the Republic of Poland* (various years), using the same categories as the personnel data in Appendix 1. Unlike the Czech and Slovak data, the Polish statistical data on average wages in the general economy do exclude the wages of state officials.

3. Interview Sample

Interviews were conducted with state administrators, politicians, and policy experts over three trips to Poland, the Czech Republic, and Slovakia from 1999 to 2001, which together added up to thirteen months in the field. I conducted 132 interviews: 57 in Poland, 34 in Slovakia, and 41 in the Czech Republic. I used an open-ended format in these interviews, tailoring the questions to the particular experience of my various interlocutors but also keeping up a certain repertoire of standard questions. Using a combination snowball / quota sampling strategy, I selected the initial interviews in order to reflect all levels of the state—top, middle, and lower—and as these interviews yielded further contacts, I followed the trail.

Table A3.1 provides a breakdown of the respondents, dividing the sample by country and the type of respondent. On one dimension it tabulates the sample in terms of the relevant level of governance, central, regional, and local. I define the meso-level here as those institutions between the central government and the local government. In Poland and Slovakia, the meso-level includes regions and districts. In the Czech Republic, it includes only districts. The table's other dimension tabulates the sample in terms

TABLE A3.1.
Interview Sample, by Country and Respondent Type

	Elected	Appointed	Experts	Central	Meso	Local
Czech Republic	8	19	18	36	5	11
Slovakia	6	7	21	31	3	10
Poland	8	31	25	39	12	19
Central	12	45	61			
Meso	1	6	13			
Local	15	10	20			

NOTE: To be clear, this table aggregates the number of respondents, not the number of interviews. Because I interviewed some people more than once, the number of interviews was greater than 132.

of elected officials, appointed officials in the state administration, and experts. This last category includes a wider group of respondents who either worked with the state administration in some area of public policy (for instance through an NGO or through an international organization such as the EU) or who worked on the subject of the state administration as journalists or academics. In a few cases, respondents fit into more than one of these categories; for instance, after several years in the state administration, a respondent may have left to work in an NGO dealing with public policy. In a number of instances, I conducted multiple interviews with the same people over successive trips to the field.

4. Data Used to Calculate Party System Fractionalization

This appendix presents the raw data used to assess the internal heterogeneity of electoral alliances (such as AWS and SDK) in calculating the party system fractionalization in Chapter 2. It presents the data on the representation of political groupings in parliament. Table A4.1 lists the internal breakdown of the major electoral alliances by their constituent political groupings, which formed a subset of the data used to calculate party system fractionalization. The rest of the data used in computing these indicators did not involve electoral alliances but single parties. Since the data on parliamentary seat shares for single parties are readily available (see, for example, the University of Essex, *Project on Political Transformation and the Electoral Process in Post-Communist Europe*, www.essex.ac.uk / elections), I do not include them here. I used the *Wykaz 2000 Osób Sprawujących Władzę w RP* (1994) to calculate party subgroupings for the 1993 Polish parliament. The figures for the 1997 Polish parliament are taken from Włodzimierz Wesołowski (2000, 134). I have simplified the SLD alliance into four subgroupings because of the limitations of the available data. For the Slovak figures, I am indebted to Kevin Deegan Krause.

Breakdown of the Parliamentary Seat Shares of the Electoral Alliances by Component Political Groupings

POLAND

Electoral Coalition Name	Party Name	Party Acronym	Number of Seats in Parliament
	1993 Elections (Sejm)		
	Social Democrats of Poland	SdRP	76
Democratic Left Alliance (SLD)	All-Poland Association of Unions	OPZZ	10
	Union of Polish Teachers	ZNP	12
	Other subgroupings		34
	Independents		39
	1997 Elections (Sejm)		
	Solidarity	S	62
	Conservative People's Party	SKL	18
	Union of Christian Nationalists	ZChN	25
Electoral Action Solidarity (AWS)	Confederation for an Independent Poland	KPN	9
	Center Understanding	PC	13
	Catholic Families	RK	18
	Christian Democratic Party	PChD	5
	Self-Governmenters	SRz	12
	Independents		13
	Social Democrats of Poland	SdRP	94
Democratic Left Alliance (SLD)	All-Poland Association of Unions	OPZZ	13
	Union of Polish Teachers	ZNP	4
	Other subgroupings		20
	Independents		33

SLOVAKIA

Electoral Coalition Name	Party Name	Party Acronym	Number of Seats in Parliament
	1990 Elections (Slovak National Council)		
Hungarian Alliance	Hungarian Christian Democratic Movement	MKDM	8
	Coexistence	ESWS	6
	1992 Elections (Slovak National Council)		
Hungarian Alliance	Hungarian Christian Democratic Movement	MKDM	5
	Coexistence	ESWS	9
	1994 Elections (Slovak National Council)		
Common Choice (SV)	Party of the Democratic Left	SDL'	13
	Social Democratic Party of Slovakia	SDSS	2
	Green Party of Slovakia	SZS	2
	Agrarian Party?	HP	1
Hungarian Alliance	Hungarian Christian Democratic Movement	MKDM	7
	Coexistence	ESWS	9
	Hungarian Civic Party	MPP	1
	1998 Elections (Slovak National Council)		
Party of the Democratic Coalition (SDK)	Democratic Party	DS	6
	Christian Democratic Movement	KDH	16
	Slovak Green Party	SZS	4
	Democratic Union	DU	12
	Social Democratic Party of Slovakia	SDSS	4

5. Countries Used in Cross-National Comparison

This appendix presents the countries used in the cross-national analysis (Chapter 7), as well as a list of how they have been coded in terms of party system type. For most countries, there are four observations, corresponding to each of the four years covered in Kaufmann, Kraay, and Mastruzzi's survey of government effectiveness (2002). For a few countries, only two observations are given because these countries were not classified as free for the full period. The criteria for classifying party system type are discussed in Chapter 7.

TABLE A5.1.
Party System Type by Country and Year

Country	1996	1998	2000	2002
Albania	DPv1	DPv1	DPv1	DPv1
Argentina	RP	RP	RP	RP
Benin	WG	WG	WG	WG
Bolivia	WG	WG	WG	WG
Brazil	WG	WG	WG	WG
Bulgaria	WG	WG	WG	WG
Cape Verde	DPv1	DPv1	DPv1	DPv2
Chile	RP	RP	RP	RP
Colombia	DPv1	DPv1	DPv1	DPv1
Croatia	DPv1	DPv1	DPv2	DPv2
Czech Republic	RP	RP	RP	RP
Djibouti	—	—	DPv1	DPv1
Ecuador	WG	WG	WG	WG
Estonia	WG	WG	RP	RP
Ghana	DPv1	DPv1	DPv1	DPv2
Guatemala	WG	WG	WG	WG
Hungary	RP	RP	RP	RP
Indonesia	—	—	WG	WG
Latvia	WG	WG	WG	WG
Lithuania	WG	WG	WG	WG
Macedonia	WG	WG	WG	WG
Madagascar	WG	WG	WG	WG
Malawi	DPv1	DPv1	DPv1	DPv1
Mali	DPv1	DPv1	DPv1	DPv1
Mauritius	DPv1	DPv1	DPv1	DPv1
Mexico	DPv1	DPv1	RP	RP
Moldova	WG	WG	WG	DPv1
Mozambique	RP	RP	RP	RP
Namibia	DPv1	DPv1	DPv1	DPv1
Niger	—	—	DPv1	DPv1
Nigeria	—	—	DPv1	DPv1

Country	1996	1998	2000	2002
Paraguay	DPv1	DPv1	DPv1	DPv1
Peru	DPv1	DPv1	DPv1	WG
Philippines	WG	WG	WG	WG
Poland	WG	WG	WG	WG
Romania	WG	WG	WG	WG
Russia	DPv2	DPv2	DPv1	DPv1
São Tomé	DPv1	DPv1	DPv1	DPv2
Senegal	DPv1	DPv1	DPv2	DPv2
Serbia	DPv1	DPv1	DPv1	WG
Seychelles	DPv1	DPv1	DPv1	DPv1
Slovakia	DPv1	DPv1	DPv2	DPv2
Slovenia	WG	WG	WG	WG
South Africa	DPv1	DPv1	DPv1	DPv1
South Korea	DPv1	DPv2	WG	WG
Taiwan	RP	RP	RP	RP
Tanzania	DPv1	DPv1	DPv1	DPv1
Thailand	WG	WG	WG	DPv1
Ukraine	DPv2	DPv2	DPv2	DPv2
Uruguay	RP	RP	RP	RP
Venezuela	WG	WG	DPv1	DPv1
Zambia	DPv1	DPv1	DPv1	DPv1

NOTE: DPv1, Dominant Party (variant 1); DPv2, Dominant Party (variant 2); RP, Responsible Party; WG, Weak Governance

Notes

INTRODUCTION

1. For simplicity, I will use Communist Party to include parties that may, for nationally idiosyncratic reasons, have had a different official title. The most prominent example in this book is the Polish United Workers' Party (PZPR), which was the title adopted by Poland's Communists prior to 1989.

2. Several scholars have noted the surprising resilience of the state bureaucracy after communism; see Robert Brym and Vladimir Gimpelson (2004), Anna Grzymała-Busse (2003), Venelin Ganev (2001), Vladimir Gimpelson and Daniel Triesman (2002), the World Bank (1999), Witold Kieżun (2000), and Jerzy Bartkowski (1996).

3. Runaway state-building does not simply describe rapid growth in state size. If a state is growing in size while making commensurate gains in effectiveness, it is not an example of runaway state-building. Unfortunately, the latter dynamic is the exception rather than the rule in postcommunist Eastern Europe. How do I measure effectiveness? How can we recognize runaway state-building when we see it? I will address these questions in further detail in Chapters 1 and 3.

4. Following Martin Shefter, I define patronage as "a divisible benefit that politicians distribute to individual voters, campaign workers, or contributors in exchange for political support" (1994, 283 n.3). These benefits may take many forms. Of primary interest here are positions within the state administration.

5. "Unconsolidated states" are states in which the state administration lacks clear political autonomy, both formally and informally. Such a deficiency is common feature of authoritarian and postauthoritarian regimes.

6. Venelin Ganev describes such state-building in Eastern Europe when he writes, "State-building in post-communism is about redrawing boundaries of existing institutions, redistribution of extracted resources, and rearrangement of strategic positions behind the seemingly intact façade of the state apparatus. It is the period when the inherent ambiguity characteristic of the very essence of the socialist state—the party-state symbiosis—must come to an abrupt and dynamic resolution. Who and what will be 'the state,' who and what will be the 'party'? This is the dilemma of the earliest stage of state-building in postcommunism" (2001, 415). This kind of state-building is found wherever new democracies must separate the state from the governing parties.

7. Chapter 7 presents a large-N cross-national analysis, though it does so not by group-

ing countries in terms of runaway state-building or no but by comparing the capacity of state administrations across different types of party systems.

8. A caveat is in order here. As I describe in Chapter 1, the rate of expansion may differ significantly among runaway states over time, taking place incrementally in some and in sudden bursts in others.

9. See Chapter 1 for the rationale behind these criteria.

10. Other indicators of effectiveness could be added, but my primary aim is to establish an analytical category that can be used to test a theory with wider cross-national comparisons, not to be descriptively exhaustive. In other contexts, both geographical and historical, different measures of state effectiveness may be more appropriate.

11. Poland, whose "shock therapy" constituted the earliest and most rapid macroeconomic reforms in Eastern Europe, is a good example of such "stateless" economic development. Undoubtedly, the shock-therapy reforms set the basis for Poland's above-average economic growth in the early and mid-1990s. It is equally clear, however, that the neo-liberal reforms at the heart of shock therapy—freeing exchange rates, opening domestic markets to trade, lifting price controls, and cutting subsidies—required relatively little administrative capacity (Nelson 2001, 236). Not to denigrate Poland's achievement, but all these reforms required was political courage. Poland's shock therapy was decidedly not the kind of strategic economic stewardship of Japan's MITI or of the South Korean state in the 1980s. Shock therapy allowed Polish companies to quickly (and profitably) identify their place in the global economy; however, it was not the kind of policy that enables a country to improve its long-term economic position, as Japan, Taiwan, and South Korea's developmental states succeeded in doing (Johnson 1982; Wade 1990; Amsden 1989). Moreover, Poland's overall economic growth has slowed significantly since 2000, and important sectors of its economy are substantially behind those of Hungary and the Czech Republic. These two nations have built up more effective state administrations since the fall of communism, and the advantages of this greater capacity are evident not only in their recent economic growth rates but also in their far better handling of administration-intensive reforms such as health care, pensions, and decentralization, which are the new order of the day, now that the macroeconomic fundamentals are in place.

12. As described in Chapter 1, Poland, the Czech Republic, and Slovakia were very similar in terms of their political institutions, economic development, proximity to EU accession, and broad political culture, yet they diverged sharply in their state-building after their democratic revolutions in 1989.

13. Because national statistical bureaus use different classification schemes for public personnel and different methodologies for counting them, it is next to impossible to gather comparable data on state size for a large cross-national sample; see Schiavo-Campo, de Tommaso, and Mukherjee (1997). By focusing on just three countries, I was able to adjust for such discrepancies and collect comparable data on the growth of the state administration; see Appendix 1 for a description of this data.

14. Public opinion surveys in postcommunist Eastern Europe have consistently shown that the public strongly disapproves of official corruption (Rose, Mishler, and Haerpfer 1998).

15. See also Epstein (1967).

16. By the "consolidation of state bureaucracies," I mean the establishment of both for-

mal and informal institutions preserving the autonomy of career bureaucrats from political and societal interest groups.

17. As one scholar described the former Communist Parties, "The formerly so admired powerful machines became 'loosely knitted anarchies,' because they had to integrate quite heterogeneous coalitions of bourgeois and working-class elements" (von Beyme 1996, 139).

18. Among other scholars working in this tradition, notable examples include Huntington (1991); Dahl (1971; 1982); and Powell (1989; 2000). Often, in emphasizing the trade-off between representativeness and government effectiveness, this school advocates what Lijphart (1999) calls majoritarian democracy.

CHAPTER 1: THE CONCEPT AND CAUSES OF RUNAWAY STATE-BUILDING

1. It is also the best operational definition for collecting accurate and comparable cross-national statistics for postcommunist Eastern Europe. Inevitably, there are differences in the classification of public personnel across countries, but the categories of central government ministries and branch offices are sufficiently delimited in each of these three that they can be meaningfully compared. In her analysis of state politicization in Eastern Europe, Grzymała-Busse (2003) uses a wider operational definition of the state: the public administration. However, the public administration includes personnel whom the national government does not appoint, most notably the local-level administration; therefore, local administration growth cannot be taken as evidence of national-party patronage. The second problem with the public administration is that it includes different categories of personnel across countries.

2. These are generally defined as department heads, deputy department heads, and other administrative staff below these levels.

3. Chapter 5 tackles local-level patronage politics and its effect on local administration.

4. For more on salaries, see below.

5. Author's interviews with Jaromír Vepřek, head of Tým DG Plus, a Czech health care policy consultancy (Prague, July 27, 2001); Zuzana Šranková, Orava Project for Democracy in Education (Bratislava, July 11, 2001); Józefina Hrynkiewicz, Instytut Spraw Publicznych (Warsaw, June 21, 2001).

6. Unfortunately, Czech and Slovak data are unavailable before 1993. Polish data are available from 1990. See Appendix 1.

7. The post-1998 numbers for Poland are adjusted to reflect personnel reassigned to regional governments after that country's 1998 decentralization. Even comparing all three countries from 1993 to 1998 to avoid this complicating factor shows the same case-ordering: Slovakia, 82 percent; Poland, 48 percent; Czech Republic, 16 percent.

8. Kaufmann, Kraay, and Mastruzzi's measure assigns a minimum value of −2.5 for the least effective states and 2.5 for the most effective ones. I have used figures from 1996 and 2000 because they most closely match the period analyzed here.

9. See the cross-national analysis in Chapter 7 for a sense of where these scores place Poland, the Czech Republic, and Slovakia relative to other new democracies in Eastern Europe and beyond.

10. These countries rate very similarly on Johnson, Holmes, and Kirkpatrick's *Index of Economic Freedom* (1999). On the index's five-point scale (with 5 being the least free), the Czech

Republic rated 2.05 in 1999, Poland 2.95, and Slovakia 3.05—scores that put them in the most free category for the region.

11. See the large-N cross-national comparison in Chapter 7 for a statistical analysis of the impact of economic development on the state administration. The analysis there shows that higher levels of economic development are, in fact, associated with greater state capacity but that the effect of the party system is still significant after controlling for differences in economic development.

12. In 1998, Czech per capita GDP was U.S.$5,170 in 1995, compared with $3,900 for Poland and $4,000 for Slovakia (World Bank 2002). If the size of the state administration is weighted by population size, Slovakia comes out with the largest state at 7.48 state personnel per 1,000 inhabitants, compared with 4.43 for Poland and 4.37 for the Czech Republic (see Appendix 1). The ratio of per capita administrative personnel to per capita GDP makes for a rough-and-ready measure of the economic footprint of the state. Again, Poland and Slovakia stand out here, with scores of 1.87 and 1.44, compared with 0.85 for the Czech Republic.

13. The additional data on the Bulgarian and Russian administrations come from Verheijen (1999, 126) and Gimpelson and Triesman (2002, 158). In Russia's case, the growth of administration came primarily at the subnational level, while the central level remained quite stable (Gimpelson and Triesman 2002, 160). The economic data are from the World Development Indicators (World Bank 2002).

14. Poland's presidency is strongest of the three, but it is more parliamentary than presidential overall (Baylis 1996).

15. There were not significant differences in the regulation of party finances among these countries for most of the period considered here. Poland was first to pass more stringent regulations, and that did not occur until 1997, well after the greatest expansion of the administration (Walecki 2000). Poland enacted additional regulations in 2000–2001, but their efficacy is dubious in light of a subsequent party finance scandal, the so-called Rywin affair. This affair centered around a July 2002 incident in which a film producer, Lew Rywin, with connections to the then governing Democratic Left Alliance (SLD) tried to solicit a $17.5 million payoff from Poland's biggest newspaper, *Gazeta Wyborcza*, in exchange for the inclusion of favorable provisions in a draft law on the media. It was alleged that he was acting on behalf of the SLD in order to raise funds. Unbeknownst to Rywin, the newspaper's editor Adam Michnik recorded the conversation. The Rywin affair became the subject of a prolonged parliamentary investigation, which itself became the subject of accusations of political corruption; for a summary of the scandal, see Smolenski (2002) and "Rywingate" (2004).

16. Ironically, this starting point of postcommunist party organization is, according to a number of scholars, also the style of party organization toward which some Western European parties are moving. Dubbed "minimal parties" in the literature on Western European politics, these parties "tend to be 'minimal' only in respect to mobilization efforts. But where penetration of the state system is concerned, the[se new] parties could be rather dubbed 'maximal parties' . . . [T]he state has been colonized by the party leaders, not via plutocratic economic power—as Pareto once suggested—but rather via penetration of the state. Meritocracy no longer plays its old role . . . The links between parties and members have become loose. Party and government leaders increasingly established communication links between the electors and themselves without resort to party organization" (von Beyme 1996, 145–46).

The similarities to the postcommunist countries are striking, though in them the reliance on a narrow circle of critical supporters rather than a wider membership base is even more extreme.

17. Ekiert and Kubik offer a caveat in their survey of protest events, suggesting that postcommunist society is more mobilized than generally recognized. As they also note, however, "the magnitude of protest is by and large lower than in more established democracies" (1997, 31). Thus, their "contentiousness" measure does not contradict the widely noted low identification with political parties.

18. See also Linz and Stepan (1996, 245–47).

19. See the National Democracies Barometer (NDB) III survey conducted in 1993–94 among nine countries of Eastern Europe, described in Rose, Mishler, and Haerpfer (1998, 85–88, 153–57).

20. The Western European figure is calculated as a simple average of the party membership figures for the 14 countries as reported in Szczerbiak (2001, 112).

21. The availability of public funding and interest groups may also impact parties' demand for patronage. Though small in size, public funding has been available in all three countries since the early 1990s and so cannot account for differences in patronage. One might also hypothesize that organized interest groups were stronger in the Czech Republic, allowing its parties to do without patronage or membership. The scholarship emphasizes these groups' weakness, however; see Orenstein and Desai (1997).

22. To reemphasize an important point, I am speaking of the administrative apparatus of the state, not the welfare state. In many ways, the communist welfare state was generous, providing nominally free health care, education, and housing—though the necessity for informal payments for these services was notorious. The state is still largely seen as the expected provider of these services. My characterization of the administrative apparatus as delegitimized is not, therefore, intended to describe the welfare state, which is excluded from the personnel data (Rose 1995, 19; Kapstein and Mandelbaum 1997; Cook, Orenstein, and Rueschemeyer 1999).

23. See also World Bank (1999, 7).

24. It is not uncommon today to hear tales, for example, of farmers or travel agents being appointed to hospital boards by the dominant local political party (Walewski 1999).

25. Guillermo O'Donnell calls this mechanism "vertical accountability." Party system institutionalization also enhances "horizontal accountability," parties holding each other accountable, especially between elections (O'Donnell 1999, 29–30, 42–44).

26. Given voter disengagement from politics in Eastern Europe, it may seem that these are uninstitutionalized systems. However, institutionalization is a continuous, not dichotomous, variable; see Mainwaring (1999, 22–26). Moreover, institutionalization varies considerably in this region, both across countries and over time (Shabad and Slomczynski 2004; Kreuzer and Pettai 2003; Toole 2000).

27. Shabad and Slomczynski (2004) have measured institutionalization in terms of interparty switching. Consonant with the analysis here, they find that the rate of party switching has decreased significantly in the Czech Republic, though not in Poland. Kreuzer and Pettai (2003) measure institutionalization in terms of the electoral success of nonestablished parties: start-ups, splinters, and mergers. On one dimension of institutionalization, the emer-

gence of career politicians, Shabad and Slomczynski (2002) offer a caveat on the Polish-Czech comparison, finding that reelection rates for MPs have been increasing in both countries.

28. See Mainwaring (1999, 89, 128–31).

29. On high volatility, see Mainwaring (1999) and O'Donnell (1999, 30); on high turnover, see Toole (2000, 458) and Mainwaring (1999, 123).

30. See Mair (1997, 199–223); Toole (2000).

31. I have in mind what Giovanni Sartori describes as "predominance": one party is significantly stronger than the rest and is supported by a winning majority (1976, 131–201). Elections matter in such systems since the strongest party can be turned out of government if it cannot find a supporting coalition.

32. This is a key difference between my conception of robust competition and Grzymała-Busse's, in whose formulation fractionalization is an unqualified good because it disperses power (2003, 1131 n.1). While overconcentration of power (such as in Mečiar's Slovakia) is harmful, too much dispersion creates its own incentives for patronage, as described above. As long as no party is dominant, some degree of concentration is beneficial because it increases vertical accountability and creates parties whose survival does not depend on winning the next elections.

33. Weimar Germany is also a good example of a weak-governance party system (Mainwaring 1995, 374), yet it has also been noted as a country with very little political patronage in the state administration (Shefter 1994, 40–41). How can this anomaly be explained? In fact, Weimar Germany is a good case to illustrate the necessary and sufficient logic of the party competition framework advanced here. Germany is the archetypal case of state consolidation before democratization (Shefter 1994, 36); therefore, it lacked the necessary conditions (the predisposition) for patronage politics. Had the sequencing worked the other way, Weimar's fragmented party system would have fueled widespread patronage politics.

34. The term "responsible-party" system, which I take from Martin Shefter (1994), has a long history in political science (Goodnow 1900). Although the word "responsible" adds a normative overtone, the idea of responsibility concerns the ability of democratic competition to produce governments that are vertically accountable to voters. In such party systems, elected parties can deliver on their policy programs because of the existence of an effective and politically independent state administration that can implement them (Shefter 1994, 61–62).

35. It is untenable for two reasons. First, the longer the formerly dominant-party machine sits in the opposition, the weaker it becomes since it becomes cut off from one of its primary tools of party-building, the ability to provide state patronage. Second, the fragility of the government coalition increases the chances that the formerly dominant party will return to power. In the former case, the logic of competition tends toward the fragmented type, and in the second case it reverts to the dominant-party type (variant 1).

36. Because of both its institutional peculiarities and its atypical exit from communism, postcommunist Russia in the Yeltsin era presents something of a challenge in terms of classification. Considering Yeltsin's superpresidential prerogatives, the political system concentrated power in a way suggesting the dominant-party (variant 1) logic. Yet the parliament was dominated by an obstructionist Communist Party: with the shelling of parliament in 1993, the conflict between president and parliament spilled over into armed conflict. Until Putin,

the result was political deadlock and so fit best within the category of dominant-party (variant 2) system. There is a more detailed analysis of the Russian case in Chapter 7.

37. Neither Germany nor Britain is a two-party system. Germany also has the left-leaning Green Party and the right-leaning Liberal Party. Britain has a significant third party in the Liberals. In both countries, however, these additional parties are considerably smaller, and the lines of party competition are drawn by the two anchor parties.

38. I am using the word "bureaucracy" in its ideal-typical sense. To quote Evans and Rauch, "Contemporary empirical analyses of rent-seeking and corruption often use the term 'bureaucracy' in its everyday pejorative sense rather than in the Weberian sense of a set of administrative organizations with specific structural features. Weber viewed bureaucracy, not as a generic collection of state officials, but as a particular kind of organizational structure, set in contrast to earlier patrimonial and prebendal forms of government administration" (1999, 749).

39. For an excellent and complementary discussion of the organization of the postcommunist state, see Ganev (2001).

40. Ganev terms this feature of postcommunist state administration "the informalization of discretion" (2001, 406).

41. Rudolph and Rudolph (1979) also made this argument long before the "new public management" school appeared.

CHAPTER 2: CONSTRAINING GOVERNMENT PATRONAGE

1. The qualifier "national-level" is important for the reasons mentioned in Chapter 1, namely, the size of the national-level state administration is determined by the policies of the national government. The local-level state administration is largely separate from those policies. Chapter 5 focuses exclusively on local-level party politics and administrative development.

2. The anticommunist opposition did not always win the first free elections, as the examples of Bulgaria and Romania show. In both countries, a reorganized and renamed Communist Party won these elections. However, the reorganized Communists also soon experienced internal splits, which, combined with a fractious opposition, led to the emergence of weak-governance party systems.

3. The decision to dissolve Czechoslovakia came after the June 1992 elections and took effect on January 1, 1993.

4. Of course, as conspicuous as the absence of nationalist and religious dimensions of party competition in the Czech Republic is, it begs the question of why it should be so. As mentioned in Chapter 1, a few deep-seated structural factors immediately suggest themselves. First, Czech society is deeply secularized, certainly in comparison with Poland and Slovakia, but even in comparison with Western Europe. The absence of religiously defined parties should come as little surprise. In light of the breakup of Czechoslovakia the absence of nationalist feeling in the Czech Republic is more curious. Here was a postcommunist nation, which politically dominated its federal state, that peacefully and nonchalantly acceded to the secession of its lesser half, Slovakia. A number of scholars have pointed out the "artificial" origins of the Czechoslovak state in the first place. Czechoslovakia was dreamed up

by a few Czech statesmen after WWI for instrumental reasons—namely for getting Czech independence from Austria, and the inclusion of Slovakia was useful for this goal. Additionally, as Janos (1997) has argued, Slovakia benefited economically from Czechoslovakia far more than the Czech Republic did, as a result of aid transfers to the less developed eastern part of the federation. For the Czechs, then, it seemed economically advantageous to be rid of their poor neighbors. Developing that logic, Innes (2001) has noted that in the early 1990s Czechs saw the less economically developed Slovak Republic as a brake on rapid economic reform and integration with Western Europe. This last argument only reinforces the primacy of economic concerns in Czech party competition: nationalism was framed in terms of economic policy.

5. Laakso and Taagepera (1979, 4).

6. Some weak-governance systems may have high vote differentials, but the important difference is that these differentials are not sustained over time. Consider the situation in which a governing party's support collapses after it takes office; a new government party may easily defeat the old in the next election, but then its support collapses too. Such a system would have, of course, very high volatility and lack institutionalized parties; Bulgaria is a good example. To distinguish between systems like Bulgaria's and the dominant-party type, I define dominant-party (variant 1) systems as those that sustain a high vote differential for the same party for at least two elections.

7. Because the formula for calculating fragmentation does not distinguish between government and opposition, it awards the same score whether the dominant machine is in the government or in the opposition.

8. Though it requires a deeper level of familiarity with a given country to disaggregate the vote of electoral alliances into their constituent parties, to treat such alliances as parties for the sake of convenience leads to distorted conclusions about the logic of competition in that country. It also leads to a distorted view of the relationship between party competition and patronage politics.

9. The volatility index measures the net change in the vote shares of all parties from one election to the next. "The [volatility] index is derived by adding the net change in percentage of seats (or votes) gained or lost by each party from one election to the next, then dividing by two" (Mainwaring and Scully 1995, 6). Because frequent splits and mergers represent lack of institutionalization, I count splits and mergers as fully new parties. This interpretation maximizes volatility but does so consistently while avoiding difficult judgment calls about party continuity.

10. I define an alternation as any recomposition of the government coalition or major restructuring of the cabinet, such as the replacement of the prime minister.

11. These are features of party organization and not of the social context in which parties operate. Thus, to say that a postcommunist party is well organized (because of its centralization, stable leadership, etc.) does not contradict my more general argument that the postcommunist legacy of demobilized society makes party-building based on popular mobilization difficult. All parties in postcommunist Eastern Europe—whether well organized or not—run up against the difficulties posed by a demobilized society.

12. Bulgaria's two main political groupings for most of the 1990s, the Union of Democratic Forces (UDF) and Bulgarian Socialist Party (BSP), complement the Polish examples of

weak internal organization. Both the BSP and the UDF were umbrella organizations comprising numerous, often fractious, political groupings (Bugajski 2002, 787–89, 793–95). Describing the internal composition of the UDF, one scholar writes, "Analysis of its inner relationships in terms of faction brings little illumination. If the political unit within which factions are to be discerned is taken to be the Union as a whole, then indeed lines of fracture are not only visible, but are constitutive of the unit. If the search is to be for lines of fracture within each component unit, then the search does not lead far. Most of the units are diminutive organizations and are in any case dominated by their leaders, and tensions within the Union often take the form of quarrels between individuals" (Waller 1995, 157). Romania's postcommunist camp began a process of fragmentation with the split of the National Salvation Front in 1992. Recalling the example of Poland's AWS, the fractious Romanian right formed an electoral alliance called the Democratic Convention, which established a shaky government in 1996 but vanished from the political scene in the following elections.

13. I do not include the 1989 elections in Poland since they were only partially free, the Communist Party having reserved a set number of seats for itself.

14. Considering the development of the Czech and Slovak party systems since 1990, one immediately faces the following question: inasmuch as these two republics were part of a single federal state until 1990, can their party systems be treated as separate over the period from the first free elections in 1989 until the break-up of Czechoslovakia on January 1, 1993? The unambiguous answer is yes (Innes 2001). It was precisely because there were two party systems in post-1989 Czechoslovakia that the institutional arrangements of the federal state broke apart. As evidence of the separate and diverging development of the Czech and Slovak party systems between 1990 and 1993, one need only consider that aside from the Communist Party—which had itself split into Czech and Slovak branches by that time—there were no parties that fielded party lists in both the Czech and Slovak republics in the 1990 and 1992 federal elections. Moreover, the disintegration of the Czechoslovak state had almost no impact on the Czech party system. The same parties predominated after the split which predominated before it. The one party whose trajectory seems to have been altered by the breakup of the federal state in 1993 is the Moravian regional party HSD-SMS; after the loss of Slovakia, the Moravians veered away from regional autonomy movements and HSD-SMS has declined into obscurity. HSD-SMS was a second-tier party to begin with, so its decline into obscurity may well have been the natural course even without the breakup of Czechoslovakia. In any case, it too had only run party lists in the Czech half of the federal state.

15. Slovakia's electoral system in the 1990, 1992, and 1994 elections mirrored that in the Czech Republic. Namely, the elections employed a proportional representation (PR) system with closed party lists and minimum thresholds of 5 percent.

16. The reason for Mečiar's conversion to nationalism is unclear. In my opinion, it was an example of astute political opportunism. In Slovakia's local elections in November 1990, which followed the national elections by five months, the vote for the nationalist parties increased dramatically while that of the dissident parties declined in equal measure. Mečiar perceived that nationalism had a better future than reform politics.

17. Previously, electoral alliances of two to three parties required 7 percent in total, and alliances of four or more 10 percent in total. For a description of HZDS's electoral ruse, see Bútora et al. (1999).

18. Slovakia's electoral volatility was on par with another dominant-party (variant 1) system of the time: Croatia's volatility averaged 48.8 percent under Tudjman (author's calculations).

19. For more on the treatment of the Tiso regime in contemporary Slovakia, see Cohen (1999).

20. These are designated by italics in Table 2.2.

21. The Communist Party had expected that the institutional arrangements negotiated in the Roundtable Agreement would preserve its leading role in politics (Latynski 1992, 98–99).

22. The fragmentation of Solidarity into squabbling factions engendered public disillusionment with politics and was evident in the declining voter turnout in national elections. Whereas the turnout in the 1989 elections had been nearly 100 percent, the figure was only 43 percent in the 1991 elections, among the lowest figure for Eastern Europe at the time (Agh 1998, 150). In the first elections in Czechoslovakia, which took place in June 1990, the turnout was 96 percent. In Hungary, where the founding elections took place in March-April 1990, the turnout was 63 percent. A public opinion survey undertaken in 1992 provides another measure of the public's apathy at this time: 33 percent of Polish respondents—more than in any other country surveyed—said they would support the suspension of parliament and political parties (quoted in Derleth 2000, 275).

23. The post-Solidarity government of Hanna Suchocka was brought down by the Solidarity MPs themselves in a misguided bluff to gain political leverage by calling a vote of no-confidence.

24. For a full description of the SLD's composition, see Szczerbiak (1999c, 1432).

25. The thresholds were 5 percent for individual parties, 8 percent for electoral committees composed of more than one party, and 7 percent for national list seats. The number of electoral districts was increased from 37 to 52, each with from 3 to 17 members (Millard 1999, 87).

26. Parenthetically, Poland's attempt to simplify the party system by changing the electoral rules has not been very successful. Before 1993—that is, before the elimination of pure PR rules—Poland's governments were formed by a constantly shifting coalition of splinter parties from the original Solidarity movement. Since 1993, Polish governments no longer comprise large coalitions of formally distinct splinter parties, social movements, and labor unions. Rather, they have been formed by large electoral committees. These electoral committees are still made up of heterogeneous splinter parties, social movements, and labor unions, but now these groups are formally united for the purpose of running election campaigns. Such committees are marriages of convenience that allow parties to ensure that they will meet the electoral laws' minimum threshold requirements. They reflect the failure of attempts to achieve party system consolidation by making electoral laws less forgiving to small parties.

27. The other right-wing party to gain parliamentary seats in the 1993 election was the Confederation for an Independent Poland (KPN). This nationalist party was not of the post-Solidarity camp, however, as it had participated neither in the Round Table talks nor in any of the governments from 1989 to 1993.

28. This is the highest "lost vote" figure for any of the post-Soviet parliamentary elec-

tions outside of the former USSR. The second highest lost vote was in Bulgaria in 1991, amounting to 35 percent of the electorate. Outside of the Bulgarian and Polish cases, however, the lost vote in the rest of post-Soviet Eastern Europe was much lower, the average being around 15 percent (Agh 1998, 126–39).

29. It was not, of course, off the charts for postcommunist Eastern Europe. In Bulgaria and Romania's weak-governance systems, volatility averaged 42.3 and 55.2, respectively (author's calculations).

30. I do not count the aborted government of 1992, though had it gained approval it would have been a partial alternation.

31. See Appendix 4 for a breakdown of the major political groupings within AWS in terms of parliamentary seat share.

32. On patronage in the Polish administration, see World Bank (1999, 9): "Other forms of high level corruption [in Poland] are manifested in nepotism in public sector appointments . . . This tendency is exacerbated by the practice of making political appointments down to medium levels in the administration"; also Matys (2001); Kieżun (2000, 8–11); and Jakubkowska (2000).

33. For another description of patronage under the SLD-PSL governments, see Vinton (1994).

34. It was remarkable that from the very beginning Klaus insisted that his grouping was a political party. He broke with Civic Forum because it was not disciplined ("party-like") enough. Without endorsing Klaus's views, it should be noted that this kind of thinking was revolutionary in postcommunist Eastern Europe at this time, when "party" was still a bad word.

35. Another such party was the Christian Democratic Party (KDS), a very minor party with 1 or 2 percent of the vote. It disappeared after 1992 when its founder and leader Václav Benda died.

36. In opinion polls between the 1992 and 1996 elections, ČSSD support ranged between 12 and 21 percent (Fitzmaurice 1998, 130).

37. Hungary's responsible-party system had similar scores on these measures of institutionalization. For example, its vote differential averaged 6.6 percent. Its volatility averaged around 25 percent and was also decreasing over time (author's calculations).

38. There was one partial exception here: the caretaker government of independents and professional bureaucrats that filled in between the 1997 vote of no-confidence in the ODS government and the next elections in 1998.

39. The one instance of partial alternation came in 1992 when the KDU-ČSL remained in the government even though its coalition partners changed.

40. For a statement of Klaus's identification with the British Conservative Party, see Havel, Klaus, and Pithart (1996).

41. He was unsuccessfully challenged for the leadership of ODS in 1998 by Jan Ruml. Ruml subsequently left ODS, and Klaus's position grew stronger.

42. Václav Klaus often disparaged the dissidents and intellectuals of Czech politics, many of whom had been placed in menial jobs after the Soviet invasion of Czechoslovakia in 1968. Klaus, who had not participated in the reform movement of the Prague Spring, and who had retained his job in the economic research institute as a result, had the following to say about

the dissidents: "Indeed a lot of people losing their jobs after the Prague Spring ended up as if in a worse state. I think this isn't quite the truth. Many among them chose those occupations in which they [would] be mentally intact. Such occupations like watchmen, stoker, and the like, affording certain regularity, time for example for studying Heidegger. I on the other hand chose work, which was very binding, immensely uninspired, and regular" (quoted in Eyal 1997, 94).

43. One does not find in accounts of Czech administrative development the same emphasis on party politicization as in Poland and Slovakia. See, for example, the country-studies by Hendrych (1993), Pomahač (1993), Vidláková (1993), and Illner (1997). Even in more critical accounts of Czech state-building, such as Abby Innes's, the claim that ODS sought patronage in the administration is tempered with the qualifier that it did so regarding the "top-flight" and "senior" positions (2001, 232). By contrast, accounts of patronage in Slovakia and Poland emphasize that patronage occurred extensively at the middle and lower levels as well.

44. Each country studied here has had its party financing scandals, with Poland's ongoing Rywin affair the latest example. Moreover, as Krause writes of the ODS scandal, "The scale of the acknowledged donations is relatively small, even by the standards of Czech politics, and only a few such donations were uncovered" (2000b, 78). The most damaging charges against ODS, that it manipulated privatization in exchange for campaign contributions, were never substantiated, even after an extensive audit by the American firm Deloitte and Touche (Stroehlein 1999, 46).

45. In his thorough analysis of the 1998–2002 government, Andrew Roberts definitively rejects the "unholy alliance" characterization: "It appears then that the last Czech government was a typical example of a minority government. ČSSD did not have the consistent support of any parliamentary party. Rather, it had to form ad hoc parliamentary majorities on almost every element of its legislative programme. It is even more clear that ODS and ČSSD did not dominate the legislative process and definitely did not dominate the process in collusion against other parties. Observers of the Czech political scene are mistaken in viewing it as anything other than a minority government and in seeing a hidden grand coalition" (2003, 1275–76).

CHAPTER 3: THE RUNAWAY STATE-BUILDING PHENOMENON

1. Because of the difficulties of collecting data on the size and effectiveness of state administrations, this chapter focuses on three core countries. The notes, however, draw parallels to other countries in the region, particularly to Bulgaria and Romania. I visited Romania in 1999 and conducted twelve interviews there with state officials and policy experts. Although I was not able to conduct interviews in Bulgaria, there is relatively more material available about it in the secondary literature.

2. As noted in Chapter 1, I define the state administration as the set of nonelected positions in the central offices and ministries along with their associated branch offices outside the capital. For Poland, these data are published yearly by the National Statistical Office (Główny Urząd Statystyczny), whereas for the Czech Republic and Slovakia, I had to request the data specifically from their respective National Statistical Offices (Národní Úřad Statis-

tiky and Národný Úrad Statistiky). For the full data and an accounting of its constituent elements, see Appendix 1.

3. The figure includes only administrative positions, not employees in state services such as education (for example, teachers), health care, the police, the courts, or army. The figures for each country include the following: the central ministries and central offices, the branch offices of the central state, state inspectorates (in construction, for example), and tax offices. For a description of how these statistics were compiled, see Appendix 1.

4. Unfortunately, ministry-level data for these countries are not available because of laws that restrict the respective national statistics offices to publishing aggregate-level data using, for example, the central administration as the unit of analysis.

5. Figure 3.1 also includes personnel data for Poland after its 1998 decentralization, indicated by the dashed line after 1998. The hoped-for reversal in the trend of administrative growth did not materialize after decentralization. The national-level positions were simply transferred to the administrative apparatuses of the regional- and district-level governments.

6. See Appendix 1.

7. As noted earlier, comparable data on the growth of the state is difficult to gather. The secondary literature provides some indications, however. For example, Hungary, which also has a responsible-party system, actually reduced the size of its national-level state administration by 16 percent between 1993 and 1997 (Nunberg 2000, 280). In contrast, Bulgaria's weak-governance system did little to constrain the runaway growth of its state administration; the number of personnel in the central state ministries and offices doubled in size between 1990 and 1995 (Verheijen 1999, 126).

8. The "government effectiveness" indicator comes from Kaufmann, Kraay, and Mastruzzi (2003). See also Table 1.1.

9. Again, I define a change of government as any reorganization of the government coalition or major restructuring of the cabinet, for example, the replacement of the prime minister.

10. This state during this period had parallels to Croatia, another dominant-party (variant 1) system. As Bugajski writes, Tudjman's Christian Democratic Union (CDU) "implanted itself in all administrative institutions. This did not simply involve the temporary appointment of key personnel, but the creation of a politically loyal *nomenklatura* not subject to independent checks and balances" (2002, 598).

11. In addition, there was one provisional government that never gained a parliamentary majority and a major government reshuffling in 2000.

12. See Jałowiecki (1999). This episode is described in greater detail in Chapter 4.

13. In my field interviews with Polish state officials, I often heard that it was difficult to fire employees in the state administration, even if it was relatively easy to hire them. In contrast, my Slovak respondents reported that it had been very easy to fire state officials under Mečiar. They noted that this situation had begun to change under the post-Mečiar government, which encountered unexpected resistance when it tried to replace the previous government's appointees.

14. Interview with the author, Warsaw, June 2001. As the World Bank report noted, "Rising employment in the [Polish] administration may soon become a problem . . . The costs of administration are rising very fast (due to increases in employment and wages), which mean

that, while budgets shrink, administration becomes a higher and higher portion of expenditure" (1999, Annex 1).

15. Figure 3.2 combines the inflation-adjusted salaries of central-and branch-level administration (together, these comprise the national-level state administration). The central-level salaries are generally higher than those at the branch level.

16. In 1999, the average Pole took in about 20,365 zł per year, which amounted to approximately $5,134. By comparison, the average central-level bureaucrat was earning 29,346 zł per year (approximately $7,397). This and the dollar figures in the following footnotes were calculated by dividing the nominal national currency by the U.S. dollar exchange rate for that year. For the raw data on wages, see Appendix 2.

17. In 1993, the average yearly Slovak salary was 64,548 Slovak crowns (Sk), or approximately $2,098. By 1998, this salary had increased to 116,214 Sk, or about $3,298 a year. In comparison, the average salary of the central-state official in 1993 would have been 106,476 Sk, approximately $3,461. By 1998, it had increased to 238,968 Sk, about $6,782.

18. The average yearly wages in the general Czech economy were 69,804 Kč in 1993, or about $2,394. By 2000, the average wage had risen to 140,346 Kč, or $4,347. As to the salaries in the state administration, in 1993 the average salary for a central-level official was 109,920 Kč, equivalent to $3,770. In 1998, this salary had grown to 198,096 Kč, or $6,156.

19. The stagnation of salaries in the welfare sector—especially for nurses and teachers—is general across the region.

20. It hardly needs to be pointed out that money spent on administration is money not spent on education or health care.

21. There is a paradox here in that much of the literature on corruption recommends higher salaries to achieve professionalization and combat corruption in the public sector. While certainly there is much truth in this proposition (as Chapter 6's analysis of the welfare system shows), it is interesting that while higher salaries *may* reduce petty corruption, they also make state jobs more valuable as a source of patronage.

22. Although this indicator also suffers from being overly broad, on closer inspection it is not as blunt as it may at first seem, at least for these countries. Because public finance is still very centralized in each of these cases—despite the rhetoric of decentralization—overall government consumption is a decent measure of the size of the national state in economic terms. If government consumption is increasing, then the national-level state is primarily to blame.

23. Figures are from 1997, the only year for which data were available for all three countries.

24. These data were compiled by the Polish Ministry of Finance from annual national budgets. It should be noted that budget data in Poland tend to understate actual spending because of the existence of extrabudgetary funds (Economist Intelligence Unit, 2001, 28).

25. Torres-Bartyzel and Kacprowicz (1999) make a similar argument.

26. As the data on "government effectiveness" presented in Table 1.1 attest, there are large-N, cross-national indices of state capacity. The most comprehensive of these show higher state capacity in the Czech Republic than in either Poland or Slovakia. The task here is not to redo these surveys but rather to complement them, to fill in the areas for which they are too broad.

27. A good example of the difficulty of interview research around charged topics like patronage is presented by anthropologists Jerome Kirk and Marc Miller who conducted field
research about the use of the drug coca by Peruvians. In their first interviews, Kirk and Miller
received the same bland responses to their question "Tell us about coca" from the vast majority of interviewees. Their respondents denied any personal knowledge of coca. Their
question was a reliable measure but not, as it turned out, a valid one. When they changed
their questionnaire to try less sensible questions like "When do you give coca to animals?"
and "How did you find out you didn't like coca?," their "bemused informants began to open
up and elaborate on their personal, if modest, commitments to coca" (1986, 26).

28. Because many of the opinions expressed in these interviews were often sharply critical of the organizational culture of the state, I do not give the names of my respondents. I
do, however, describe the position of the interlocutor where useful.

29. See Appendix 3 for a breakdown of the interview sample.

30. The secondary literature on state-building in the formerly communist region strongly
indicates that the Polish and Slovak experience is more the rule than the exception; see, for
example, Ganev (2001), Verheijen (1997, 1998, and 1999), and Nikolova (1998) on Bulgaria;
Pasti (1997) and Stan (2002) on Romania; and Way (2003) on Moldova. In Bulgaria's and Romania's weak-governance systems party competition did little to constrain the predisposition
to patronage politics. Describing the pattern one would expect in a weak-governance regime,
Stan (2002) argues that the (poor) performance of Romania's state administration bore little
relation to whether the former communists or the anticommunists were in the government,
a situation recalling developments in Poland.

31. To put this in a larger perspective, Romania and Bulgaria's weak-governance systems
also facilitated the politicization of the state administration. As one government official told
me in an interview in Romania, "The positions in the state are dispersed according to party
power, and appointments are purely political. The spoils system is entrenched. When a ministry changes hands, between parties or between factions of the one party, the replacement
of personnel often extends down to the third or fourth level of the state bureaucracy. This
is different than in the Western parliamentary democracies, where a change in ministry
leadership means a rotation of only the highest level." Bulgarian specialist Krassimira Nikolova described the relationship between parties and the state in the postcommunist period as follows: "The [Bulgarian] civil service has been constantly reminded of its uncertain
position: each government of the day has tried to change as many of the old civil service
personnel as it could on political grounds, without bothering too much to define the dividing line between political appointees and professional administrators" (1998, 66). Nikolova
also notes that administrative reform is a favorite topic of incoming Bulgarian governments,
leading to contradictory reforms that serve to further politicize and destabilize the administration (1998, 69).

32. These findings of administrative politicization closely correspond to the assessment
of a recent study of the Slovak central state administration. In 2000, the post-Mečiar government commissioned an outside audit of the central state to make recommendations for
public administration reform (INEKO 2001). The INEKO report noted the absence of standard regulations and modus operandi across different institutions of the central state, ministries, agencies and so on. With almost exaggerated understatement, the report observed

that the allocation of financial resources between different ministries was "not always defined only by objective factors but also by the political strength of the ministry, its minister, and other subjective factors." "The result is a substantial difference in average salary conditions of individual ministries and their organizations" (22). This, in very halting language, is a description of a clientelistic and personalized principle of state organization.

33. In a paper assessing public perceptions of petty corruption in Bulgaria, the Czech Republic, Slovakia, and Ukraine, English researchers placed Bulgaria at approximately the same level as Slovakia. They noted that both countries were closer to the Ukraine than to the Czech Republic, where respondents showed the least amount of personal experience with corrupt officials (Grodeland, Koshechkina, and Miller 1997).

34. My interviews in Romania suggested that career paths in the state administration there were not stable or predictable. As one respondent noted, "Well, the main problem is that shortness of the time horizon for a party expert. The risk of being replaced in two or three years is great. The result of the Romanian system is that you attract either inferior people to the ministries or else people that intend to make the most of their two to three years of power to enrich themselves because their time horizons are so short." For more on the unpredictability of administrative appointments in Romania, see Pasti (1997, 127). In his assessment of the Bulgarian state administration, public administration expert Tony Verheijen noted, "Promotions in the administration do not generally follow established patterns. Even though it is theoretically possible to have a gradual career in the administration, this is still an exception rather than the rule. The best way to make a fast career is by being politically 'close' to the minister, which on the other hand is a risky strategy if a civil servant wants to stay in the administration in the long term. Many top civil servants 'survive' by playing the political game with each minister in the hope to remain in office for as long as possible" (1997).

35. I coded this interview as one expressing the view that career paths were stable and predictable since that was the respondent's perception of the situation at the time of the interview.

36. The Slovak National Party was HZDS's main coalition partner during its 1994–1998 government.

37. Again, these interview responses largely accord with other evaluations of the Slovakia's state administration. According to one study in 1999, "As many as 50 percent of officials do not meet the requirements of their job descriptions" (Nižňanský, Petráš, and King 1999, 109).

38. Most of the other state ministries such as Education, Health, even Foreign Affairs (which built on the Slovak branch of the Czechoslovak military) had already existed as full Slovak branches because of Czechoslovakia's federal constitution. After Slovakia gained independence in 1993, they simply changed their official titles and continued along in their old capacity.

39. Compare these responses with the INEKO (2001) report on Slovakia's central state administration cited earlier. That report offered a detailed look at the inner workings of the Slovak state bureaucracy and, overall, a sharply critical assessment of the state administration's effectiveness: "Several factors do not allow the transformation of ministries to institutions in which the government program is translated into concepts and laws and where decisions are made on the creation of conditions and instruments. Under the pressure of

administrative and operational activities, and partly voluntarily, central authorities waste opportunities to make decisions concerning strategic and conceptual matters. The fragmentation of activities among numerous institutions, the absence of a clear definition of responsibilities for a lot of areas, and constraints due to the current remuneration system and structure account for over-staffing, marked duplication, and fragmentation within the state administration framework, and its inefficiency" (4).

40. I need hardly point out that this is not the Weberian sense in which I use the term "bureaucratization."

41. My interviews in Romania echoed the Polish and Slovak ones quite closely here. To quote one Romanian official, "Many new agencies have been set up, but they have only people, no resources. We were looking at the regional development area the other day, and I think we counted five agencies working on the same area. This kind of problem is endemic to the Romanian state. There is a replication of function among different agencies (committees, ministries) and no effective coordination among them. Or if there is coordination, it occurs only at the highest level possible, for example in the meetings of the government. This has the result of overburdening the highest levels, so that there is no effective control of the activity of the agency. In practice, then, the different agencies often work independently of each other."

42. The MFA is one of the most desirable ministries in which to work in all three countries. Besides prestige, it offers employees the opportunity to work abroad in a diplomatic post in the normal course of their careers. While abroad, their salaries are adjusted upward to reflect the other country's price levels. The desirability of MFA posts makes it a good place to look for patronage politics. The disadvantage, one might argue, is that it overstates the problem for that very reason. There are, however, other factors that mitigate against patronage in this particular institution. First, these posts require very concrete and easily testable professional competencies, most obviously foreign language skills. In countries where knowledge of foreign (especially Western) languages is not high, this is a big constraint. Second, that these ministry officials will be representing national interests abroad, very publicly, would seem to mitigate against the appointment of obviously incompetent officials. Overall, the MFA is one of the most important and visible ministries in any state; if a bureaucratic order is to take hold anywhere, it will take hold here. Finally, even in consolidated states such as the United States a certain amount of patronage is tolerated in the appointment of ambassadorships; however, that patronage is clearly demarcated from the operation of the rest of the ministry. The question for evaluating postcommunist MFAs is whether such a demarcation exists.

43. I was able to interview the one who did return, and he felt quite certain that he would not be around after the next elections if HZDS returned to power. As he said, he could take the risk because he was still young and did not have a family.

44. One of my respondents at the Czech MFA fit this profile exactly. He entered the ministry in 1994 with no previous experience in diplomacy and by the time of the interview (2001), he was among its most senior officials.

45. For an example of the radical conservative position, see Barski and Lipkowski (1996).

46. PHARE was an aid program to help Eastern European countries in the process of EU accession.

CHAPTER 4: REMAKING THE REGIONS

1. For statements of the influence of the EU on postcommunist states, see Nunberg (1998 and 2000) and Torres-Bartyzel and Kacprowicz (1999).

2. By "regional governance reform," I am referring to the restructuring of the division of powers and tasks between subnational elected governments (at the local, regional, and district levels) and the branch offices of the central state administration (at the local, regional, and district levels). Of course, genuine reform is in the eye of the beholder: some of the "reforms" that I describe fully deserve to be in quotations.

3. For a broader view of EU influence in Eastern Europe, see Janos (2001).

4. For a description of the cognitive-socializing element of EU integration, see Laffan (2001).

5. Jan Zahradil, foreign affairs spokesman of the conservative Civic Democratic Party (ODS), quoted in Green (2003).

6. As variegated as regional reforms have been in Poland, the Czech Republic, and Slovakia, there has been much less movement in many other countries in the region. There have been no significant regional reforms in Bulgaria or Romania (Djildjov 2002; Batt 2002). As Djildjov suggests, one reason for the absence of such reform in Bulgaria was that EU accession appeared on the political agenda relatively later there (2002, 78); the same logic would apply for Romania, which, like Bulgaria, was not among the first round of EU accession countries. Second, Bulgaria and Romania both underwent profound economic crises in the mid-1990s, during which time an issue like regional reform no doubt seemed a lot less pressing. Finally, as in Slovakia, the presence of sizeable and geographically concentrated ethnic minority populations made the issue of devolution much more politically contentious. In Slovakia's dominant-party (variant 2) period following the fall of Mečiar, the ethnic issue was exploited to block a change to the regional status quo, just as occurred in Romania and Bulgaria (Djildjov 2002, 87; Batt 2002).

7. Deconcentration "entails the transfer of limited responsibility to lower levels of administration"; whereas devolution "is the transfer of authority to relatively autonomous bodies outside the direct control of central authorities" (Yoder 2003, 264). As Jonah Levy notes, deconcentration differs fundamentally from devolution in that it offers a singular advantage to the government, "the preservation of central state control" (2001, 106).

8. Earlier enlargements had allowed new members to adjust policies after accession.

9. There were, formally speaking, decentralized regional structures under communism, but what really mattered was the Communist Party, which was extremely centralized. The territorial administration of the state was essentially the same in Poland and Czechoslovakia. In both, the provincial state apparatus consisted of four levels (the government, the region, the district, and the municipality or commune), each of which was subordinated to the Communist Party. Elections to these subnational institutions amounted to a pro forma ratification of the candidates nominated by the appropriate party-level committee. Within this system, the role of subnational institutions was to implement directives from above.

10. For a description of the initial, unsuccessful attempts to reform Poland's regional level, see Gorzelak and Jałowiecki (1999).

11. The structural funds target Objective 1 regions whose per capita GDP is less than 75 percent of the EU average, Objective 2 regions facing economic restructuring, and Objective 3 regions to combat unemployment (Faro 2004; Marek and Baun 2003, 897; Hughes, Sasse, and Gordon 2003, 4–5).

12. From la Nomenclature des Unités Territoriales Statistiques.

13. For a complete list of the regional policy requirements, see Commission of the European Communities, "Enlargement of the European Union: Guide to the Negotiations Chapter by Chapter" (March 2002): www.europa.eu.int/comm/enlargement/negotiations/chapters/negotiationsguide.pdf.

14. As one example of such variation, in its version of regional reform, the Czech Republic chose to create elected regional governments whose boundaries did not qualify as NUTS 2 regions; instead, it created NUTS 2 regions as separate, purely statistical entities for the purposes of implementing structural funds projects. In Poland's regional reform, on the other hand, the boundaries of regional self-governments and NUTS 2 regions were coterminous.

15. As Yoder admits, however, the effect of these two influences may not be decisive. Regarding the institutional legacies of regional institutions, there are at least two at play in Eastern Europe, the precommunist and the communist. Second, regional sentiments do not appear to be highly developed in these countries. On the second point, see also Jałowiecki (1999).

16. Among extant analyses of regional reform in Eastern Europe, Yoder pursues domestic politics the farthest, arguing that where the transition from communism was negotiated (as in Poland), Communist successor parties were better able to constrain reforms (2003, 267). She also notes, however, that the beliefs of noncommunist parties did not neatly align in favor of regional devolution. While sympathetic to these points, my argument takes a different tack, focusing on regional state reform as a political tool by which governing coalitions seek to secure institutional advantages in the process of party-building. In this conception, the relative balance between the government and opposition becomes the crucial factor.

17. According to opinion polls conducted in Poland from 1990 to 1998, the percentage of the public who considered decentralizing the public administration an urgent priority never exceeded 9 percent. Moreover, the same polls showed that most respondents considered either that this reform could be postponed or that it was unnecessary altogether (Falkowska 1999, 282). Though not as extensive, public opinion research on regional decentralization in the Czech Republic indicates a similar lack of public interest. A survey conducted in June 2000 found that only 37 percent of the public claimed to have a clear idea of what the reform meant, and only 45 percent considered regional decentralization a step in the right direction ("Většina lidí" 2000).

18. Hughes, Sasse, and Gordon also note the close connection between regional state reform and political advantage, finding, for example, that interview respondents felt that "regionalization in Hungary was corruptly manipulated by the Fidesz government of prime minister Orban to secure its patrimony and political position" (2003, 23).

19. Before 1989, there had been regional offices in Slovakia (as well as in the Czech Republic). These offices were abolished in both republics in the spring of 1990 (Falt'an and Krivý 1999, 105). The Czechs did not follow the Slovaks in recreating them a few years later.

20. Data requested from the Slovak Statistical Office's Infoservis, Bratislava, July 2001.

21. To give one example, the reform charged each regional self-government with formulating regional policy but entrusted the centrally appointed regional prefect with monitoring that policy and with negotiating regional policy contracts with the central government ministries. In the words of one vice-regional governor, this led to "competency battles" and, in many cases, a struggle to determine who was more important, the prefect or the self-government (author's interview, Cracow, August 2001).

22. These administrative units were subordinate to the central government and headed by its appointees.

23. Sixty-five of the new districts were larger cities that took on the powers of district governments in addition to those of local governments.

24. The exceptions to this rule were the SLD and PSL, which had kept many of the organizational resources of their predecessors in the old regime.

25. Author's interview with Michał Kulesza, Warsaw, October 1999.

26. Mirosław Sekula, Chair of the Polish Parliamentary Committee on Administration and Internal Affairs (quoted in Kerlin 2001, 14–15).

27. KDU-ČSL and ODA were more supportive of regional decentralization, yet ODS was able to consistently override its coalition partners on this issue (Korecký 2000), highlighting the essentially bipolar character of Czech party competition.

28. See Andrew Roberts (2003) for an excellent description of the ODS's opposition during the ČSSD's minority government of 1998–2002.

29. The ČSSD tried in 1999 to amend the number of regions once again, from the 14 enacted in 1997 to the nine that regional policy specialists argued would be optimal. Illustrating again the power of the political opposition in the Czech system, this attempt failed (Korecký 2000).

30. Recall Slovakia's second round of regional reform, where the government was unable to win support for abolishing the district-level state administration to compensate for the new regional governments.

31. There are eight NUTS 2 regions in the Czech Republic that do not have elected institutions. They are purely administrative entities for the implementation of structural funds programs.

CHAPTER 5: LOCAL CONTROL

1. Kitschelt has some trouble locating Slovakia within his state typology since during the communist era it shared the same state as the Czechs but has developed very differently since 1989. In the end, he assigns it to a hybrid bureaucratic-patrimonial category.

2. Kitschelt does not use national administrative tradition to explain the rate of postcommunist state expansion. His concern is rather the quality of democracy in postcommunist countries.

3. See, for example, Ekiert (1996 and 2003) and Linz and Stepan (1996).

4. I will focus on the period from 1990 to 1998 because after regional governance reform happened, local politics became less directly comparable in Poland, the Czech Republic, and Slovakia.

5. Thus, local governments enjoyed a very different fate from that of regional and district governments immediately after 1989. Although the dismantling of regional and district governments was rapid, vehement, and total, local government was the one level of subnational governance that was strengthened rather than weakened after 1989. In 1990, the Solidarity government passed legislation that established self-government at the local level. As in Poland, the first major act of postcommunist state-building in Czechoslovakia was to establish a democratic basis for local government. Local government was encouraged by political elites in the national government because local self-government was seen as completing the democratic revolution and, at the very least, further breaking up the communist power structure (Grabowski 1996; Illner 1997).

6. The decision to treat local and national politics as analytically separate fits with the work of other scholars on this region. For example, the political scientist Jan Kubik has written of Poland that "the reactivation of local elites (through Citizens' Committees) and the decentralizing administrative reform, led to the *decoupling* of national and local / regional politics. This, in turn, shields local social, political, and—most importantly—economic process from the volatility of central politics" (1994, 339, emphasis in the original).

7. Judging by articles in the press, there may be some local-level political machines in these countries, but they are a decided minority and too small to much affect the size of local state administration in the aggregate (Pleśniak and Kowalski 2001).

8. For more on local-level social demobilization and political apathy in these countries, see Paradowska (1994a), Balicka (1994), Gorzelak et al. (1999, 96–99), Grabowski (1996), and Kisiel and Taebel (1994).

9. The sources for the voter turnout rates cited in this paragraph are as follows: (1) the Czech Republic—*Statistical Yearbook of the Czech and Slovak Federal Republics* (1991, 631) and *Statistical Yearbook of the Czech Republic* (1995, 600; 1999, 696); (2) Poland—Janicki (1998c) and Paradowska (1998a); and (3) Slovakia—*Statistical Yearbook of the Czech and Slovak Federal Republics* (1991, 631) and *Statistical Yearbook of the Slovak Republic* (1995, 512) and Krivý (1999, 72).

10. To calculate the party statistics, I have averaged the combined results of national-level parties, local-level parties, and independents across the three sets of local elections in the 1990s. Because election results were reported with varying degrees of precision across the countries, in the case of Poland I have had to combine the "independents" and "local parties" categories. The averages for Slovakia are computed only from the 1990 and 1994 local elections. The figures for Poland are computed from the 1990 and 1998 local elections. Aggregate results for the 1994 Polish elections are not available. The sources used in the calculations are as follows: (1) the Czech Republic—*Statistical Yearbook of the Czech and Slovak Federal Republics* (1991, 631) and *Statistical Yearbook of the Czech Republic* (1995, 600; 1999, 696); (2) Poland—Regulska (1993, 229–31) and Szczerbiak (1999a, 90); and (3) Slovakia—*Statistical Yearbook of the Czech and Slovak Federal Republics* (1991, 631) and *Statistical Yearbook of the Slovak Republic* (1995, 512).

11. Based on my interviews with local politicians in Slovakia, I believe that the relatively greater presence of national parties at the local level in that country was a result of the machine-style politics of the HZDS. Because the HZDS viewed local government as a refuge of the opposition parties, it often intervened heavy-handedly to influence local election results. According to one former mayor I interviewed, the HZDS-controlled utility company

threatened to turn off the power if the town did not elect the HZDS candidate. Not surprisingly, such tactics raise the stakes and sharpen party identities.

12. The published results for the 1990 Polish local elections distinguished between local party and independent candidates. In those elections, independents won 38 percent of the seats (Regulska 1993, 229–31).

13. Both the Czech Republic and Slovakia used PR rules for their local elections (Illner 1998, 79 n. 20; Krivý 1999; Galanda et al. 1999, 90–91). Slovakia's local rules did differ from the Czech ones in one respect, however. Mayors were directly elected by the townspeople, not nominated and confirmed by the town councilors as in both the Czech Republic and Poland. This direct election of mayors may also help account for the relatively greater presence of national parties in Slovakia's local politics. The Polish system employed different rules for cities than for small towns. Municipalities with voting districts of more than 40,000 citizens— a small minority of both towns and the local races—used a proportional representation system. Smaller-sized municipalities used a majoritarian system, with candidates competing in single-member districts and the largest vote-getter winning the seat (Regulska 1993, 225). Proportional representation in the bigger cities encouraged the development of political parties, whereas the electoral systems of smaller towns reinforced the tendency toward a personalized, candidate-based politics.

14. These figures provide further evidence of the greater organizational advantage of postcommunist parties at the local level. Almost 80 percent of the winning candidates sponsored by the Czech Communists (KSČM) were members of that party. For the two main parties created after 1989, ČSSD and ODS, a far smaller portion of these candidates were actually party members, 39.4 percent for the Social Democrats and 48.6 percent for ODS (*Statistical Yearbook of the Czech Republic* 1995, 600).

15. The Communists themselves believed this; for example, the Polish Communist Party agreed to partially free elections in 1989 because it seemed unlikely that the Solidarity movement could win more than a few seats in a contest against its own far more developed party organization (Latynski 1992, 98–99).

16. These and the following data on the number of local party organizations are Grzymała-Busse's estimates for the years 1992 to 1999 (2002, 77–78). The data on the number of municipalities are from *The Statistical Yearbook of the Czech Republic, The Statistical Yearbook of the Republic of Poland,* and Bryson and Cornia (2000, 510).

17. The KDU-ČSL was a reorganized version of the communist-era People's Party.

18. The extensive local network of the HZDS, which was the most popular Slovak party for most of the 1990s, helps explain Slovakia's higher percentage of national party candidates who successfully contested local elections.

19. For example, the staffing decisions of locally elected politicians in Poland are beyond the regulation of such bodies as the National Civil Service Office. Author's interview with Witold Krajewski, Polish Office of the Civil Service, Warsaw, June 2001.

20. These data include only administrative posts that were appointed or hired by governments at the local level, not the national government. For a full description of the data, see Appendix 1.

21. Czech and Slovak data are not available before 1993.

22. For example, the introduction of the new system of district and regional offices by

Mečiar, described in Chapter 4, was perceived by local governments as an attack on their autonomy.

23. There were 4,104 Czech municipalities in 1989 and 6,244 in 1999 (*Statistical Yearbook of the Czech Republic*, various years).

24. The number of Polish municipalities rose from 2,122 in 1989 to 2,489 in 1999 (*Statistical Yearbook of the Republic of Poland*, various years).

25. Author's interview with Marcin Tomalak, Instytut Badań nad Gospodarką Rynkową (Institute for Market Economy Research), Warsaw, July 2000.

26. Author's calculations for 1999 using data from Kameničková (2000), Kňažko (2000), and the Polish Ministry of Finance.

27. According to budget data, Polish, Czech, and Slovak local governments do not much differ in the allocation of budget resources—even given the differing amounts of resources they have at their disposal. In all three, local government expenditures are dominated by current spending (approximately two-thirds of budgets), which is short-term spending going mainly to payrolls. Capital expenditures, or longer-term investments, constitute roughly the remaining third of the budget (Kameničková 2000; Kňažko 2000; Tomalak interview). Slovak local governments' behavior with the money they did have suggests that they would have been expanding as rapidly as their Czech and Polish counterparts if they had had the same financial resources.

CHAPTER 6: A RUNAWAY WELFARE STATE?

1. On welfare universalism, see Esping-Andersen (1990).

2. As a preface, it must be emphasized that policy failure and underperformance are relative concepts. Compared to the rest of the region, the development of the welfare state has gone reasonably well in the Czech Republic and even in Poland and Slovakia. Welfare protections have not been trivialized by inflation and lack of funding or overwhelmed by general economic crisis—as they have been in, say, Russia, Bulgaria, and Romania (Lynch 2005; Hassan and Peters 1996; Ringold 1999). Romania is also anomalous for its very low social spending in the Ceausescu era, the legacy of which carried over into the postcommunist period (Ringold 1999, 30). To use cases of complete collapse as the comparative referent, however, is to set the bar for policy success too low. The Polish, Czech, and Slovak welfare states do not face the problem of irrelevance as do some of the other East European states. The problem, rather, is to assert government control over the welfare sector, to close the gap between the legal entitlements of citizens and the actual benefits provided, and to ensure fairness and equity in the administration of those benefits. Comparisons between Poland, the Czech Republic, and Slovakia may be less enlightening for countries that delayed macroeconomic reforms in the early to mid-1990s or which faced macroeconomic crises—countries like Russia, Bulgaria, and Romania. That said, I will provide in the notes comparative referents to these countries where relevant.

3. As noted in Chapter 1, there are three main reasons why welfare states have proved less open to traditional patronage politics—that is, personnel-based patronage—than the state administrations have. First, the welfare state agencies were less directly linked to the *nomenklatura* system in the communist era. There were not the same advantages for nurses and

teachers as there were for administrative *nomenklatura*. Thus, the administration had a tradition of pervasive patronage that the welfare system lacked. Second, even the lower-level positions in the welfare system require a greater degree of specialized knowledge and professional expertise than those in the administration. It is easier to play at being a bureaucrat than at being a doctor. Third, welfare state personnel were not well paid under communism, which mattered less then, but mattered a lot once a free-market system was introduced. For the most part, these have not been attractive patronage positions in the postcommunist era.

4. The expansion of social expenditures has been most dramatic in Poland, where such expenditures rose from 17 percent of GDP in 1989 to 32 percent in 1995. By comparison, Czech and Slovak social expenditures in 1995 accounted for approximately 25 and 26 percent of GDP, respectively. Romania, as noted above, had much lower social spending—about 17 percent of GDP in 1995—in part as a result of the legacy of low spending under Ceausescu (Ringold 1999, 29–30). In all of these countries, social expenditures were increasing.

5. Relative to the underlying level of economic development, these welfare states were some of the most extensive in the world (Connor 1997).

6. Cain and Surdej (1999) make a similar argument about the expansion of the postcommunist social security systems, though their terminology differs from that of collusion adopted here. They argue that the explosion of social security system is the product of *both* the weakness of governments in the face of narrow interest groups and the prevalence of petty corruption and administrative failure inherited from the previous system (what I call collusion).

7. Reflecting the much more difficult macroeconomic situation mentioned earlier, official health care expenditures were lower in Bulgaria, Romania, and Russia. Where the Polish, Czech, and Slovak expenditures trended toward 6–7 percent of GDP, in Bulgaria they ranged between 5 and 4 percent of GDP from 1990 to 2000. In Romania, they rose from 3 to 4 percent of GDP, and in Russia they rose from roughly 2 to 3 percent (World Health Organization, *Health For All* database, http://hfadb.who.dk/hfa/).

8. The incidence of informal payments in Bulgaria seems surprisingly low in Lewis's study. Another study, which focused on Bulgaria alone, made a higher estimate, reporting that 42.9 percent of a large sample of Bulgarians reported having paid for nominally free medical services (Delcheva, Balabanova, and McKee 1997). The volume of informal payments in the Romanian health care system has been estimated at as high as 60 percent of total health expenditures (Bara, van den Heuvel and Maarse 2002, 451).

9. As Lawson and Nemec write of the WHO ranking, "Although some of [the countries'] poor performance is due to access variations induced by the move to an insurance-based system, much of it is due to the necessary, but illegal, co-payments to gain access to adequate treatment" (2003, 225).

10. There are more detailed public opinion data available on the incidence of informal payments in Poland, and they paint a similar picture. For example, Poland's Center for Public Opinion Research conducted yearly polls on health care from 1993 to 1997. One of the questions asked, "Do you think it could be said of the state health care system that it ensures free treatment?" Each year fewer and fewer respondents answered "yes," from 51 percent in 1993 to 32 percent in 1997. The number of respondents answering "yes" to a second question, as to whether "everyone has the same chance of getting health care," dropped from 45 per-

cent to 26 percent between 1993 and 1997 (Centrum Badania Opinii Społecznej [CBOS], quoted in Falkowska 1999, 319).

11. For more on informal health care payments in Poland, see Lewis, Chawla, and Shahriari (2000).

12. According to public opinion research conducted by the Statistical Office of the Slovak Republic in 1997, two-thirds of Slovaks believe that is necessary either to have good connections or to bribe health professionals to receive good treatment (Demeš et al. 1998, 144).

13. According to another study, Slovak respondents were twice as likely as Czech ones to state that "they would expect to have to bribe hospital doctors to get treatment" (Miller et al. 1998, quoted in Lawson and Nemec 2003, 224). According to yet another study, "Only five percent of Czech doctors confessed to accepting 'something more' than a small gift but between 18 percent and 21 percent in the other countries" (Miller, Grødeland, and Kosheckhina 2000, 307). These results fit well with Lewis's description of the informal health care sector in the Czech Republic, which notes that in the Czech Republic—as well as Slovenia—side payments to physicians are rare (2000, 7, 28).

14. According to data from the Polish Center for Public Opinion Research, the Polish public rated the performance of the health service increasingly poorly over the course of the 1990s (quoted in Falkowska 1999, 319). Only in 1998, when the promise of health care reform appeared on the horizon, did this appraisal improve, albeit briefly. In a subsequent CBOS survey in 1999, however, a full 79 percent of respondents evaluated the results of the AWS-led government's health care reform negatively (quoted in Fandrejewska-Tomczyk 2000, 199).

15. Each year, the Ministry of Health made a list of all medical procedures and services, assigning each a certain number of points depending on each one's complexity, time to execute, and material requirements. Doctors then accumulated points based on the procedures they performed. At the end of the year, the total available health budget was divided by the number of points to determine the value of each point. Private doctors and medical facilities were compensated by the health funds for the number of points they accumulated. In theory, such a system should encourage doctors to increase their services in order to collect more points, at the same time driving the price of those services down because the global budget is fixed.

16. Initially, there were 26 private health funds, which was surely too high a number. Previous to the introduction of the private funds, an estimated 90 percent of Czechs were registered with the GHIC in 1993. After the private funds entered the market, this number dropped to about 66 percent. The remaining 34 percent were registered with one of the private health funds. By 1996, within three years of their founding, 11 of the private funds either had run into serious financial difficulties or had gone bankrupt altogether. In the wake of their collapse, many Czechs went back to the GHIC, bringing its share of insured back up to 75 percent of the population (Marrée and Groenewegen 1997, 61). In 1999, there were nine private health funds (Lawson and Nemec 2003, 228).

17. Bulgaria and Romania also continued to fund their health care systems through the national budget for most of the 1990s. Like Poland, Romania undertook to switch to a third-party payer system in 1998 (Bara, van den Heuvel, and Maarse 2002, 451).

18. Author's interview with Michał Kulesza, Warsaw, October 1999.

19. Politically appointed boards were inclined to use political and not economic criteria

in their decision to fund hospitals (Walewski 2000): why close down an unnecessary hospital if doing so might cost the fund's board members their seats in the next election?

20. Assessments of the AWS reform by policy experts and the public in general were very negative (Włodarczyk 2000; Tymowska 2000; Fandrejewska-Tomczyk 2000).

21. One difference from the Polish health care system, according to some sources, is that the hand of patronage politics has often been evident in personnel matters. According to Martin Demeš (1997), the reform of health care policy in Slovakia was stalled by the problem of massive personnel turnover under the Mečiar governments. From 1990 to 1992, Slovakia had been moving in close tandem with the Czech Republic in the field of health care policy. After Mečiar's election as prime minister in June 1992, however, these efforts came to an abrupt halt. In addition to halting the planned reforms, the new government also undertook "unforeseen personnel changes at all levels of health care management." More than half of the professional personnel were dismissed from the Ministry of Health apparatus, including the management and reform working groups appointed by the previous government (Demeš 1997, 155). In short, the new government conducted a personnel purge in the state health care apparatus, replacing them with party loyalists.

22. The dramatic growth of social security spending in some countries is another illustration of the surprising proclivity for state expansion after communism. The volume of pension expenditure is great across Eastern Europe, accounting for a very large portion of state spending. In Poland, for example, pension spending represented nearly half of all social spending and some 14 percent of GDP at the end of the 1990s (Cain and Surdej 1999, 149). Similarly, in Slovakia pension spending accounted for 42.3 percent of social spending in 2000 (Gonda and Jakoby 2001, 774). These levels of pension spending are very high, matching (sometimes even exceeding) levels of spending in Western Europe and far exceeding the spending of countries at comparable income levels in Latin America and Asia (Ringold 1999, 41).

23. The pension statistics in the next few paragraphs are taken from Gomułka (1999, 8–9), Gonda and Jakoby (2001), and Fultz (2001).

24. See Chapters 1 and 7 for a description how.

25. Author's personal communication with Linda Cook, Cambridge, Massachusetts, April 2004.

CHAPTER 7: EXPORTING THE ARGUMENT

1. It should be noted that, as a form of comparative statics, this analysis demonstrates a correlation among the main variables but does not test the direction of causality. Again, the goal is to show that the data for a larger set of countries are consistent with my interpretation. The case studies in the earlier chapters strongly indicate that the direction of causality runs from party system competition to state administrative performance.

2. Although my sample includes the majority of new democracies that fit the following criteria, it is not exhaustive. For some cases, there were insufficient data on party system institutionalization to allow me to comfortably fit them within the typology, so they were excluded.

3. There are two exceptions here. Ecuador, which democratized in 1979, is included because it is so close to the cutoff point. The second exception is Venezuela, which democratized in 1958. Long considered one of the most institutionalized and stable democracies in Latin America, its party system quickly unraveled in the 1990s, culminating in the election of populist demagogue Hugo Chavez. Thus, Venezuela offers an ideal opportunity to observe the causal logic of the argument in reverse: instead of more robust party competition leading to a more effective state, what happens to the state when the party system moves from more to less organization and stability? It also serves as a lesson that even responsible-party systems are not bulletproof: a severe economic shock such as that sustained by Venezuela can undo them (Levitsky and Cameron 2003).

4. The one exception to this rule was Russia, which, according to Diamond's typology, switched from "ambiguous" to "competitive authoritarian" regime with the rise of Putin. I include it anyway because it is such an important case and was considered a democracy for most of the 1996–2002 period.

5. Because data on vote share were not available for all of the countries in the larger sample, I measure the vote differential here in terms of the seat share in the lower house of each country's legislature.

6. As discussed below, examples include Bulgaria, Romania, Madagascar, and Guatemala.

7. See Kreuzer and Pettai (2003).

8. The precise scale used by the different authors in building aggregate indices of institutionalization differs slightly—Kuenzi and Lambright (2001), Riedl (2005), and Stockton (2001) use a nine-point scale of institutionalization while Mainwaring and Scully (1995) use a twelve-point one—but the overall methodology is very consistent. For the Eastern European party systems, I do my own assessment of institutionalization based on the criteria discussed in the main text.

9. As noted above, in some cases a weak-governance system may also exhibit a high vote differential because of the generally high level of electoral volatility. What differentiates this from a dominant-party system is that the governing party loses the next election, usually by a very substantial margin. These kinds of serial electoral landslides are a sign of party system instability rather than consolidation. Each new government is elected more as a protest against the incumbents rather than as an endorsement of the challenger's program; soon after taking office, the new governing party's support quickly recedes.

10. Another variation of the dominant-party (variant 2) type, which appears in Russia until 2000 and Ukraine until the most recent election, is an institutional one. Here one finds superpresidentialism combined with an extremely fluid legislature dominated by a Communist Party that does not cooperate with the president. Institutionally, power is concentrated in the president; politically, however, the opposition of the largest parliamentary party is enough to produce deadlock.

11. Brazil is noted as one of the preeminent examples of an underinstitutionalized, or "inchoate," party system in the literature; see Mainwaring (1999) and Mainwaring and Scully (1995).

12. The source for these data is the World Bank's *World Development Indicators* (2002).

13. Roeder's data are from 1985, somewhat earlier than would be ideal, but since popula-

tions change relatively slowly, they certainly are acceptable for almost all cases. For the former Yugoslav cases, these data will overstate ethnic heterogeneity in the 1990s.

14. This variable has a score of zero if the president is directly elected, a score of one if he/she is strong but elected by an assembly, and a score of two if the system is parliamentary. These data are from the World Bank's "Database of Political Institutions," in which the variable used here is labeled "SYSTEM" (http://paradocs.pols.columbia.edu:8080/datavine/MainFrameSet.jsp). I use the data from 1995, the most recently available.

15. Because these are cross-sectional time-series data, OLS does not provide the best estimates of the standard errors for the regression. To correct for problems of heteroskedasticity and first-order autocorrelation, I have used a fixed-effects model with panel-corrected standard error (PCSE) estimates produced by Prais-Winsten regression (Beck and Katz 1995; Greene 2000). Practically speaking, the interpretation of the coefficients is the same as in the familiar OLS technique; the difference is better estimates of the standard errors and, so, better hypothesis testing.

16. Substantively, this is a significant difference: to illustrate using some other countries in Kaufmann, Kraay, and Mastruzzi's analysis, it is equivalent to going from the effectiveness of government in the United States to that in Portugal, or from Portugal to Jordan, or from Jordan to the Dominican Republic.

17. More formally, H_0: $\alpha_{\text{Responsible-Party}} = \alpha_{\text{Weak-Governance}} = \alpha_{\text{Dominant-Party (Variant 1)}} = \alpha_{\text{Dominant-Party (Variant 2)}}$.

18. The F-test statistic for this hypothesis test is 7.067, which has a p-value of 0.0002132.

19. This alternative hypothesis can be written, H_A: $\alpha_{\text{Responsible-Party}}$; $\alpha_{\text{Weak-Governance}} = \alpha_{\text{Dominant-Party (Variant 1)}} = \alpha_{\text{Dominant-Party (Variant 2)}}$.

20. The F-test statistic for this hypothesis test is 15.665, which has a p-value of 0.0001068.

21. See Table 1.1. The Hungarian state administration also receives a very positive evaluation by Meyer-Sahling (2001).

22. For most of the 1990s, there were two main political groupings, the postcommunists and the UDF. However, as noted, the volatility of their vote share and their weak internal organization—each contained numerous factions and, in the case of the UDF, parties—meant that the overall logic of party competition tended more toward the weak-governance variety (Bugajski 2002, 787–89, 793–95).

23. To quote from one report on Macedonia, "Political party membership is the determining factor for employment in Macedonia . . . Thus, the country's workforce is by and large untrained and lives on patronage. The politicians in power are only too happy to comply with this Faustian bargain because it keeps them in office" (Pearson 2002, 3).

24. Kreuzer and Pettai (2003) offer an alternative to this characterization, arguing that despite the high volatility the Lithuanian and Latvian party systems have been becoming more orderly over time. In making this argument, however, they use different measures than the rest of the literature on party system institutionalization. As useful as these measures are for comparing the Baltic countries, they are difficult to extend beyond the postcommunist region.

25. On the contrary, in the contemporary Russian political scene, it is difficult to find politicians who will publicly disagree with Putin's policies; see Myers (2004) and Neilan (2004).

26. The average government effectiveness score for the Latin American countries in this sample was −0.170, compared with 0.002 for Eastern Europe.

27. Costa Rica would also nicely fit into the responsible-party category. Its party system is anchored by two parties, one on the left and one on the right, which enjoy near parity in vote share. It also scores at the top of the Latin American region in terms of government effectiveness. However, since it has been democratic since 1949, I do not include it in the analysis of new democracies. Arguably, it is the stability and accountability generated by the party system that has insulated Costa Rica from the tendency to frequent regime change that has characterized the rest of the region.

28. Mexico ranks at the upper middle of Mainwaring and Scully's (1995) institutionalization index.

29. Peru receives the lowest ranking in Latin America on Mainwaring and Scully's (1995) institutionalization index.

30. Some scholars have questioned the use of the terms "political parties" and "party systems" in Africa, noting that the practical meanings of both terms may vary substantially from country to country; see McHenry (2004).

31. In the country's 1992 parliamentary elections, the Frelimo party won 129 out of 250 seats, compared to its contender Renamo's 112. Frelimo retained its edge over Renamo in the following 1999 elections, but only by a slim margin of 133 to 117. Riedl (2005) gives Mozambique a score of eight on her nine-point scale of party system institutionalization, placing it at the top of the 22 African countries in her sample.

32. Benin's electoral volatility in this period was 85 percent (Kuenzi and Lambright 2001, 450).

33. Though noting that Indonesia lacks key features of the ideal-typical institutionalized party system, Tan believes it is actually more stable than it appears because the salience of ethnic and religious cleavages provides politicians with easily tapped resources for popular mobilization. Given the exploitation of such cleavages and identities in Eastern Europe by populist demagogues (think of Slovakia or even of the religious-nationalists in Poland), I feel considerably less sanguine about this as the basis for party system stability and vertical accountability.

34. The constitution of 1991 ended Thailand's most recent in a long series of bouts with military rule.

CONCLUSION

1. At around the time of the Rywin affair, Polish politics was also roiled by corruption scandals surrounding the oil industry, "Orlengate," and links between the SLD and organized crime, the Starochowicki affair.

2. Incidentally, Slovakia has also shown signs of democratic disillusionment since 2000. In the 2004 presidential elections, Mečiar was nearly elected; under considerable outside pressure, Mečiar's former right-hand man, Ivan Gašparovic, was elected instead. Meanwhile, outsider parties with antisystem tendencies, such as Robert Fico's *Smer* (Direction) party, have steadily gained ground.

3. A certain skepticism about electoral tinkering is also healthy. After all, Poland's switch

to a minimum-thresholds PR system in 1993 only superficially reduced party system fragmentation; as Chapter 2 notes, it gave rise to the "electoral confederation," the pre-election bandwagon of many small parties who act independently once entering parliament. Likewise, although Grzymała-Busse (2003) argues that party financing regulation is more stringent in Poland, it did not really take effect until as late as 2000, was practically nonexistent previously (Walecki 1999), and, given the recent Rywin affair, has been of dubious efficacy since.

4. Positions in regional, district, and local level administrations were not covered by the law and so were still not regulated by any standardized selection and promotion procedures.

5. Author's interview with Maria Gintowt-Jankowicz, Warsaw, June 2001.

6. Verheijen (2001, 29) also provides a tepid assessment of KSAP's influence on the Polish state administration.

7. In its rush to quantify the EU enlargement process, the European Commission has overemphasized formal and technical attributes of administration for the reason that they seem more objective and easier to compare across cases. (The reports are available at http://europa.eu.int/comm/dg1a/index.htm.) The analysis here would suggest, however, that the salutary effects of membership will not come quickly or easily, for example, through the importing of bureaucratic codes from the *acquis communautaire*. As Chapter 4 shows, such superficial administrative modernization may, in fact, provide the cover for reforms that benefit parties more than they do state personnel.

8. Just to show that this argument should not be pushed too far, I should note that Mečiar did make it to the final round of that country's most recent presidential election, which his former associate Ivan Gašparovič—not one of the more "West-friendly" candidates—won. Similarly, one of the dominant figures on the Polish political scene at the time of this writing is the so-called Polish Le Pen, Andrzej Lepper.

9. In a recent paper comparing the effect of EU accession on state politicization and bureaucratic reform in Greece, Spain, and Portugal in the 1970s and 1980s, Ziblatt and Biziouras (2005) come to conclusions that strongly echo the argument here. First, they find that party system institutionalization generally corresponds with less politicization and slower state expansion. Second, they find that this relationship holds even after accession to the EU, which, if anything, increased the state's resources for political patronage.

10. Doing so has the effect of understating the true fractionalization.

11. The number of effective parties is calculated using the Laakso-Taagepera index described in Chapter 2. The values given here are taken from Norris (2004, 87). If the fractionalization index is calculated using the constitutive parties *within* the electoral confederations, Poland receives a much higher score, around nine effective parties (see Chapter 2).

12. Author's calculations. They do not include volatility between the first and second elections after the fall of communism, which generally saw big spikes in volatility.

References

Amsden, Alice. 1989. *Asia's Next Giant: South Korea and Late Industrialization*. New York: Oxford University Press.

Andrews, Emily, and Mansoora Rashid. 1996. "The Financing of Pension Systems in Central and Eastern Europe." World Bank Technical Paper no. 339. Washington, DC: World Bank.

Arian, Alan, and Samuel Barnes. 1974. "The Dominant Party System: A Neglected Model of Democratic Stability." *Journal of Politics* 36(3): 592–614.

Balicka, Mariola. 1994. "Tyłem do gminy" [With Their Backs to Local Government]. *Polityka* (May 28): 3.

Bara, Ana-Claudia, Wim van den Heuvel, and Johannes Maarse. 2002. "Reforms of the Health Care System in Romania." *Croatian Medical Journal* 43(4): 446–52.

Barany, Zoltan. 1997. "Democratic Consolidation and the Military: The East European Experience." *Comparative Politics* 30(1): 21–43.

Barbone, Luca, and James Hicks. 1995. "Local and Intergovernmental Finances in Poland." In *Decentralization of the Socialist State*, ed. Richard Bird, Robert Ebel, and Christine Wallich. Washington, DC: World Bank.

Barski, Jarosław, and Kazimierz Lipkowski. 1996. *Unia Europejska Jest Zgubą dla Polski* [The European Union Means Ruin for Poland]. Warsaw: Wydawnictwo Polskie.

Bartkowski, Jerzy. 1996. "Państwo i wielka przemiana" [The State and the Great Transformation]. In *Naród, Władza, Społeczeństwo* [Nation, Power, Society], ed. A. Jasińska-Kania and J. Raciborski. Warsaw: Scholar.

Bartoníček, Radek. 1999. "Praha je v reakcích nevyzpytatelná, říká náměstkyně ministra vnitra." *Mladá Fronta Dnes* (November 19): 2.

Barzelay, Michael. 1992. *Breaking Through Bureaucracy: A New Vision for Managing Government*. Berkeley: University of California Press.

Batt, Judy. 2002. "Between a Rock and a Hard Place: Multi-ethnic Regions on the EU's New Eastern Frontier." *East European Politics and Societies* 15(3): 502–27.

Baylis, T. A. 1996. "Presidents versus Prime Ministers: Shaping Executive Authority in Eastern Europe." *World Politics* 48(3): 297–323.

Beck, Nathaniel, and Jonathan Katz. 1995. "What to Do (and Not to Do) with Time-Series Cross-Section Data." *American Political Science Review* 89(3): 634–47.

Beckman, Andreas. 1999. "The Big Yawn: Decentralization in the Czech Republic." *Central Europe Review* (September 20). www.ce-review.org/99/13/beckmann13.html.

Bercik, Peter, and Juraj Němec. 1999. "The Civil Service System of the Slovak Republic." In

Civil Service Systems in Comparative Perspective, ed. Tony Verheijen. Cheltenham, UK: Edward Elgar.

Bielecki, Jędrzej. 1998. "Polska traci 34 miljony ecu" [Poland Loses 34 Million ECU]. *Rzeczpospolita* (May 26): 3.

Blahož, Josef, Lubomír Brokl, and Zdenka Mansfeldová. 1999. "Czech Political Parties and Cleavages After 1989." In *Cleavages, Parties, and Voters: Studies from Bulgaria, the Czech Republic, Hungary, Poland, and Romania,* ed. Kay Lawson, Andrea Römmele, and Georgi Karasimeonov. Westport, CT: Praeger.

Boduszyński, Mieczysław. 1997. "From United Workers to Social Democrats: The Case of the Polish SdRP." B.S. thesis, University of California, San Diego.

Bogdanor, Vernon. 1990. "Founding Elections and Regime Change." *Electoral Studies* 9(4): 288–94.

Bogusz, A., Macieja D., and Z. Wojtkowska. 2000. "Jak urządza się SLD" [How the SLD Governs Itself]. *Wprost* (June 25): 21–23.

Boston, Jonathan, ed. 1991. *Reshaping the State: New Zealand's Bureaucratic Revolution.* Oxford: Oxford University Press.

Bowornwathana, Bidhya. 1997. "Thailand: Bureaucracy under Coalition Governments." Paper presented at "Civil Service Systems in Comparative Perspective," School of Public and Environmental Affairs, Indiana University, Bloomington, April 5–8, 1997.

Brokl, Lubomír, and Zdenka Mansfeldová. 1999. "How the Voters Respond in the Czech Republic." In *Cleavages, Parties, and Voters: Studies from Bulgaria, the Czech Republic, Hungary, Poland, and Romania,* ed. Kay Lawson, Andrea Römmele, and Georgi Karasimeonov. Westport, CT: Praeger.

Brusis, Martin. 1999. "Re-creating the Regional Level in Central and Eastern Europe: An Analysis of Administrative Reforms in Six Countries." In *Central and Eastern Europe on the Way into the European Union,* ed. Eric von Breska and Martin Brusis. Munich: Center for Applied Research.

Brym, Robert, and Vladimir Gimpelson. 2004. "The Size, Composition, and Dynamics of the Russian State Bureaucracy in the 1990s." *Slavic Review* 63(1): 90–112.

Bryson, Phillip and Gary Cornia. 2000. "Fiscal Decentralisation in Economic Transformation: The Czech and Slovak Cases." *Europe-Asia Studies* 52(3): 507–22.

Bugajski, Janusz. 2002. *Political Parties of Eastern Europe: A Guide to Politics in the Post-Communist Era.* New York: M. E. Sharpe.

Bukowski, Andrzej. 1996. "Citizens' Committees in the Process of Formation of Local Power: A Polish Case Study." In *Transformation from Below: Local Power and the Political Economy of Post-Communist Transitions,* ed. John Gibson and Philip Hanson. Cheltenham, UK: Edward Elgar.

Burgess, Katrina, and Steven Levitsky. 2003. "Explaining Populist Party Adaptation in Latin America: Environmental and Organizational Determinants of Party Change in Argentina, Mexico, Peru, and Venezuela." *Comparative Political Studies* 36(8): 881–911.

Bútora, Martin, et al., eds. 1999. *The 1998 Parliamentary Elections and Democratic Rebirth in Slovakia.* Bratislava: Institute for Public Affairs.

Bútorová, Zora, and Martin Bútora. 1995. "Political Parties, Value Orientations and Slovakia's Road to Independence." In *Party Formation in East-Central Europe,* ed. Gordon Wightman. Aldershot, UK: Edward Elgar.

Cain, Michael, and Aleksander Surdej. 1999. "Transitional Politics or Public Choice? Evaluating Stalled Pension Reforms in Poland." In *Left Parties and Social Policy in Postcommunist Europe*, ed. Linda Cook, Mitchell Orenstein, and Marilyn Rueschemeyer. Boulder, CO: Westview Press.

Carnahan, R., and J. Corley. 1992. "Czechoslovakia, June 8 and 9, 1990." In *The New Democratic Frontier: A Country by Country Report on Elections in Central and Eastern Europe*, ed. L. Garber and E. Bjornlund. Washington, DC: National Democratic Institute for International Affairs.

Carpenter, Michael. 2002. "The Politics of Identity and the Breakthrough to Liberal Democracy in Poland." Ph.D. diss., University of California, Berkeley.

CBOS (Centrum Badania Opinii Społecznej). 2004. "Preferencje Partyjne w Maju: Kommunicat z Badań" [Party Preferences in May: A Research Bulletin]. Warsaw: CBOS.

Central European Opinion Research Group. 2002. "Public Opinion on Health Care in Central Europe: Czechs More Satisfied than Poles and Hungarians; Not Much Improvement Seen in 2002." www.ceorg-europe.org/research/2002_12.html.

Chancellery of the Prime Minister of the Republic of Poland. 1998. "Effectiveness, Openness, Subsidiarity: A New Poland for New Challenges." 3rd ed. Pamphlet of the Government Plenipotentiary for the Systemic Reform of the State. Warsaw.

Charlton, Roger, Roddy McKinnon, and Lukasz Konopielko. 1998. "Pensions Reform, Privatisation and Restructuring in the Transition: Unfinished Business or Inappropriate Agendas?" *Europe-Asia Studies* 50(8): 1413–46.

Cielecka, Anna, and John Gibson. 1996. "Polish Local Government: Whither the Second Stage of Reforms?" In *Transformation from Below: Local Power and the Political Economy of Post-Communist Transitions*, ed. John Gibson and Philip Hanson. Cheltenham, UK: Edward Elgar.

Cohen, Shari. 1999. *Politics Without a Past: The Absence of History in Postcommunist Nationalism.* Durham, NC: Duke University Press.

Conaghan, Catherine. 1995. "Politicians Against Parties: Discord and Disconnection in Ecuador's Party System." In *Building Democratic Institutions: Party Systems in Latin America*, ed. Scott Mainwaring and Timothy Scully. Stanford: Stanford University Press.

Connor, Walter D. 1997. "Social Policy under Communism." In *Sustaining the Transition: The Social Safety Net in Postcommunist Europe*, ed. Ethan Kapstein and Michael Mandelbaum. New York: Council on Foreign Relations.

Cook, Linda, and Mitchell Orenstein. 1999. "The Return of the Left and Its Impact on the Welfare State in Poland, Hungary, and Russia." In *Left Parties and Social Policy in Postcommunist Europe*, ed. Linda Cook, Mitchell Orenstein, and Marilyn Rueschemeyer. Boulder, CO: Westview Press.

Cook, Linda, Mitchell Orenstein, and Marilyn Rueschemeyer, eds. 1999. *Left Parties and Social Policy in Postcommunist Europe.* Boulder, CO: Westview Press.

Copi, Irving. 1961. "Causal Connections and Mill's Methods of Experimental Inquiry." In *Introduction to Logic*, 2nd ed. New York: Macmillan.

Craig, Ann, and Wayne Cornelius. 1995. "Houses Divided: Parties and Political Reform." In *Building Democratic Institutions: Party Systems in Latin America*, ed. Scott Mainwaring and Timothy Scully. Stanford: Stanford University Press.

"Czarnecki bez teki" [Czarnecki Loses His Portfolio]. 1998. *Rzeczpospolita* (July 28): 3.

Czerwińska, Iwona. 2002. "Reforming Reform." *Warsaw Voice* (February 17). www.warsawvoice .pl/archiwum-phtml/1881/.

Czubiński, Antoni. 2000. *Historia Polski XX Wieku* [A History of Poland in the Twentieth Century]. Wydawnictwo Poznański: Poznań.

Dahl, Robert. 1971. *Polyarchy: Participation and Opposition.* New Haven: Yale University Press.

———. 1982. *Dilemmas of Pluralist Democracy: Autonomy vs. Control.* New Haven: Yale University Press.

Darski, Jozef. 1991. "Slovakia: The Power Game." *Uncaptive Minds* 4(2): 80–88.

Delcheva, Evgenia, Dina Balabanova, and Martin McKee. 1997. "Under-the-Counter Payments for Health Care: Evidence from Bulgaria." *Health Policy* 42: 89–100.

Demeš, Martin. 1997. "Health Care." In *Global Report on Slovakia: Comprehensive Analyses from 1995 and Trends from 1996,* ed. Martin Bútora and Péter Hučík. Bratislava: Institute for Public Affairs.

Demeš, Martin, et al. 1998. "Health Care." In *Slovakia 1996–1997: A Global Report on the State of Society,* ed. Martin Bútora and Thomas Skladony. Bratislava: Institute for Public Affairs.

Derleth, J. W. 2000. *The Transition in Central and Eastern European Politics.* Upper Saddle River, NJ: Prentice-Hall.

Diamond, Larry. 2002. "Elections Without Democracy: Thinking about Hybrid Regimes." *Journal of Democracy* 13(2): 21–35.

Djildjov, Aleko. 2002. "Methods and Techniques of Managing Decentralization Reforms in Bulgaria." In *Mastering Decentralization and Public Administration Reforms in Central and Eastern Europe,* ed. G. Péteri. Budapest: Open Society Institute.

Economist Intelligence Unit. 2001. "Poland: Country Profile 2001." www.eiu.com/schedule.

Ekiert, Grzegorz. 1996. *The State Against Society: Political Crises and Their Aftermath in East Central Europe.* Princeton, NJ: Princeton University Press.

———. 2003. "Patterns of Postcommunist Transformation in Central and Eastern Europe." In *Capitalism and Democracy in Central and Eastern Europe: Assessing the Legacy of Communist Rule,* ed. G. Ekiert and S. Hanson. Cambridge: Cambridge University Press.

Ekiert, Grzegorz, and Jan Kubik. 1997. "Contentious Politics in New Democracies: Hungary, Poland, Slovakia, and the Former East Germany since 1989." Central and Eastern Europe Working Paper Series No. 41. Cambridge, MA: Center for European Studies, Harvard University.

———. 1998. "Contentious Politics in New Democracies: East Germany, Hungary, Poland, and Slovakia, 1989–93." *World Politics* 50: 547–81.

Epstein, Leon. 1967. *Political Parties in Western Democracies.* New York: Praeger.

———. 1980. "What Happened to the British Party Model?" *American Political Science Review* 74(1): 9–22.

Esping-Andersen, Gøsta. 1990. *The Three Worlds of Welfare Capitalism.* Princeton: Princeton University Press.

Evans, Peter, and James Rauch. 1999. "Bureaucracy and Growth: A Cross-National Analysis of the Effects of 'Weberian' State Structures on Economic Growth." *American Sociological Review* 64: 748–65.

———. 2000. "Bureaucratic Structure and Bureaucratic Performance in Less Developed Countries." *Journal of Public Economics* 75: 49–71.

Eyal, Gil. 1997. "The Break-up of Czechoslovakia: A Sociological Explanation." Ph.D. diss., University of California, Los Angeles.

Falkowska, Macieja. 1999. "Społeczeństwo wobec reform." [Society's Opinion of the Reforms] In *Druga fala polskich reform* [The Second Wave of Polish Reforms], Lena Kolarska-Bobińska, ed. Warsaw: Instytut Spraw Publicznych.

Falt'an, Lubomír, and Vladimír Krivý. 1999. "Slovakia: Changes in Public Administration." In *Decentralization and Transition in the Visegrad: Poland, Hungary, the Czech Republic and Slovakia*, ed. Emil Kirchner. New York: St. Martin's Press.

Fandrejewska-Tomczyk, Aleksandra. 2000. "Przyczyny niskiej akceptacji społecznej reformy powszechnych ubezpieczeń zdrowotnych w 1999 r" [Causes of the Low Social Acceptance of the Reform of Health Insurance in 1999]. In *Cztery reformy: od koncepcji do realizacji* [The Four Reforms: From Conception to Realization], ed. Lena Kolarska-Bobińska, ed. Warsaw: Instytut Spraw Publicznych.

Faro, Jeremy. 2004. "Europeanization as Regionalisation: Forecasting the Impact of EU Regional-Policy Export upon the Governance Structure of Slovenia." Center of International Studies, Cambridge University.

Filinson, Rachel, Piotr Chmielewski, and Darek Niklas. 2003. "Back to the Future: Polish Health Care Reforms." *Communist and Post-Communist Studies* 36(4): 385–403.

Fish, M. Steven. 1995. *Democracy from Scratch: Opposition and Regime in the New Russian Revolution*. Princeton: Princeton University Press.

———. 1999. "The End of Meciarism." *East European Constitutional Review* (winter/spring): 47–55.

Fisher, Sharon. 1993. "Economic Developments in the Newly Independent Slovakia." *RFE/RL Research Report* 2(30): 42–48.

———. 1994a. "New Slovak Government Formed after Meciar's Fall." *RFE/RL Research Report* 3(13): 7–13.

———. 1994b. "Controversy in Slovakia over Budget Proposal." *RFE/RL Research Report* 3(3): 23–27.

———. 1994c. "Slovakia." *RFE/RL Research Report* 3(22): 68–71.

———. 1994d. "Slovak Government's Personnel Changes Cause Controversy." *RFE/RL Research Report* 3(27): 10–15.

Fisher, Sharon, and Stefan Hrib. 1994. "Political Crisis in Slovakia." *RFE/RL Research Report* 3(10): 20–26.

Fitzmaurice, John. 1998. *Politics and Government in the Visegrad Countries*. New York: St. Martin's Press.

Friedman, Steven. 2004. "South Africa: Building Democracy after Apartheid." In *Democratic Reform in Africa: The Quality of Progress*, ed. E. Gyimah-Boadi. Boulder, CO: Lynne Rienner Publishers.

Fultz, Elaine, and Markus Ruck. 2001. "Pension Reform in Central and Eastern Europe: Emerging Issues and Patterns." *International Labour Review* 140(1):19–44.

Gadomski, Witold. 2000. "Korupcja nasza powszednia: rozmowa z Janem M. Rokitą" [Our Everyday Corruption: Interview with Jan Rokita]. *Gazeta Wyborcza* (March 16): 15.

Galanda, Milan, Andrea Földesová, and Marek Benedik. 1999. "Rule of Law, Legislation and Constitutionality." In *Slovakia 1998–1999: A Global Report on the State of Society*, G. Mesežnikov, M. Ivantyšyn, and T. Nicholson. Bratislava: Institute for Public Affairs.

Gamarra, Eduardo, and James Malloy. 1995. "The Patrimonial Dynamics of Party Politics in Bolivia." In *Building Democratic Institutions: Party Systems in Latin America,* ed. Scott Mainwaring and Timothy Scully. Stanford: Stanford University Press.

Ganev, Venelin. 2001. "The Separation of Party and State as a Logistical Problem: A Glance at the Causes of State Weakness in Postcommunism." *East European Politics and Societies* 15(2): 389–420.

Geddes, Barbara. 1994. *Politician's Dilemma: Building State Capacity in Latin America.* Berkeley: University of California Press.

Gilowska, Zyta. 2000a. "Reforma samarządowa a reforma finansów publicznych" [The Self-Government Reform and the Reform of the Public Finances]. In *Cztery reformy: od koncepcji do realizacji* [The Four Reforms: From Conception to Realization], Lena Kolarska-Bobińska, ed. Warsaw: Instytut Spraw Publicznych.

———. 2000b. "Regionalne Uwarunkowania Reform Strukturalnych" [Regional Conditions of the Structural Reforms]. *Studia Regionalne i Lokalne* 2: 21–34.

Gilowska, Zyta, and Wojciech Misiąg. 1995. "Decentralizacja Polskiego Systemu Budżetowego" [The Decentralization of the Polish Budgetary System]. Gdańsk: Instytut Badań nad Gospodarką Rynkową.

Gimpelson, Vladimir, and Daniel Triesman. 2002. "Fiscal Games and Public Employment." *World Politics* 54 (January): 145–83.

Golinowska, Stanisława. 2001. "Health Care Reform in Poland After Three Years: Challenges for New Authorities." Warsaw: Center for Social and Economic Research (CASE). www.case.com.pl/upload/publikacja_plik/sg_en.pdf.

Gomułka, Stanisław. 1999. "Comparative Notes on Pension Developments and Reforms in the Czech Republic, Hungary, Poland, and Romania." Center for Social and Economic (CASE) Research Studies and Analyses Series no. 182. Warsaw.

Gonda, Peter, and Marek Jakoby. 2001. "Dôchodková reforma"[Pension Reform]. In *Slovensko 2001: Súhrnná správa o stave spoločnosti,* ed. Miroslav Kollár and Grigorij Mesežnikov. Bratislava: Institute for Public Affairs.

Gonda, Peter, et al. 2002. "Analýza dôchodkového systému na Slovensku" [An Analysis of the Pension System in Slovakia]. Bratislava: MESA 10 (Center for Economic and Social Analysis). www.mesa10.sk/vs/index.asp.

Goodnow, Frank. 1900. *Politics and Administration: A Study in Government.* New York: Macmillan.

Gorzelak, Grzegorz and Bogdan Jałowiecki. 1999. "Reforma teritorialnej organizacji kraju" [Reform of the Territorial Organization of the Country]. In *Druga Fala Polskich Reform* [The Second Wave of Polish Reforms], ed. Lena Kolarska-Bobińska. Warsaw: Instytut Spraw Publicznych.

Gorzelak, Gregorz et al. 1999. *The Dynamics and Factors of Local Success in Poland.* Trans. Krzysztof Kaczyński. Warsaw: Center for Social and Economic Research (CASE).

Grabbe, Heather. 2003. "Europeanisation Goes East: Power and Uncertainty in the EU Accession Process." In *The Politics of Europeanisation,* ed. K. Featherstone and C. Radaelli. Oxford: Oxford University Press.

Grabowski, Tomasz. 1996. "The Party That Never Was: The Rise and Fall of the Solidarity Citizens' Committees in Poland." *East European Politics and Societies* 10(2): 214–54.

Green, Peter. 2003. "On Eve of Vote, Czechs Seem to Lean Toward Joining Europe." *New York Times* (June 13): A-15.

Greene, W. 2000. *Econometric Analysis.* 4th ed. Upper Saddle River, NJ: Prentice-Hall.

Grodeland, Ase, Tatyana Koshechkina, and William Miller. 1997. "Alternative Strategies for Coping with Officials in Different Postcommunist Regimes: The Worm's Eye View." *Public Administration and Development* 17: 511–28.

Gross, Jan. 1989. "Social Consequences of War: Preliminaries to the Study of Imposition of Communist Regimes in East Central Europe." *East European Politics and Societies* 3(2): 198–214.

Grzymała-Busse, Anna. 2002. *Redeeming the Communist Past: The Regeneration of Communist Parties in East Central Europe.* Cambridge: Cambridge University Press.

———. 2003. "Political Competition and the Politicization of the State in East Central Europe." *Comparative Political Studies* 36 (December): 1123–47.

Gyimah-Boadi, E. 2004. "Africa: The Quality of Political Reform." In *Democratic Reform in Africa: The Quality of Progress,* ed. E. Gyimah-Boadi. Boulder, CO: Lynne Rienner Publishers.

Hassan, Fareed, and Kyle Peters. 1996. "The Structure of Incomes and Social Protection during the Transition: The Case of Bulgaria." *Europe-Asia Studies* 48(4): 629–46.

Haughton, Tim. 2001. "HZDS: The Ideology, Organisation and Support Base of Slovakia's Most Successful Party." *Europe-Asia Studies* 53(5): 745–69.

Hausner, Jerzy. 1994. "Reprezentacja interesów w społeczeństwach socjalistycznych i postsocjalistycznych" [Interest Representation in Socialist and Postsocialist Societies]. In *Od socjalitycznego korporacjonizmu do . . . ?* [From Socialist Corporatism to . . . ?], ed. J. Hausner and P. Marciniak. Warsaw: Polska Prace Foundation.

———. 2001. "Security Through Diversity: Conditions for Successful Reform of the Pension System in Poland." In *Reforming the State: Fiscal and Welfare Reform in Post-Socialist Countries,* ed. János Kornai, Stephan Haggard, and Robert Kaufman. Cambridge: Cambridge University Press.

Havel, Václav, Václav Klaus, and Petr Pithart. 1996. "Civil Society after Communism: Rival Visions." *Journal of Democracy* 7(1): 12–23.

Hendrych, Dušan. 1993. "Transforming Czechoslovakian Public Administration: Traditions and New Challenges." In *Administrative Transformation in Central and Eastern Europe,* ed. Joachim Hesse. Cambridge, MA: Blackwell.

Hirsz, Zbigniew. 1998. *Historia Polityczna Polski, 1939–1998* [A Political History of Poland, 1939–1998]. Białystok, Poland: PPUH Book House.

Hood, Christopher. 1991. "A Public Management for All Seasons?" *Public Administration* 69(1): 3–20.

Hoopengardner, Tom. 2000. "Disability and Work in Poland: Disability Pensions and Programs to Encourage the Employment of People with Disabilities." World Bank Internal Report, Version 3 (October 18). Washington, DC: World Bank.

Horn, Miriam. 1990. "Campaign Carnival: A Velvet Election." *New Republic* 203(6): 11–13.

Howard, Marc. 2003. *The Weakness of Civil Society in Post-Communist Europe.* Cambridge: Cambridge University Press.

Hríb, Stefan. 2001. "Čo sme to za reformátorov?" [What Kind of Reformers Are We? (Interview with Viktor Nižňanský)]. *Domino-Forum* (July 12–18): 5–6.

Huber, John, and G. Bingham Powell. 1994. "Congruence Between Citizens and Policymakers in Two Visions of Liberal Democracy." *World Politics* 46(3): 291–326.

Hughes, James, Gwendolyn Sasse, and Claire Gordon. 2003. "EU Enlargement and Power Assymetries: Conditionality and the Commission's Role in Regionalisation in Central and Eastern Europe." ESRC "One Europe or Several?" Programme Working Paper 49(2003). London: ESRC.

Huntington, Samuel. 1968. *Political Order in Changing Societies.* New Haven: Yale University Press.

———. 1991. *The Third Wave: Democratization in the Late Twentieth Century.* Norman: University of Oklahoma Press.

———. 1997. "After Twenty Years: The Future of the Third Wave," *Journal of Democracy* 8(4): 3–12.

Illner, Michal. 1997. "The Territorial Dimension of Public Administration Reforms in East Central Europe." Working Paper. Prague: Institute of Sociology, Academy of Sciences of the Czech Republic.

———. 1998. "Local Democratization in the Czech Republic After 1989." In *Participation and Democracy East and West: Comparisons and Interpretations,* ed. D. Rueschemeyer, M. Rueschemeyer, and B. Wittrock. Armonk, NY: M. E. Sharpe.

———. 1999. "Territorial Government in the Czech Republic." In *Decentralization and Transition in the Visegrad: Poland, Hungary, the Czech Republic and Slovakia,* ed. Emil Kirchner. New York: St. Martin's Press.

Innes, Abby. 2001. *Czechoslovakia: The Long Goodbye.* New Haven: Yale University Press.

Institute for Economic and Social Reforms (INEKO). 2001. "Central Government Audit." www.ineko.sk/english/audit.htm.

"Internal Bickering Plagues Poland's Ruling Party Ahead of Crucial Meeting." 2003. *RFE-RL* (June 24). www.hri.org/news/balkans/rferl/2003/03-06-24.rferl.html#39.

Jacoby, Wade. 1999. "Priest and Penitent: The European Union as a Force in the Domestic Politics of Eastern Europe." *East European Constitutional Review* 8(1–2): 62–67.

Jakubkowska, Ewa. 2000. "Corruption in Procurement in Poland: Analysis and Recommendations." Stefan Batory Foundation. www.batory.org.pl/ftp/program/przeciw-korupcji/publikacje/corruption_procurement.rtf.

Jałowiecki, Bogdan. 1999. "Ruchy regionalne czy bunt elit? Obserwacja protestów społecznych" [Regional Movement or Revolt of the Elites? Observations About the Social Protests]. In *Decentralizacja terytorialnej organizacji kraju: założenia, przygotowanie, ustawodawstwo* [Decentralization of the Territorial Organization of the Country: Principles, Preparation, Legislation], ed. Grzegorz Gorzelak. Center for Social and Economic Research (CASE) Report no. 21. Warsaw: CASE.

Janicki, Mariusz. 1994. "Pawlak a jego drużyna" [Pawlak and His Retinue]. *Polityka* (November 12): 3.

———. 1998a. "Słaba siła" [A Weak Strength]. *Polityka* (November 21): 22–24.

———. 1998b. " 'S', kadra" [Of the Solidarity Cadre]. *Polityka* (October 10): 24–26.

———. 1998c. "Lista obcych nazwisk" [List of Unknown Names]. *Polityka* (October 3): 34–35.

———. 1998d. "Maska-rady" [Masquerade: The Mask of the Local Council]. *Polityka* (November 14): 32–33.

Janos, Andrew. 1997. "Czechoslovakia and Yugoslavia: Ethnic Conflict and the Dissolution of Multinational States." Exploratory Essays, no. 3. Berkeley: Institute of International and Area Studies, University of California.

———. 2001. "From Eastern Empire to Western Hegemony: East Central Europe under Two International Regimes." *East European Politics and Societies* 15(2): 221–49.

Jędrzejewska, Katarzyna. 1999. "Budżet się kurczy, administracja rośnię" [Budgets are Shriveling, Administration is Growing]. *Rzeczpospolita* (March 22): 15.

Jelonkiewicz, Wanda. 2000. "Diseased Health Funds." *Warsaw Voice* (October 29). www .warsawvoice.pl/archiwum.phtml/4402.

Johnson, Bryan, Kim Holmes, and Melanie Kirkpatrick. 1999. *Index of Economic Freedom.* Washington, DC: Heritage Foundation and Dow Jones.

Johnson, Chalmers. 1982. *MITI and the Japanese Miracle: The Growth of Industrial Policy, 1925–1975.* Stanford: Stanford University Press.

Jowitt, Ken. 1992. *New World Disorder: The Leninist Extinction.* Berkeley: University of California Press.

Kalinowska, Beata. 2001. "Nie ma rozrostu biurokracji: rozmowa z Józefem Płoskanką wiceministrem spraw wewnętrznych i administracji" [There Is No Growth of Bureaucracy: An Interview with Jozef Płoskanka, Deputy Minister of the Interior and Administration]. *Wspólnota* (January 27): 17.

Kameničková, Vera. 2000. "Municipal Finance and Governance in Selected Eastern European Countries." Unpublished report. (April). Prague: Czech Ministry of Finance.

Karasimeonov, Georgi. 1996. "Bulgaria's New Party System." In *Stabilising Fragile Democracies,* ed. G. Pridham and P. Lewis. London: Routledge.

Kaufmann, Daniel, Aart Kraay, and Massimo Mastruzzi. 2003. "Governance Matters III: Governance Indicators for 1996–2002." World Bank Policy Research Working Paper 3 106. Washington, DC: World Bank. www.worldbank.org/wbi/governance/pubs/ govmatters3.html.

Kennedy, Michael, and Ireneusz Białecki. 1989. "Power and the Logic of Distribution in Poland." *East European Politics and Societies* 3(2): 300–328.

Kerlin, Janelle. 2001. "The Politics of Decentralization in Poland: Influences and Outcomes." Paper presented at the Annual Meeting of the American Political Science Association, San Francisco, August 31.

———. 2002. "The Political Means and Social Service Ends of Decentralization in Poland: The Story of Poland's Mid-Level Public Administration Reform and Its Effect on Social Service Delivery." Ph.D. diss., Syracuse University.

Kieżun, Witold. 2000. "Czterej jez'dz'cy apokalipsy polskiej biurokracji" [The Four Riders of the Polish Bureaucratic Apocalypse]. *Kultura* (March): 3–12.

———. 2001. "Krańcowa gigantomania" [Extreme Meglomania]. *Rzeczpospolita* (February 6): 3.

Kim, Young-Pyoung. 1997. "The Korean Civil Service System." Paper presented at "Civil Service Systems in Comparative Perspective," School of Public and Environmental Affairs, Indiana University, Bloomington, April 5–8, 1997.

Kirchner, Emil. 1999. "The Role of the EU in Local and Regional Government." In *Decentralization and Transition in the Visegrad: Poland, Hungary, the Czech Republic and Slovakia,* ed. E. Kirchner. New York: St. Martin's Press.

Kirk, Jerome, and Marc Miller. 1986. *Reliability and Validity in Qualitative Research.* Beverly Hills, CA: Sage Publications.

Kisiel, Wieslaw, and Del Taebel. 1994. "Poland's Quest for Local Democracy: The Role of Polish Mayors in an Uncertain Environment." *Journal of Urban Affairs* 16(1): 51–66.

Kitschelt, Herbert. 1992. "The Formation of Party Systems in East Central Europe." *Politics and Society* 20(1): 7–50.

———. 1999. "Accounting for Outcomes of Post-Communist Regime Change: Causal Depth or Shallowness in Rival Explanations." Paper presented at the Annual Meeting of the American Political Science Association, Atlanta, September 1–5, 1999.

———. 2000. "Linkages Between Citizens and Politicians in Democratic Polities." *Comparative Political Studies* 33(6/7): 845–79.

Kitschelt, Herbert, Zdenka Mansfeldova, Radoslaw Markowski, and Gábor Tóka. 1999. *Post-Communist Party Systems: Competition, Representation, and Inter-Party Cooperation.* Cambridge: Cambridge University Press.

Klesner, Joseph. 2001. "Electoral Competition and the New Party System in Mexico." Paper prepared for the meeting of the Latin American Studies Association, Washington, DC, September 6–8, 2001.

Kňažko, Miroslav. 2000. "Municipal Finance and Governance." (April). Bratislava: MESA 10 (Center for Economic and Social Analysis).

Kochanowicz, Jacek. 1997. "Incomplete Demise: Reflections on the Welfare State in Poland after Communism." *Social Research* 64: 1445–69.

Kopecký, P. 1995. "Developing Party Organizations in East-Central Europe." *Party Politics* 1: 515–34.

Koral, Jolanta. 2000. "Sukcesy i porażki wdrażanej reformy" [Successes and Setbacks of the Reform]. In *Cztery reformy: od koncepcji do realizacji* [The Four Reforms: From Conception to Realization], ed. Lena Kolarska-Bobińska. Warsaw: Instytut Spraw Publicznych.

Korecký, Miroslav. 2000. "Osm let se bojovalo hlavně o počet krajů" [For Eight Years They Fought Mainly about the Number of Regions]. *Lidové noviny* (March 10).

Kornai, Janos. *The Socialist System: The Political Economy of Communism.* Oxford: Oxford University Press, 1992.

Krause, Kevin. 2000a. "Public Opinion and Party Choice in Slovakia and the Czech Republic." *Party Politics* 6(1): 23–46.

———. 2000b. "Accountability and Party Competition in Slovakia and the Czech Republic." Ph.D. diss., University of Notre Dame.

———. 2003. "Slovakia's Second Transition." *Journal of Democracy* 14: 65–79.

Kreuzer, Marcus, and Vello Pettai. 2003. "Patterns of Political Instability: Affiliation Patterns of Politicians and Voters in Postcommunist Estonia, Latvia, and Lithuania." *Studies in Comparative International Development* 38(2): 76–98.

Krivý, Vladimír. 1998. "Slovakia and Its Regions." In *Slovakia 1996–1997: A Global Report on the State of Society,* ed. Martin Bútora and Thomas Skladony. Bratislava: Institute for Public Affairs.

———. 1999. "Election Results 1998–1999." In *Slovakia 1998–1999: A Global Report on the State of Society,* ed. G. Mesežnikov, M. Ivantyšyn, and T. Nicholson. Bratislava: Institute for Public Affairs.

Kroupa, Aleš and Tomáš Kostelecký. 1996. "Party Organization at the National and Local Level in the Czech Republic since 1989." In *Party Structure and Organization in East-Central Europe*, ed. Paul Lewis. Cheltenham, UK: Edward Elgar.

Kubik, Jan. 1994. "Decentralization and Cultural Revival in Post-communist Transformations: The Case of Cieszyn Silesia, Poland." *Communist and Post-Communist Studies* 27(4): 331–56.

Kuenzi, Michelle, and Gina Lambright. 2001. "Party System Institutionalization in 30 African Countries." *Party Politics* 7(4): 437–68.

Kukliš, Peter, and Peter Bercík. 1999. "The Framework for Public Management in Slovakia." In *Innovations in Public Management: Perspectives from East and West*, ed. Tony Verheijen and David Coombes. Cheltenham, UK: Edward Elgar.

Kulesza, Michał. 1994. "Szanowny Panie Premierze" [Esteemed Mr. Premier]. *Polityka* 22 (May 28): 1, 6.

Kunder, Peter. 2001. "Vyhrali politici: porazili reformu" [The Politicians Won: They Defeated the Reform]. *Sme* (July 6): 1.

Kurski, Jarosław. 2004. "Kraksa polskiej polityki: Aleksander Smolar w rozmowie z Jarostawem Kurskim." [The Implosion of Polish Politics: An Interview with Aleksander Smolar]. *Gazeta Wyborcza* (April 11): 13–14.

Kusý, Miroslav. 1998. "Slovakia '97." *Perspectives* 9: 45–51.

Laakso, Markku, and Rein Taagepera. 1979. " 'Effective' Number of Parties: A Measure with Application to West Europe." *Comparative Political Studies* 12(1): 3–27.

Laffan, Brigid. 2001. "The European Union Polity: A Union of Regulative, Normative, and Cognitive Pillars." *Journal of European Public Policy* 8: 709–27.

Latynski, Maya. 1992. "Poland: May 27, 1990." In *The New Democratic Frontier: A Country by Country Report on Elections in Central and Eastern Europe*, ed. Larry Garber and Eric Bjornlund. Washington, DC: National Democratic Institute for International Affairs.

Lawson, Colin, and Juraj Nemec. 2003. "The Political Economy of Slovak and Czech Health Policy: 1989–2000." *International Political Science Review* 24(2): 219–35.

Lawson, Kay, Andrea Römmele, and Georgi Karasimeonov. 1999. *Cleavages, Parties, and Voters: Studies from Bulgaria, the Czech Republic, Hungary, Poland, and Romania*. Westport, CT: Praeger.

Lebovič, Peter. 1999. "Political Aspects of the Election Law Amendments." In *The 1998 Parliamentary Elections and Democratic Rebirth in Slovakia*, ed. Martin Bútora et al. Bratislava: Institute for Public Affairs.

Letowski, Janusz. 1993. "Polish Public Administration Between Crisis and Renewal." In *Administrative Transformation in Central and Eastern Europe*, ed. Joachim Hesse. Cambridge, MA: Blackwell.

Levitsky, Steven, and Maxwell Cameron. 2003. "Democracy Without Parties? Political Parties and Regime Change in Fujimori's Peru." *Latin American Politics and Society* 45(3): 1–33.

Levy, Jonah. 2001. "A Revolution in the Provinces? Territorial Politics after Decentralization." In *Developments in French Politics 2*, ed. Alain Guyomarch, Peter Hall, Jack Hayward, and Howard Machin. London: Macmillan.

Lewis, Maureen. 2000. "Who Is Paying for Health Care in Eastern Europe and Central Asia?" Washington, DC: World Bank.

Lewis, Maureen, M. Chawla, H. Shahriari, and P. Belli. 2000. "The Theory and Practice of Informal Payments in Health: Evidence from Poland." Washington, DC: World Bank.

Lewis, Paul. 1999. *Patterns of Democracy: Government Forms and Performance in Thirty-Six Countries.* New Haven, CT: Yale University Press.

———. 2000. *Political Parties in Post-Communist Eastern Europe.* London: Routledge.

Lijphart, Arend. 1999. *Patterns of Democracy: Government Forms and Performance in Thirty-Six Countries.* New Haven: Yale University Press.

Linz, Juan, and Alfred Stepan. 1996. *Problems of Democratic Transition and Consolidation: Southern Europe, South America, and Post-Communist Europe.* Baltimore: Johns Hopkins University Press.

Lipset, Seymour Martin, and Stein Rokkan. 1967. "Cleavage Structures, Party Systems, and Voter Alignments: An Introduction." In *Party Systems and Voter Alignments: Cross-National Perspectives,* ed. S. M. Lipset and S. Rokkan. New York: Free Press.

Lynch, Allen. 2005. *How Russia Is Not Ruled: Reflections on Russian Political Development.* Cambridge: Cambridge University Press.

Mainwaring, Scott. 1995. "Brazil: Weak Parties, Feckless Democracy." In *Building Democratic Institutions: Party Systems in Latin America,* ed. Scott Mainwaring and Timothy Scully. Stanford: Stanford University Press.

———. 1999. *Rethinking Party Systems in the Third Wave of Democratization: the Case of Brazil.* Stanford: Stanford University Press.

Mainwaring, Scott, and Timothy Scully, eds. 1995. *Building Democratic Institutions: Party Systems in Latin America.* Stanford: Stanford University Press.

Mair, Peter. 1997. *Party System Change: Approaches and Interpretations.* Oxford: Clarendon Press.

Mandelbaum, Michael. 1997. *Sustaining the Transition: The Social Safety Net in Postcommunist Europe,* ed. Ethan Kapstein and Michael Mandelbaum. New York: Council on Foreign Relations.

Marek, Dan, and Michael Braun. 2002. "EU as Regional Actor: The Case of the Czech Republic." *Journal of Common Market Studies* 40: 895–919.

Markowski, Radoslaw. 1997. "Political Parties and Ideological Spaces in East Central Europe." *Communist and Post-Communist Studies* 30: 221–54.

Marrée, Jörgen, and Peter Groenewegen. 1997. *Back to Bismarck: Eastern European Health Care Systems in Transition.* Brookfield, VT: Avebury.

Massaro, T., J. Nemec, and I. Kalman. 1994. "Health System Reform in the Czech Republic: Policy Lessons from the Initial Experience of the General Health Insurance Company." *Journal of the American Medical Association* 271(23): 1870–74.

Matałowska, Anna. 1994. "Kuszenie z listy" [Temptation from the List]. *Polityka* (July 9): 3.

Matys, Michał. 2001. "Nie możesz byc' niczyj" [You Can't Be No One's]. *Gazeta Wyborcza* (June 2–3): 18–19.

Mazulo, Brazão. 2004. "Mozambique: The Challenge of Democratization." In *Democratic Reform in Africa: The Quality of Progress,* ed. E. Gyimah-Boadi. Boulder, CO: Lynne Rienner Publishers.

McHenry, Dean. 2004. "Political Parties and Party Systems." In *Democratic Transitions in East Africa,* ed. Paul Kaiser and F. Okumu. Burlington, VT: Ashgate.

Mesežnikov, Grigorij. 1999. "Domestic Politics." In *Slovakia 1998–1999: A Global Report on the*

State of Society, ed. G. Mesežnikov, M. Ivantyšyn, and T. Nicholson. Bratislava: Institute for Public Affairs.

Meyer-Sahling, Jan-Hinrik. 2001. "Getting on Track: Civil Service Reform in Post-Communist Hungary." *Journal of European Public Policy* 8(6): 960–79.

Millard, Frances. 1995. "Changes in the Health Care System in Post-Communist Poland." *Health and Place* 1(3): 179–88.

———. 1999. *Polish Politics and Society.* London: Routledge.

Miller, William, Åse Grødeland, and Tatyana Koscheckina. 2000. "If You Pay, We'll Operate Immediately." *Journal of Medical Ethics* 26(5): 305–11.

———. 2001. *A Culture of Corruption? Coping with Government in Post-Communist Europe.* Budapest: CEU Press.

"Minister zdravotníctva Roman Kováč: Snahou je splatiť všetky dlhy do budúcich volieb" [Health Minister Roman Kováč: 'We Will Attempt to Pay Off All Debts by the Next Elections']. 2001. *Trend* (July 4): 8.

Mlynář, Vladimír. 1994. "Jen pro otrlé: koalice se opět přela o správní reformu" [Only for the Cynical: The Coalition Again Skims Over Administrative Reform]. *Respekt* (July 4–10): 3.

Montinola, Gabriella. 1999. "Parties and Accountability in the Philippines." *Journal of Democracy* 10(1): 126–40.

Moravcsik, Andrew, and Milada Vachudova. 2003. "National Interests, State Power, and EU Enlargement." *East European Politics and Societies* 17(1): 42–57.

Mydans, Seth. 2004. "As Expected, Putin Easily Wins a Second Term in Russia." *New York Times* (March 14): 3.

Myers, Steven Lee. 2004. "9 Candidates Run to Praise Putin, Not to Beat Him," *New York Times* (January 9): A-3.

"Najgorzej ze zdrowiem: Cztery reformy społeczne rządu Buzka" [The Worst Is Health Care: The Four Social Reforms of the Buzek Government]. 2000 *Rzeczpospolita* (January 25): 3.

Neilan, Terence. 2004. "Putin Fires Premier and Cabinet Ahead of March 14 Election," *New York Times* (February 24).

Nelson, Joan. 2001. "The Politics of Pension and Health-Care Reforms in Hungary and Poland." In *Reforming the State: Fiscal and Welfare Reform in Post-Socialist Countries,* János Kornai, Stephan Haggard, and Robert Kaufman. Cambridge: Cambridge University Press.

Nicholson, Tom. 2005. "SDKÚ-HZDS deal mooted." *Slovak Spectator* (February 14–20). http://slovakspectator.sk/clanok-18668.html.

Nikolova, Krassimira. 1998. "The Framework for Public Management Reform in Bulgaria: A View from the Inside." In *Innovations in Public Management: Perspectives from East and West,* ed. T. Verheijen and D. Coombes. Cheltenham, UK: Edward Elgar.

Nižňanský, Viktor, and Miroslav Kňažko. 2001. "Public Administration." In *Slovakia 2000: A Global Report on the State of Society,* ed. G. Mesežnikov, M. Kollár, and T. Nicholson. Bratislava: Institute for Public Affairs.

Nižňanský, Viktor, Milan Petráš, and Jaroslav King. 1999. "Public Administration." In *Slovakia 1998–1999: A Global Report on the State of Society,* ed. G. Mesežnikov, M. Ivantšyn, and T. Nicholson. Bratislava: Institute for Public Affairs.

Nižňanský, Viktor, and Ol'ga Reptová. 1999. *From Common to Private: 10 Years of Privatization in Slovakia*. Bratislava: MESA 10.

Norris, Pippa. 2004. *Electoral Engineering: Voting Rules and Political Behavior*. Cambridge: Cambridge University Press.

"Nové kraje mají přiblížit úřady k občanům." 2000. *Hospodářské noviny* (April 18): 13.

Nunberg, Barbara. 2000. "Ready for Europe: Public Administration Reform and European Union Accession in Central and Eastern Europe." World Bank Technical Paper no. 466. Washington, DC: World Bank.

———, ed. 1999. *The State after Communism: Administrative Transitions in Central and Eastern Europe*. Washington, DC: World Bank.

Nunberg, Barbara, and Luca Barbone. 1999. "Breaking Administrative Deadlock in Poland: Internal Obstacles and External Incentives." In *The State after Communism: Administrative Transitions in Central and Eastern Europe*, ed. Barbara Nunberg. Washington, DC: World Bank.

"Od 1. kwietnia będzie mniej urzędów centralnych" [Starting April 1st There Will Be Fewer Central Offices]. 2002. *Gazeta Wyborcza (April 1)*.

O'Donnell, Guillermo. 1999. "Horizontal Accountability in New Democracies," *The Self-Restraining State*, ed. A. Schedler, L. Diamond, and M. Plattner. Boulder: Lynne Rienner Publishers.

OECD. 1999. *OECD Economic Outlook 66* (December). Paris: Organization for Economic Co-operation and Development.

———. 2002. *OECD Economic Outlook 70* (December). Paris: Organization for Economic Co-operation and Development.

———. 2003. "Making High Quality Health Care Fiscally Sustainable." In *OECD Economic Surveys: Czech Republic*. Paris: Organization for Economic Cooperation and Development.

Offe, Claus. 1991. "Capitalism By Democratic Design? Democratic Theory Facing the Triple Transition in East Central Europe." *Social Research* 58(4): 865–81.

"Oficjalne dane o zatrudnieniu" [Official Data About Employment]. 2001. *Wspólnota* (January 20): 11.

Orenstein, Mitchell. 1996. "The Failures of Neo-Liberal Social Policy in Central Europe." *Transition* 2(13): 16–20.

———. 2000. "How Politics and Institutions Affect Pension Reform in Three Postcommunist Countries." World Bank Policy Research Working Papers no. 2310. Washington, DC: World Bank.

———. 2001. *Out of the Red: Building Capitalism in Postcommunist Europe*. Ann Arbor: University of Michigan.

Orenstein, Mitchell, and Raj Desai. 1997. "State Power and Interest Group Formation." *Problems of Post-Communism* 44(6): 43–52.

Papakostas, Apostolis. 2001. "Why Is There No Clientelism in Scandinavia? A Comparison of the Swedish and Greek Sequences of Development." *Clientelism, Interests, and Democratic Representation*, ed. Simona Piattoni. Cambridge: Cambridge University Press.

Paradowska, Janina. 1994a. "Bitwa na górze, milczenie na dole" [A Battle on High, Silence Below]. *Polityka* (June 4): 1.

———. 1994b. "Spazmy gminne" [Spasms of Local Government]. *Polityka* (July 23): 7.

———. 1998a. "Rebus z trzema szczeblami" [A Riddle with Three Levels]. *Polityka* (October 31): 20–21.

———. 1998b. "Kto ma teczki, ten ma władzę" [Whoever Has the Dossier Has Power]. *Polityka* (November 21): 3–6.

———. 2000. "Imperium ministra Kropiwnickiego: O dalszy rozwoj" [Minister Kropiwnicki's Empire: For Further Development]. *Polityka* (July 8): 22–23.

———. 2000. "Jedność' ma swoją cenę" [Unity Has Its Price]. *Polityka* (October 28): 16–17.

———. 2001. "Pełniący obowiązki" [Fulfilling Their Duties?]. *Polityka* (June 2): 22–24.

Paradowska, Janina, and Mariusz Janicki. 1994. "A publiczność' bije brawo" [And the Public Cries Bravo]. *Polityka* (December 31): 6.

Paradowska, Janina, and Ewa Wilk. 1998. "Układ warszawski" [The Warsaw System]. *Polityka* (November 28): 27–29.

Pasti, Vladimir. 1997. *The Challenges of Transition: Romania in Transition.* Boulder: East European Monographs.

Pearson, Brenda. 2002. "Putting Peace into Practice: Can Macedonia's New Government Meet the Challenge?" Special Report no. 96. Washington, DC: U.S. Institute for Peace.

Piattoni, Simona. 2001a. "Clientelism in Historical and Comparative Perspective." In *Clientelism, Interests, and Democratic Representation,* ed. Simona Piattoni. Cambridge: Cambridge University Press.

———. 2001b. *Clientelism, Interests, and Democratic Representation.* Cambridge: Cambridge University Press.

Pierson, Paul. 1994. *Dismantling the Welfare State? Reagan, Thatcher, and the Politics of Retrenchment.* Cambridge: Cambridge University Press.

Plenipotentiary for the Reform of the Public Administration. 1999. "Strategy of Public Administration Reform in the Slovak Republic." (July). Bratislava: Government of Slovakia. www.mesa10.sk/vs/index.asp?id=1.

Pleśniak, Rafał, and Marcin Kowalski. 2001. "Sitwokracja" [Network-ocracy]. *Wprost* (June 3): 26–33.

Podgórska, Janina. 1994. "Piłowania stołu" [Sawing the Table]. *Polityka* (July 9): 3.

Pomahač, Richard. 1993. "Administrative Modernization in Czechoslovakia: Between Constitutional and Economic Reform." In *Administrative Transformation in Central and Eastern Europe,* ed. Joachim Hesse. Cambridge, MA: Blackwell.

Powell, G. Bingham. 1989. "Constitutional Design and Citizen Control." *Journal of Theoretical Politics* 1(2): 107–30.

———. 2000. *Elections as Instruments of Democracy: Majoritarian and Proportional Visions.* New Haven, CT: Yale University Press.

Pytlakowski, Piotr. 2000. "Wybrałeś, to sie męcz" [You've Chosen, Now Suffer the Consequences]. *Polityka* (July 8): 26–29.

Raciborski, Jacek. 1997. *Polskie Wybory: Zachowania wyborcze społeczeństwa polskiego 1989–1995* [Polish Elections: The Electoral Behavior of Polish Society, 1989–1995]. Warsaw: Wydawnictwo Naukowe "Scholar."

"Raport 1990–1999: Krajowa Szkoła Administracji Publicznej" [Report 1990–1999: National School of Public Administration]. 1999. Warsaw: Krajowa Szkoła Administracji Publicznej.

Regulska, Joanna. 1993. "Democratic Elections and Restructuring in Poland, 1989–91." In *The New Political Geography of Eastern Europe*, ed. John O'Loughlin and Herman van der Wusten. London: Belhaven Press.

Regulski, Jerzy. 1999. "Building Democracy in Poland: the State Reform of 1998." Local Government and Public Services Reform Initiative Discussion Papers no. 9. Budapest: Open Society Institute.

Reszka, Paweł. 2000. "Poseł do wynajęcia" [MP for Rent]. *Rzeczpospolita* (July 27): 4.

Riedl, Rachel. 2005. "Party Systems in New Democracies: Variations in Institutionalization in Africa." Paper presented at "Bridging Disciplines, Spanning the World," Princeton Institute for International and Regional Studies, Princeton University, April 8–9.

Ringold, Dena. 1999. "Social Policy in Postcommunist Europe: Legacies and Transition." In *Left Parties and Social Policy in Postcommunist Europe*, ed. Linda Cook, Mitchell Orenstein, and Marilyn Rueschemeyer. Boulder CO: Westview Press.

Roberts, Andrew. 2003. "Demythologising the Czech Opposition Agreement." *Europe-Asia Studies* 55: 1273–1303.

Roeder, Philip. 2001. *Ethnolinguistic Fractionalization (ELF) Indices, 1961 and 1985*. http// :weber .ucsd.edu\~proeder\lf.htm.

Rose, Richard. 1995. "Mobilizing Demobilized Voters in Post Communist Societies." Studies in Public Policy, no. 246. Glasgow: University of Strathclyde.

Rose, Richard, William Mishler, and Christian Haerpfer. 1998. *Democracy and Its Alternatives: Understanding Post-Communist Societies*. Baltimore, MD: Johns Hopkins University Press.

Rose, Richard, and Neil Munro. 2002. *Elections Without Order: Russia's Challenge to Vladimir Putin*. Cambridge: Cambridge University Press.

Rothchild, Donald, and Naomi Chazan, eds. 1988. *The Precarious Balance: State-Society Relations in Africa*. Boulder: Westview Press.

Rudolph, Lloyd, and Susanne Rudolph. 1979. "Authority and Power in Bureaucratic and Patrimonial Administration: A Revisionist Interpretation of Weber on Bureaucracy." *World Politics* 31(1): 195–227.

Rueschemeyer, Marilyn, and Sharon Wolchik. 1999. "The Return of Left-Oriented Parties in Eastern Germany and the Czech Republic and Their Social Policies." In *Left Parties and Social Policy in Postcommunist Europe*, ed. Linda Cook, Mitchell Orenstein, and Marilyn Rueschemeyer. Boulder CO: Westview Press.

"Rywingate—Majority Report." 2004. *Warsaw Voice* (April 14). www.warsawvoice.pl/view/ 5307.

Sartori, Giovanni. 1976. *Parties and Party Systems: A Framework for Analysis*. Volume 1. Cambridge: Cambridge University Press.

Šafaříková, Katarina. 2003. "Co přinese sobota 14. června?" [What Will Saturday June 14th Bring?]. *Respekt* 24:3.

Scherpereel, John. 2002. "Renewing the Socialist Past or Moving Towards the European Administrative Space? Inside Czech and Slovak Ministries." Paper presented at the Annual Meeting of the American Political Science Association, Boston, August 29–September 1.

Schiavo-Campo, Salvatore, Giulio de Tommaso, and Amitabha Mukherjee. 1997. "An International Statistical Survey of Government Employment and Wages." World Bank Policy Research Working Paper no. 1806. Washington, DC: World Bank.

Schumpeter, Joseph. 1950. *Capitalism, Socialism, and Democracy.* 3rd ed. New York: Harper.

Scott, James. 1969. "Corruption, Machine Politics, and Political Change." *American Political Science Review* 63 (December).

Sepioł, Janusz. 2000. "Reforma samorządowa w działaniu" [The Self-Government Reform in Action]. In *Cztery reformy: od koncepcji do realizacji* [The Four Reforms: From Conception to Realization], ed. Lena Kolarska-Bobińska. Warsaw: Instytut Spraw Publicznych.

Shabad, Goldie, and Kazimierz Slomczynski. 2002. "The Emergence of Career Politicians in Post-Communist Democracies: Poland and the Czech Republic." *Legislative Studies Quarterly* 27(3): 333–59.

———. 2004 "Interparty Mobility among Political Elites in Post-Communist East Central Europe." *Party Politics* 10(2): 151–76.

Shefter, Martin. 1994. *Political Parties and the State: The American Historical Experience.* Princeton: Princeton University Press.

Silberman, Bernard. 1993. *Cages of Reason: The Rise of the Rational State in France, Japan, the United States, and Great Britain.* Chicago: University of Chicago Press.

Skocpol, Theda. 1985. "Bringing the State Back In: Strategies of Analysis in Current Research." In *Bringing the State Back In,* ed. Peter Evans, Dietrich Rueschemeyer, and Theda Skocpol. Cambridge: Cambridge University Press.

Skowronek, Stephen. 1982. *Building the New American State.* New York: Cambridge University Press.

Smolar, Aleksander. 1998. "Poland's Emerging Party System." *Journal of Democracy* 9(2): 122–33.

Smoleński, Paweł. 2002. "Ustawa za łapówkę czyli przychodzi Rywin do Michnika." *Gazeta Wyborcza* (December 27): 3.

Sochacka, Ewa, and Tadeusz Krasko. 1996. *Rzeczpospolita Demokracji Lokalne: rozmowy z prof. Jerzym Regulskim, prof. Michałem Kuleszą, sen. Jerzym Stepniem, prof. Piotrem Buczkowskim* [The Republic of Local Democracy: Interviews with Jerzy Regulski, Michał Kulesza, Jerzy Stepień, and Piotr Buczkowski]. Foundation for the Development of Local Democracy. Warsaw: Wydawnictwo Samorządowe.

Solnick, Steven. 1998. *Stealing the State: Control and Collapse in Soviet Institutions.* Cambridge, MA: Harvard University Press.

Spiro, Nicholas. 2000. "Unfinished Business: The Limitations of Poland's Regional Reforms." *Business Central Europe* (June): 45.

Stan, Lavinia. 2002. "Comparing Post-Communist Governance: A Case Study." *Journal of Communist Studies and Transition Politics* 18(3): 77–108.

Statistical Yearbook of the Czech and Slovak Federal Republics. 1991. Prague: Český spisovatel.

Statistical Yearbook of the Czech Republic. 1994–2000 (various editions). Prague: Český spisovatel.

Statistical Yearbook of the Republic of Poland. 1990–2000 (various editions). Warsaw: Główny Urząd Statystyczny.

Statistical Yearbook of the Slovak Republic. 1994–1998 (various editions). Bratislava: Štatistický úrad Slovenskej republiky.

Stockton, Hans. 2001. "Political Parties, Party Systems, and Democracy in East Asia: Lessons from Latin America." *Comparative Political Studies* 34(1): 94–119.

Stroehlein, Andrew. 1999. "The Czech Republic 1992 to 1999." *Central Europe Review* (September 13). www.ce-review.org/99/12/stroehlein12.html.

Suruszka, Wisla. 1996. "Local Revolutions in Central Europe, 1990 to 1994: Memoirs of Mayors and Councilors from Poland, Slovakia, and the Czech Republic." *Publius* 26(2): 121–40.

Świaniewicz, Paweł. 1996. "The Policy Preferences and Ideologies of Candidates in the 1994 Polish Local Elections." *International Journal of Urban and Regional Research* 20(4): 733–43.

Szczerbiak, Aleks. 1999a. "The Impact of the 1998 Local Elections on the Emerging Polish Party System." *Journal of Communist Studies and Transition Politics* 15(3): 80–100.

———. 1999b. "Testing Party Models in East-Central Europe: Local Party Organization in Post-Communist Poland." *Party Politics* 5: 525–37.

———. 1999c. "Interests and Values: Polish Parties and their Electorates." *Europe-Asia Studies* (58)1: 1401–32.

———. 2001. "Party Structure and Organizational Development in Post-Communist Poland." *Journal of Communist Studies and Transition Politics* 17(2): 94–130.

Tan, Paige. 2004. "Party Rooting, Political Operators, and Instability in Indonesia: A Consideration of Party System Institutionalization in a Communally Charged Society." Paper presented at the annual meeting of the Southern Political Science Association, New Orleans, January 10.

Taras, Wojciech. 1993. "Changes in Polish Public Administration, 1989–1992." In *Administrative Transformation in Central and Eastern Europe,* ed. Joachim Hesse. Cambridge, MA: Blackwell.

Tarrow, Sidney. 1977. "The Italian Party System Between Crisis and Transition." *American Journal of Political Science* 21(2): 193–224.

Thompson, Mark. 1996. "Off the Endangered List: Philippine Democratization in Comparative Perspective." *Comparative Politics* 28(2): 179–205.

Thomson, David. 1969. *Democracy in France since 1870.* New York: Oxford University Press.

Tilly, Charles. 1984. *Big Structures, Large Processes, Huge Comparisons.* New York: Russell Sage Foundation.

———. 1985. "War Making and State Making as Organized Crime." In *Bringing the State Back In,* ed. Peter Evans, Dietrich Rueschemeyer, and Theda Skocpol. Cambridge: Cambridge University Press.

Toole, James. 2000. "Government Formation and Party System Stabilization in East Central Europe." *Party Politics* 6: 441–61.

Torres-Bartyzel, Claudia, and Grazyna Kacprowicz. 1999. "The National Service System in Poland." In *Civil Service Systems in Central and Eastern Europe,* ed. Tony Verheijen. Cheltenham, UK: Edward Elgar.

Transparency International. 1996–2000. "Corruption Perceptions Index." www.gwdg.de/~uwvw/.

Tymowska, Katarzyna. 2000. "Założenia i rzeczywistość' w reformowaniu opieki zdrowotnej" [Assumptions and Reality in the Health Care Reform] In *Cztery reformy: od koncepcji do realizacji* [The Four Reforms: From Conception to Realization], ed. Lena Kolarska-Bobińska. Warsaw: Instytut Spraw Publicznych.

Tyrański, Władysław. 1999. "Bez hipokryzji proszę: rozmowa z Markiem Nawarą, marszał kiem województwa małopolskiego" [Without Hypocrisy Please: An Interview with Marek Nawara, Speaker of the Małopolska Regional Parliament]. *Wspólnota Małopolska* (March 27): 1–2.

Vagovič, Marek. 2001. "Reformné K.O.: Skutočnú reformu verejenej správy parlament odmietol" [Reform Knockout: Parliament Rejects the Real Sense of Public Administration Reform]. *Domino-Forum* (July 12–18): 2.

Vajdová, Z., and T. Kostelecký. 1997. "The Political Culture of Local Communities: The Case of Three Towns." *Sociologický časopis* 33(4): 445–65.

Večerník, Jiří. 1996. *Markets and People: The Czech Reform Experience in Comparative Perspective.* Aldershot: Avebury.

Velecký, Milan, and Jaroslav Biehunek. 2001. "Prezident Združenia zdravotných poist'ovní Peter Kvasnica: O transformácii sa viac hovorí, ako koná" [President of the Association of Health Funds Peter Kvasnica: There Is a Lot of Talk about Transformation, but Little Done]. *Trend* (July 4): 9.

Vepřek, Jaromír, et al. 2000. "Koncepce reformy systému zdravotní péče v České Republice po r. 2000" [Concept for Health Care Reform in the Czech Republic after 2000]. Prague: Tým DG Plus.

Verheijen, Tony. 1997. "The Civil Service System of Bulgaria: In an Ever Deeper Crisis?" Paper presented at "Civil Service Systems in Comparative Perspective," School of Public and Environmental Affairs, Indiana University, Bloomington, April 5–8.

———. 1998. "Reform of Central and Local Government in Bulgaria: A New Start?" In *Innovations in Public Management: Perspectives from East and West,* ed. T. Verheijen and D. Coombes. Cheltenham, UK: Edward Elgar.

———. 1999. "The Civil Service System of Bulgaria: Hope on the Horizon." In *Civil Service Systems in Central and Eastern Europe,* ed. Tony Verheijen. Cheltenham, UK: Edward Elgar.

———. 2001. "Public Administration Reform: A Mixed Picture." In *Diversity in Action: Local Public Management of Multi-Ethnic Communities in Central and Eastern Europe,* ed. Anna-Mária Bíró and Petra Kovács. Budapest: Open Society Insitute.

"Většina lidí zatím ne ví, co jim přinese vznik nového kraje" [The Majority of People Still Don't Know What the New Regions Will Mean for Them]. 2000. *Právo* 30 (June 30): 14.

Vidláková, Olga. 1993. "Administrative Reform in the Czech Republic." In *Administrative Transformation in Central and Eastern Europe,* ed. Joachim Hesse. Cambridge, MA: Blackwell.

Vinton, Louisa. 1994. "Power Shifts in Poland's Ruling Coalition." *RFE/RL Research Report* (March 18): 7–10.

Von Beyme, Klaus. 1996. "Party Leadership and Change in Party Systems: Towards a Post-Modern State?" *Government and Opposition* 31(2): 135–59.

Wade, Robert. 1990. *Governing the Market: Economic Theory and the Role of Government in East Asian Industrialization.* Princeton, NJ: Princeton University Press.

Wagner, Adolf. 1883. *Finanzwissenschaft.* 3rd ed. Leipzig: C.F. Winter. Excerpted in *Classics in the Theory of Public Finance,* ed. Richard Musgrave and Alan Peacock. London: Macmillan, 1958.

Walecki, Marcin, ed. 2000. *Finansowanie polityki: Wybory, pieniądze, partie polityczne.* Warsaw: Wydawnictwo Sejmowe.

Walewski, Paweł. 1999. "Swój w radzie" [Their Own on the Governing Board]. *Polityka* (November 6): 22–25.

———. 2000. "Szpital powiatotwórczy" [The Hospital That Makes the District]. *Polityka* (January 1): 83.

Waller, Michael. 1995. "Making and Breaking: Factions in the Process of Party Formation in Bulgaria." In *Factional Politics and Democratization,* ed. R. Gillespie, M. Waller, and L. Nieto. London: Frank Cass.

Wawrzewska, B., P. Aleksandrowicz, and K. Gottesman. 2000. "Chcemy dokończyc' ten remont" [We Want to Finish This Reconstruction: Interview with Marian Krzaklewski]. *Rzeczpospolita* (July 19): 6–7.

Way, Lucan. 1978. *Economy and Society.* Ed. Guenther Roth and Claus Wittich. Trans. Ephraim Fischoff et al. Berkeley: University of California Press.

———. 2003. "Weak States and Pluralism: The Case of Moldova." *East European Politics and Societies* 17(3): 454–82.

Weber, Max. 1978. *Economy and Society: An Outline of Interpretive Sociology,* Guenther Roth and Claus Wittich, eds. Berkeley: University of California Press.

Wesołowski, Włodzimierz. 1995. "Formowanie się partii politycznych w postkomunistycznej Polsce" [The Formation of Political Parties in Post-Commmunist Poland]. *Studia Polityczne* 4: 7–28.

———. 2000. *Partie: Nieustanne Kłopoty* [Parties: Endless Difficulties]. Warsaw: IFiS PAN.

White, Gordon. 1990. "Democratizing Eastern Europe: The Elections of 1990." *Electoral Studies* 9(4): 277–87.

Wiatr, Jerzy. 1999. "Political Parties and Cleavage Crystallization in Poland, 1989–1993." In *Cleavages, Parties, and Voters: Studies from Bulgaria, the Czech Republic, Hungary, Poland, and Romania,* ed. Kay Lawson, Andrea Römmele, and Georgi Karasimeonov. Westport, CT: Praeger.

Wightman, Gordon. 1990. "Czechoslovakia." *Electoral Studies* 9(4): 319–26.

———. 1995. "The Development of the Party System and the Break-up of Czechoslovakia." In *Party Formation in East-Central Europe,* ed. Gordon Wightman. Aldershot, UK: Edward Elgar.

Włodarczyk, Cezary. 1999. "Reforma Opieki Zdrowotnej" [Health Care Reform]. In *Druga fala polskich reform* [The Second Wave of Polish Reforms], ed. Lena Kolarska-Bobińska. Warsaw: Instytut Spraw Publicznych.

———. 2000. "Cely reformy opieki zdrowotnej" [The Goals of the Health Care Reform]. In *Cztery reformy: od koncepcji do realizacji* [The Four Reforms: From Conception to Realization], ed. Lena Kolarska-Bobińska. Warsaw: Instytut Spraw Publicznych.

Woleková, Helena, and Iveta Radičová. 2001. "Social Policy." In *Slovakia 2000: A Global Report on the State of Society,* ed. G. Mesežnikov, M. Ivantšyn, and T. Nicholson. Bratislava: Institute for Public Affairs.

World Bank. 1996. *World Development Report 1996: From Plan to Market.* Oxford: Oxford University Press.

———. 1999. "Corruption in Poland: Review of Priority Areas and Proposals for Action." (October 11). Warsaw: World Bank. www.worldbank.org.pl/html/corruption.html.

———. 2000. "Anticorruption in Transition." www.worldbank.org.pl.

———. 2002. *World Development Indicators.* CD-ROM. Washington, DC: World Bank.

World Health Organization (WHO). 2001. *World Health Report 2000, Health Systems: Improving Performance.* Geneva: WHO.

Wróbel, Renata, and Filip Frydrykiewicz. 1999. "Co dziesiąta złotówka na administrację" [Every Tenth Zloty on Administration]. *Rzeczpospolita* (March 22): 16.

Wykaz 2000 Osób Sprawujących Władzę w RP [List of 2,000 Persons Governing the Polish State]. 1994. Warsaw: Wydawnictwo Wiejska.

"Yesterday's Men: 2,000 Members of Slovakia's Former Government Have Been Dismissed." 1999. *Economist* (January 16): 48.

Yoder, Jennifer. 2003. "Decentralisation and Regionalisation after Communism: Administrative and Territorial Reform in Poland and the Czech Republic." *Europe-Asia Studies* 55: 263–86.

Zagrodzka, Danuta. 2000. "Czterech jez'dz'ców biurokracji" [The Four Riders of Bureaucracy: Interview with Professor Witold Kieżun]. *Gazeta Wyborcza* (October 28–29): 17–18.

Zajac, Rudolf, and Peter Pažitný. 2001. "Zdravotníctwo" [Health Care]. In *Slovensko 2001: Súhrnná správa o stave spoločnosti,* ed. Miroslav Kollár and Grigorij Mesežnikov. Bratislava: Institute for Public Affairs.

Zaluska, Wojciech. 2000. "Nie ma pogody dla AWS: rozmowa z Ryszardem Czarneckim (ZChN)" [Not the Weather for AWS: An Interview with Ryszard Czarnecki (ZChN)]. *Gazeta Wyborcza* (August 3).

Zarycki, Tomasz. 1999. "Wybory samorządowe w 1998 r" [The Subnational Elections in 1998]. In *Decentralizacja terytorialnej organizacji kraju: założeżia, przygotowanie, ustawodawstwo* [The Decentralization of the Territorial Organization of the Country: Foundations, Preparation, Legislation], ed. Gregorz Gorzelak. Reports of the Center for Social and Economic Research no. 21. Warsaw: CASE.

———. 2000. "Politics in the Periphery: Political Cleavages in Poland Interpreted in Their Historical and International Context." *Europe-Asia Studies* 52(5): 851–73.

Ziblatt, Daniel, and Nick Biziouras. 2005. "The State in the Shadow of the European Union: The Undermining of State Capacity in Southern and Eastern Europe." Paper presented at the European Union Studies Association Biennial International Conference, Austin, Texas March 31–April 2.

Index

Page numbers followed by *f* refer to figures; page numbers followed by *t* refer to tables.

acquis communautaire, 101, 121, 201, 239n13, 250n7

administration, schools of public, 195, 197–99

Africa: dominant-party logic in, 174, 185–87; in large-N analysis, 171–72, 176t, 185–88, 249n30; patronage, ix, 2, 185–87; sequencing of state-building and democratization in, x, 185

African National Congress (ANC), 186–87

Albania, 174, 180

All-Poland Trade Union (OPZZ), 57, 163

Argentina, 182–83, 190

Asia, ix–x, 171–72, 176t, 188–90

Association for Civic Understanding (SOP), 49–50, 114

Association of Workers of Slovakia (ZRS), 48, 50

autonomy, state, 5, 82–83t, 84–87, 93

Balcerowicz, Leszek, 38, 164

Belgium, 204

Benin, 187–88, 249n32

Berisha, Sali, 180

Bielecki, Krzysztof, 56, 197

Bolivia, 183–84

Brazil, 2, 174, 183–84, 247n11

Britain, 28, 57, 227n37

Bulgaria: Bulgarian Socialist Party (BSP), 228–29n12; character of state-building, 179–80, 235nn30–31, 236n34; Communist Party, 227n2; electoral volatility, 179, 231n29; regional de-centralization, 238n6; state expansion, 17, 233n7; Union of Democratic Forces (UDF), 179, 228–29n12, 248n22; weak-governance logic, 179, 184, 228n6, 228–29n12; welfare state, 169, 243n2, 244n7, 245n17

bureaucracy, 8, 29, 33, 80, 82–83t, 227n38

bureaucratization, 5, 87–89, 93, 99, 170–71, 194–95

Buzek, Jerzy, 56

capacity, state. *See* effectiveness, state

Cape Verde, 174, 186

career paths, state administration, 82–83t, 87–89, 93

Čarnogurský, Jan, 51

Center Understanding (PC), 131

Charter 77, 129

Chavez, Hugo, 183

Chile, 18, 182–83, 189

Christian Democratic Movement (KDH), 45–46, 48–51, 114

Christian Democratic People's Party (KDU-ČSL), 38, 59–60, 132, 167, 203, 231n39

Christian National Party (ZChN), 72, 98, 131

chronology of government alternation, 46–47t

Citizens' Committees, 128–29

Civic Democratic Alliance (ODA), 59–60

Civic Democratic Party (ODS), 36, 59–62, 97, 203; local-level institutionalization, 132; pa-tronage, 232nn43–44; regional decentraliza-tion, 110, 118–20; welfare state, 155, 163, 167–68

Civic Forum (OF), 20, 37, 43, 59, 61, 126–28

civil service, 17, 22–23, 58, 97, 195–97

civil society, 7, 22

cleavages, social, 28, 36–39, 131, 195, 202, 227–28n4

closure, party system, 24f, 40–43, 44t, 49–50, 56, 60; local level, 125–26; party system institu-tionalization, 25, 170